FICTIONS OF POWER IN ENGLISH LITERATURE:

1900–1950

Studies in Twentieth-Century Literature

Series Editor:
Stan Smith, Professor of English, University of Dundee

Published Titles:
Rainer Emig *Modernism in Poetry: Motivation, Structures and Limits*
Lee Horsley *Fictions of Power in English Literature: 1900–1950*

Fictions of Power in English Literature: 1900–1950

Lee Horsley

Longman
London and New York

Longman Group Limited,
Longman House, Burnt Mill,
Harlow, Essex CM20 2JE, England
and Associated Companies throughout the world.

*Published in the United States of America
by Longman Publishing, New York*

First published 1995

ISBN 0 582 09094 6 CSD
ISBN 0 582 09095 4 PPR

British Library Cataloguing-in-Publication Data

A catalogue record for this book is
available from the British Library

Library of Congress Cataloging-in-Publication Data

Set by 5 in 10/12 pt Bembo

Transferred to Digital Print on Demand 2002
Printed and bound by Antony Rowe Ltd, Eastbourne

For Tony

Contents

Preface

This book is about fictional representations of political power in the first half of the twentieth century. Although British domestic politics did not provide much scope for romantic conceptions of political action, Britain nevertheless, given its imperial role and the pressures of continental totalitarianism, was closely involved with compelling and disruptive myths of power. Two forms of romantic power in particular left their impress on the early twentieth-century political imagination. The adventure hero could still, at the turn of the century, be thought of as flourishing, unchecked by conventional political methods and constraints, in the 'action territory' of Empire. Then, in the decades following the First World War, the messianic figure of the self-deified charismatic leader, fascinating but also deeply worrying, came increasingly into public consciousness with the rise of European totalitarianism, serving collective rather than individualistic ideals and challenging the whole ethos of secular-libertarian political life.

Both kinds of political power excite strong and ambivalent reactions, and the first four chapters of this study survey some of the contradictory responses to highly personalised, masculine and aggressive exercises in domination. Amongst the central themes explored are the problematic nature of imperial adventure and of the hopes for renewal engendered by nationalistic cults of power, the stereotypical assumption of male mastery and female submission in the political movements of the time, and the dilemmas faced by Britain in responding in totalitarian aggression. Impersonal modes of political control can be seen as a safeguard against the excesses and irrationalism of charismatic leaders. But, as became all too apparent in the decades between the wars, dictatorial regimes can be secured and even vested with a spurious impartiality by an ostensible maintenance of legal forms, just as they can by an appearance of technological rationality. My last two chapters deal with law and technopower, and the texts chosen for discussion explore abuses of impersonal power structures under both liberal and totalitarian systems. These are narratives which build tension around the opposition between the individual conscience and the state, focusing, for example, on individual resistance to brutal extensions of the area of legal authority or of technological organisation, which are seen as threatening to eradicate the boundaries of the ethical private self.

Most of the novels and plays included are by British writers, and one of the main questions addressed concerns the construction of a distinctly 'British' political identity, and the way in which this affected the vision of contemporary political mythology. The writers' whose work is examined in most detail are Conrad, Shaw, Chesterton, Lawrence, Forster, Wells, Huxley, Orwell, Wyndham Lewis and Graham Greene. Comparisons are also drawn with the work of continental writers (most importantly, Thomas and Klaus Mann, Yevgeny Zamyatin and Arthur Koestler), and throughout the study narrative patterns are considered in relation to such popular forms as the adventure story, the thriller, the romance and science fiction, with close discussion of key novels by Rider Haggard, Buchan, E.M. Hull (*The Sheik*), Household and Ambler and of a range of dystopian science fiction.

I am very grateful to the University of Lancaster, which gave me sabbatical leave to write this book, and to the colleagues who have given me advice, in particular to David Carroll, Tess Cosslett and Greg Myers. When the project was in the planning stage, I benefited greatly from discussions and correspondence with Francis Dodds of Longman Academic. I am also indebted to Gerry Weston, of Weston Booksellers, whose knowledge of science fiction and generous loan of books helped me considerably. Most of all, I want to express my thanks to the members of my family, who have buoyed me up throughout – to my daughter, Katharine, for her many ideas, lively interest and encouragement, to my sons, Daniel and Samuel, for sharing with me their enthusiasm for adventure stories and science fiction, and to their grandmother, Hilda Drewery, whose help has enabled me to find time for writing. I relied especially on Tony Horsley, whose patience in reading the manuscript and suggestions on how to improve it have been invaluable.

Introduction: The Cult of Power

For thousands of years now . . . there have been two opposed ideals or visions of human society struggling for the allegiance of men's minds. The first is based on superstition and magic; it appeals to primitive tribal instincts, fear, hatred . . . . The other is based on freedom, intelligence, and co-operation; its appeal is to reason and scepticism, tolerance, and humanity.

(Leonard Woolf, *Quack, Quack!*, 1936)

Power is beyond us. Either it is given us from the unknown, or we have not got it. And better to touch it in another, than never to know it. Better to be a Russian and shoot oneself out of sheer terror of Peter the Great's displeasure, than to live like a well-to-do American, and never know the mystery of Power at all. Live in blank sterility.

(D.H. Lawrence, *Reflections on the Death of a Porcupine*, 1925)[1]

The first half of the twentieth century witnessed the collapse of old empires, the failure of parliamentary governments, the rise of totalitarian dictatorships, violent revolutions and the devastation of two world wars. At a time when democratic governments seemed unable to act effectively, the great personalities of the day, almost all of whom were critics of democracy (Stalin, Mussolini, Hitler, Dollfuss, Primo de Rivera), made sweeping promises, which appeared to offer decisive ways of dealing with despair and crisis – with the severe economic problems that ultimately led to the Great Depression (as Keynes said, to 'the greatest economic catastrophe' of modern times), with the ethnic and class conflicts and the widespread social disruption that were destabilising so many European states. As old orders and certainties crumbled, it became increasingly apparent that there were widely divergent ideals of political life – not just the clash between left- and right-wing solutions but opposing ideas about the

1

way in which power is to be exercised. Leonard Woolf's anti-fascist polemic is just one of many attempts to represent this division as a fundamental difference between rational and irrational modes of power. On the other side of the political spectrum, D.H. Lawrence takes for granted the same division, but rejects as 'lifeless' all political relationships not based on the 'unending inequality' of 'real power' – 'the old divine power' that arouses 'real fear' and 'real passion'. The opposition can also be characterised as a split between 'soft' and 'hard' political methods: Oswald Spengler, for example, in *The Decline of the West* (1922), contrasts democratic mediocrity and a debilitating liberal belief in reason, toleration and individual rights with the power of a strong, militantly nationalistic movement dominated by a great leader and an iron-willed elite.

For those looking back on the totalitarian excesses of the mid-twentieth century, the worship of iron-willed power has seemed culpable in the extreme. Thus Bernard Crick, in *The Defence of Politics* (1962), defines his subject with an eye to excluding altogether the kinds of power – anti-liberal, romantic, irrationalist – admired by Spengler and Lawrence. In argumentation of this kind, the word 'politics' is given very different meanings, sometimes all-inclusive, sometimes either exclusive or excluded: Spengler, having dismissed ordinary party politics as spineless and limited, grandly declares that '*All living is politics*, in every trait of instinct, in the inmost marrow'; Lawrence prefers his romantic gestures to be untainted by the word 'politics' (as Ramón says in *The Plumed Serpent*, 'I don't want to acquire a political smell').[2] Crick, on the other hand, valuing politics highly, harbours the somewhat impracticable hope that the word might be reserved for something much closer to the traditions of the British parliamentary system: the politics he wants is *not* religion, totalitarian ideology, nationalism or any other faith that ignores two of the most essential characteristics of political activity, the diversity of group interests and a concern with personal identity; neither is politics spontaneous or dramatic; rather, it relies on a kind of 'deliberate and continuous individual activity' which, as Crick himself observes on his opening page, is often dismissed as boring and inconsequential.[3] In these competing partisan vocabularies, what we see is an effort to define the existence of a fundamental polarity. Each writer, in his own way, is describing what can, particularly in times of political turmoil, seem to be an irreconcilable opposition between two models of power believed to be perpetually in conflict with one another.

Political scientists, striving to create a more objective picture of (in a wide sense) political life, instead of seeing diametrically opposed types of polity, tend to think in terms of a continuum – placing regimes, for example, on a liberal-totalitarian or pluralist-monist continuum. One of the most helpful models, outlined by David Apter in *The Politics of Modernization*, uses the labels secular–libertarian and collective-sacred. Broadly, the secular–libertarian model is identified with Western concepts of democracy, with a market economy and a system that (ideally) maximises opportunities for exercising rationality and individualistic behaviour within a framework designed to minimise coercion and tyranny – in short, the classic liberal picture of a political community, the values of which are (like those defended by Leonard Woolf) centred on individual liberty protected by common law and custom. In contrast, the essential elements of the sacred–collective model are a stress on the unity rather than the diversity and individualism of the people, a preoccupation with communal, consummatory values, a disciplined concentration on utopian or spiritual objectives, rather than on diversity of opinion and a free flow of ideas, and a preference for strong personal leadership which is directed towards arousing mass excitement and exploiting collective effort. Cast in an heroic mould, the collective-sacred system offers a 'mobilising' form of power that holds out the prospect of renewed conviction and regeneration: to this end, it sets itself against moral ambiguity, uncertainty and compromise; it polarises issues and mythologises grievances during what Apter calls periods of political fantasy. With their marked millennial quality, these periods emphasise ultimate ends (understood as religion) as opposed to intermediate ends (secularity). These different models of power will obviously be associated with quite different kinds of leadership. The talents of the charismatic leader are particularly important in periods of political fantasy. His leadership often takes the form of a dramatic acting out of messianic or heroic or 'Robin Hood' roles, and the dynamism of his self-definition ensures the construction of national identity and the clear identification of enemies.[4]

Within the liberal counter-tradition, there are also, of course, outlets for romantic political fantasies, but in the British political life of this century, except in time of war, such possibilities have been mainly created by departure to the action territory of Empire. In his famous Oxford lecture of 1870, Ruskin called on England to send her 'most energetic and worthiest men' to serve the Empire.[5] It was a 'call to duty' that evoked the ideals of chivalry and heroic action. Like the American frontier, the imperial enterprise provided an escape-route, allowing the adventurous individual to leave behind the stifling security of a well-regulated Western political system. Those subscribing to the values of the Western system have, of course, been deeply divided about whether the imperial impulse should be countenanced, and the enthusiasm for imperial adventure, strong though it was in the late nineteenth and early twentieth centuries, had begun to fade by the time of the First World War, when there was a widespread loss of confidence in the whole notion of heroism. But however discredited by the realities of modern warfare, the myths and the language of heroism retained much of their potency, and heroic fictions of power often surfaced again in European political life, both in literary adventure and in the rhetoric of challenge and crisis – whether in the communist call to heroic revolutionary activity, in Hitler's 'heroism of the Will', or Churchill's 'Come then: let us to the task, to the battle . . . .' As Valentine Cunningham argues, the continuing importance of the language of heroism and lofty endeavour is evident in the fact that the conflicts of the day were so often couched in terms of heroic stature – which rival was morally bigger, and which would prove to be militarily the stronger?[6]

In the decades following the First World War, calls for heroic action were assimilated to quite different kinds of rhetoric – to the collectivist, anti-individualist creeds of the great competing ideologies that were coming to dominate European politics. What increasingly gripped the European political imagination was 'the cult of power' – or, as it was variously called, the cult of violence, the cult of leadership, the cult of personality, the cult of the divine nation. This brand of power (whether located in Nazism, Italian or Spanish fascism, Soviet communism, or, more generally, in any form of nationalism or totalitarianism) was seen by many as the politics of regression. But it was also an event-making form of political engagement – the politics of mobilisation and excitement.[7] Even before the rise to power of Mussolini (1922) and Hitler (1933) or totalitarian unification under Stalin in the thirties, intellectual debate repeatedly brought to the fore the question of whether 'weak' liberal-democratic states were better supplanted by another kind of power altogether – of whether the romantic vision of a self-determining charismatic personality leading a movement of national renewal could be translated into political reality. Since the turn of the century, there had been throughout Europe growing approval of Nietzschean calls for a 'natural' leader and for the replacement of 'politics' (in a liberal sense) by nationalism and appeals to the blood, the iron Will and 'Northern' values; the younger generation everywhere seemed to be 'in search of an ideal and a faith'. Disillusioned with conventional, bureaucratic political methods, many responded to the Nietzschean idea of 'strong, imperious natures', artist–politicians who are 'incalculable . . . like lightning: too terrible, too sudden, too compelling and too "different" even to be hated'.[8] Attention was focused on the nature of power itself, and, whatever their political orientations, writers were often preoccupied with the attractions and the dangers of such a visible exercise of power, not hidden and constrained within impersonal bureaucratic structures but striding arrogantly onto a very public stage. Most of the texts included in this study reflect in one way or another on the ramifications of romantic political action, individualistic (the imperial adventure hero) as well as collectivist (the would-be messiah or prophet). The first four chapters look, respectively, at heroic action, charismatic leadership, male dominance and totalitarian violence. Some of the writers included fictionalise myths of power in a relatively straightforward way, whereas others, by rewriting adventure, thriller or romance motifs, raise fundamental questions about the moral and psychological implications of an aggressive, masculinist species of power and about the romantic conception of personality. The final two chapters focus on impersonal aspects of political life, paying particular attention to the way in which law and technological control can be manipulated and abused under any type of government, though most devastatingly within a collective-sacred system of power.

Fascination with the stories generated by political romanticism is abundantly apparent in both the serious and the popular literature of the time. Shaw, in *Everybody's Political What's What?* (1944), says that lovers and practitioners of literature appreciate better than anyone the romantic attractions of heroic barbarism,[9] and one implication is clearly that atavistic forms of power satisfy an imaginative hunger for bold action. Crick, as we have seen, honestly admits that the procedures of liberal politics may reduce the spectator to a state of boredom. But what Spengler calls the two Faustian instincts – the spirit of the Teutonic knights (rooted in the soil and subordinating the will of the individual to the will of all and to the charismatic authority of Christ) and the Viking spirit (an equally aggressive tradition, but founded on a free-roving, seafaring predatory instinct)[10] – generate the excitement at the core of many narratives that are political in the widest sense. In popular fiction, leaders appropriate to these two modes of power can be found, for example, in the novels of John Buchan and H. Rider Haggard. Buchan's charismatic villain, Prester John, is Christ's earthly representative, the priest-king who feels the armies of Heaven behind him and mesmerises his followers with 'God's message to His own'. Rider Haggard's heroic Sir Henry Curtis, the Viking individualist, would look, if given a battle-axe and horn mug,

5

the very picture of an ancient Dane.[11] Buchan's black preacher has all of the world-altering qualities attributed by Spengler to the great personality, whom he explicitly compares to the Christian martyr – the living exemplar who can unify thousands and render them collectively capable of 'deeds to which they could never otherwise have risen'.[12] Rider Haggard's Viking-style hero, on the other hand, is more suggestive of a romantic-individualist conception of political life, such as that theorised by Hannah Arendt, who (though not well disposed to anything of a sanguinary or imperialistic nature) prefers politics to be a colourful and vital process of individual choice and action. In keeping with her dramatic view of political activity, Arendt emphasises that without stories we cannot understand political action: 'Action reveals itself fully only to the storyteller.'[13] Conversely, without romantic political action, whether led by messianic or heroic figures, there would be less vivid stories to feed the popular hunger for narrative excitement: as Chesterton said, although it is clearly possible to argue that romance can take dangerous and damaging forms, it would be hard to maintain that it could disappear altogether.[14]

The imaginative lure of such action is readily apparent in a range of early twentieth-century popular literary forms: not only adventure stories, like those of Buchan and Rider Haggard, but romances, thrillers and science fiction all find a major source of narrative excitement in the dynamism and hazards of romantic political action. The texts included in this study negotiate the political space between a familiar (rational, legally structured) domestic sphere and alien scenes dominated by larger-than-life men of power, whether imperialist adventurers or self-deified charismatic figures. In the first chapter, we will look at the heroic adventurer who performs his role in one of the most basic myths of originating action. An important part of the English political imagination (but removed to a safe distance), he is valued for his energetic assertion of individual responsibility. Outside of the popular adventure story, however (in, say, the novels of Conrad), his virtues are seen to be shadowed by less amiable traits, marred by the violence inherent in the martial ideal or weakened by moral *naïveté* and a tendency towards arrogant domination, qualities which, even when displaced into a dark double, undercut imperial presumption. Men who claim godlike powers, being decidedly un-British, have frequently, as in Buchan's fiction, been cast as the charismatic villains of adventure narratives; by contrast, a writer like Lawrence, hostile to the British political establishment, ponders the possibility that political salvation might reside in some messianic figure far removed from what Lawrence saw as the anaesthetising dullness of English political life. The ambivalent handling of such figures, analysed in the second chapter, conveys a sense of their attractions (offering transcendence of the mundane political world) and of their dangers (absolute, divinely-sanctioned power demanding complete sacrifice of individual volition).

The romance and the thriller centre on two of the most evident perils of political romanticism – oppressive domination and violence. Erich Fromm, describing, in *The Fear of Freedom* (1942), the contemporary eruption of the 'dark and diabolical forces of man's nature', says that not even the insights of Nietzsche and Freud had prepared people for 'such lust for power, such disregard for the rights of the weak, or such yearning for submission'.[15] The phrases he uses here – 'the lust for power', 'the yearning for submission' – are commonplaces reflecting what many have seen as a sexual dynamism at the heart of charismatic power. This double-edged comparison, gesturing towards 'sexual politics' as well as towards the political exploitation of redirected sexuality, will be discussed in Chapter 3, with reference both to the 'brutal male power' clichés of popular romantic fiction and to various reshapings of these fantasies – in the work of Lawrence, who adapts the clichés for political, or quasi-political, ends; in the satires of Wyndham Lewis and Aldous Huxley; and in feminist texts which challenge stereotypes of sexual difference and male political dominance. In the thrillers of the thirties, another popular formula is modified to allow exploration of current political preoccupations. With war imminent, the more serious thriller-writers of the period (Greene, Ambler and Household, whose work is discussed in Chapter 4) reject the sensational thriller's unashamed aggression, constructing instead narratives that oppose civilised restraint to savage aggression, imaging British hopes of avoiding war in their deferral of the conventionally violent action of the thriller.

The terrifying possibilities of totalitarian regimes are obviously not confined to brutal domination and violence; a more insidious threat is the prospect of an alliance between primitive impulse and sophisticated forms of political control – an unbounded lust for power secured by a repressive strengthening and perversion of the legal framework and advanced technology. Historically, the abuse of such institutions as the legal system and of modern technological and scientific developments served, as Orwell said, to make totalitarianism oppressive on an unimagined scale. The clash between the individual conscience and impersonal systems of control, which is one of the main subjects of the fifth and sixth chapters, is a recurrent theme in narratives of trial and inquisition, and is still more indispensable to the science fiction dystopia. In a novel such as Koestler's *Darkness at Noon* (in which the 'crime' is constituted by the process of inquisition) and in the large body of dystopian science fiction, we see the state's usurpation of all individual space, curbing the power not only of independent action but of narrative construction. The isolated individual's struggle to regain freedom of thought and movement is in part a struggle to re-establish the right to narrate his own story. The dystopia, with its suppression of all individual volition, eliminates both politics and narratives. For stories set in this static future world to start at all, the character who possesses a surviving spark of sheer oddness or energetic individualism (inherited from adventure heroes of old) must try to assert his independent will. Many of the best-known dystopian narratives (such as *Nineteen Eighty-Four* and *Brave New World*) end with pessimistic closure – with the story stopping because the impulse of adventure has been effectively suppressed by those in power; if the narrative is to hold open (as, for example, Zamyatin's *We* does) the possibility of escape from dystopia, it will also be a potential foundation myth – a new story of political origins.

From a British perspective, the dystopian future-world is invariably 'foreign' to a nostalgically viewed native landscape – the product either of rootless, mechanised modernity or of a continental totalitarian creed. There was, as Rex Warner said, a complacent British conviction that European movements were 'wholly alien from ourselves'. The belief in an island of Englishness was very strong, and much that was written during this period served to reinforce the notion of an absolute separation between English and non-English – most commonly during this period, of course, between English and German. This creation of an imagined community and the articulation of national differences can be seen, for example, in Ernest Barker's influential study, *National Character and the Factors in its Formation* (1927), which, though it rejects the idea of racial essences (as a Germanic notion likely to lead to tyranny), insists upon the embodiment of the English way in a great, unifying cultural tradition and clarifies the terms of the English tradition by delineating the non-English. The definition of essential Englishness included such traits as moderation, independence and individualism, whereas the German character was identified with innate aggression, devotion to the state and crude power-mongering: as L.T. Hobhouse writes in *Questions of War and Peace* (1916), 'Follow German thought down through the century, and you will only find more and more insistence on force, power, ascendancy, and more and more repudiation of any binding law . . . .'[16] The large, bold gestures animating the continental cults of power, inconceivable in 'the cosy littleness of the English landscape', were omitted from the more 'English' definitions of political activity – indeed, a liberal-humanist politics, from which the spurious attractions of more provocative forms of power are strictly banished, might in some ways be taken as an image of Britain itself in the period between the wars. Lawrence, in describing Aaron Sisson's reactions abroad, captures in less approving terms this sense of detachment: 'Aaron stared out of the window, and played the one single British role left to him, that of ignoring his neighbours, isolating himself in their midst, and minding his own business. Upon this insular trick our greatness and our predominance depends – such as it is.' Inspecting the boldness of the Italian landscape, Aaron is 'fascinated and impressed'. Here, in the contrast between English tameness ('such as it is') and foreign vitality ('as if the walls of life had fallen'), we can see in miniature the romantic's response to a parochial, patriotically constructed image of Englishness.[17] But at the end of the day, even those writers most inclined to see 'strong men' as an antidote to debilitating British liberalism tended to find something risible and unsatisfactory in the continental leaders who came to power in the twenties and thirties. Lawrence, though proclaiming that 'We're sick of being soft, and amiable, and harmless', ridiculed Mussolini as 'a little harmless Glory in baggy trousers'; Wyndham Lewis, retracting the more favourable opinions expressed in his earlier series of newspaper articles, set out in *The Hitler Cult* (1939) to demonstrate why the English were not cut·out to follow in the footsteps of the National Socialists and why they were unlikely to suffer gladly any home-grown 'Führers' who took to imitating the inferior marching-songs and tacky Hollywood sets of the Third Reich.[18] Such caricatures are in themselves symptomatic not only of an identity crisis faced by many on the extreme Right but of the widespread English difficulty in taking seriously the real dangers of totalitarianism – a difficulty which, for those who were not enamoured of the cult of power, often sprang from an inability to grasp the overwhelming attraction for such a large mass of people of political religions and their prophet figures. As conflict came to seem inevitable, however, the absurdities of the enemy nation tended to recede under pressure of wartime rhetoric. Churchill's speeches, naturally enough, do not dwell on baggy trousers and Hollywood sets but on 'the more serious, darker and more dangerous aspects of the vast scene of the war':

> We must all of us have been asking ourselves: What has that wicked man whose crime-stained regime and system are at bay and in the toils – what has he been preparing during these winter months . . . . What fresh assault will he make upon our Island home and fortress;

which – let there be no mistake about it – is all that stands between him and the dominion of the world?[19]

One of the things that Churchillian rhetoric sweeps aside is the way in which, during the thirties, many had felt that their whole concept of Englishness would be compromised by entry into another war. Some of the essential elements in the English character were seen as anything but 'military'. As Spenser Wilkinson wrote at the beginning of the First World War, a native inclination to 'make no fuss', a shyness about 'using large language' and a preference for such offhand phrases as 'playing the game' did not accord well with the necessary bellicosity; perhaps, another writer of the time suggested, one had to distinguish between militarism (held to be a German quality) and warlike pugnacity: 'There is no fear that we shall ever become militarist, but we *are* a fighting race.'[20] Others expressed fears, however, before both the world wars, that by engaging in combat Britain would reveal a darker face, much more closely resembling that of the enemy it was setting out to defeat. This impasse, considered in detail in Chapter 4, was only one of many contradictions troubling those caught up in the oppositional rhetoric of the time. In a period of crisis, of course, the language of conflict – its polarised vocabulary, its hostile and defensive metaphors – is sharpened, confirming the boundaries between 'us' and 'them'; the narration of the coming war accentuates and clarifies the images of England's political system and produces a stronger sense of difference. Such turmoil also, however, has the effect of disturbing the certainties of dichotomous thinking, and one of the things most evident throughout this period is a persistent sense of unease about the terms used to structure and explain the clash between secular-libertarian and collective-sacred models – for example, Left/Right, liberal/totalitarian, civilised/barbarous, rational/irrational, scientific/Stone Age, impersonal/personal.

It was common during the thirties for people to think of the extreme Left and the extreme Right as the sole alternatives, given the apparent failure of parliamentary democracies to cope effectively with economic and social crises. If liberal political systems were doomed (and the West, as Spengler declared, was in decline), then communism may well be the only defence against fascism. And vice versa: for those who feared that the communists would come to dominate the world, a fascist saviour-leader for a time seemed the only hope. In the thirties, one immediate predicament faced by many left-wingers was that their own pacifist principles made it difficult to contemplate effective resistance to the fascist menace. But there were more fundamental problems. Aldous Huxley expresses the dilemma felt by those who, hoping to find a 'direct and inspiring' form of opposition to fascism, nevertheless hesitated to commit themselves to the alternative political religion on offer: 'For any anti-Fascist religion, if it is to be successful, must be at least as intolerant as Fascism itself.' The English, he says, generally decline to make this 'uncomfortable choice', with people instead 'trying to squeeze their way between the spikes'.[21] As Huxley implies, one of the more disturbing problems (for both left- and right-wing extremists) was that the ends of the political spectrum actually appeared not to be opposed but kindred. Wyndham Lewis, in *The Art of Being Ruled* (1926), suggests that fascism was really just a faction of the militant Left that 'burst round and through to the right – circumnavigated, boxed the compass'. In more ways than this, it was increasingly recognised that the conventional antithesis between left- and right-wing totalitarianism concealed important similarities, particularly evident in the creation of all-embracing faiths. Both clearly favoured a collective-sacred model of political life and gradually came to be seen as what Eric Voegelin calls political religions, combining a sense of religious absoluteness with the promise of an eventual community and a militant antagonism to political unbelievers.[22]

One of the enemies most obviously common to these competing versions of totalitarian faith is the temporising of those whom Huxley characterises as trying to squeeze between the spikes – the dithering and 'softness' of liberal-humanitarian political leaders and institutions – and this shared hostility often added to the confusions of the Left–Right divide. From the 1870s on – and more dramatically with the First World War – there had been signs of a change of consciousness, a loss of confidence in the nineteenth-century individualist philosophy, in established political institutions and in the liberal vision of progress. What some demanded was 'a new political savagery'. Sir Oswald Mosley, for example, saw the parliamentary atmosphere as robbing 'a people's champion of his vitality and fighting power', draining him of his revolutionary ardour and turning the warrior into 'the lap-dog of the lobbies'. This debilitating ambience of clerks and talkers could only be resisted by the doer, the fighter, the new man who stood not for 'a difference of method or points of policy' but for a different spirit.[23] Mosley, who, like many of his followers, had moved from the political Left to fascism, attracted a certain amount of intellectual support from those on the Left who saw in his politics both a collectivist creed and a belief in the strong man who is not trammelled by conventional parliamentary politics: as Shaw wrote in his Fabian lecture, 'In Praise of Guy Fawkes' (1933), 'The moment things begin to break up and something has to be done, quite a number of men like Mosley will come to the front . . . .'[24] In the unstable enthusiasms of a writer like Shaw, whose representations of combative heroes and prophets are discussed in Chapters 1 and 2, it is apparent that anti-liberalism in itself produced some strange bedfellows. The notion of the strong man's readiness for crisis and his challenge to what were dismissed as moribund liberal traditions had great appeal for those on both ends of the political spectrum, with radical writers on the Right and Left alike responding, for example, to Georges Sorel's representation of proletarian violence (in contrast to 'bourgeois force') as the heroic means of regaining energies sapped by soft humanitarianism.[25]

Amongst British intellectuals, however, it was perhaps less common to hunger after the leadership principle than to remain bemused by it. The difficulty of grasping political irrationalism is examined in some detail by George Orwell in an essay called 'Wells, Hitler and the World State'. Writing in 1941, the year the conflict with Germany widened to become a world war, Orwell poses the question of why so many English writers and intellectuals seemed unable to understand the nature of totalitarianism. The essence of the difficulty, he argues, is the habit of thought which smugly assumes that rationally planned, orderly political life is somehow immune to the romantic attractions of adventure heroism, nationalistic emotion, political religion and leader-worship. The displays of the military adventurer – of Napoleon, say – are dismissed by writers like H.G. Wells as anachronistic: 'The thunder of guns, the jingle of spurs, the catch in the throat when the flag goes by, leave him manifestly cold. He has an invincible hatred of the fighting, hunting, swash-buckling side of life, symbolised in all his early books by a violent propaganda against horses.' This Wellsian way of thinking opposes, for example, science, order and progress to war, nationalism and religion, assuming that in any 'reasonable', planned form of society control will be exercised by scientists rather than witch-doctors.

Orwell's argument is that, at the very least, it is essential to recognise the power of the irrational impulses which appear to be determining the course of European history. So, for example, Churchill's propagandistic vision of Bolsheviks as 'monsters dripping with blood' is judged by Orwell as, in its very extremity, nearer the mark than Wells's suggestion that the Russian revolutionaries are merely ushering in a scientifically controlled, commonsensical regime from which 'flag-wavers like Churchill' would be excluded: 'The early Bolsheviks may have been angels or demons, according as one chooses to regard them, but at any rate they were not sensible men. They were not introducing a Wellsian Utopia but a Rule of the Saints, which, like the English Rule of the Saints, was a military despotism enlivened by witchcraft trials.' Wells's misconception, Orwell says, can also be seen, in an inverted form, in his attitude to Nazism: assuming that Hitler is 'all the war-lords and witch-doctors in history rolled into one', Wells wrongly concludes that such a 'ghost from the past' will simply disappear. The truth, however, is that it is foolish either to delude oneself into believing that these archaic forces are no longer powerful or to think in terms of any simple antithesis between rational planning and primitive impulse. Modern Germany is much more 'scientific' than England, but also 'far more barbarous'; in looking at Nazi Germany, it is perfectly clear that 'the order, the planning, the state encouragement of science, the steel, the concrete, the aeroplanes' can all be made to serve 'ideas appropriate to the Stone Age'. England itself, in resisting fascist aggression, has been kept going less by 'some vague idea about a better future' than by 'the atavistic emotion of patriotism'.[26] Implicit in Orwell's argument, then, is a breaking down of the antitheses between the rational and the irrational and between scientific advance and 'Stone Age' attitudes: England must, apparently, abandon its reasonable detachment if it is to resist fascism; and Germany's role in the conflict seems to owe as much to the technological application of reason as to the irrationalism of its ideology.

The polarising habits of mind to which Orwell is referring are apparent in many propagandistic uses of anthropological and evolutionary vocabulary to construct an opposition between the 'civilised' or 'cultured' and the 'primitive', 'savage' and 'barbarous' – perhaps the most pervasive anti-totalitarian (and particularly anti-fascist) language of the interwar years. Churchill's speeches put the matter in an unequivocal light, representing the fight against Nazism as a crusade to preserve civilisation and to defend moral progress, enlightenment and mankind's future – the 'urge and impulse of the ages, that mankind will move forward towards its goal'.[27] British political essays of the thirties and forties – whether written by left- or right-wing writers – recurrently point to barbarity itself as a root cause of strife. They explore the nature of political atavism, explaining its emergence and its attractions, warn of its dangers – and, of course, castigate such earlier writers as Lawrence, whose primitivist leanings could be plausibly likened to fascist ideology. On the Right, Wyndham Lewis, for example, maintains that in Germany the present coexists with a past which is like another dimension, 'a mirage', blended with a more modern landscape; Hitler himself is an irrational emanation 'of the old many-schlossed, spiky and bosky landscapes'; on the Left,

Shaw represents human society as naturally divided into barbarians and civilised citizens and maintains that he sees clearly the persistence of the 'ancient moral valuations' of primitive tribes, which dictated that no woman would marry a man unless he could produce trophies.[28] Leonard Woolf (in *Quack, Quack!*) analyses at length the way in which the 'great army of primitive men and barbarians', temporarily submerged by the 'full tide' of civilisation, come to the fore at times of crisis: 'The half-atrophied beliefs of the savage rise to the surface of the mind in individuals and in society, and the minority in whose hands is the future of civilisation betray it by encouraging its enemies, the quacks, the witch-doctors, the spell-binders, the miracle workers, and the rain-makers.' In elaborating the manifestations of 'political quacking', Woolf develops detailed comparisons between Stone Age and fascist rituals, gesticulations and beliefs. To clinch his point, he juxtaposes photographs of Mussolini and Hitler with an effigy of an Hawaiian war-god, demonstrating the way in which the fascist leaders have managed to make their faces convey not individual but generalised emotions, 'the savage emotions of the savage's mask' (pp. 25–47). But, as we have seen in Orwell's analysis, contradictory elements emerge. Virginia Woolf, for example, in her 1937 polemic *Three Guineas* (discussed in Chapter 3), represents primitive, repressive male power as no less dominant in British than in German society. And, as Orwell says, Germany can be seen as Janus-faced – dark and barbarous, but also itself an advanced civilisation. Mechanisation is perceived as an instrument of force, but also as a cause of fascist barbarism, with machine civilisation creating the conditions that allow totalitarianism to flourish. These are contradictions central to such later diagnoses of mass society as Wilhelm Reich's *Mass Psychology of Fascism* (1946), which argues that Prussian military displays, for example, show the characteristics of the 'mystical machine-man', exemplifying the paradoxical phenomenon of a primitive cult of the machine.[29] Totalitarianism is thus not only an extreme response to technologically advanced modern society, but its apotheosis.

This union between the worship of power and the worship of technology – 'Leviathan on wheels' – is what transforms the imagined future into dystopia. Or rather, transfixes it, since the chief paradox of the science fiction dystopia is that technological progress and all-embracing political change have engendered political paralysis. In a period of dizzying instability, of violent conflict and revolution, the dystopian vision is a realisation of the fairytale motif of the rash wish – the change to end changes – and it drives home its point by inventing a future world in which some of the most persistent anxieties of the age have achieved their 'perfected' expression. Although it is often explicitly anti-fascist or anti-communist, the deepest fears expressed in the dystopia are the same ones that plagued those who seemed most inclined to favour totalitarian solutions − fears evident in the figuring of modern political life as the product of the machine, as impersonal system and as the expression of mass mentality. The recurrent metaphoric representations of the malaise of modern society are also the defining characteristics of dystopia: man is an automaton, a cog that is part of an anonymous social machine; all life is reduced to function (as opposed to 'being'); people are 'flung in masses through the streets or through underground tunnels in engine-driven vehicles' that are taken as emblematic of the rootlessness and flux of modernity; the 'mass' of mankind, carried along in this mindless fashion, is figured as less than human, an indiscriminate swarm or herd with no will of its own; modern mass society is supported and controlled by the 'iron cage' of an impersonal bureaucracy; the ever-increasing rationalisation and efficiency of social systems leads only to the 'cage of bondage' of technical rationality (Weber's *'Gehäuse der Hörigkeit'*) and to a desert of disenchanted, 'parcelled-out' souls − what Lawrence calls 'blank sterility'.[30] It can be argued that the lure of European authoritarianism in the 1920s and 1930s is to be explained less by its blueprints for the future than by its 'great anti-positions', its promises of salvation from the evils of modernisation. In the movement from present discontents to the thought of future remedies we see one of the most telling contradictions in the political thinking of the time. Intellectuals who were appalled by the shape of modern society saw themselves as a subversive force, acting against the established systems that served impersonal, mechanised mass society and against liberal-democratic ineffectuality; whether they looked towards a revolution from the Right or from the Left, they hoped for release and renewal. But the individual impulse of revolt was not so easily accommodated by movements that had to satisfy a simultaneous need for critique and for political identification and solidarity:

> The consequences of emancipation called for new certainties, and these were offered mainly by those 'philosophies' which seemed to overcome not only (rationally) the permanent crisis of liberal democracy but also (irrationally) the vacuum of a value orientation by means of new certainties. Face to face with the frightening openness of secularized society it was the proclaimed 'closed nature' that contained the greatest seductive appeal. Not rational logic and harmony but an irrational assurance of salvation held together the large disparate elements . . . .[31]

The realised blueprint of dystopia maps the disturbing certainties of a collective-sacred creed on to the ossified form of modern mass society, and vests whatever slender hope there is for regeneration in individual protest of a secular-libertarian variety – the heroic individual (Spengler's Viking) capable of inserting himself into the world and beginning 'a story of his own'. This preoccupation with political action (in the sense of setting in motion, or originating) will be seen in many of the narratives we will be discussing, whether the focus is on the nature of action itself, on the replacement of individual action by collective spiritual purpose, or on the political and institutional constraints on action. Nietzsche, in *Twilight of the Idols* (1888), asserted that the West was no longer capable of the kind of action which could accomplish the renewal of political institutions: 'In order that there may be institutions, there must be a kind of will, instinct, or imperative, which is anti-liberal to the point of malice . . . . The whole West no longer possesses the instincts out of which institutions grow, out of which the future grows.' Often sharing something of Nietzsche's and Spengler's pessimism about the undercutting of instincts – and of the heroic virtues of manliness, resolution and courage – in modern society, the writers of the time repeatedly explored the possibility of romantic political action and the problems attendant on trying to 'begin a story of one's own'.[32]

NOTES

1. Woolf L. *Quack, quack!* 1936 p. 108; Lawrence D.H., Blessed are the powerful (1925) in *Reflections on the death of a porcupine* 1988 p. 327.
2. Spengler O. *The decline of the West* 1922 vol. 2 p. 440; Lawrence D.H. *The plumed serpent* (1926) 1990 p. 259.
3. Crick B. *In defence of politics* 1971 pp. 15–16.
4. Apter D. *The politics of modernization* 1967 pp. 15–35, 290–2, 321–3 and 379–80.
5. Ruskin J., Inaugural lecture (8 February 1870), *Works* ed Cook E.T., Wedderburn A., vol. 20 p. 41, quoted by Girouard M. *The return to Camelot: chivalry and the English gentleman* 1981 pp. 222–3.
6. Cunningham V. *British writers of the thirties* 1989 Chapter 6; Stern J.P. *Hitler* (1975) 1979 p. 27; Churchill W.S., Let us to the task (27 January 1940) in *Churchill speaks* 1981 p. 701.
7. Lee S.J. *The European dictatorships* 1987 pp. 2–23.
8. Hughes H.S. *Consciousness and society* 1979 pp. 337–44; Bracher K.D. *The age of ideologies* 1985 pp. 94–100; Nietzsche F. *Beyond good and evil* (1886)

in Hollingdale R.J. (selected and trans.) *A Nietzsche reader* Penguin 1986 p. 229; Nietzsche F. *On the genealogy of morals* (1887) quoted by Stern *Hitler* pp. 44–7.

9. Shaw G.B. *Everybody's political what's what?* 1944 pp. 131–8.
10. Spengler O. *Preussentum and sozialismus* (1919), quoted by Fischer K.P. *History and prophecy* 1989 p. 219. On the contradictory elements of individualism and collectivism in political romanticism, see Woodring C. *Politics in English Romantic poetry*. Harvard University Press, Cambridge, Massachusetts 1970 p. 40.
11. Buchan J. *Prester John* (1910) 1956 pp. 106–7; Haggard H.R. *King Solomon's mines* (1885) 1992 pp. 11–12.
12. Spengler *Decline* vol. 2 p. 443.
13. Arendt H. *The human condition* 1958 pp. 191–2.
14. Chesterton G.K. *Shaw* (1909) 1935 pp. 272–3.
15. Ibid p. xxxi; Fromm E. *The fear of freedom* (1942) 1966 pp. 4–6.
16. Warner R. *The cult of power* (1947) 1969 p. 16; Pick D. *War machine* 1993 pp. 132–8, 147–8 and 158.
17. Lawrence D.H. *Aaron's rod* (1922) 1950 pp. 238–9.
18. Blessed are the powerful pp. 323–4; Lewis W. *Hitler.* Chatto & Windus 1931; Lewis W. *The Hitler cult* 1939 pp. 45–7.
19. Churchill W., Give us the tools (9 February 1941). In *Churchill speaks* p. 739.
20. Wilkinson S. *The coming of war* (1914) and Warren H. *Poetry and war* (1914), quoted by Pick *War machine* p. 148.
21. Bracher *Age of ideologies* p. 32; Huxley A., The prospects of Fascism in England (3 March 1934) in Bradshaw D. (ed) *The hidden Huxley* 1994 pp. 140–1.
22. Lewis W. *The art of being ruled* (1926) 1989 pp. 70–1.
23. Skidelsky R. *Oswald Mosley* 1981 pp. 45f and 311–12.
24. Shaw G.B., In praise of Guy Fawkes, *The new clarion* 3 and 10 December 1932, quoted by Skidelsky *Mosley* pp. 348–9.
25. Winegarten R. *Writers and revolution* 1974 pp. 281–2.
26. Orwell G., Wells, Hitler and the world state (1941) in *Collected essays* (1946–53) 1975 pp. 161–6.
27. Churchill, We shall never surrender (4 June 1940) in *Churchill speaks* pp. 708–13; and Charmley J. *Churchill* 1993 p. 401.
28. Lewis *Hitler cult* p. 49; Shaw *Everybody's political* pp. 131–8.
29. Reich W. *The mass psychology of fascism* (1946) 1991 p xv; Pick *War machine* p. 211.
30. Playne C. *The pre-war mind in Britain* (1928), quoted by Pick *War machine* p. 199; Carey J. *The intellectuals and the masses* 1992 pp. 23–5; Mitzman A. *The Iron cage* 1985 pp. 189–91.
31. Bracher *Age of ideologies* p. 99.
32. Arendt *Human condition* pp. 177–86; Nietzsche F. *The twilight of the idols* (1888) in Kaufmann W., selected and trans. *The portable Nietzsche* (1954) Chatto & Windus 1971 pp. 543–4.

CHAPTER ONE

Heroic Action: Narratives of Imperialism

This scene of impotence and futility was ended by the entrance of the remarkable man who had raised the party from the dust, and had led them from one success to another until it had seemed that the victory was won. Silence fell upon the assemblage; some stood up in respect; everyone wondered what he would say . . . . Above all, what course would he propose? . . .

His nervous temperament could not fail to be excited by the vivid scenes through which he had lately passed, and the repression of his emotion only heated the inward fire. Was it worth it? The struggle, the labour, the constant rush of affairs, the sacrifice of so many things that made life easy, or pleasant – for what? A people's good! That, he could not disguise from himself, was rather the direction than the cause of his efforts. Ambition was the motive force, and he was powerless to resist it . . . . To live in dreamy quiet and philosophic calm, far from the noise of men . . . was, he felt, a more agreeable picture. And yet he knew he could not endure it. 'Vehement, high, and daring' was his cast of mind. The life he lived was the only one he could ever live; he must go on to the end.

(Winston Churchill, *Savrola*, 1900)[1]

Savrola, Winston Churchill's only novel, was written when he was in his mid–twenties, serving as a subaltern in South India. The eponymous hero is the romantic leader of the National Party, which is fomenting a revolution against a dictatorship in the republic of Laurania. He is a great orator, a 'remarkable man' whose energy is apparent in his ability to transform a scene of 'impotence and futility' into one of breathless expectation. Here, at the centre of the narrative, in the theatrical moment when the populace waits for the hero to speak or act, our attention is fixed on the great man's character and his bearing. We see the paramount importance of public performance, the necessary sacrifice of other areas of his life and the intensity of experience represented by the man of action choosing dangerous commitment over private contentment. Savrola's self-conception bears a distinct resemblance to that of Churchill himself, who told his mother that he had put 'all my philosophy . . . into the mouth of my hero'.[2] Throughout his life, Churchill was preoccupied with heroic adventure and the concept of the great man. With his taste for conquest, fame and glory, he liked to see himself in the tradition of the great commanders: Cromwell and Nelson were amongst his chief heroes; he kept a white porcelain bust of Napoleon on his desk all his life. The public figure of 'Winston Churchill' was created on an almost equally heroic scale.

However great the disillusionment with heroic attitudes after the First World War, the heroic ideal proved in some ways to be remarkably resilient. The rhetoric of heroism – gallant deeds, ardent warriors, swift steeds and base foes – could not again be used with the innocence of a prewar world in which 'everyone knew what Glory was, and what Honour meant'.[3] But the disjunction between pre- and post-1914 was by no means absolute: this is not only to say that what we would think of as 'modern consciousness' is already latent in nineteenth-century thought, but that many of the values, myths and fantasies of the prewar period persisted. What Valentine Cunningham calls the postwar 'vacuum of glory' was, after the anti-heroic twenties, filled by new claimants to heroic stature and exemplars of the greatness of a life of action.[4] Churchill was, of course, amongst those who worked hardest to keep alive Britain's heroic traditions. For him, the sacrifices of the First World War made it incomprehensible that 'we should now throw away our conquests and our inheritance, through sheer helplessness and pusillanimity'. The greatness of a life of action retained in his mind its martial aspect. Some accused him of finding war alone interesting: 'I don't believe Winston takes any interest in public affairs', Viscount Cecil said, 'unless they involve the possibility of bloodshed. Preferably he likes to kill foreigners . . . .'[5] The way in which he expressed his belief in personal and national greatness, which to many seemed absurdly heightened and archaic, again came into its own when he was appointed prime minister in May 1940. In a passage from his war memoirs on becoming prime minister, Churchill says, 'I felt as if I were walking with destiny, and that all my past life had been but a preparation for this hour and this trial.'[6] Crisis and conflict had once more provided scope for romantic egoism. As Isaiah Berlin writes, Churchill was a leader whose strength of character and single-mindedness inevitably aroused the suspicion of those committed to more conventional forms of political activity: 'he thinks it a brave thing to ride in triumph through Persepolis; he knows with an unshakeable certainty what he considers to be big, handsome, noble and worthy of pursuit by someone in high station, and what, on the contrary, he abhors as being dim, grey, thin, likely to lower or destroy the play of colour and movement in the universe.'[7]

In the period before the First World War, the whole notion of heroic adventure was most closely bound up with the excitement of empire-building. Churchill saw himself as heir to the heroic ethos of a Victorian era when Britain's position on the seas was unrivalled, 'and when the realisation of the greatness of our Empire . . . was ever growing stronger'. He was determined that the imperial heritage, secured by the great men of the past, should not be lost by the 'small men' of the present.[8] Although Savrola is a national rather than an imperial hero, his qualities are those which the Victorians admired in the men of action who served on the frontiers of Empire. Remote from England, the republic of Laurania can, like Asia and Africa, be imagined as the right setting for the bold, colourful movement and noble pursuits which are, as Berlin suggests, seen as the antithesis of the grey, dull round of ordinary political life. From the time of the scramble for Africa in the closing decades of the nineteenth century until the outbreak of the First World War, the imperialist enterprise provided a context for heroic action. In Edward Said's phrase, 'The colonial territories are realms of possibility.'[9]

If Empire provided the territory for romantic action (and often for personal redemption), it also, of course, provided territory to be possessed and exploited. Imperialism was motivated by a drive towards economic expansion. It was generally less acceptable, however, to celebrate a capitalist commitment to economic growth than to glory in the moral and imaginative possibilities inherent in the imperial adventure. As J.A. Hobson argued in his influential turn-of-the-century study of imperialism, although the dominant direct motive for imperialist expansion was an urgent economic demand for markets, those pursuing imperial policies most often championed objectives other than commercial gain, appealing to motives grander than a predatory search for greater wealth and new investment possibilities. There was, in Hobson's judgement, a confusion of motives that did not, on the whole, involve hypocrisy or the deliberate simulation of false motives, but rather a kind of 'psychical departmentalism'. Imperialism had been 'floated on a sea of vague, shifty, well-sounding phrases'. The 'cheery optimism' of the undertaking was founded on a general belief in 'national destiny'. It relied upon appeals to the mission of civilisation, to what Kipling called the 'white man's burden' and the spirit of adventure. For those who saw themselves as upholding the values of the gentleman, serving the Empire was emphatically dissociated from making money: the businessman who was in the Empire for profit was a 'box-wallah'.[10] This imaginative recuperation of imperialism was facilitated by what Hannah Arendt calls England's tradition of men 'who went enthusiastically into far and curious lands to strange and native peoples to slay the numerous dragons that had plagued them for centuries'. The figure of St George presided over the chivalry of the Empire, his role in rescuing those in distress symbolising what many believed Empire was all about. A latter-day adventurer like T.E. Lawrence (Lawrence of Arabia) conformed to the same pattern in being equipped by an extensive acquaintance with the literature of chivalry and romance: Lawrence told Liddell Hart that he had read nearly every manual of chivalry plus Morris and Tennyson's romances and sagas; he carried a copy of Malory's *Morte d'Arthur* with him into the desert.[11] The colonies were a perfect realm for dragon-slayers, a testing-ground for the sense of sacrifice and duty, and for the virtues of chivalry, nobility, fidelity and bravery – for 'dreams which contained the best of European and Christian traditions, even when they had already deteriorated into the futility of boyhood ideals'. The colonial services, Arendt argues, tended to enlist those who, having never outgrown such boyhood ideals, were most fit for the task in hand, and the challenges posed by remote and unfamiliar places provided an outlet for larger, more romantic kinds of action than were allowable in a domestic political sphere in which revolution (one of the most obvious outlets for heroic action) was decidedly undesirable. Imperialism thus provided an opportunity to escape 'a society in which a man had to forget his youth if he wanted to grow up', and the departure of the more adventurous young men to distant lands allowed the continued toleration of boyhood ideals, while at the same time preventing a conversion of these ideals into a more mature form of political action: 'Strange and curious lands attracted the best of England's youth since the end of the nineteenth century, deprived her society of the most honest and the most dangerous elements, and guaranteed, in addition to this bliss, a certain conservation, or perhaps petrification, of boyhood noblesse which preserved *and* infantilized Western moral standards.'[12]

The association of high moral standards with the activities of the energetic, event-making man is central to the tradition of hero-worship which runs through the nineteenth century. The ideal can clearly be expressed in military action, but its martial aspect is invariably coupled with moral or spiritual inspiration: the imperialist Remington, for example, in Wells's *New Machiavelli*, lamenting England's 'lethargy of soul', says that he prays for 'a chastening war' and would not mind seeing England's flag in the dirt 'if only her spirit would come out of it'.[13] Carlyle writes of 'the leaders of men, the great ones', as having a dual function, both creating history and acting as patterns or 'modellers' for other men to imitate. They are metaphorically represented by the light of rectitude: the great individual is 'a natural luminary shining by the gift of Heaven; a flowing light-fountain . . . of native original insight, of manhood and heroic nobleness; – in whose radiance all souls feel that it is well with them'. The hero, whose values are antithetical to those of commercial society, is identified as a man who boldly chooses intuition over reflection, preferring ardour and temerity to detachment and caution. The British are seen as a chosen people with a special mission, and the hero as a manifestation of national destiny.[14]

Hero-worship and the excitement of Empire were sustained by the late nineteenth-century proliferation of tales of adventure, both non-fiction and fiction. Adventuring heroes are shown meeting the challenge of unknown and savage places. Their stories testify to the innate greatness of individual character and at the same time embody 'the exaggerated sense of responsibility' that the British felt for foreign peoples, inferiors in need of special protection.[15] The exploits of contemporary adventurers were widely circulated. Nineteenth-century adventurers like Chinese Gordon and Conrad's model, James Brooke, the white rajah of Sarawak, were readily assimilated to the imperial myth. As the ill-fated Dan Dravot tells his friend Peachey in Kipling's *The Man who would be King* 'we shall be Emperors – Emperors of the Earth! Rajah Brooke will be a suckling to us. I'll treat with the Viceroy on equal terms.'[16] In the early twentieth century, T.E. Lawrence, though he came on the stage at a time when it seemed that heroes might be a disappearing breed, manufactured his own myth of heroic endeavour, and his elevation to the status of a national hero was encouraged by many of the leading men of the day, including Churchill, Shaw and Buchan. Much popular fiction of the time contributed to the legend of the imperial adventurer. In spite of his reputation as the poet of the white man's burden, Kipling himself is very far from presenting an uncritical characterisation of the imperial hero: many of the men in his stories are, like Dravot and Peachey, greedy or weak or deficient, failing to measure up to the ideals of heroic adventure. But others fictionalised the myth in a more straightforward way. From 1876 on, George Alfred Henty published dozens of novels on English and Imperial history, achieving sales in 1898 as high as a quarter of a million. H. Rider Haggard's

King Solomon's Mines appeared in 1885, billed as 'THE MOST AMAZING BOOK EVER WRITTEN'. The young Winston Churchill, who read every novel he could of Haggard's, wrote to tell him that he liked his next novel, *Alan Quatermain*, even better than *King Solomon's Mines*: 'it is more amusing. I hope you will write a good many more books.'[17] This, of course, is just what Haggard did, becoming one of the most enduringly popular of all adventure writers.

In *King Solomon's Mines* we see the way in which the romantic elements in the imperialist tale are entwined with, but also differentiated from, commercial concerns. Allan Quatermain, the comparatively unheroic teller of heroic tales, is allowed to have an underlying financial motive: '"I am a trader, and have to make my living, so I accept your offer about those diamonds . . . ."' A central thread in the narrative is obviously the quest for the mine itself, and we, as readers, would be loathe to see Quatermain *fail* to obtain at least some of the fabulous diamonds. At the same time, however, the journey undertaken leads towards the fulfilment of a heroic mission. Motives are clearly distinguished, and the narrative places heroic adventure on a much higher plane than commercial interests. The 'great men' of the story are Sir Henry Curtis and his African counterpart, Ignosi, rightful King of the Kukuanas. The history of Sir Henry's family involvement in Africa in a sense contains a progression from materialistic to idealistic motives – from Sir Henry's lost brother to his own warrior-brotherhood with Ignosi. His original objective in undertaking the journey is to rescue his brother, who has come to grief whilst trying to make his fortune in South Africa; Curtis is, however, diverted into a task of heroic restoration, enlisted to fight on the side of a good native ruler who is seeking to regain a kingdom lost to a wicked usurper. It is essential that Sir Henry, the very type of the heroic adventurer (a Viking figure resembling an 'ancient Dane'), is detached from the quest for material gain. When the path of the white adventurers crosses that of Ignosi, Sir Henry rejects the inducement of diamonds as implying a motive unworthy of an English gentleman: 'he mistakes an Englishman . . . a gentleman will not sell himself for wealth'. Instead, the gentleman undertakes the task of helping the noble savage out of good fellowship and a virtuous antipathy to the evil represented by the usurping king: 'It will be very pleasant to me to try and square matters with that cruel devil, Twala.'[18]

In coming to Africa, the adventure hero is able to test to the full his heroic daring and resolution. There is a shedding of civilised inhibitions, suggested in *King Solomon's Mines* by the kinship of the European hero with Ignosi. What he *brings* to the scene of the

23

adventure is a degree of moral superiority, allowing him to hope he will influence for the better the conduct of affairs in the kingdom he has helped to save. The third member of Quatermain's expedition, the immaculately dressed and gentlemanly Captain Good, provides Haggard with a comic version of white supremacy, holding the natives in thrall with a half-shaven face, false teeth which inexplicably 'come and go' and his 'beautiful white legs'. Quatermain, with sudden inspiration and 'an imperial smile', tells the 'astonished aborigines' that all three white men have descended from 'the biggest star that shines at night' (pp. 113–15). An impressive moment, but not, Haggard implies, an act that can be sustained for long. The morally ascendant adventurers must soon, like Good's magical teeth, move and melt away.

The territory of the adventure is above all a space of possibility and performance. Huge assemblies of men, great set-piece battles and fierce man-to-man combats require the hero to speak and act, but it is neither necessary nor desirable for him to stay once the crisis has passed. It is not finally a space to be possessed by the adventurers, either physically (all the fabulous riches of the mine itself) or politically and morally. The help afforded by white power is given on condition that Ignosi accept something closer to European standards of just rule, promising to do away with the 'smelling out of witches' and with 'the killing of men without trial' (p. 176), but this establishment of European moral influence is secured only by the inherent goodness of Ignosi. In the end, the white adventurers must recall their English identities and depart from the land of the Kukuanas, dismissing any suggestion of a permanent role in the country they have aided. The hero's task is to originate, to found a new order or to restore a lost one. The home to which he returns, of course, is only a temporary resting-place: as Quatermain says, in the Introduction to Haggard's next novel, he had a 'great craving' to 'go away from this place where I lived idly and at ease, back again to the wild land where I had spent my life .... The thirst for the wilderness was on me' (p. 3).

The tensions running through *King Solomon's Mines* – between possession and performance, commercial motives and heroic morality, home territory and action territory – are present in countless other tales which communicated to a wide readership the exhilaration of Empire. These oppositions are important as well to the more sophisticated, ironic or comic versions of romantic adventure-heroism. The three writers included in this chapter – Joseph Conrad, G.K. Chesterton and George Bernard Shaw – are all ambivalent in their representation of the character and role of the heroic adventurer, and their handling of the heroic mythos reflects not only their divided judgements of imperialism but their wider conceptions of political life – for example, of the exercise of power by the romantic egoist and of the relationship between the individual political actor and the larger community. All three writers, although opposing imperialism in essential respects, sympathetically dramatise the lives of men who are to some extent heroes of Empire: white men gaining pre-eminence in imperial outposts; a hero whose victory establishes the Empire of Notting Hill; historical heroes asserting imperial power in, say, Italy or Egypt. At the same time, however, they explore the inherent violence and moral *naïveté* of the heroic ethos, and the corruption of the heroic quest by the drive towards imperial conquest, by greed and possessiveness, political rationalisation and aggrandisement.

Conrad, Chesterton and Shaw clearly spoke for very different political positions and often disagreed with one another (Shaw and Chesterton over a long period in their seventeen years of public debates). None of them held views that can be easily slotted into conventional political categories: to relate them, respectively, to conservatism, distributism and socialism does not give us any very complete sense of their preferences and judgements; more individual labels (for example, Conrad as sceptical romantic, Chesterton as radical populist, Shaw as creative evolutionist) perhaps create a slightly fuller picture, but still are not entirely adequate. Each writer has been a controversial figure, in his own time and subsequently, partly because of the complex, often contradictory nature of his political beliefs. Conrad has been variously classed as an aristo-royal apologist, an old-fashioned conservative and a repressed revolutionary; several recent critics (for example Fleishman and Said) have developed analyses designed to explain the tensions in his political thinking, between anarchism and conservatism, community and individual, and so on. Chesterton's contemporaries sometimes expressed puzzlement over whether he was a radical or a conservative, since he attacked the exploitation of the poor by the rich but at the same time stood against current social reform and loved nothing more than the patriotism, chivalry and romance that are contained in the 'direct tradition of the Past'. Chesterton maintained that Shaw was 'the least social of all Socialists': 'I pity the Socialist state that tries to manage with him.' What Chesterton calls Shaw's 'anarchism' made it difficult for any political group to feel wholly at ease with him, and he was often at odds with fellow socialists and Fabians, not least over his tendency to make laudatory comments about strong individual leaders like Mussolini or even, at times, Hitler.[19] But however diverse the political convictions of the three writers, it is possible to find common ground amongst them in their romantic conceptions of political action, which entail a passionate stress on individual identity and initiative and an anti-deterministic belief in the possibility of political choice. Each to some extent avoids pessimism by asserting the value in political life of individual action. The dynamism of the hero or great man is seen as redemptive – a hope (even if only a 'tragic hope') for salvation from the dull, unimaginative mediocrity and restrictiveness of bureaucratic politics.

Conrad's novels are often included in studies of adventure tales because his rewritings of adventure motifs, though they are in many respects sardonic reversals of the genre, are at the same time powerful expressions of the virtue inherent in heroic assertion.[20] His narratives of loss and ironic disillusionment depart from popular versions of the adventure form in order to examine in a more complex way the motives, standards of behaviour and code of honour that the European hero takes with him to far-flung lands. The most difficult trials the Conrad hero faces are, of course, moral and psychological rather than physical: he is a carrier of strongly positive values, but, instead of facing the straightforward choices confronting a Haggard adventurer, he must cope with unsettling self-doubt, anxiety and uncertainty; the slick resolutions possible in Haggard's novels – a final satisfying victory, a little wealth, a modicum of influence and a hasty departure from a 'wild land' that continues to fascinate – are not available to Lingard, Lord Jim or Nostromo. When Conrad writes directly about military conflict it is evident that he is very far from seeing combat itself as a stimulating test of valour: in *Autocracy and War*, for example, war, personified, receives homage from states which cannot bear the thought of ceasing to grow in territory, wealth and influence; it harnesses science to its gun-carriages; it enriches the arms manufacturers and devours 'the first youth of whole generations', reaping 'its harvest of countless corpses'.[21] In his novels, the protagonists are not (in contrast to Haggard's heroes) generally represented engaging in acts of violence, but this is by no means to say that Conrad avoids confronting the destructive implications of the heroic ideal. Betraying their own ideal images at crucial moments, his heroes can end by leading others, distorted reflections of the hero (the ghost-like Jörgenson, for example, or Jim's dark double, Gentleman Brown), to perpetrate violence which is to them 'unthinkable'. The death and devastation with which the novels close are far more disturbing than the routine carnage of Haggard's novels, and ensure that readers feel unease about the violence at the core of heroic action.

More superficially and comically created hero figures – hero as Life Force and hero as romantic warrior – play a central role in the work of Shaw and Chesterton. Not as burdened with thoughts of their own responsibility as Conrad's heroes, they face the moral dilemmas of heroic action with a certain equanimity. Shaw's admiration for heroic intensity of will and vitality of mind is an essential aspect of his faith in 'creative evolution', in human advancement inspired by the man fearless, energetic and subversive enough to rise above the encumbrance of established political institutions and shape his own destiny. In choosing to represent the great imperial military commanders – Napoleon and Caesar - Shaw pursues his task of relieving the hero of his traditional (and typically English) moral baggage. The romantic paragon, serving an outmoded chivalric code and engaged in 'fighting single combats in a monotonous ecstasy of heroism', is to be supplanted by someone more like Carlyle's 'true hero', beyond 'the mere *preux chevalier,* whose fanatical personal honour, gallantry, and self-sacrifice, are founded on a passion for death born of inability to bear the weight of a life that will not grant ideal conditions'. Shaw often expresses a dislike of war, but his detestation is reserved for the moral hypocrisy of romantic militarism – for the propagandistic representation of war 'as a simple and heroic scene of knight errantry, with England as Lancelot-Galahad'. In 1917, for example, his speeches are combative (with Shaw wanting, as Lytton Strachey said, to beat the Germans 'again, and again, and again!'), but favour a war that is waged without patriotic illusions.[22] In his plays, the realistic man of action acknowledges that spectacular military victories are expected of the hero by the people, and is ready to give them what they want. Instead of bonds of responsibility between hero and public, Shaw sees bonds created by the devious, manipulative capacities of a hero who has been divested of the adventure hero's childlike innocence and has discarded the ethical content of the heroic ideal.

Like Conrad, Chesterton is disturbed by the views of such progressive intellectuals as Shaw and Wells: Conrad is unsettled by the rationalistic confidence of their 'hopeful industry', Chesterton alarmed at the sheer scale of their optimistic projections. Chesterton had begun by sympathising with socialist idealists, but had then, by his own account, become 'uneasily conscious that some of the things that they wanted to destroy were those that I wanted most to preserve. Little things; Neighbourly things . . . .'[23] In *The Napoleon of Notting Hill,* his championing of the common people against large-scale political institutions (whether imperialist or socialist) prompts him to reach back to an essentially knightly conception of the hero, a flamboyant

27

figure from the 'Land of Youth' drawing his 'great sword' in the cause of popular politics – a fantasy in which London is miraculously transformed into a realm of romantic possibility. Although Chesterton acknowledges that heroic action might itself pave the way for some form of systematic domination or exploitation, he is unquestionably more given to simple political nostalgia than either Conrad or Shaw, and more inclined to glorify both martial violence and the 'infantilised' morality of adventure heroism. But, as I have suggested, Conrad and Shaw as well, for all their reservations and revisions, greatly value the heroic impulse: with its connotations of youthful energy, fresh starts and 'big, handsome' actions, it can be seen as a vital preventative, working against passive acquiescence in the status quo and countering deterministic modes of thought. Conrad's thwarted idealists and Shaw's cynical realists stand equally above the sluggish conformity of modern political life, an implicit reproach to a civilisation that seems to leave no room for independent, courageous initiatives.

HEROIC ACTION IN *THE RESCUE*

Reading *The Rescue*, which was begun in the closing years of the nineteenth century and completed some twenty years later (in 1918–19), gives us a strong impression of the continuity of Conrad's views and of his commitment to treating moral action in traditional moral language. The finished novel, in providing a sustained representation of so idealised a central character as Tom Lingard, illuminates Conrad's conception of the nature of the hero and the problems of heroic action that so often preoccupied him, defining with clarity the underlying ethos of adventure-heroism which is repeatedly challenged, tested and ironised in the novels Conrad wrote between the inception and the completion of *The Rescue* – most importantly, in *Lord Jim* and *Nostromo*. When Conrad depicts political action in the context of advanced European society, it tends to be compromised and doomed from the start: in *Under Western Eyes*, for example, we see the anguished conflict experienced by the good and gentle Haldin when he sees the discrepancy between his heroic mission and the means of its accomplishment ('reckless – like a butcher – in the middle of all these innocent people – scattering death – I! I! . . . I wouldn't hurt a fly!').[24] In *Nostromo*, Conrad also animates his hero figure within a quite highly developed social-political world – one which is remote enough to be the scene of romantic political action, but which is still sufficiently complex to limit and qualify the nature of the hero's influence, allowing Conrad to bring out very fully the strengths and weaknesses of his character. In *The Rescue*, on the other hand, the qualities of the hero are thrown into relief by bringing civilised society *to him*. The representatives of an older, more sophisticated form of political life are compelled to meet Lingard on his own terms, so that our attention is repeatedly drawn to the contrast between the realm of action – of political origins – and those established authority systems which have found a substitute for action, escaping from 'the frailty of human affairs into the solidity of quiet and order'. This description of settled political systems, from Hannah Arendt's *The Human Condition*, captures a sense of both the attractions and the perplexities of a commitment to action, as opposed to the safety and dullness implied by 'solidity of quiet and order'. Arendt's definition of some of the basic elements in a life of action has been of central usefulness in this discussion. The ideal of political action that she expounds, though idiosyncratic, is similar, in its strenuous individual engagement and moral responsibility, to the romantic political thinking that is both sceptically and sympathetically viewed by Conrad (on whom she draws heavily in her discussion of imperialism). Like Conrad, she is consistently alert to potential problems and contradictions in an ideal of political action, such as the danger of moral *naïveté*, the temptation to retain full control by denying others the right to act and the difficulty of separating action from violence.[25]

Conrad sets the scene in *The Rescue* by explaining the conjunction of primitive political structures and the archetypal Western man of action. The Malay Archipelago, 'the scene of adventurous undertakings', is a place which, in spite of European conquest, has not lost 'the mystery and romance of its past'. Although the narrator sees the imminent prospect of advancing civilisation winning the long struggle, the Archipelago still retains the characteristics of its own earlier phase of political life. Rapid changes in 'the ideas of the world' are also rendering obsolete the type of Western man, the true adventurer, initially involved in these struggles. The bond between the adventurer and the people he befriends is anachronistic: he fights alongside them for a cause which, as the narrator observes with irony, 'had no right to exist in the face of an irresistible and orderly progress', being guided by a simple feeling and tinged with romance. The rajah and princess aided by Lingard, and natives of Wajo generally, are similarly described in terms of their youthful heroic capacity, a vitality that gives Mrs Travers 'a sudden glow and exhaltation impossible in viewing the affairs of her

29

own society'. The Shore of Refuge, where most of the action takes place, is as removed as possible from established and bounded political communities: it is 'land without form', presenting a blurred outline, having no specific name on the charts, omitted from the geography manuals.[26] It is, for Lingard, 'the circle of another existence', in which he can live 'governed by his impulse, nearer his desire'. His world is, in one sense, 'cut off from the rest of the earth', but in another, clearly, a surviving fragment of earth's most powerful primitive myths of foundation (pp. 89, 134).

The contrast with more advanced Western political and social arrangements is made more explicit by the introduction of the heavily caricatured Travers, the conceited, impenetrable Englishman who, having happened upon the scene of Lingard's massing forces, presents himself as 'a very great man'. Travers represents those political systems which substitute modes of settled regularity for action. His concerns are with commerce, administration and conventional politics; he regards with intense suspicion and growing disgust the inexplicable intrusion of Lingard, 'a disgrace to civilisation' who looks 'as if he had stepped out from an engraving in a book of buccaneers' (pp. 107–11). The coast on which the adventure takes place is to Travers merely a fragment of colonial territory, covered by official treaties and regulations. His inflexible 'official verbiage' , as he talks of international understandings and the duty to civilise, captures the absurd presumption of his conceptions. In Travers's mind, the imperial position can be defined with pedantic precision: 'This coast . . . has been placed under the sole protection of Holland by the Treaty of 1820. The Treaty of 1820 creates special rights and obligations' (p. 127). There is never any question of acknowledging the separate 'rights and obligations' established amongst themselves by the inhabitants of this alien society. The nature of Travers's sphere is reflected most clearly in his relationship with his wife, who scornfully acquiesces in 'the shallowness of events and the monotony of a worldly existence' which life with Travers has meant for her (p. 108). Having married him in the hope of attaching herself to a passionate and sincere ideal, she has found only the respectability of the kind of cold careerist who is able to ascend in the power structure of advanced society. Travers is the embodiment of politics as method and as dry, calculating cynicism. A man who assiduously winds his watch even when it is broken, he is committed to the regularity of civilised routine, as opposed to the seizure of the moment that is at the heart of romantic action: his approach to power is not the picturesque, energetic, above-board action of Lingard, but the circumspect deviousness of diplomacy. The two men are both dealing in 'matters of high policy and local politics', but the political worlds they come from are so entirely separated that neither recognises the other as a man of power. Mrs Travers assures her husband that Lingard has no idea of his importance: 'He doesn't know anything of your social and political position and still less of your great ambitions' (pp. 225–7).

The Rescue is centred around an emotionally-coloured myth of action that, to borrow T.E. Lawrence's phrase, serves 'the wish to quicken history . . . as the great adventurers of old had done'. The story Lingard tells to Mrs Travers establishes him as quintessentially an 'actor', in the sense that Arendt gives the word. Such action, in her analysis, has the 'startling unexpectedness' that is 'inherent in all beginnings and all origins': man's capacity for genuine political action 'means that the unexpected can be expected from him, that he is able to perform what is infinitely improbable'. Action is the disclosure of who you are, the hero being the agent who sets in motion the process which eventually produces the series of events that together form a story.[27] What Conrad gives in *The Rescue* is a fully embodied sense of the initial impulse behind the imperial adventure: 'The headlong fierceness of purpose invested his obscure design of conquest with the proportions of a great enterprise' (pp. 138–9). We see the energy of Lingard in imposing his will on the world as he finds it, but the adventurer's naïve idea of greatness is also shadowed by reminders of the later phase of established imperialist rule. The high valuation placed on the impulse is apparent, as are the qualifications and ironising perceptions of the limitations of vision, the folly that goes hand in hand with the generous energies. A roving seaman like Lingard, conquering the 'kingdom' of the jungle, has a primitive purity of motive, innocent of later betrayals of the ideal. Though his involvement in itself creates dangers for those he leads, he is explicitly dissociated from the materialistic objectives that can be seen to operate behind commercial-capitalistic imperialism. Mrs Travers rightly tells her husband that the thought of wealth would be the last thing to enter Lingard's head. As an individual adventurer, he is the enemy of established imperial power, which is in the hands of the Dutch, to whom the Malays pay tribute. Though he disclaims any intention of interfering with the Dutch, Lingard's Wajo expedition is to be undertaken in the teeth of Dutch colonial intentions. As in *Savrola* and *King Solomon's Mines*, the objective is the slaying of a dragon: the restoration of a good ruler, Hassim, requires the defeat of the corrupt, arbitrary power of the Rajah Tulla, who 'smokes opium and is sometimes dangerous to speak to' (p. 90). Again, we can see

31

an affinity with the aims pursued by Lawrence of Arabia: it is the same kind of self-image we find, for example, in his account of his intentions in the Arab rising, to 'make a new nation, to restore a lost influence'. 'Naturally', he told Liddell Hart, 'it would be a crusade in the modern form – the freeing of a race from bondage.'[28]

Such resolute political initiative presupposes a hero who is marked off in a qualitatively unique way from ordinary men, the kind of man described by Sidney Hook as an event-making man, that is, someone whose actions are not just accidents of position but are the consequences of outstanding capacities of character, will, tenacity and audacity. He is a man who is able to exert some control over events, as opposed to the mediocre 'eventful' man, who may be lucky enough to be at the right place at the right time, but who has no controlling conception of the effects of his decisions.[29] Tom Lingard is the embodiment of the event-making man, identified by his devotion to impulse, high-mindedness, purity of heart and commitment to an ideal of foundation (to 'lay the foundation of a flourishing state on the ideas of pity and justice'). Though in early middle age, Lingard is consistently characterised by youthful, active qualities. A man of great stature, he is 'erect and supple', with hair like 'gold wire', an unwrinkled brow and remarkable eyes, which give a 'scrutinising ardour' (*The Rescue*, pp. 15–20). His primitive vitality is evident throughout, as when he lifts his big arm and shakes his fist, proclaiming his determination to shape the lives of others: 'He would wake up the country! That was the fundamental and unconscious emotion on which were engrafted his need of action, the primitive sense of what was due to justice, to gratitude, to friendship . . .' (pp. 94–5). Lingard is seen as a chivalric knight errant by the perceptive d'Alcacer: 'A knight as I live! A descendant of the immortal hidalgo errant upon the sea' (p. 123). Representing not only physical action but rhetorical force, he is a charismatic figure, but one who makes manifest the human and moral dimensions of this role rather than the quasi-religious aspects of charismatic leadership. His 'great voice' which, like his great strength, fills all the space around with its 'undeniable authority', is as appealing as that of a fine actor, but, unlike the actor, Lingard speaks only for himself, persuading and moving with his truth and sincerity: 'this man was nothing in the world but his very own self' (pp. 323, 342).

This inherent truthfulness proceeds from Lingard's 'simple-minded brain' and 'guileless breast' (p. 234). Conrad confronts here, as he does elsewhere, the question of whether such simplicity is finally indistinguishable from stupidity – and, if so, whether even stupidity can in some sense be praiseworthy. The romantic answer, of course, is that it may well be admirable if it is on a grand enough scale. As Mrs Travers observes to d'Alcacer, Lingard's obtuseness is of an utterly different kind to that of her husband, who is so completely a creature of his social-political world that he lacks all intuitive human understanding; Lingard, on the other hand, possesses the kind of 'colossal' stupidity which is 'indistinguishable from great visions that were in no sense mean and made up for him a world of his own' (p. 259). When Lingard, by falling in love with Mrs Travers, loses his simplicity and his childlike perception of the world, he loses his direction: he can still see 'the visible surface of life open in the sun to the conquering tread of an unfettered will', but whereas before the facts that assailed him could be 'discerned clearly, mastered and despised' they are now clouded by 'the wavering gloom of a dark and inscrutable purpose' (p. 177). He eventually comes to recognise a conflict within himself, in which he has to face 'unsuspected powers, foes that he could not go out to meet at the gate' (pp. 270–1). Jörgenson, reflecting on the relative value of 'Tom's integrity' and 'that woman', laments that the intrusion of a woman into the male world of adventure has taken all the hardness out of Lingard: a man's commitment to a woman has nothing to do with the essential heroic qualities of 'sincerity and good faith and honour' (pp. 313, 337). He has been defined by his adventure, 'which made him in his own sight exactly what he was'. For Lingard to lose his energetic purposiveness is for him to cease to be himself (p. 185).

Having lost purposiveness, Lingard is imaged as a ship becalmed. He sinks into 'perfectly appalling' listlessness, and we see his immobility as 'the dreadful ease of slack limbs in the sweep of an enormous tide' (pp. 346, 353). Lingard's captaincy of his ship is initially the metaphoric embodiment of his sense of his own individual power to determine the course of events. His romantic partnership with the brig suggests complete autonomy and confident, independent motion: 'the swiftest country vessel in those seas', his brig is the emblem of action as passion and represents to him 'the incomparable freedom of the seas' (p. 20). In his analysis of the sea as the national symbol of the English, Elias Canetti observes the close connection between the Englishman's relationship to the sea and his 'famous individualism'. The decisive conception is that the sea is there to be ruled, and the isolated individual, captain of his ship, has a power of command that is absolute and undisputed: 'The captain decides on the goal, and the sea . . . carries him there, though not without storms and other manifestations of hostility.' As is also apparent in such later adventure tales as C.S. Forester's Hornblower stories, the command of a ship provides many opportunities for decisive individual action, and hence for heroism. Lingard's free stride on board his brig is contrasted with the wary, circumscribed motion that might be expected of a man more aware of the constraints on freedom of action for someone standing on the 'cramped decks of a small craft, tossed by the caprice of angry or playful seas'. Like many romantic egoists, he suffers from the false impression that he has greater control and power of self-determination than is humanly possible. It is not the case, however, that Conrad disbelieves in the determining power of heroic action. Although *The Rescue* very fully explores the illusions of the heroic personality and the limitations of his power, the narrative repeatedly demonstrates that the hero's actions can decisively influence the course of human affairs.[30]

The notion of heroic action implies a belief that the fate of peoples can hang on what one person decides or does, as against the determinist's conviction that the outcome of events is decided by historical laws or by the exigencies of the period in which the hero lives. The feeling that there is a *need* for a hero 'to initiate, organise, and lead' grows out of the conviction that choices are open, that where the historical situation permits of major alternative paths of development, heroic action can count decisively. One of the key images associated with such a belief is that of the forking path. Both the 'eventful' and the event-making man appear at 'the forking points of history' and, in the case of the event-making man, he not only finds the fork but helps to create it, making his own luck and increasing the odds of success for his chosen alternative by virtue of his own extraordinary qualities: 'At the very least, like Caesar and Cromwell and Napoleon, he must free the path he has taken from opposition and, in so doing, display exceptional qualities of leadership. It is the hero as event-making man who leaves the positive imprint of his personality upon history . . . .'[31] The forking path, both literally and as a metaphor for choices made, is one of the main structural elements in *The Rescue*. As in many tales of adventure, the actual direction travelled determines the course of events, as when Lingard decides to sail to Wajo, where his speedily executed plan of action rescues Hassim from imminent death, or when he finally sets his course in the opposite direction to that taken by the schooner carrying Mrs Travers. At the beginning of the novel, we have one of Conrad's strong natural images of an idealised path, clear and unmistakable, but surrounded by threatening darkness, by forebodings of malign fate. Some of the characters, in particular the Malaysians, tend to see the hand of fate at work in all of the choices made, and there are undeniably changes of direction forced by blind fate (for example, when Carter blunders on Lingard's brig in the dark). At the same time, however, the main actors have an acute sense of the obligation to choose and of their responsibility for the choices made. Although much of what Lingard does seems to spring from impulses not fully grasped at the time, he is not mistaken in feeling that the fate of many other lives depends upon his decisions. After he rescues Hassim and Immada, he does not know where he is going, but feels certain that something is expected of him. The unconscious direction of his commitment is imaged in the brig itself, which hesitates just as he does, lingering on the road, until Lingard's deepening commitment puts an end to indecision, and, working in accord with his vessel, he follows the path of the adventurers of two centuries ago to the Shore of Refuge. During the next two years, as Lingard works to help Hassim reconquer his country, the brig continues to express his commitment in its movements, 'travelling fast . . . passing east, passing west . . . flying with masts aslant . . . forging ahead . . . battling ,with a heavy monsoon . . . lying becalmed . . . or gliding out suddenly . . . .' (*The Rescue*, p. 88). Others also make key decisions which, it is stressed, could as easily go either way. Belarab observes to Lingard, of his arrival on the Shore of Refuge, 'I said "welcome" – it was as easy for me to say "kill him"' (p. 97). Such choices are crucial to the whole of the narrative. As the disaster of the end approaches, Lingard tells Mrs Travers, 'The road was plain but I saw you in it and my heart failed me' (p. 281).

Whereas the determinist can shift moral responsibility from the acts of individual men to the impersonal course of history, it is fundamental to the heroic ethos that the human agent accept responsibility for his own actions.[32] One of Lingard's strongest characteristics is this sense that he is answerable for the lives of those whose paths have crossed his own. The utterly unheroic man, Travers, habitually refuses to take responsibility; he withdraws increasingly during the course of the narrative, until finally he is back on his yacht, his vanity soothed and his sense of the importance of his own 'superior mind' restored: 'He was not responsible. Like many men ambitious of directing the affairs of a nation, Mr Travers disliked responsibility. He would not have been above evading it in case of need, but with perverse loftiness he really, in his heart, scorned it' (p. 371). Lingard, on the other hand, is all too acutely aware of his conflicting obligations and the heavy burden of responsibility he bears, not only for Hassim and Immada but for the Europeans on board the yacht and all the others on the Shore of Refuge. His love for Mrs Travers has loosened his grip on earthly responsibility. Having cast his eyes through 'the gates of Paradise' he has been 'rendered insensible . . . to all the forms and matters of the earth', and his night of perfect rest, with his head on Mrs Travers's knee, removes him at the most crucial juncture from 'all those questions of freedom and captivity, of violence and intrigue, of life and death' (pp. 339–43).

This 'infinite ease' of paradisal contentment is linked by Conrad with the private as opposed to the public realm. According to Arendt, the courage which we tend to see as an indispensable quality of the hero is in its origins simply the willingness 'to insert one's self into the world and begin a story of one's own'; it consists 'in leaving one's private hiding place and showing who one is, in disclosing and exposing one's self'. The man of action establishes his reality in a public space of appearance before an audience of fellow men. Action itself creates this space, 'which can find its proper location almost any time and anywhere'. Once Jaffir dies at the end of *The Rescue*, there is no one left either to reproach Lingard or to witness the greatness of his intentions. Action is never possible in isolation. Strength, which is 'the natural quality of an individual seen in isolation', is to be contrasted with power, which 'springs up between men when they act together and vanishes the moment they disperse' (*Human Condition*, pp. 186–201). If a man isolates himself he forfeits power and becomes impotent, no matter how strong he is and how valid his reasons for choosing separation.

Tom Lingard's power lies in his ability to bring into being what Arendt calls a space of appearance. Here again, the distinction between Lingard and Travers is a telling one. Travers, the overly civilised man, is helpless far from home, whereas Lingard has the dynamism to create *himself* outside 'the wall of the *polis*': 'I belong where I am. I am just Tom Lingard, no more, no less, wherever I happen to be . . .' (p. 107). It is 'the world of his creation', in which all who look at him recognise him for who he is. Only in the frigidly civilised atmosphere of the yacht does he seem at first unable to generate the kind of followership which has been the essence of his self-definition: his inability to create belief bewilders him 'as if he had suddenly discovered that he was no longer himself' (pp. 238, 112). For those who do 'recognise' him, and so belong to the world he dominates, the problem is that of too complete a dependence on 'Rajah Laut'. They have lost their power of independent action, and so, when Lingard withdraws his prestigious presence, there is a disastrous power vacuum. The determining sign in the moments before the final catastrophe is vacancy, an absence of any message from Lingard, or any manifestation of his continuing commitment and power: 'there was nothing there, not even a flag displayed . . .' (p. 365).

Lingard's failure to achieve his aims is in large part a failure to keep promises. The importance of the promise in a narrative of heroic action is apparent. To use the formulation in Arendt's *The Human Condition*, which is couched in terms strongly echoing Conrad's own imagery:

> Without the fulfilment of promises, we would never be able to keep our identities; we would be condemned to wander helplessly and without direction in the darkness of each man's lonely heart, caught in its contradictions and equivocalities – a darkness which only the light shed over the public realm through the presence of others, who confirm the identity between the one who promises and the one who fulfils, can dispel.
>
> (p. 237)

The keeping of promises, which is the foundation of Lingard's good name, is also comprehended in the wider conception of honour, as represented, for example, by the values of d'Alcacer; it is an essential safeguard against the unpredictability of action and the fatality which constantly threaten to undermine human purposes. The final disaster is in a sense caused by the central importance of promise-making in Lingard's life. Unlike the heroes of a simple adventure narrative such as *King Solomon's Mines* (who pledge exactly what they are able to perform), Lingard is a man who finds himself compelled to promise too much. The night-time confidences imparted to Mrs Travers lead to his insistence that he will keep his word in his dealings with her. This is not, as is sometimes suggested, evidence that he is now acting according to the civilised code of the gentleman. Rather, it is an effort on Lingard's part to put his own simple ethic of heroic action into a context that his listener will understand. A gentleman, he asserts, would keep his word wherever given: 'Well, I am going to do that. Not a hair of your head shall be touched as long as I live!' Like the gold ring that passes between Hassim and Lingard, this remembered promise is 'a charm of great power', a talismanic pledge that seems to hold unpredictability at bay (*The Rescue*, pp. 140, 308).

Trust is one of the novel's most recurrent themes. Its power repeatedly seems to dispel darkness, as, for example, when Wasub's 'vain offer of fidelity' makes the darkness Lingard has to combat 'as if by some enchantment . . . less overpowering to his sight' (pp. 169–70). The curse that the Traverses and their yacht bring upon Lingard is that the bonds of trust begin to dissolve. Even Hassim and Immada begin to doubt him – 'And by heavens they may be right.' As the crisis deepens, the political conflict is carried forward by the growing suspicion that Lingard is false, that his allies can no longer rely on him being 'the very embodiment of truth and force'. Lingard has 'only one word',

37

and for him to lose that is to unloose 'suspicion, dread, and revenge, and the anger of armed men' (pp. 269–74). It is the absence of his word at the end that turns events to tragedy. Without the shaping force of the actions undertaken by a trustworthy leader, there is a reversion to the formlessness of the landscape itself, mere chaos, with 'no shape for the eye to rest upon, nothing for the hand to grasp', obscurity without apparent limit submerging the universe 'like a destroying flood' (p. 201).

The other defence against formlessness is the story itself, and, as Arendt says, the general meaning of an action is only available in those dramatic narratives which 'glorify a deed or accomplishment and, by transformation and condensation, show some extraordinary event in its full significance' (*The Human Condition*, p. 187). From the outset Lingard is seen as a man whose actions generate stories of legendary proportions. The stories of the first meeting of Lingard and Hassim (with Lingard hurling men about 'as the wind hurls broken boughs') and of how Lingard saved the rajah and princess at the time of the Wajo civil war are regularly told: in fact, the first point at which we know that the romantic attempt to restore Hassim will fail is when we hear the traditional account of a chief and his sister rescued by the art of magic by a ship which appeared to have sailed down from the clouds (*The Rescue*, pp. 67, 79). Some of the most important events in the novel hinge on the telling of stories of the great actions of the past. At its centre there is the crucial retelling of Lingard's own personal legend in his first extended encounter with Mrs Travers. She is 'fascinated by the simplicity of images and expressions', and he recognises in her his perfect listener (p. 135). The telling of the tale is to her the revelation of his completely different world, dominated by the legendary scale of Lingard's own personality. She sees herself becoming the figure in a story, like a woman in a ballad or in some tremendous drama in which Lingard is the tragic hero. Her husband, on the other hand, dismisses her, when she has dressed herself in the clothes of the princess, as wearing a 'most appropriate costume for this farce' (p. 220). We judge characters on the basis of whether or not they could conceivably rise to a role in Lingard's heroic drama: the romantic side of Conrad's nature leads him to admire most highly those capable of committing themselves to such a role, however strongly his pessimism suggests a tragic outcome. So d'Alcacer, for example, though he has a spectator's reluctance to participate in the play and does not relish the thought of having his throat cut by 'gorgeous barbarians', ultimately feels a preference for being involved in a story that at least has some dignity and meaning. Instead of being a player in the production that Travers sees, in which he would merely be swindled, he prefers to be the victim 'of a rough man naïvely engaged in a contest with heaven's injustice' (p. 284). Part of the disaster which overtakes Lingard is that the story which he has been creating begins to disintegrate, to lose its shape and to become unintelligible. Although it is not he who commits the final violence, he knows full well both the extent of his responsibility for Jörgenson's gesture of 'mad scorn' and the impossibility of incorporating this knowledge into a coherent heroic narrative. He finds that he is unable to explain things to Carter because the shape of the story is no longer clear to him: 'Tell him everything? . . . Only yesterday! . . . only six hours ago I had something to tell. You heard it. And now it's gone . . . . There's nothing to tell any more' (p. 194). Conrad gives us a sense that all of life's energy and warmth is contained in narratives such as those of Lingard's adventure – though, if the purposes of the hero are ultimately defeated, they can be almost too much for the audience to endure. At the end, Lingard himself cannot bear the thought of hearing the preternaturally faithful Jaffir's narrative, and, in the closing pages, d'Alcacer is alarmed at the thought that Mrs Travers might have anything more to tell him: 'Don't let us tell each other anything . . .' (pp. 372–3).

THE HERO IRONISED: *LORD JIM* AND *NOSTROMO*

The telling of an heroic story is even more centrally important to *Lord Jim*. Conceiving of the events of his life as a story and wishing to confer on them his own shape and meaning, Jim is deeply unsettled by accident, unpredictability and all other hindrances to a well-ordered and impeccable performance. One of the things about which he cares most of all is the account that he gives to Marlow, and that Marlow, in turn, will give of him to 'the world at large', but he is not finally able to find an arrangement of words adequate to the purpose. His sudden cry of 'Tell them' is followed by 'no message', and he is 'overwhelmed by the inexplicable' when he tries to commit to paper the events in Patusan. This final failure to narrate is in part a symptom of the insufficiency of the literary models of Jim's boyhood. It is his appetite for a good adventure story which has itself generated the main events of the novel. His 'course of light holiday literature' has filled him with visions of 'a stirring life in the world of adventure' where he could be 'as unflinching as a hero in a book'. He has in a sense been narrating his own 'exalted' story since he was 'quite a little chap' – 'elaborating dangers and defences, expecting the worst, rehearsing his best . . . A succession of adventures, so much glory, such a victorious progress!' In Patusan, he creates himself as a fictional stereotype, so that when Marlow last sees him, there is 'a legend of strength and prowess forming round his name as though he had been the stuff of a hero'.[33]

Jim's struggle to understand the events of his life in relation to idealised stories of heroism and romance is overlaid with Marlow's more sophisticated efforts to create a narrative that will do justice both to the facts as he knows them and to the forms and visions which Jim himself sees 'in the glow of the west' (*Lord Jim*, p. 290). This complex narrative frame, which qualifies and darkens our response to Jim as a pattern of heroic virtue, also has the effect of simplifying and exaggerating key elements in the story, bringing to the fore the regressive nature of the adventure narrative. Jim's gifts are undeniable. He is able to establish himself in Patusan as brave, true, just and utterly trustworthy; his alertness, readiness and even his capacity for speech (not eloquent but dignified and persuasive) are all fully acknowledged. But in comparison to Lingard, who is every inch the hero, Jim can only claim a heroic stature that is 'an inch, perhaps two', under the true heroic height of six feet. The satiric edge, evident in the mock-heroic phrasing (absent from descriptions of the more mature heroism of Lingard or Nostromo), does not lessen our affection for Jim, but alerts us from the outset to the dangerous self-deception involved in his romantic egoism. The fixed stare, powerful, bull-like forward movement and 'deep, loud' voice of this promising 'clean-limbed, clean-faced' boy establish at once his limitations as well as his strengths. Conrad's gentle mockery catches the romantic hyperbole of 'his many-sided courage' and his 'valorous deeds', which have a 'gorgeous virility, the charm of vagueness', passing before him 'with a heroic tread' and making his soul 'drunk with the divine philtre of an unbounded confidence in itself' (pp. 45–58, 72).

Such phrasing is matched by images of height and depth and by scenes of swift descent from illusion to disenchantment, as when, aboard the *Patna*, we witness the bathetic fall of the hero from soaring idealism to sordid complicity in the most comically embodied human inadequacy. Constantly fixing his vision on what is so high as to be unattainable, Jim renders himself as unable at the end as at the beginning to see 'the shadow of the coming event' (p. 57). In Patusan, the approach of this shadow, the ugly fact of Brown's character, is as invisible to Jim as the underwater hazard with which the *Patna* collides, and as unpalatable as the 'facts' with which he is tortured at the enquiry. The simple naïveté of his romantic nature emerges as a fatal obtuseness about the real nature of things. Like a true Carlylean hero, Jim abhors the idea of compromise, imagining that there must be an absolute distinction between the scoundrel and the hero. Conrad repeatedly stresses Jim's conviction that he belongs to a heroic realm which excludes base natures, and, in both halves of the novel, his own sense of identity is shattered by circumstances which force him to acknowledge kinship with those who 'did not belong to the world of heroic adventure' (p. 61). The extreme moral fastidiousness of this white-clad, 'immaculate, don't-you-touch-me sort of fellow' betokens the unreadiness of an innocent for the sullying compromises of adult experience. Cornelius, with the contempt of the wholly cynical, dismisses him as 'a very great man, but all the same, he knows no more than a child . . . . He is like a little child' (pp. 322–7).

Childlike innocence and the commitment to boyhood ideals suggest a regression which is closely linked to the direction of the narrative as a whole. As he retreats from the judgements of the larger world, moving 'towards the rising sun' (p. 46), Jim journeys back to a simpler stage of society, although not, as is sometimes argued, to an untarnished, idyllic world. Riven by strife and betrayals, Patusan suffers from the cruelty and rapacity of Rajah Allang and the incursions of Sherif Ali. It is, however, in its utter isolation, a survival of the sort of primitive world in which there is still scope for heroic action, offering to Jim 'a totally new set of conditions for his imaginative faculty to work upon'. Although the natives of Patusan are trading people, their engagement in trade is primarily a manifestation of youthful excitement 'beating in the blood'. In contrast to greed-driven imperial conquest, this earlier expansive impulse is a romantic enthusiasm for the challenge of unknown places, carrying men 'in the hot quest of the Ever-undiscovered Country over the hill, across the stream, beyond the wave' (pp. 203–9, 292).

In Patusan, then, Jim finds a society naturally responsive to his own romantic nature, and it is clear that his rapport with the people does not involve inculcating 'the morality of an ethical progress', or trying to establish 'the truth of ideas racially our own', in the manner of presumptuous European civilisers (pp. 292–3). Jim's role in a sense is, like that wished by Lingard, one of restoration – or at least, of helping this 'lost corner of the earth' to retain its fresh, youthful integrity and pure spirit of adventure. Ironically, however, his 'example' inspires European attentions of a less exalted kind, the predatory, unprincipled depredations planned by Gentleman Brown, a 'great man' who has attained his greatness by virtue of a 'satanic gift of finding out the best and the weakest spot in his victims' (p. 328). This 'latter-day buccaneer' wolfishly sets out for Patusan in the hope of acquiring provisions and is eventually led to think of 'stealing the whole country'. His piracy is a broadly caricatured form of colonial exploitation: 'gloating over the view of Patusan, which he had determined in his mind should become his prey', he is the epitome of treachery and greed, scheming to take for himself the 'possession, security, power' that he imagines Jim to have. We see quite different kinds of hunger behind these opposing motives for seeking dominance. When Jim asks Brown what made him come to Patusan, he replies succinctly, 'Hunger. And what made you?' – a question that for Jim could only be answered, if at all, with reference to the imaginative hunger which, in the wider world, he had failed to satisfy (pp. 303–24). Jim has indeed become 'virtual ruler of the land', possessing unquestionable power: 'in his new sphere there did not seem to be anything that was not his to hold or to give'. His 'possession' of Patusan, however, is moral and emotional rather than material. It is in a sense true, as Said argues, that Jim's position, isolated at the centre of an empire he rules, is analogous to that of the European coloniser, but it is clear that we must distinguish Jim's guardianship of his 'magic totality' from the kind of possessive relationship sought by Gentleman Brown. The legend of the mysterious white man carrying about with him an emerald of enormous size, obtained by strength and cunning from the ruler of a distant land, is only ironically applicable to Jim, since the truth contained in it is his love for Jewel, the antithesis of a materialistic 'ravishment' (pp. 244–50).

Jim's confrontation with Gentleman Brown takes place 'perhaps on the very spot' where Jim had taken the 'desperate leap' that carried him into the life of Patusan. Brown taunts Jim with 'jumping off', by chance hitting on the very phrase most likely to resonate in his mind, and Jim's abrupt decision to let Brown have a 'clear road' is another such crucial juncture, from which events move 'fast without a check, flowing from the very hearts of men like a stream from a dark source' (pp. 324–6). In contrast to *The Rescue*, with its forking paths and connected journeys, *Lord Jim* images choices between alternatives as sudden leaps or jumps, creating a much stronger sense of either–or decisions made in moments of impulsive movement, unpredictable and irreversible. The energy of youth, essential to heroic readiness, is in Jim's case governed by motives he is too immature to understand and control. His unconsidered actions may result in good or ill. Both the early experience during the gale (when he springs up but is stopped from leaping into the sea to help) and the disastrous jump from the *Patna* show his inability to grasp the nature of actions which can, in a split-second, change the hero's self-perception with devastating finality. The more rewarding decisions of Jim's life are, equally, headlong leaps into the unknown. After Marlow proposes that he 'jump into the first gharry' to get his instructions from Stein regarding Patusan, Jim flings out of the room and commits himself totally to the venture (p. 214). His early days in Patusan are also notable for their examples of abrupt, impulsive action. He leaps over the stakes of the stockade 'at once, without any mental process as it were', going over like a bird, picking himself up instantly and then (in his second leap) 'flying through the air', though in this case into the slime of the creek mouth, from which he is just able to extricate himself with a supreme effort (pp. 228–30). Unreflective though it is, of course, the propensity for leaping in itself marks Jim out as a potential hero. In contrast to the massive and immobile Doramin and the treacherous, diplomatic Kassim, Jim is able to seize the situation in an active way, seeing what has to be done and acting swiftly and audaciously, as when he takes Sherif Ali's 'impregnable' camp by mounting cannon, Napoleon-like, on the top of the hill.

For Jim as for Lingard, the hero's extraordinary energies come to nothing when, at a crucial moment, he fails in his responsibilities to the people who depend on him, first abandoning the pilgrims on the *Patna*, then bringing destruction on his closest allies in Patusan. Like Lingard, although he has not committed violence himself, he has failed to foresee and prevent it, and the consequence is the disintegration of the triumphant heroic narrative that was almost within his grasp. Jim has, by his strength and daring, established a sphere in which he can be trusted, and for this secure public space he feels totally accountable: 'I am responsible for every life in the land' (p. 335). However bookishly stereotypical Jim's conception of the heroic role, he knows that he must test 'the secret truth of his pretences', and this determined 'authenticity' is the indispensable foundation of his heroic display (p. 50). When his assembled people assent to his will and demonstrate their belief in him, it is the testimony to his faithfulness that makes him in his own eyes the equal of 'the impeccable men who never fall out of the ranks' (p. 234). In the last scene, an equally attentive audience watches him make good his promise to answer with his life, and, in keeping with the best traditions of the romantic hero, this final act is both an expression of the hero's inner integrity and a superb performance: 'They say that the white man sent right and left at all those faces a proud and unflinching glance' (p. 351).

In the remote, 'suspended' realm of Patusan, Jim's storybook heroism has shown itself able to transform life in a temporary realisation of the chivalric virtues of nobility, fidelity and bravery. Until demoralising reality intrudes, undermining his self-conception, he is able to achieve the 'immensity' of his ambitions within his own miniature realm. In *Nostromo*, Conrad tests the ideals of adventure heroism in a much more complex setting. Sulaco is a place on the verge of being drawn into connection with the modern world, with its 'civilised business', steamers, railways and telegraph-cables. It has long been ensconced behind the natural barriers of the mountains, 'repelling modern enterprise', but, in contrast to Patusan, it is very far from being a repository of primitive virtues, or of any simple goodness that can be rescued or restored by the idealistic hero. Rather, it is thoroughly corrupt, plagued by senseless civil wars, arbitrary imprisonment, barbarous executions and 'officialdom with its nightmarish parody of administration without law, without security, and without justice'.[34] The primitive itself, in *Nostromo*, suggests ignorance, baseness, political immaturity and mental darkness: however highly valued courage may have been, popular lore testifies that bodily strength, duplicity and cunning were held by primitive mankind to be even more important heroic virtues. The 'material interests' which have designs on the wealth of the silver mine are not just marauding pirates like Gentleman Brown but potential allies of civilised form; it is not the lone romantic hero but the structures of an advanced society which now present themselves as the guardians of a peacefully organised way of life: 'the San Tomé mine was to become an institution, a rallying point for everything in the province that needed order and stability to live. Security seemed to flow upon this land from the mountain-gorge' (*Nostromo*, pp. 119–20).

The germ of the idea for the novel, as Conrad explains it, came to him in with the recognition that the actual theft of a lighter-full of silver need not have been committed by a confirmed rogue but might actually have been accomplished by 'a man of character, an actor and possibly a victim in the changing scenes of a revolution' (p. 31). In developing this thought, Conrad persistently returns to the question of whether imperialistic theft can in truth often be committed by men whose involvement is altogether more principled and high-minded; and, conversely, of whether the adventuring hero, however apparently noble, can ever be entirely free from the taint of materialism. Departing from the simpler social-political contexts of *The Rescue* and *Lord Jim*, he throws into doubt any sharp contrast between commercial concerns and heroic sentiment – between the territory to be possessed and the action territory of heroic legend. Throughout *Nostromo*, there is a blurring of the distinctions between the high-minded adventurer and the exploiter who wants merely to break into the 'treasure-house' of South America. From the time of Spanish rule, South America has been cursed, Decoud maintains, by the confusion of grand ideals and sordid commercial realities: 'Don Quixote and Sancho Panza, chivalry and materialism, high-sounding sentiment and a supine morality, violent efforts for an idea and a sullen acquiescence in every form of corruption' (p. 166). The Gould Concession, the 'Imperium in Imperio', is likewise the focus of both greed and moral enthusiasm. In the eyes of Nostromo and Mrs Gould the mine takes on the oppressive personality associated with human abuses of power. Nostromo sees it as a curse and a master, binding him with 'silver fetters' which are 'hateful and immense'; to the wholly unmercenary Mrs Gould, it seems first a 'fetish', then 'a monstrous and crushing weight', ultimately a soulless tyrant (pp. 416–17, 204–5). The mine is also, however, sentimentalised, both by Charles Gould, the incorrigible idealist, and by the financier Holroyd, the Protestant ethic incarnate. Gould, for whom life is a 'moral romance', has a contagious faith in the mine; Holroyd, high priest of 'the religion of silver and iron', takes all commercial gain to be an affair of the spirit, according with American destiny and fulfilling 'an insatiable imagination of conquest' (pp. 89–95). For Gould and Holroyd, there is no conflict between commercial and idealistic motives, since the wealth of the colonial world is in itself the instrument of a heroic moral crusade. With his English heritage, Charles Gould inevitably sees himself as 'the descendant of adventurers'. But whereas his 'poor uncle' carried a sword when he entered the senseless fray, Charles's only weapon in his defence of the decencies of organised society is the wealth of the mine, which is 'more far-reaching and subtle than an honest blade of steel . . . . More dangerous to the wielder, too . . . tainting the very cause for which it is drawn' (p. 311).

Nostromo is more explicitly preoccupied than *Lord Jim* with the conflict between romantic and sceptical ways of viewing political life. Charles Gould, too practical and too idealistic to look on political affairs with an ironic eye, is unable to find amusement in the elements of farce and absurdity apparent to more sceptical observers like Decoud, who finds in Costaguanan intrigues the exaggerated gestures and comical self-importance that seem to him to characterise all political action. With its 'atmosphere of opera-bouffe' such a scene is 'screamingly funny, the blood flows all the time, and the actors believe themselves to be influencing the fate of the universe' (*Nostromo*, p. 152). Conrad uses

Decoud's cynicism to provide a detached perspective on the posturings of would-be heroes. As Decoud himself, however, becomes involved as 'the Journalist of Sulaco' his responses are also used to suggest the limitations of the ironic stance. Unlike Travers, who also dismissed heroic gestures as pure farce, Decoud is not wholly without redeeming human characteristics; his scepticism is more intelligent, and at the same time his capacity for human involvement is greater. As he comes closer to political action, through his attachment to Antonia, he realises that it is 'not possible to dismiss their tragic comedy with the expression, "*Quelle farce!*"' (p. 169). The reality of political action acquires 'poignancy' for him once he is no longer able to contemplate revolutions from a distance. The reserves of passion he finds, however, are not sufficient to give him a sustaining faith when he confronts the darkness of the gulf, a situation 'too exasperating to be looked upon with irony' (p. 248).

If the character of Decoud is used to define the limits of civilised mockery, the satiric voice is nevertheless indispensable in shaping our response to heroic action. The large canvas of *Nostromo* gives Conrad room to include a range of caricatured 'great men', whose antics very effectively expose the 'opera-bouffe' nature of much that is mistaken for heroism. Conrad's observation about the primitive respect accorded such 'heroic virtues' as cunning and deceit is amply born out in the chapter describing the arrival of Montero's forces in Sulaco. The combination of burlesque descriptions and ironic commentary creates a grimly humorous impression of ludicrous bravado masquerading as dashing leadership. Pedro Montero is followed into Sulaco by an 'armed mob of all colours, complexions, types, and states of raggedness . . . like a torrent of rubbish, a mass of straw hats, ponchos, gun-barrels . . .'. Success is their only criterion of morality, and they willingly follow a leader who is able 'to deliver their enemies bound, as it were, into their hands' (pp. 326–7). As the Montero take-over of Sulaco gets into full swing we are given vignettes of the various 'bad actors' on the stage of Sulaco. There is a grotesquely comic victory procession and speeches, with broad physical caricature of everyone involved. Pedrito secures a hero's reception by speaking on tip-toe, arms flung above his head, eyes rolling, mouth opening and shutting, striking his breast and uttering 'detached phrases'. He is followed by Gamacho, who is big and hot, grinning with yellow fangs in 'stupid hilarity', howling an anti-imperialist oration 'delectable to popular ears' before he falls into a drunken stupor. The ascendancy of Pedrito is ascribed to 'a genius for treachery' which appears as 'the perfection of sagacity and virtue' to 'violent men but little removed from a state of utter savagery' (pp. 327–32). Amongst the immediate causes of the Monterist revolution is Pedrito's conception of an ideal existence for himself, in which he would imitate the Duc de Morny, conducting political affairs in such a way that he could command every pleasure. Like an outrageously distorted version of Lord Jim, he harbours immense ambitions shaped principally by the 'absurd visions' put into his head by literary models: he has devoured 'the lighter sort of historical works in the French language', and his actions are thus generally 'determined by motives so improbable in themselves as to escape the penetration of a rational person'. He speaks in what he imagines to be the manner of a grand seigneur: 'Pedrito elevated his hand jerkily to help the idea of pinnacle, of fame' (p. 342). His brother, General Montero, is a less literate hero, but 'the glorious victor of Rio Seco' achieves his eminence by being the epitome of martial display, playing on his reputation as a savage fighter. Extravagantly guying Nostromo's physical vanity, he parades with a jingling steel scabbard and gorgeous uniform, a 'mass of gold on sleeves and breast', plumed hat, enormous spurs and shining boots. With his bull neck, hooked nose, working nostrils, dyed moustache and 'imbecile and domineering stare', his appearance has 'the exaggeration of a cruel caricature, the fatuity of solemn masquerading'. As Decoud comments, 'Not the two Monteros put together would make a decent parody of a Caesar' (pp. 126–9, 164).

The Montero brothers, Gamacho, Sotillo, Barrios and others are used, like distorting mirrors, to reveal the many possible perversions of the character of the hero. Alongside such figures as these, Nostromo himself looks to be the genuine heroic article. Captain Mitchell, whose narrative comes closest to seeing events in terms of the traditional patterns of heroism, attests with comic pomposity to Nostromo's claims to fame. His famous ride to Cayta saved Sulaco 'intact for civilisation – for a great future, sir' (pp. 401–2). Even those less infatuated than Captain Mitchell reflect on his character in ways that confirm his heroic credentials as the 'undoubted Great Man' of the people, exercising his personal powers to make himself feared and admired, and to make the populace sensible of his courage, fidelity and resourcefulness (p. 33). We repeatedly see Nostromo through the eyes of others, as is appropriate to a man whose main need in life is for others to witness his deeds and his qualities. His considerable abilities are all directed towards creating a hero's appearance and reputation. The famous Capataz de Cargadores has, as Decoud observes, a sure instinct for catching the popular imagination, a talent for appearing whenever something 'picturesque' needs to be done. Riding a silver-grey mare and immediately recognisable to everyone in the town, Nostromo twists his moustache and displays a muscular neck and bronzed chest; he is dressed in snowy linen, with red silk sash, embroidered leather jacket and enormous silver buttons. His overriding concern is not with the cause he champions but with maintaining his public identity, and in defining himself, as Decoud reflects, he unfailingly places the outward show of approval above inner judgement, making no distinction 'between speaking and thinking'. Reproached by Giorgio's wife's because he has been away fighting for what does not concern him, the baffled Nostromo replies, 'It concerns me to keep on being what I am: every day alike' (p. 224).

In contrast to *Lord Jim* and *The Rescue*, *Nostromo* does not involve the central hero figure in a series of independent decisions and self-determined actions (whether leaps or forking paths), but instead represents him as being constantly called upon to meet the needs of others and so win their praise. His assistance is necessary and decisive, but his need for others to witness his greatness means that he is never an entirely free agent: he is not 'his own man' but 'our man'. Having been singled out by Captain Mitchell on the strength of his looks, he is 'lent out', becoming a sort of universal factotum to the Europeans of Sulaco, who use for their own ends his 'genius' for dominating 'the destinies of great enterprises'. Nostromo has, in theory, the choice of whether to accept a task or not. In reality, however, as Monygham observes when Nostromo is required for the mission to Barrios, the only alternative to embarking on this dangerous enterprise (and thereby retrieving his great reputation) is stealing 'ingloriously' away from Sulaco (*Nostromo*, pp. 378–81).

The function of Sulaco for Nostromo, as the arena in which he can display his magnificence and thus create his identity, is thrown into relief by the central adventure in the gulf, when Nostromo takes charge of the lighter containing the treasure of silver ingots. The gulf, in contrast to Sulaco, is a space of non-appearance. Embarking on the adventure is like 'being launched into space'. Unable to see one another, Nostromo and Decoud move into the deep darkness of the gulf, a place of such obscurity and blackness that even Nostromo's voice 'seemed deadened by the thick veil of obscurity'. They are invisible and inaudible as they move through the 'featureless night'. Nostromo boasts of his good eye and steady hand, but exclaims, '*por Dios*, Don Martin, I have been sent into this black calm on a business where neither a good eye, nor a steady hand, nor judgement are any use'. In the gulf, there is no scope for heroic traits; there are no witnesses and no chances for public performance. Only the negative action of not being seen or heard is of any value, if they are to save the treasure from the steamer full of soldiers. Nostromo has lived 'in splendour and publicity' up to this moment, but in the gulf the necessity of concealment makes everything that has gone before seem 'vain and foolish, like a flattering dream'. The fact that he can no longer display himself on the streets of Sulaco makes it appear to him 'as a town that had no existence', and his own non-appearance makes him feel destitute, 'deprived of certain simple realities, such as the admiration of women, the adulation of men, the admired publicity of his life' (pp. 348–53).

In the remainder of the narrative, after he has been forced to hide the silver on the island, Nostromo has the chance to reshape a public identity for himself, but now with the devastating knowledge of a secret link between the heroic performance and material possession. Having accidentally acquired a fabulous share in the European wealth which before was only a vague promise for him, he must conceal his connection with the very emblem of the 'material interests' of Sulaco. The consequence of having to hide the material fact which now possesses him is a fatal separation between Nostromo's self and the image others have of him. We have known all along that a certain amount of money was requisite to Nostromo's heroic display: 'One must pay in some way or other for such a solid thing as individual prestige' (p. 204). Once he is in possession of the stolen silver he need never again be short of funds, but equally, he will never want reminders of his insincerity in acting a false role in public while drawing in secret on his hidden resources of silver. Such humiliating deception and stealth undermine both his peace of mind and his sense of heroic integrity: 'the genuineness of all his qualities was destroyed . . . . His courage, his magnificence . . . everything was as before, only everything was a sham' (p. 432). No heroism, perhaps, can survive the triumph of material interests.

JESTERS AND HEROES: CHESTERTON, SHAW AND NAPOLEON

Carlyle calls Napoleon 'our last Great Man'. Although he can be taken to foreshadow twentieth-century megalomania and to symbolise the potential of modern man, the image of heroism associated with

Napoleon is in some ways an anachronism. As Jenni Calder suggests, he was perhaps 'less the inspirer of a new age of great achievement than the last of the heroes for which a new, democratic, cash-nexus age would have no room'. The vigour and grandeur of the flamboyantly great warrior and challenger of decrepit authoritarian systems could inspire passionate admiration. Equally, Napoleonic bloodshed and excess could arouse detestation, even in those who responded to the fascination of the Napoleonic myth.[35] The figure of Napoleon calls to mind, more unavoidably than a purely fictional hero, the slaughter as well as the excitement of heroic adventure. Conrad, for example, in introducing *A Set of Six*, says that he had as a boy heard 'a good deal of the great Napoleonic legend' and that he had 'a genuine feeling that I would find myself at home in it'; he planned a Napoleonic novel and devoted much time to studying the memoirs and history of the period. He also, however, in *Autocracy and War*, harshly condemns Napoleon for promoting national hatred, political tyranny and violence – not an eagle, but a vulture preying on the corpse of Europe. Shaw was similarly divided, and in *Everybody's Political What's What?* he diagnoses his own contradictory response to Napoleonic military heroism. Like Hitler, Napoleon leads crusades which leave 'men dying in millions, cities crashing in ruins'. And yet, he is idolised: Napoleon found glory 'readymade for him by all the bards and all the romancers', and Shaw not only identifies in himself a boyhood attraction to invincible fighters but admits to having been 'astonished and scandalised' to find 'traces of war excitement' stirring in him at the outbreak of the First World War, when he was nearly sixty.[36] Even when he has stripped his heroes of all their romantic trappings, what Shaw responds to in them is the excitement of seeing a combative disposition forcing its way in the world. Chesterton, too, finds contradictory elements in the Napoleonic myth, particularly in the dichotomy between the original, youthful impulse of heroic assertion and the establishment of imperial rule. But Chesterton's political nostalgia is of a kind that leads him to look back, much more uncritically than either Conrad or Shaw, to the sheer exuberance of military conquest, and in *The Napoleon of Notting Hill* (1904) the mood is dominated by a boyish enthusiasm for flags and swords, hand-to-hand combat and manning the barricades.[37] Both Shaw and Chesterton structure their narratives around the confrontation between a Napoleon figure and a jester (the King in *The Napoleon of Notting Hill* and the Strange Lady in Shaw's *Man of Destiny*), staging lengthy debates on the nature of heroism in which Chesterton lightheartedly sentimentalises and Shaw mischievously undermines such key elements in the heroic mythos as youthful innocence, moral rectitude and noble deeds.

Chesterton's romanticism about fighting goes hand in hand with a weakness for romantic nationalism, as can readily be seen in his reactions to the Boer War, which had only recently ended when he wrote *The Napoleon of Notting Hill*. Shaw, who argued that there was no moral distinction between the Boers and the British in their predatory fight for the possession of South Africa, was strongly opposed to the war, but, in *Fabianism and the Empire*, sought to heal the division in the Fabian Society by arguing that control of South Africa by a Great Power like Britain was more likely to pave the way for an internationalised future than was control by small and irresponsible 'communities of frontiersmen'. Conrad also felt revulsion at the 'appalling fatuity' of the war, an 'imbecile' affair likely to bring prolonged suffering, but, like Shaw, declined to sentimentalise the Boers.[38] In contrast, Chesterton, who resigned from the Fabian Society at the time of the Boer War, was genuinely pro-Boer, opposing the war out of sympathy with little nations. Shaw's compromise position of grafting international socialism onto British Imperialism involved, in Chesterton's view, a repugnant conviction that it was necessary to eliminate political communities which were too small to be economically viable. As Chesterton commented when he attended a peace rally, he was wholly unmoved by the dry economic details which supported the anti-Imperialist arguments of a progressive theorist like J.A. Hobson. What he warmed to, on the other hand, was the speech of Conrad's friend Cunninghame Graham, who presented a historical picture which was 'like a pageant of Empires'. Chesterton's romantic bellicosity and his anti-Imperialism both reflected his preference for political life characterised by the vitality of 'a raid and a rescue'.[39]

As a writer, Chesterton revelled in the narrative excitement, the colour and energy of adventure fiction. His antipathy to progressive ideas of evolutionary transcendence often led him towards medievalism and towards the sentimental celebration of earlier values, capable of satisfying human needs in a way he felt to be impossible in the modern, well-planned socialist state. In *The Napoleon of Notting Hill*, Chesterton reverses the conventions of the adventure tale by transferring the elements of the adventure story to London itself, creating a futuristic fantasy which allows him to project heroic action within an overly civilised context. The future imagined in England, 1984, is one in which the spirit of heroism has departed. It is 'now practically a despotism', led by a King chosen by rotation from a dull, mechanical official class (heirs of a soulless socialist belief in 'Evolution'). The

King is no more than a kind of universal secretary and everyone relies on things 'happening as they have always happened'. People have forgotten the possibility of political choice, and their spiritual and emotional impoverishment has increased as more and more things have 'dropped out of sight'. In the beginning of the novel, the only reminder of a lost world of political possibility is the President of Nicaragua, the stock adventure-story figure of the deposed ruler. In every respect the antithesis of the tedium of British officialdom, he brings the spirit of a recalcitrant imperial outpost into the heart of London. As when Lingard confronts Travers, we see the collision between opposing conceptions of politics. The brilliant green of the President's military uniform, glittering with decorations, and his indefinable air of simplicity and arrogance give him, to a sublime extent, the quality of a leader whom all men follow. Against the ethos of a pacific, utilitarian, cosmopolitan modern world he sets a way of catching wild horses emblematic of all that disappeared from the world when Nicaragua was civilised; against 'a mere business routine of government' he sets a heroic politics of revolutionary fervour, choice and danger. With a melodramatic gesture, he stabs his hand, so that the red of a blood-drenched handkerchief can complete his display of the Nicaraguan colours.[40] As in Conrad, public performance is the essence of heroic politics.

The dramatic narrative of *The Napoleon of Notting Hill* is set in motion when the eccentric jester Auberon Quin becomes King and, his imagination stimulated by the fantastic figure of the Nicaraguan President, issues a Charter of the Free Cities which restores local autonomy and medieval pageantry to the different districts of London. In a chance encounter, he inspires a boy called Adam Wayne, who takes Quin's joke with passionate seriousness: 'the King . . . with a few words flung in mockery, ratified for ever the strange boundaries of his soul' (pp. 70–2). When he has grown up to become Provost of Notting Hill, Wayne announces himself as heir to Quin's scheme, 'the child of the great Charter'. With his flaming red hair, high features, violent gestures and chivalrous eloquence, Wayne strides forward as someone who takes Notting Hill seriously, ready to raise his sword against the enemies who are scheming to encroach upon the local rights of his inviolate city. Having tried to compose a burlesque, Quin is astonished when Wayne turns it into an epic by living 'the life for which the Iliad is only a cheap substitute' (pp. 54–65).

The tone of the novel is suspended between the romantic effusions of the glorious fanatic and the mockery of the humorist. Both Quin and Wayne are admirable in being free from conventional modes of thought and behaviour, and the subversive alliance between playfulness and passion is established in the warm relationship between the two men. They speak the same heightened language, even though they often fail to understand one another: when they talk at cross purposes we see, for example, that such superlatives as 'immense' and 'splendid' can refer either to a prodigious jest or to a glorious conception worthy of a hero (p. 58). They share a taste for whatever is excessive and out of the ordinary, though Wayne's militant dedication and blind fanaticism have greater transformative power. Quin can mischievously overturn commonplace, bureaucratic forms, but even his humorous apprehension of life can be suspended by the vision of a new and overwhelming force, 'the conqueror, with his face flung back, and his mane like a lion's' (p. 99). What Chesterton in the end suggests is that Quin's farce and Wayne's tragedy are not, after all, the fruit of such very different perceptions of the world, but are essentially allied in their challenge to the sheer inertia of a routinely ordered political world, and that they share a genius for originating new courses of action: 'we have been opposite like man and woman, aiming at the same moment at the same practical thing' (p. 162). Both are characterised by their childlike freshness and their capacity for 'infantile wonder' and enthusiasm – more associated by Chesterton with new beginnings than with, say, immature political judgements. His ideal body politic rejoices 'in something fresher than progress' (p. 159). The child–hero is part and parcel of his anti-deterministic opposition to the idea that there can be any inevitable line of historical development, or that the evolution of humankind can carry society beyond the heroic stage of man's life. As he says in his book on Shaw, he continues to support the case he made 'against Mr Shaw's depreciation of chivalry or the romantic tradition. There is a case for saying that romance will reappear in a damaging or dangerous form; there is no case at all for saying it will disappear.'[41]

Chesterton's presentation of the heroic impulse, though distanced by fantasy and comedy, is overwhelmingly sympathetic. Blood runs in the streets, but bloodshed remains an epic spectacle, never represented in a way which would suggest the horrors of modern mechanised warfare, or anything more distasteful than knightly combat. The one darker irony lies in his sense that all ideals risk being corrupted – it being hard 'to make a thing good without it immediately insisting on being wicked' (pp. 147–8). We have seen that one of the main elements in his antipathy to imperialist expansion is his conviction that mammoth political organisations will crush the highly individual capacity for action. In the local events of *The Napoleon of Notting Hill*, we see, in microcosm, the conflict between heroic self-assertion and Empire-building, and, at the same time, see the way in which the liberating romantic nationalism of the small political unit can, over time, be transformed into the repressive force of imperial aggression. Adam Wayne's territorial kingdom is a modest affair, extending to about nine streets, but his spiritual kingdom encompasses all of the changes wrought in others by his 'roaring, unreasonable soul' (p. 118). In defending his territorial kingdom of Notting Hill, Wayne is determined not to allow the original impulse of his crusade be tainted by victory. When his forces capture the Waterworks, he vows that he will never use his triumph 'for any of those repressive purposes' which others have entertained against him (p. 137). But twenty years after the vast army of South Kensington has surrendered to him and the Empire of Notting Hill has begun, the nature of his spiritual influence has gone beyond the inspiration of local patriotism and chivalric conduct: while Wayne sits with his sword by the fire, crowds have been 'intoxicated by the spreading over the whole city of Wayne's old ways and visions', so that 'they try to meddle with everyone, and rule over everyone, and civilise everyone'. Hoping to restrain their misguided zeal, Wayne tells his people that in trying to overreach themselves they will lose the glory of their original achievement: 'Notting Hill is a nation. Why should it condescend to be a mere Empire?' In the end, though the larger ideals represented by Wayne and Quin ('the pure fanatic, the pure satirist') are declared eternal, the originating spirit of Wayne himself is 'swallowed up by the vast armies of a new world' (pp. 145–52).

In *The Napoleon of Notting Hill*, Quin's joke is the occasion for Wayne's heroic action; in Shaw's plays, heroic action is the occasion for many jokes. The great man is repeatedly viewed through the humorist's mocking eye, though he can at the same time be seen as having a serious function to fulfil if, gifted with energy and realism, he can become an instigator of political progress. Around the turn of the century, at the time when he was writing *The Man of Destiny*, *The Perfect Wagnerite* and *Caesar and Cleopatra*, Shaw was losing his faith in the inevitability of the gradual progress hoped for by the Fabians. He began, as Michael Holroyd says, to recognise the need for 'a more romantic figure than that of the civil servant and political researcher', and to recognise the importance of appearance in political life, of a heroic figure to fire the popular imagination; he began to vest his hopes for political change in 'the order of Heros'.[42] In considering candidates for the transformative hero, however, Shaw was looking for great men who had something to recommend them other than romantic conceit, moral arrogance and strutting storybook magnificence. His comedies are thus an assault on both conventional respectability and clichéd notions of heroism. In Chesterton's novel, the playfulness of comedy is a boyish exuberance of spirit closely related to the original impulses of adventure and heroism; in Shaw's plays, the comedy that arises from the incongruity between adult realism and immature pretence is designed to strip heroism of its juvenile illusions.

Written and performed in the late 1890s, *The Man of Destiny* represents the youthful Napoleon of the Italian campaign as capable of being genuinely heroic, of showing the qualities of will and daring that won him the Battle of Lodi two days earlier; at the same time, with a combination of high comedy and darker irony, Shaw punctures the hero's legendary status. Like Conrad, he juxtaposes the male ethos of adventure heroism with the quite different standards and attractions of feminine enchantment and civilised society. In *The Man of Destiny* the whole sphere of action is reduced to the scale of the polite drawing room, and the Strange Lady is given not only female allure but the wit and rhetorical power to wage her own mocking and aggressive battle with the 'Corsican adventurer' over the possession of a packet of letters and despatches. The noble language of battle – courage, generosity to the vanquished, resolution in the face of the enemy – is borrowed by Napoleon as he seeks to create the impression of martial 'force and decision', only to be teased for attitudinising and pulled up short by the Lady's 'mocking curtsey'. She is a worthy opponent, effectively revealing both the grown-up cunning and the childlike pique in the hero's make-up: 'I have often seen persons of your sex getting into a pet and behaving like children; but I never saw a really great man do it before.'[43]

In spite of occasionally behaving like a child, Shaw's Napoleon is not by any means akin to the romanticised worldly innocents we have encountered elsewhere. On the contrary, Shaw stresses the shrewd realism he has acquired in the process of maturing. Now, as a young officer, he is not incapable of ideals – having 'swallowed them all in his boyhood' – but, having outgrown such boyish misapprehensions and having 'a keen dramatic faculty', he is, as Shaw says in his introductory note, 'extremely clever at playing upon them by the arts of the actor and stage manager' (*The Man of Destiny*, pp. 163–4). Shaw's satire is directed against those qualities which he regards as irrelevant to true greatness, and true greatness is represented as having a sure instinct for the creation of an image which will please the common man. In his commentary on English attitudes towards Empire in 'Civilization and the Soldier', Shaw derides 'the visions of Jingo romance' and urges that a sincere defence of martial action be distinguished from pronouncements made from behind the 'entrenchments of rhetoric and blarney'. He also acknowledges, however, that rhetoric and blarney are what the hero's public demands, and in creating the young Napoleon he imagines a man who fully understands both the real nature of military conquest ('devastation is a soldier's business') and the art of pandering to more romantic popular expectations.[44] The Shavian historical hero sees clearly that heroic action itself divides into real, pragmatic action and play-acting. In spite of being a tough-minded realist who shares his creator's contempt for those who judge life by the standards of stage romance, the young Napoleon, 'called on, as a man who had won battles, to cast himself for Emperor', recognises what he must do to satisfy the human hunger for heroes, 'since the audience will have its ideal king, its President, its statesman, its saint, its hero . . .'[45] He knows the value of displays of pluck and is well aware of the importance for the hero of creating a space of appearance, his lion's den within which he can develop an appropriately romantic role. The overriding importance of popular reputation is comically caught in the Lady's search for reasons that will persuade Napoleon to change his course of action – lost honour ('Nothing worse than that?') and happiness ('the most tedious thing in the world to me') count for nothing; it is 'you will cut a very foolish figure in the eyes of France' that makes him pause and reconsider (pp. 186–7).

In Conrad's novels, the hero's efforts to adhere sincerely to the heroic ideal are undermined by his human weakness, and he must try as well as he can to live with 'the knowledge of his moral ruin locked up in his breast'.[46] In Shaw's plays, however, the gap between the real and the ideal does not produce a fatal weakness; rather, knowledge of the gap is a source of strength. The Napoleon represented by Shaw is himself a debunker of political myths, not only a man with a 'clear realistic knowledge of human nature in public affairs', but a 'merciless cannonader of political rubbish' (*The Man of Destiny*, pp. 163–4). He recognises the falsity of all of the positive attributes stereotypically associated with the role of the hero – moral innocence and simplicity, integrity, honour, selflessness, responsibility and concern for others. In *The Man of Destiny*, innocence and simplicity are given instead to the Lieutenant, who is not only gullible enough to allow the disguised Lady to steal the letters and despatches, but who, adhering to a gentlemanly moral code, is outraged at the betrayal of trust involved. The only kind of simplicity manifested by Napoleon, on the other hand, is the 'strong simplicity' which seizes on precisely those actions which will fulfil his purpose (pp. 203–4). This single-minded pursuit of action and victory is like a devouring devil which is both his genius and his doom. He is enslaved not by any sense of responsibility to the people he commands but by his own inner drive towards mastery. When the Lady catches Napoleon offguard, though he quickly 'pulls himself piously together' to protest that his role is as a servant of the French people, humbly winning battles for humanity, his nationalism is shown to lack foundation. He can adopt a solemn attitude, modelled on heroes of classical antiquity and take a high moral tone in affirming his self-sacrificing commitment to the interests of others, but his real strength, as the Lady observes, lies only in his belief in himself. Integrity and unselfishness ('love . . . pity . . . the instinct to save and protect someone else'), she suggests, are to be seen as cowardice, womanliness, slavishness and want of character; true greatness resides in 'being really, strongly, positively oneself' (pp. 181–4). Similarly, in *Caesar and Cleopatra*, Caesar's special quality of mind, his originality, enables him to see through things and evaluate them without relying on 'convention and moral generalisation'. Thus, like other great men, he knows how to produce 'an impression of complete disinterestedness and magnanimity', but in fact accomplishes this by acting with 'entire selfishness', which is, Shaw maintains, 'perhaps the only sense in which a man can be said to be *naturally* great'.[47]

Shaw's undercutting of the traditional attributes and higher morality of the hero is closely related to his representation of the conventional imperialist narrative. The historical situation is in a sense not dissimilar to that found in Conrad and Haggard, but the moral import of the hero's task is rather different. Napoleon's troops have the ostensible objective of rescuing the Italians 'from the tyranny of their Austrian conquerors' and of conferring republican institutions on them – but what this means is that 'in incidentally looting them [France] merely makes free with the property of its friends, who ought to be grateful to it, and perhaps would be if ingratitude were not the proverbial failing of their country' (*The Man of Destiny*, pp. 164–5). This mocking commentary on the relationship between commercial motives and moral sentiment is explicitly related to English Imperialism in the final conversations between Napoleon and the Lady, with the implication that the English, unlike Napoleon, are taken in by their own propaganda. The play is rounded off by his speech about the 'vulgar scruples' of conscience. Napoleon explains that the English suffer from such scruples not only amongst the 'middle people' but amongst the low and high people as well:

> . . . every Englishman is born with a certain miraculous power that makes him master of the world. When he wants a thing, he never tells himself that he wants it. He waits patiently until there comes into his mind, no one knows how, a burning conviction that it is his moral and religious duty to conquer those who possess the thing he wants. Then he becomes irresistible . . . . He is never at a loss for an effective moral attitude. As the great champion of freedom and national independence, he conquers and annexes half the world, and calls it Colonization.

> (pp. 204–5)

The Englishman sends a missionary when he wants a market, he sails to the ends of the earth and destroys anyone who disputes his control of 'the empire of the seas'; he will never admit that he is in the wrong and acts only on principle: 'He fights you on patriotic principles; he robs you on business principles; he enslaves you on imperial principles; he bullies you on manly principles.' The lady's behaviour, Napoleon concludes, has been a small-scale embodiment of English imperialist hypocrisy: she has spent the morning stealing the letters from Napoleon and the rest of the day putting him in the wrong about them.

The Man of Destiny is a comic acknowledgement of the universality of hypocrisy and betrayal, in sexual as well as political affairs, and those who emerge well from their combats are those who are most strong-willed, clear-sighted and free from encumbering principles. Shaw's post-First World War judgements of Napoleon were often more negative. But even in *Everybody's Political What's What?* (1944), in which Shaw provides a damning 'offhand' summary of Emperor Napoleon's many shortcomings, the achievements of Lieutenant Bonaparte are judged as they are in *The Man of Destiny* – as the contributions of a man who has some claim to be classed as 'the world's greatest realist', a military genius who was actually capable of restoring order even if he was also 'a snob, a cad, an assassin, and a scoundrel'. He is a hard-headed commander who sees through but also knows that he must fulfil the expectations of a public which demands heroic displays on a grand scale, thus forcing him to carry on in his role as 'a glory merchant'. Shaw's revulsion at 'bloodshed and destruction', here as elsewhere, is vigorously expressed, as are his reservations about government by great men: 'No one', he observes tartly, 'can feel any assurance of where they will stop', and there is thus ultimately 'no hope for civilisation in government by idolised single individuals'. At the same time, however, he hedges by saying that, when legitimate governments fail, there may be no alternative to strong arms: leaders like Napoleon, Mussolini and Hitler 'have won their eminence by doing certain things that everybody wanted to have done, and been idolised accordingly'.[48]

Similarly, in Part IV ('Tragedy of an Elderly Gentleman') of *Back to Methuselah* (1921), the Napoleonic character, though made to cower by the alarming Oracle, is represented as the type of the great man. Possessing exceptional energy and will, he is driven to make use of his extraordinary gifts, even while himself recognising (just as in *Everybody's Political What's What?*) that the dilemma to be confronted is one of limits: that is, the fighting which secures his triumphant greatness must go on until the victors themselves are ruined and depopulated. Entering with audacity and introducing himself as the Man of Destiny, he makes it clear that he never stops, never waits and belongs only to himself. He has the strongest mesmeric field ever seen in a 'shortliver', and, in spite of the fact that the Oracle is a more devastating female than the Strange Lady, he quickly recovers his composure and makes the case for putting into action his exceptional talent as a military commander. It is a talent which possesses him and demands expression, since without it he would 'cut no particular figure in the world' – he is great when he exercises it, nobody without it. Superiority, he argues, will make itself felt, and, ironically, people adore him for 'the shedding of oceans of blood' and 'the death of millions of men'. As in *The Man of Destiny*, his heroic force is inextricably related not only to his power of imagining things as they are but to his capacity for creating a romantic illusion: 'If you kill me, or put a stop to my activity (it is the same thing), the nobler part of human life perishes.'[49] The playwright's own disgust at military excess is more strongly apparent in *Back to Methuselah* than in *The Man of Destiny's* brief opening gibe about the cheapness of blood, but in both plays what we are being shown is an event-making man who sees clearly but is not unduly troubled by the human cost of his effectiveness.

In Shaw's sketches of Napoleon one sees a conception of the great man which is also to some extent reflected in his favourable comments on Mosley, Hitler and Mussolini, and in his lifelong belief in the greatness of Stalin. As he wrote of his support of Mussolini in the twenties: 'All dictators begin as reformers and are encouraged by all sensible people until they find that their subjects do not understand their reforms and respond to nothing but military glory. I applauded both Hitler and Musso while they were in their reform phase, just as Churchill did.' Some have seen Shaw's support for extremist leaders as simply 'an eagerness to shock British Liberals' – and no doubt shock value was, as always, important to Shaw – but such opinions are also very much a reflection of his conviction that only heroic realists are capable of implementing strong and effective measures.[50] For similar reasons, Shaw early recognised Churchill's potential for leadership, keeping, as Holroyd says, his eye on Churchill 'as someone who might emerge in Europe as a Shavian-permeated superman'. Even when Churchill moved towards the Tory party, Shaw continued to value his adventurousness and strength of character. 'You have never been a real Tory', Shaw told him in the forties; his qualities as a leader were confirmed by the fact that the 'Blimps and Philistines and Stick-in-the-Muds' had always dreaded him, precisely because he seemed to offer some prospect of bringing revival to moribund political institutions. For his part, Churchill valued Shaw's provocative sparkle and originality. During wartime, however, Churchill's sense of the seriousness of the great man's task meant that he was short of patience with what he saw as the fundamental irresponsibility of the incorrigible jester. The satiric perspective of the humorist seemed an irrelevant nuisance to the chivalric hero caught up in the heat of battle: 'When nations are fighting for life', Churchill wrote, 'when the Palace in which the Jester dwells not uncomfortably, is itself assailed, and everyone from Prince to groom is fighting on the battlements, the Jester's . . . witticisms and commendations, distributed evenly between friend and foe, jar the ears of hurrying messengers, of mourning women and wounded men.'[51] Churchill's complaint about the jester is a deflection of blame that recalls Chesterton's description of the hero's necessary gravity. Action may, as Arendt insists, be confined to speech, but its physical and violent aspects are hard to gainsay, and, as it is the heroic leader who is charged with responsibility for those dying on the battlements, it is perhaps understandable that he resents the jester's reminder of what Shaw called his tragic dilemma. The dilemma lies in part in the nature of his responsibility (battle, once joined, cannot simply be abandoned), but it also lies in the demands of his reputation: the hero possesses a talent which, as Napoleon says in *Back to Methuselah*, involves the shedding of 'oceans of blood, the death of millions of men' in the 'great game of war', but he must nevertheless go on playing because if he stops he will 'commit suicide as a great man and become a common one' (pp. 226–8).

NOTES

1. Churchill W.S. *Savrola* (1900) 1973 pp. 34 and 40.
2. Churchill W.S., quoted by Charmley J. *Churchill* 1993 p. 17.
3. Fussell P. *The Great War and modern memory* 1990 pp. 21–3.
4. Cunningham V. *British writers of the thirties* 1986 pp. 156–7; Pick D. *War machine* 1993 pp. 189–204.
5. Churchill to Beaverbrook (23 September 1930) and Lord Cecil of Chelwood Papers, Add. Mss. 51079 Cecil to Irwin (7 June 1927) quoted by Charmley *Churchill* pp. 252 and 236.
6. Churchill W.S. *The gathering storm* Cassell 1948 (vol. 1 of *The Second World War*) pp. 526–7.
7. Berlin I. *Personal impressions* 1980 pp. 6–8; Payne R. *The great man* 1974 pp. 11–13, 92 and 130–1; Jablonsky D. *Churchill* 1991 pp. 6–17.
8. Churchill W.S. *My early life: a roving commission* (1930) Mandarin 1990 p. 11; Charmley *Churchill* p. 251.
9. Said E.W. *Culture and imperialism* 1993 p. 75.
10. Hobson J.A. *Imperialism* (1902) 1938 pp. 206–14; and see Arendt H. *The origins of totalitarianism* (1951) 1967 p. 132; Girouard M. *The return to Camelot: chivalry and the English gentleman.* Yale University Press, New Haven 1981 p. 226.
11. Girouard *Return to Camelot* pp. 219–30; Green M. *Dreams of adventure* 1980 p. 326; Stewart D. *T.E. Lawrence* Paladin 1977 p. 246.
12. Arendt *Origins* pp. 207–11.
13. Wells H.G. *The new Machiavelli* (1911) 1994 p. 255.
14. Carlyle T. *On heroes* (1841) 1897 pp. 1–2; Bentley E. *The cult of the superman* 1947 pp. 17–18.
15. Arendt *Origins* pp. 180–1 and 207–11.
16. Kipling R. *Selected stories* 1987 pp. 131–2.
17. Churchill to Haggard, quoted by Manchester W. *The last lion: Winston Spencer Churchill: visions of glory 1874–1932* Michael Joseph 1983 p. 128; Introduction to Haggard H.R. *King Solomon's mines* (1885) 1992 p. vii.
18. Haggard *King Solomon's mines* pp. 11 and 152–6.
19. Fleishman A. *Conrad's politics* 1967 pp. vii-ix; Canovan M. *G.K. Chesterton* 1977 pp. 8–9; Chesterton G.K. *Shaw* (1909) 1935 pp. 272–3 and 177–8; Holroyd M. *Bernard Shaw* 1991 vol. 3 pp. 143–4; Wisenthal J.L. *Shaw's sense of history* 1988 p. 67.
20. Green M. *Seven types of adventure tale* 1991 p. 161.
21. Conrad J. *Autocracy and war* (1905), in *The works of Joseph Conrad* 1925 vol. 19 p. 109.
22. Shaw G.B., Bernard Shaw and the Heroic Actor, in *The Bodley Head Bernard Shaw: collected plays with their prefaces* ed Laurence Dan H., The Bodley Head 1970–4 vol. 2 307; Shaw quoted by Wisenthal *Shaw's sense of history* pp. 58–62; and see Holroyd *Shaw* vol. 2 pp. 12–20 and 362–3.
23. Gérard J.-A. (ed) *Joseph Conrad: life and letters* vol. 2 p. 12 (16 February 1905) quoted by Fleishman *Conrad's politics* p. 31; and Titterton W.R. *G.K. Chesterton: a portrait* (Douglas Organ 1936) pp. 44–5, quoted by Canovan *Chesterton* pp. 102–3. Canovan argues effectively for the

appropriateness of the label 'radical populist'. Chesterton had been a member of the Fabian Society until the Boer War.

24. Conrad J. *Under Western eyes* (1911). Penguin 1985 pp. 69–70.
25. Arendt H. *The human condition* 1958 pp. 194–5 and 220ff.
26. Conrad J. *The rescue* (1920) 1950 pp. 15–16 and 61–5.
27. Lawrence T.E., quoted by Green *Dreams of adventure* p. 327; Arendt *Human condition* pp. 177–8 and 185.
28. Hart L. *T.E. Lawrence: in Arabia and after* Jonathan Cape 1934 p. 80; Green *Dreams of adventure* pp. 326–7.
29. Hook S. *The hero* 1943 pp. 26 and 151–64.
30. Canetti E. *Crowds and power* 1973 pp. 199–200; Calder J. *Heroes* 1977 pp. 18–22; and see Hunter A. *Joseph Conrad and the ethics of Darwinism* 1983 pp. 96ff, for a discussion of Conrad and determinism.
31. Hook *The hero* pp. 12–15, 59, 109, 114 and 156–7.
32. *Ibid.* pp. 64 and 74.
33. Conrad J. *Lord Jim* (1900) 1989 pp. 215, 288–94 and 112–13.
34. Conrad J. *Nostromo* (1904) 1990 pp. 221–5, 63–4 and 103.
35. Carlyle *On heroes* p 243; Calder *Heroes* pp. 22–4.
36. *A set of six* (1908) p. x, quoted by Baines J. *Joseph Conrad* 1986 pp. 411–12; *Autocracy and war* p. 86; Shaw G.B. *Everybody's political what's what?* 1944 pp. 133–4.
37. See Canovan *Chesterton* pp. 102–9 on the nature of Chesterton's patriotism.
38. Holroyd *Shaw* vol. 2 pp. 40–4; Conrad to Garnett (15 January 1900), and see other letters quoted by Baines *Conrad* pp. 289–90, and Fleishman *Conrad's politics* pp. 31–2.
39. Chesterton G.K. *Autobiography* Hutchinson and Co 1936 pp. 270–1.
40. Chesterton G.K. *The Napoleon of Notting Hill* (1904) 1994 pp. 11–27.
41. Chesterton *Shaw* pp. 272–3.
42. Shaw G.B. The Perfect Wagnerite (1909), quoted by Holroyd *Shaw* vol. 2 pp. 11–12.
43. Shaw G.B. *Man of destiny* (1897), in *Plays pleasant* (1898) 1946 pp. 191 and 207.
44. Shaw G.B., Civilization and the soldier (January 1901) in Crawford F.D. (ed) *Shaw offstage* 1989 p. 107; and see Shaw, A dramatic realist to his critics (July 1894) in *Selected non-dramatic writings of Bernard Shaw* ed Laurence Dan H., p. 338; and see Berst C.A. *The man of destiny*: Shaw, Napoleon and the theater of life, in Turco A. (ed) *Shaw: the neglected plays* 1987 p. 89.
45. Shaw G.B. How to become a man of genius (6 December 1898) in *Selected non-dramatic writings* p. 343; and see Berst *The man of destiny* p. 90. A man without illusions, Napoleon is not himself deceived by the role he plays but simply believes that even high-minded moral pretence is justifiable on the grounds of pragmatic effectiveness.
46. Conrad *Nostromo* pp. 32–3.
47. Shaw G.B. *Caesar and Cleopatra* (1898). In *Three plays for Puritans* (1901) 1946 pp. 251–4.
48. Shaw *Everybody's political* pp. 338–40.
49. Shaw G.B. *Back to Methuselah* (1921) 1990 pp. 223–31.
50. Shaw, In praise of Guy Fawkes, quoted by Skidelsky *Mosley* p. 349.

51. Holroyd *Shaw* vol. 3 p. 350; Shaw and Churchill, quoted ibid. pp. 226–7, 143–4 and 227.

CHAPTER TWO

Superhuman Arts: Narratives of Nationalistic Faith

The term 'charisma' will be applied to a certain quality of an individual personality by virtue of which he is considered extraordinary and treated as endowed with supernatural, superhuman, or at least specifically exceptional powers or qualities. These are such as are not accessible to the ordinary person, but are regarded as of divine origin or as exemplary, and on the basis of them the individual concerned is treated as a 'leader'. In primitive circumstances this peculiar kind of quality is thought of as resting on magical powers . . . .

It is recognition on the part of those subject to authority which is decisive for the validity of charisma. This recognition is freely given and guaranteed by what is held to be proof, originally always a miracle, and consists in devotion to the corresponding revelation, hero worship, or absolute trust in the leader . . . .

Pure charisma is specifically foreign to economic considerations. Wherever it appears, it constitutes a 'call' in the most emphatic sense of the word, a 'mission' or a 'spiritual duty'. In the pure type, it disdains and repudiates economic exploitation of the gifts of grace . . . .

(Max Weber, *Economy and Society*)[1]

Max Weber's definition of charisma encompasses the exceptional powers of the hero, and the charismatic warrior-hero of the feudal aristocracy plays an important role in his theories. But the term can also imply a belief in powers of a higher order, that is, in endowments taken to be of divine origin. In its full sense, charisma refers to a dimension of leadership beyond 'heroism' in the sense of a merely human capacity for independent, energetic action, and beyond the human virtues of courage and honour. We have seen, in *Lord Jim*, the creation of the 'amazing Jim-myth', the legend which 'gifted him with supernatural powers', attributing his heroic defeat of Sherif Ali to his magical ability to throw down the gates of the stockade with just a touch of one finger. But however much Jim is idolised by his people, he never perceives himself as a bearer of divine authority or as a representative of god on earth. He has a wholly human sense of fate, which can act for or against him, and of his human responsibility to the community that looks to him for leadership. When he fails them, though there is an element of martyrdom in his determination to take all that has happened upon his own head, the moral meaning of his end is entirely in keeping with Conrad's secular turn of mind. For Conrad, a man who seeks godlike status, or indulges in self-deification, has perverted the role of heroic leader. So Kurtz, for example, in *Heart of Darkness*, is said to have 'the power to charm or frighten rudimentary souls into an aggravated witch-dance in his honour'. The frenzied adoration and the self-abasement of Kurtz's followers ('They would crawl . . .') are a demonic inversion of the religious dimension of charismatic domination.[2] The charismatic leader is often regarded, either literally or metaphorically, as a god or a devil. To the devoted follower, longing for a transcendent prophet figure, such a leader will appear to be a messiah in the literal sense of being, in Carlyle's phrase, a messenger 'sent from the Infinite Unknown'. Political activity guided by such a leader takes on a millennial quality; it is directed towards ultimate goals, utopian and spiritual in nature, but also very often rooted in the collective identity of the imagined community of the nation. Nationalism, having emerged as a surrogate religion at a time (in the late eighteenth century) when orthodox religious belief was declining, is precisely the kind of militant and emotional faith which can be mobilised by the dynamism of the charismatic leader.[3]

The fascination exerted by men thought to be endowed with supernatural or superhuman qualities has been at the heart of some of the most frightening developments in twentieth-century political life, and there have been numerous efforts to elucidate the relationship between totalitarianism and charismatic authority. In part, this has involved looking back to nineteenth- and early twentieth-century expressions or analyses of quasi-mystical and irrationalist political thought – for example, Nietzsche's apotheosising of the emotional intensity of the *Übermensch*, the wilful genius opposed to the constraints of civilisation. In the decade between 1910 and his death in 1920, Weber developed the typology of this alternative political realm, opposing charismatic power to the 'iron cage' of the increasing rationalisation and efficiency of social systems. Charisma connotes grace, which has the theological sense of divine election but which also, in a psychological sense, refers to inner assurance and compelling attractiveness for others. It can be seen as a kind of extraordinary political authority, free from any conventional framework, unpredictably interrupting the normal processes of government and temporarily suspending or transfiguring all institutional routines and legal–rational authority. Although Weber also discussed institutional charisma, which legitimises and maintains what exists, he distinguished 'primal charisma' as an emotionally intense, revolutionary and creative force which emerges in times of social crisis. In contrast to Nietzsche, who sees the genius as isolated, Weber takes charismatic power to be a kind of personal authority that can only exist in relation to adoring followers. The basis of legitimation is the recognition of the leader's miraculous quality by followers who are lost in complete devotion. For people caught up in charismatic movements, self-sacrifice is the greatest virtue, selfishness the greatest vice.

In Weber's analysis, charismatic power is set against a waste-land vision of modern political life. Like so many of his contemporaries, he was preoccupied with the sterility of impersonal (legal–rational) political control systems, seeing them as alienating and destructive of individual autonomy and setting against them some form of heroic vitalism – 'a religion of Dionysian life and energy'. The 'emotional life force' of charisma seemed to offer the possibility of renewed vitality and meaning, though Weber himself was pessimistic about the possibility of withstanding the bureaucratic domination and centralisation of the modern power state. He expressed contempt for the 'swindle' and 'self-deception' of those modern intellectuals who hungered after substitute religions – who credited the redemptive rhetoric of bogus prophets and based their literary careers on mystical experiences they had manufactured. Artificial attempts to generate alternative spiritual satisfactions had, he argued, no chance of succeeding in a public world that was thoroughly disenchanted – '*entzaubert*'. Yet even this Puritan ascetic to some extent fell prey to the Dionysian concept of charisma, tempted, despite himself, towards worship of the charismatic leader, 'questioning his own rationalist heritage and coming to terms with the "vitalist" breakthrough, which dominated the intellectual culture of Europe in the years before World War I'.[4]

Although the general thrust of Weber's work was on the side of civilised constraint, he saw such constraint as destructive of all that is glorious and emotionally compelling. Those he designates as prototypical charismatic leaders, like the shaman, the demagogue and the prophet, are all marked by an innate capacity to display highly coloured emotions, and so are imagined by Weber, as by Nietzsche, to be more vivid, appearing to exist in an intensified state of consciousness, more potent than ordinary emotional life. Their power is associated with enhanced physical expressiveness – eyes and voice, for example, acting to intensify and transmit a heightened emotional state, infecting onlookers with enthusiasm and a feeling of vitality. Such techniques of ecstasy as frenzied dancing, singing and oratory offer a kind of participatory communion which has absolute value for followers. The excitement generated, like that evoked by the heroic man of action, is closely associated with the idea of political origins. Early twentieth-century crowd psychologists, like Gustave Le Bon and Gabriel Tarde, link the beginning of all society with the charismatic figure's expressive emotionality and ability to generate belief by means of 'contagious' volition. In more advanced societies, although the bureaucratised world would seem to run counter to the rise of charismatic movements, the circumstances of modernity can also be seen as increasing the desire for charismatic involvement as an escape from alienation and as compensation for the erosion of religious belief and disappearance of a vitalising *telos*.[5]

Immersion in the charismatic group was seen by many – by Freud, for example, as well as by Le Bon and Tarde – as a form of regression, allowing members of the group to 'throw off the repressions of the unconscious instinctual impulses' and approach more primitive states of consciousness.[6] Both Freud and the crowd psychologists argued that the idea of this primitive state of consciousness was akin to the mind of the somnambulist. Hypnotic trance is taken to provide one of the most telling images of the charismatic group, since the crowd, like the mesmerised individual, appears to be passive, credulous, emotional and suggestible, to experience the blurring of personal boundaries and to undergo identity shifts. Paradoxically, though mesmerised individuals characteristically surrender volition, they believe that they are acting spontaneously: both the crowd and the somnambulist need an inspiring leader to stimulate their actions, and thus are human puppets with an illusion of will. Other images associated with the experience of charismatic power similarly connote the forfeiture of individual will. The follower, for example, is 'magnetically' attracted, and the leader 'possessed' by a higher power which speaks through him. The leader's messianic role frees him of personal responsibility for the content of his visions, and his followers are moved by an 'irresistible' power to worship and imitate his intensely expressed beliefs.[7] These metaphors of charismatic domination are also a reflection of the close relationship between politics and the theatre. Heroic action is theatrical in the sense that it implies a narrative with a strong dramatic shape; in the case of the charismatic leadership of a political substitute religion, the comparison is more to do with the actor's ability to 'master' his audience, the performances of both actor and demagogue being described in language which suggests a loss of independent volition – 'spellbinding', 'captivating', 'enthralling' (a thrall being a slave or bondman).

The longing for charismatic leadership was, of course, most disturbingly evident in the rise of Hitler, whose public performances have time and again been described in the language of 'the Will' of the leader and the surrendered volition of his followers. Charismatic leadership played an important role in communist as well as fascist totalitarian regimes, and, in spite of Marxist hostility to personalised politics, both Lenin and Stalin were the objects of personality cults: Stalin, for example, 'invested himself with an image of colossal proportions – so that he might appear to the Soviet people as a father, a hero, a king, and a God'.[8] He was, however, the leader of a party which already had a monopoly of power and therefore, although the establishment of his personal image and authority was important, he did not need to court popularity in order to appeal to a large electorate. For Hitler, on the other hand, it was necessary to go to the people, and, even though he set no more store by democratic politics than did Stalin, he had to learn the techniques of persuading a popular following to support him. Although the rise of Hitler may have been less abrupt and inevitable than the Nazi propaganda machine tried to suggest, it would be hard to gainsay his extraordinary ability to manipulate mass audiences or his confidence in his power to sway people by the assertion of his 'constant Will'. Historians use phrases like 'a wave of acclamation', 'swept away' and 'magnetic field'; the testimony of those caught up in the experience, and compelled to believe in Hitler's charismatic powers, repeatedly draws upon the imagery of trance and possession. Statements by devotees give some impression of the feeling of communion listeners felt: 'The intense will of the man, the passion of his sincerity, seemed to flow from him into me. I experienced an exaltation that could be likened only to religious conversion.'[9] Those present at Nazi rallies felt themselves to be revitalised, powerful and filled with devotion. Joachim Fest describes people 'springing from their seats with raised arms, shouting wildly – overwhelmed in the double sense of being manipulated and ecstatic: now HE was here'. This was, in part, the performance of a man who proudly claimed the title of 'the greatest actor in Europe', meticulously planning his performances and studying the theories of crowd psychologists about ways of submerging individual beliefs in the collective experience of 'deindividualising mass consciousness'.[10] Under this self-conscious theatricality, however, there was also a belief that he was an authentic prophet whose feelings and thoughts derived from some higher source, a saviour endowed by Providence with special powers. A sense of divine mission was at the heart of the Hitler myth ('I go the way that Providence dictates with the assurance of a sleep-walker'). Like Joan of Arc he heard voices calling on him to rescue the nation. As Alan Bullock says, 'No one took the Hitler myth more seriously than Hitler himself.' His messianic role was reflected not only in Nazi ceremonies but in the polarising eschatology of Nazi ideology, based on a conception of the world as a cataclysmic battle between gods and demons, with the ultimate millennial promise of a Thousand Year Reich. What he required of his followers in return was unconditional loyalty: 'My first demand from you, therefore, is blind obedience.' The 'paltry worm' of an individual would thus become part of 'a great dragon' and could, by submitting, shed all sense of individual responsibility.[11]

Germany's 'God-sent leader' thus in many ways seemed to fill the role of Nietzsche's 'superman' or Weber's 'new prophet', with such devastating consequences that the experience made people, contemporary writers as well as later social theorists, highly suspicious of positive evaluations of charismatic experience. We will look, at the end of this chapter, at two of the most forceful attacks by German writers on the nature and consequences of charismatic domination: Thomas Mann's parable, *Mario and the Magician*, written in response to the rise of Mussolini, and Klaus Mann's *Mephisto*, a darkly satiric portrait of Nazi Germany.

The horrifying spectacle of the aggressive collective emotions, the grandiosity, paranoia and violence of Hitler-led National Socialism, not only engendered great suspicion of charismatic power itself but led to the condemnation of those thinkers whose work might be seen to have prepared the ground for Nazi ideology and manipulation of mass psychology. Thus Weber's attraction to the notion of a charismatic prophet is sometimes taken (rather unfairly) as evidence of proto-fascism. Of the writers included here, it was D.H. Lawrence in particular, with his dark gods and blood mysticism, who was most vulnerable to the charge of having been an unwitting precursor of Nazism. On the one hand, there is good evidence that Lawrence would have disliked all actual fascist movements; on the other, his efforts to think of political life on the model of religious experience did produce some very extreme ideas, no sooner passionately proclaimed than problematised. His deep desire for some kind of political role created certain intractable problems for Lawrence, absorbing much his creative energy during the decade after the First World War.

There are fluctuations and contradictions in his views which spring directly from his effort to find a public, political belief worthy of his immensely serious moral passions. In part, what we see is a tension between self and society. He says, for example, in 'Democracy' that 'the singleness of the clear, clean self' must keep itself out of 'people melted into a oneness . . . *En Masse*' – and yet, elsewhere, he would seem to celebrate charismatic immersion in the 'being' of the whole. There is also the difficulty of actually giving a political shape and location to his vague longing for the non-rational satisfactions of a political substitute religion. Amongst the things he rails against in 'Democracy' are the idealised collective activities of all governments, nations, empires 'and so forth': nationalism, he says, should lose every scrap of its 'ideal drapery'.[12] This leaves Lawrence with the question of what exactly, in concrete political terms, he was hoping to find. His notions of blood-consciousness, for example, clearly have none of the nationalistic implications of '*Blut und Boden*' (Mother Earth and the mystical substratum of the blood); that this is so distances Lawrence's views from those of the Nazis, but at the same time suggests a political desire with very little by way of specific content. Charismatic belief is difficult to imagine outside a particular cultural and political milieu, since the deep sources of conversion and attachment to the charismatic leader are to be found in the common symbols and myths of a shared cultural heritage. Lawrence's restless travels during the 1920s were all in search of the right soil for the 'new shoot' he wanted to send out into the life of mankind. His failures to find what he was seeking are, in a sense, what he records in *Aaron's Rod*, *Kangaroo* and *The Plumed Serpent*. As Paul Fussell says, it was Lawrence's intense feeling for the spirit of place that ultimately cured him of his earlier hopes of promulgating a more all-embracing creed.[13]

Lawrence's need to travel was prompted by his sense that 'one's native land' itself was too restrictive to accommodate 'a bigger gesture . . . a certain grandeur', to provide scope for any political revitalisation. London, he told Russell, did not really exist and should be pulled down; in the late twenties, when he had returned to Europe, he lamented the city's deathly dullness and the 'pervasive anaesthetic' of niceness and easiness that destroyed the vitality of everyone in England.[14] Lawrence was not, of course, alone in his conviction that England was not very fertile ground for fundamental political transformations. Orwell, for example, in 'The Lion and Unicorn', makes the case in terms not dissimilar to Lawrence's own, though with more sympathy for English 'niceness'. Whilst the future is by no means fixed, some alternatives, Orwell maintains, are possible and others not; what he sees as characteristically English (and of crucial importance in determining 'what part England *can play* in the huge events that are happening') is the privateness of English life, and a gentleness which means that 'the power-worship which is the new religion of Europe, and which has infected the English intelligentsia, has never touched the common people'.[15]

Orwell often represents himself as an isolated figure on the English intellectual landscape – one of the only writers not feeling the need to commit himself to a political or religious faith. The craving for belief in novelists of the thirties has been analysed in Richard Johnstone's *The Will to Believe*, which presents a very full picture of the romantic aspirations of those young writers who rejected rational, humanistic solutions, turning instead to Catholicism or Communism. In the work of older writers of the time, as well, there is ample evidence, as Johnstone says, that what Wyndham Lewis called a 'crisis of belief' was not confined to a single generation. One manifestation of this search for belief substitutes is a recurrent interest in charismatic power figures who seem to offer a spiritual dimension absent from English political life – an interest often combined with considerable scepticism about the kind of political role played by such leaders and with an implicit recognition that they would seem wholly out of place in the ordered, familiar English setting. Just as the young novelists of the thirties tended to be attracted to beliefs that were foreign in origin and alien to their own insular traditions,[16] so other writers were fascinated by visionary leaders of decidedly un-English national causes. Amongst popular writers, one of the most striking examples is John Buchan, in many ways a conventional, establishment political figure (an MP for Scottish Universities, who took the Tory whip). Buchan often dwelt on the idea of the lost leader and, in his thrillers, repeatedly represents the brilliant, charismatic figure destroyed for dark reasons, perhaps alongside a non-committed hero finding inspiration through passionate commitment to a dream. The image of great powers perverted produces some of Buchan's most striking villains, men with an appearance of exceptional goodness, established by means of considerable gifts – for example, the splendid Reverend John Laputa in *Prester John* (1910), a vivid, prophetic tale of an African rising that is one of Buchan's best novels. In other novels as well one can see his weakness for charismatic villains: Muckle John Gib, in *Salute to Adventurers* (his last novel to be written before the First World War), uses biblical language and is an extraordinarily effective preacher; Moxon Ivery in *Mr Standfast* is capable of holding an audience spellbound but exercises his immense talents to serve evil ends. At the other end of the political spectrum, in Shaw's *St Joan* (1923), we can also see the attraction exerted by the charismatic figure whose vision seems too disruptive to be accommodated by existing systems of government. Shaw's view of the merits of British political rule was obviously far more critical than Buchan's but, like Buchan, he saw in the prophetic leader a kind of political passion that was both alluring and dangerous. In Ra's Prologue, added to *Caesar and Cleopatra* in 1912, Shaw represents Caesar as allied with the gods, participating in a divine will larger than his own. This sense of divine mission is not particularly in keeping with Shaw's earlier image of Caesar, in the body of the play, as an adept and realistic military commander who is not very successful in converting those around him to his way of thinking. It can, however, be seen as much more applicable to the inspiring conqueror-saint of his later play, written at a time when he was increasingly taken with the idea of the prophet motivated by faith in an idea and capable of inspiring others to follow.[17] This is, for Shaw, another intimation of the evolutionary role that might be played by the great man (or woman): whereas Buchan represents this kind of compelling but destabilising power as a threat to a system he wants to preserve, Shaw reflects on the possibility of an alliance between the visionary personality and man's appetite for progress.

In narratives which revolve around political faith and conversion our attention is perhaps most often drawn to the creation of belief, as well as to attendant uncertainties and doubts: how far is it possible to believe? What are the consequences of belief? In narratives of heroic action, the focus, as we have seen, is most often on individual moral issues of choice and responsibility; here, on the other hand, the central concern is more likely to be an inner process of conversion, the surrender of individual choice and responsibility to a collective will mediated by the charismatic leader. The same is true of actual charismatic movements, that is, that the inwardness of belief and the necessity of surrender are paramount ('it was chiefly in an "inner" sense that Hitler was presented as the revealer of a new meaning to life, one which absorbed his followers' need to surrender themselves, to serve and submit to him, to shed their weariness of responsibility'). Both chivalric action and charismatic domination can be seen as regressions to more primitive patterns of political engagement, but the one is a pursuit of worldly goals remote from mysticism, the other, a question of the presence (or absence) of an inner certainty inspired by God's chosen leader.[18]

MARTYRED PROPHETS: BUCHAN'S *PRESTER JOHN* AND SHAW'S *ST JOAN*

'Oh, do not come back . . . Give us peace in our time, O Lord!' De Stogumber's plea at the end of *St Joan* expresses a sense of ineradicable opposition between the settled, conventional political framework and the imperious demands of the charismatic prophet. Joan redeems the faith 'their worldlinesses have dragged through the mire', but all spring to their feet in consternation at the thought that she might rise from the dead. They may adore her now, but if she were brought back to life she would be burned again within six months. Political necessities, however 'erroneous', are imperative.

John Buchan, who looks with a far more favourable eye on established political structures, nevertheless, like Shaw, sees the charismatic leader as representing a powerful, almost overwhelmingly attractive force which is excluded from normal political life. In *Prester John*, he centres the whole of the narrative on the problematic relationship of a thoroughly decent young man to a dynamic but irresponsible African leader who seems to possess an almost vanished human capacity for conferring spiritual meaning on public life. Like St Joan, the Reverend John Laputa is doomed; like her, he polarises the judgements of those who come into contact with him. In contrast to Shaw, however, Buchan is not considering the charismatic leader as a potential ally of human progress, but rather as a great primitive force which threatens to undermine Western colonialism – just as later charismatic African leaders, such as Nkrumah in Ghana, did in fact lead their countries to independence from British colonial rule. Within the context of the thriller form, this leader is the demon-villain who must be defeated before order can be restored, though the simple conflict between the forces of native darkness and civilised progress is complicated by the role of the narrator, David Crawfurd, through whom Buchan conveys something of the power of the political faith for which Laputa speaks.

The political context of *Prester John* is an Africa in which Buchan sees unprecedented opportunities for giving satisfactory form to the relationship between the native and the European population. He does not doubt that 'the solvent and formative influences of civilisation' must ultimately prevail,[19] but at the same time this is an unsettled enough territory to allow quite opposed political possibilities to flourish. The Empire was for Buchan a secular, practical ideal, but one which, with his strongly religious background, he hoped to

73

integrate with a spiritual ideal – an ideal that is needed to 'satisfy the hunger in our hearts', since 'Everything shades sooner or later into metaphysics'.[20] The son of a Free Church minister, Buchan drew on his Calvinist background in creating Laputa's political religion, working out in political terms a dualism he saw in Calvinism itself, 'a strong creed – capable of grievous distortion sometimes, too apt, perhaps, to run wild in dark and vehement emotions, or in the other extreme to dwarf to a harsh formality', though at its best offering a combination of form and spirituality, and so crystallising a moral ideal in the life of a 'visible society'. It seems clear that he at times feels a romantic attraction to more primitive faiths. So, for example, of the Turkish and Arab desire to 'live face to face with God without a screen of ritual', he writes, 'There are times when it grips me so hard that I'm inclined to forswear the gods of my fathers!'[21] Ideally, perhaps, Buchan has in mind a union of primitive spiritual passion and civilised form. At the same time, however, he has a horror of fanaticism, and the standard role of the Buchan hero is to thwart the plans of fanatical, Nietzschean rebels against the established order. This conflict within Buchan creates a complex tension at the heart of *Prester John*, between the passionate, disruptive figure of a charismatic spiritual–political leader and David Crawfurd, fulfilling his role in defending civilised order but at the same time experiencing with great intensity the stirrings of faith that would be felt by a convert to the cause of the Reverend John Laputa.

The revivalist passions released by Laputa are a response to his attempt to reanimate the kingdom of Prester John, a legendary fifteenth-century king of Abyssinia under whom the empire of Ethiopia had extended far to the south. The legend is in part one of military conquest, but the strong religious element in the movement is symbolised by an all-important fetish, a sacred collar handed on by Prester John. The cult is a 'bastard' blend of Christianity and paganism, and these elements in Laputa's own psyche seem to Crawfurd to make him a mixture of god and demon: his heart harbours 'all the black lusts of paganism', but he sees himself as pursuing a divine mission. As Laputa, having recovered the lost fetish, seeks to revive the legend, he himself regresses, first exchanging his Western for native clothes and then stripping off his leopard skin to stand stark naked: 'At the full moon when the black cock was blooded, the Reverend John forgot his Christianity. He was back four centuries among the Mazimba sweeping down on the Zambesi. He told them, and they believed him, that he was . . . the incarnated spirit of Prester John.' To Laputa, this regressive movement is one of simplification and purification. In answer to Crawfurd's charge that in awakening 'aboriginal passions' he wants to convert everyone into savages, he makes an almost Lawrentian plea for turning from the 'bitterness' of civilisation to a world that is 'simpler and better', purged and 'awakened to a new hope'. This romantic element in the rising does not ultimately, Crawfurd notes, find its way into the official Western narrative of the black rising.[22]

Laputa's charismatic powers are presented as essential to the success of the rising, and, through Crawfurd, they are very fully established for us. An aristocratic figure of Zulu blood and high stock, he is a man of genius, nobility and splendid proportions, a fine natural orator with a wonderful voice, resonant and full of magic: 'If it be the part of an orator to rouse the passion of his hearers, Laputa was the greatest on earth.' This king–priest delivers an 'amazing discourse' – 'God's message to His own' – which Crawfurd says that he cannot hope to reproduce in his 'prosaic words' (*Prester John*, p. 107). Thus, although Laputa is capable of any villainy, Crawfurd would 'hesitate to call him a blackguard'. Marred though he is by egoism and fanaticism, he is impressive even in death – 'strange, and great, and moving, and terrible'. His dying words awaken in Crawfurd 'a wild regret': his death is like 'the fall of a great mountain' or 'the fall of Lucifer' (pp. 79, 178–80).

At the centre of the narrative is a scene in which Crawfurd feels the emotions of a convert to the cause and an intense desire for communion. It is not *his* cause, and we know that a Buchan hero can be in no real danger of total immersion in a collective devotion to pan-Africanism. Temporarily, however, and in the heart of the enemy camp, Crawfurd experiences an impulse to surrender individual free will to a god-like (or satanic) power, and we sense the fascination with the idea of complete submission that Buchan expressed elsewhere as well: 'Everything lay in the hands of God, though men fussed and struggled and made a parade of freedom. Might not there be a more potent strength in utter surrender?'[23] Crawfurd embodies a more thoroughgoing ambivalence towards the charismatic villain than is evident in any of Buchan's other novels. From the outset, his relationship with the mysterious figure of Laputa is marked by a combination of attraction and repulsion which is irrational and impossible to articulate. He feels nameless fear coupled with devouring curiosity. He is 'horribly impressed' (p. 103). Even as a boy, when he by chance sees the black minister practising 'strange magic' on the Dyve Burn sands, he feels compelled to watch the man, 'feeling somehow shut in with this unknown being in a strange union' (pp. 13–15).

This 'strange union' is crucial to the narrative, which is organised around a series of encounters between Crawfurd and Laputa. In Africa, Crawfurd is drawn to an uncanny place, the Cave of the Rooirand, which hides sacred, repressed forces that enter his mind as the uncanny sound of an underground river, a muffled groaning coming up from he rocks, 'eerie and unearthly'. He follows a man who seems 'as old as Time itself' until he is terrified by and flees from the terrible moaning of an 'imprisoned river' in his ears (pp. 49–50). Returning to the spot, he enters the vast cave in which he will discover the inner workings of Laputa's mystery, in ceremonies conducted in a gigantic chamber within which torchlight makes the 'sheer stream glow and sparkle like the battlements of the Heavenly City' (p. 96). The imagery of possession and hypnotism establishes the nature of Laputa's power: his audience is in 'a sort of trance, their eyes fixed glassily on Laputa's face'; there is 'the air of mad enthusiasm', with 'wild eyes and twitching hands', song and incantation; the worshippers are shaken by 'a kind of sobbing' and the assembly rocks 'with a strange passion'. Crawfurd is unable to resist the spell. Though his blood 'should have been boiling', he has to confess that his mind is 'mesmerised by this amazing man . . . . Indeed I was a convert.' Crawfurd is in effect taken over by the spirit of the great man, and his own regression is the counterpart to the historically regressive character of the cause championed by Laputa: he finds that he 'longed for a leader who should master me and make my soul his own, as this man mastered his followers'; hearing tones that remind him of his father's voice, he feels himself regressing to a state of childlike admiration (pp. 100–8).

Even after Laputa's death frees him and he has 'come out of savagery', there is a final moment when his antagonist's powers of leadership seem to animate Crawfurd's effort to secure peace, enabling him to speak 'like a man inspired', telling the followers of Laputa that 'His spirit approves my mission.' Seeing the course of his experiences in an explicitly Calvinist light, Crawfurd is convinced that his following of Laputa has been in some sense providential. Throughout, he has sought evidence of 'the workings of Omnipotence', in which it is necessary to believe if you are to do anything but 'bide sluggishly at home'. One of the central questions he has had to face has been whether Providence speaks through Laputa or whether it is, on the contrary, embodied by a providential opposition in which Crawfurd himself is instrumental. In the event, he interrupts what was seen as a 'destined' course and, reasserting his free will, secures an alternative. But even if the white colonial forces have ultimately proven to have providence on their side, Crawfurd is left to ponder the ways in which his triumph is as a 'follower' of Laputa. In the physical act of following (tracking down) Laputa he has actually experienced the emotional state of one of his followers (converts), but has in the end, instead, followed Laputa's example, in the sense of himself becoming inspired in his resistance, in the course of which, without consciously planning to do so, he has managed to 'cut off' Laputa from his people. Crawfurd's function has in a way been to separate the messianic force embodied in Laputa from the planned black rising – or, in more general terms, to separate the powerful and attractive force of charismatic leadership from its nationalistic context. In effect, Crawfurd has appropriated something of Laputa's spirit for a white race which, although it cannot achieve such intensity of effect, can graft a sense of divine destiny on to 'the gift of responsibility', which confers 'the power of being *in a little way* a king'. This moderated or qualified power is presented as being sympathetic to the grievances of the natives but constrained by civilised standards ('the white man's duty') – the best compromise that can be hoped for. What has been preserved in the successful resistance to Laputa, then, is precisely this sense of responsibility, the special 'gift' of the white race, and what, in essence, is thought to separate British political rule from the dark, dynamic attractions of a complete regression to charismatic domination (pp. 196–8).

From Buchan's perspective, Fabian socialism was almost as threatening to the established fabric of traditionally ordered Western society as the revolutionary zeal of a charismatic African nationalist: the Fabians, he wrote, saw the state as having the power to 'sell you up, lock you up ... in short abolish you, if you lift your hand against it'.[24] As we have seen in Shaw's case, there were perhaps enough contradictory elements in his political views to lend a certain amount of credence to accusations of authoritarianism. Beatrice Webb, for example, contrasted the idealisation of rebellion by Shaw as a young social reformer with his later idealisation of dictators: 'What he really admires in Soviet Communism is the *forceful* activities of the Communist Party. He feels that this party has a powerful collective personality that imposes itself willy-nilly on the multitude of nonentities.'[25] What this leads him towards is a dilemma curiously like the one we have explored in Buchan's thinking. That is, there is a hankering after a political religion which can reach further and offer more than ordinary politics is capable of doing, and a concomitant willingness to contemplate the subordination of individual judgement to the force of a personality capable of changing the world. Shaw, who described himself as having no religion whatever in the sectarian sense, saw in Christ just such a personality – one of the Shavian Supermen, whose appearance in history points the way towards the future of human evolution and who is alternately perceived by Shaw as a comparatively isolated rebel and as a megalomaniac king. St Joan, whose advent was like another coming of Christ, was, he said, a much more satisfactory example of the power of the 'miraculous' personality, since, to the modern mind, she speaks for heresies with which we sympathise, whereas Christ's claims seem to us the delusions of a madman.[26] Much of Shaw's 'Preface' is given over to an effort to bring Joan's 'voices and visions' into line with modern beliefs and a twentieth-century 'evolutionary appetite'.

If we compare St Joan to Napoloen, we see an important shift in Shaw's conception of personal leadership, a preference, in the years after the First World War, for prophet figures rather than warrior-heroes. Whereas Napoleon is driven by fierce ambition and an appetite for conquest, Joan is driven by her passion for a higher idea and her certainty of divine revelation, a religious vision with which she inspires those around her. As J.L. Wisenthal says, her effectiveness is like that which Shaw attributed to Cromwell and Stalin: 'they were carrying a conception of the world into the realm of action'.[27] Although Joan, like Prester John, is a semi-legendary medieval figure, Shaw's emphasis is not on the regressive nature of her example but on the possibility of assimilating her religious purpose to a progressive conception of political change, and on the modernity of her disruptive energies. The careful distinctions of his 'Preface' allow him to steer a course between idolatry and scepticism, creating a heroine far more admirable than his knowing, cynical Napoleon, who, in comparison to Joan, was 'neither frank nor disinterested': she is Shaw's 'one foray into popular myth-making, undefaced by his usual ironic graffiti'. Though she has also been described as 'the only woman who ever managed to wipe the smirk from Shaw's face', he imagines her in predominantly masculine terms – a rational dresser and masculine worker on the heroic scale, not 'peculiar' except for 'the vigour and scope of her mind and character, and the intensity of her vital energy'.[28] Representing the perennial force of direct, subversive individual intuition, Joan is for Shaw one of the self-selected saints and prophets who demonstrate that the law of God is and always has been 'a law of change' (*St Joan*, p. 34). Since all evolution in human thought and conduct makes its first appearance as heresy, it is clear that we must privilege heresy. The self-chosen mission of the innovatory saint is simply what, in secular terms, we would class as courageous originality and independence of mind, shrewdness, realism and common sense. Her genius has given her 'a different set of ethical valuations' from those of other people, as well as the energy to give effect to her vision (p. 10).

Joan's powers, however, do not spring simply from the stubborn individuality of her rebellion but from her extraordinary ability to inspire a collective movement. Her heretical version of medieval Catholicism thus merges not only with Protestant individualism but with conversion to the collective cause of a nascent nationalism. The divisions in Shaw's own mind are apparent in the competing judgements of Joan, who is not by any means left in the simple role of admirable free spirit and agent of progressive change. She is in many ways a dangerous, destructive force. In the context of a post-First World War world, she speaks both for modern warfare and for the nationalism that, in its developed form, could be seen as the cause of the war. Her championship of effectively destructive, chauvinistic militarism is in part what makes her a leader too threatening to be contained by a stable, well-ordered society. Her nationalism, which was no part of a medieval conception of a Christian society, is rightly perceived by Cauchon to be a 'most dangerous idea': fragment the unity of 'Christ's kingdom', he argues, and 'the world will perish in a welter of war'. The simple, unshakeable conviction that stands behind her nationalistic crusade is touching but also frightening: 'I am a servant of God. My sword is sacred' (pp. 83, 99).

At the same time, however, Joan represents the kind of dynamic force without which institutionalised political life would simply ossify: looked at from this angle, Joan's capacity to stir collective emotions is a vital corrective to corporate uniformity. In contrast to *Prester John*, *St Joan* does not represent villains who must be defeated before a normal civilised order can be re-established, but Joan is, equally, a heroine who has no chance of gaining a victory against the defenders of the status quo. Joan's opposition to all established, institutional ways of thinking – her 'unbounded and quite unconcealed contempt for official opinion, judgement, and authority' (p. 7) – sets her against the combined powers of Church and state. Cauchon condemns her for usurping the authority of the Church – bringing a direct message from God and writing letters such as those written by 'the accursed Mahomet', which speak, with monstrous conceit, only of God and herself (p. 94). In Warwick's view, she endangers the position of the aristocracy by putting forward the idea that kings should reign as God's bailiffs. Both men are very clear about the menace to institutional authority posed by personal charismatic power. They agree that Joan's failure to mention the Church and her failure to mention the aristocracy are the same idea at bottom, being the individual soul's protest against priests or peers interfering in a man's private relationship with God: it is therefore inevitable that she will be, as the Inquisitor says, 'crushed between these mighty forces, the Church and the Law' (p. 139).

The panic caused by Joan's heretical views is inextricably related to the power of the charismatic leader to compel belief. It is Joan's power to fire men with devotion and generate a new faith amongst the populace that makes her so alarming a phenomenon. In the five scenes leading up to Joan's trial, our attention is focused on her miraculous ability to inspire the soldiers who follow her, filling them with absolute confidence that they are serving the cause of a divinely-chosen leader. As Shaw says in the 'Preface', most people want to be saved the trouble of thinking for themselves. In the normal course of things, these obediences are 'carefully arranged and maintained' and their slavishness facilitates the smooth and continuous operation of the system. The question Shaw addresses is how, without either authority or prestige, Joan could have commanded such obedience, ordering everybody about without offering either rational solutions or expressions of her own (as opposed to God's) will (pp. 37–8). The play establishes the nature of her control over others by presenting a range of responses to her. She is not represented as a mesmerising orator or as a glamorous heroic figure (like Napoleon, say, or Nostromo), but unquestionably radiates 'pure charisma' in Weber's sense of 'a "call" . . . a "mission" or a "spiritual duty"'. The metaphorically miraculous effect of the charismatic leader on his followers is in Joan's case, of course, the actual working of miracles – the hens laying or the wind changing – which, though Shaw allows a naturalistic explanation, are amongst the things which inspire ardent faith. A miracle, as the Archbishop says, is an event that creates faith, allowing people to 'feel the thrill of the supernatural, and forget their sinful clay in a sudden sense of the glory of God' (pp. 70–1).

A capacity for transforming men into something else is perhaps most strikingly manifested in Joan's ability to turn the Dauphin into a king ('a miracle that will take some doing, it seems'), but throughout the play key scenes turn on the question of whether people will follow her (p. 77). So, for example, at the very beginning, we want to know whether she can compel the belief of the sceptical Robert de Baudricourt, who at the end of the first scene falls on his knees and acknowledges that she did come from God. When Robert first demands of his steward why his men-at-arms will not throw Joan out, the steward replies that she puts courage into them by being so positive and unafraid. The comedy of Robert trying to assert himself in the face of Joan's confidence establishes her at the outset as someone who can compel others to do her (or God's) will; it also allows us to see the contrast between Joan's charismatic authority and a 'great man's' more bullying form of power, the 'self-assertive, loud-mouthed, superficially energetic' approach of someone who gets his way by 'storming terribly' and by threatening the use of his boot (pp. 49–55). In the same way, juxtaposition with the Dauphin serves to place her alongside the decidedly unimpressive representative of officially sanctioned authority, a 'poor creature physically', wearing the expression of 'a young dog accustomed to be kicked' (p. 65); and juxtaposition with the stock hero-figure, Dunois, gives us a measure of her superiority to a mere hero. Dunois, although he comes well out of the play, is only a brave and beautiful conqueror, not a saint. For all his fine qualities, he lacks the potency of Joan's leadership, which is capable of putting 'fresh spunk' into his troops where he is not. In the first meeting with Dunois, in which he declares that not a man will follow Joan in her attack on the forts, he is answered by her sublime self-confidence: 'I will not look back to see whether anyone is following me.' As Joan later says, the knights and captains of Dunois do not follow her, but the townsfolk and common people do, showing his troops 'how to fight in earnest' (pp. 82, 108–9).

Joan's claim of divine authority ensures complete commitment on the part of those 'infatuated' with her but also creates 'no end of trouble', since, to those who do not accept her as a messenger of God, she is an 'insufferable' and 'blasphemous impostor'. Like Buchan's Laputa, Joan is accused of practising the black arts, of sorcery as well as of a heretical distortion of the Christian faith. Shaw's view of heresy, as I have suggested, is quite different to that of Buchan, but both are inclined to accept that the heretic cannot hope to escape crucifixion in the world as it is, which is not in the least likely to embrace a simple call to spiritual regeneration. Joan's commitment to her faith, and the power of her 'dramatic imagination' to transmit that faith to others, thus requires dedication and sacrifice far beyond what men would suffer in 'the selfish pursuit of personal power'. The excessiveness of her primal charisma – her pursuit of ultimate goals, impatience with institutional authority and readiness for self-sacrifice – seals her fate but also gives her immortality as a symbol of aspiration. Shaw argues in his 'Preface' that the 'hallucinations' centring on legendary personages embody forces (aspiration and conscience) that are matters of fact 'more obvious than electro-magnetism'. It is thinking in terms of 'celestial vision' that makes the world's popular religions (and political religions) apprehensible and allows the human imagination to dramatise 'superpersonal forces' (pp. 13–16). This is a dangerous but compelling form of power, discontinuous with the ordinary functioning of government. The duly authorised obediences necessary to the operation of the social system are replaced by devotion to someone with no authority and no claim to deference other than a flat appeal to a higher authority ('God says so'). 'Leaders who take that line', as Shaw says, 'need never fear a lukewarm reception' (pp. 38–9) – though in England of the twenties it would have been difficult for anyone to anticipate the full extent of the passionate devotion and fierce hatred that such a leader could generate.

'SOME QUEER DARK GOD': LAWRENCE'S 'LEADERSHIP' NOVELS OF THE TWENTIES

Lawrence, too, thinks of political and religious experience as fundamentally related, though in his work it might be more accurate to say that what is represented is less a pseudo-religious form of political activity than a pseudo-political form of religious experience: it is almost invariably the transcendent possibilities rather than policy and praxis that seize his attention. As in *St Joan*, the sense of what is transcendent in political experience is partly captured by the opposition between power and authority. These are words associated in his mind with two sorts of human nature, the aristocrats ('those that feel themselves strong in their souls') and the democrats ('those that feel themselves weak'). In *Apocalypse*, for example, he reflects at length on the dire consequences of a self-glorification of the weak and a concomitant hatred of men who are 'obviously' strong. A failure to recognise and give homage to the natural power in a greater man leads to the loss of your own potency; it means that the mass of men (who need to be ruled and governed) 'must grant *authority* where they deny power'. When authority takes the place of power, 'we have "ministers" and public officials and policemen', and democratic impoverishment rather than the 'brave power' that fulfils the human need for 'splendour, gorgeousness, pride, assumption, glory, and lordship'.[29]

No one could accuse Lawrence of having proposed a practical political programme centring on the power of the 'supreme master and lord and splendid one' – and, as Richard Aldington says in his Introduction to *Apocalypse*, we read him for his own 'glow and warmth' rather than for sound theories of political world-organisation (pp. 20, xxv–xxvi). Lawrence himself, however, was greatly troubled by his inability to join effectively in the larger male world of politics, and his 'savage pilgrimage' enabled him both to escape the disheartenment, 'ugly pettiness' and 'mass funk' that he saw in England and to search for some place where 'the natural proud self of power' might flourish.[30] Having left England in November 1919, he embarked on his travels to Italy, Australia, New Mexico and Mexico. Like the fashionable drifters in *Aaron's Rod*, he hated 'the house we live in – London – England – America! . . .', but sought, in his leadership novels – *Aaron's Rod*, *Kangaroo* and *The Plumed Serpent* – to find some more positive response to disillusionment than simply 'Pulling the house down'. All three are novels which have continued to generate controversy because of the intensity of Lawrence's efforts to imagine a world not governed by 'politics' in the ordinary sense of the word, one in which men might find 'living power' rather than the barren tedium of conventional authority. The power he valorises resides in a profoundly irrationalist political faith which is not constrained either (as in Buchan) by any balancing respect for 'responsible' political traditions or (as in Shaw) by the notion that the political visionary is in the service of mankind's progressive, evolutionary appetite. Unlike Buchan and Shaw, Lawrence was some distance from actual political involvement, and the sort of charismatic leadership that fascinated him was correspondingly more extreme, more eccentric and far less grounded in any actual experience of public life. In each of his leadership novels, a political 'seeker' (such as Lawrence himself was) is brought together with a messianic political figure who might or might not be able to 'make a break' from what he calls, in *Apocalypse*, 'the weakness of a multitude of weak men' (pp. 21–2). This is not a very clearly defined quest. Even the word 'seeker' sometimes strikes Lawrence as implying too fixed a purpose or goal – and it does indeed suggest a more definite objective than we see in the vacillations and uncertainties of Aaron Sisson, Richard Lovat Somers and Kate Leslie. Each character, however, searches for some deeper experience, for personal and political transformation of a kind apparently impossible in the dead, unimaginative world of English politics. Vacillations are caused primarily by the difficulty of finding such a transcendent experience in *any* real political world, and also by the fact that the various seekers carry with them civilised self-definitions, making them resistant to whatever 'queer dark gods' they may encounter.

Thus Aaron, for example, who abandons wife, family and eventually England, carries with him to Italy much of the Englishness which he must leave behind if he is to be capable of acting on his 'great dynamic urges'. As we have seen, he readily falls into the British role of ignoring neighbours, closing his mind to others and attending only to his own affairs, content in the cosy littleness of his English identity. He also, however, as he travels to Florence, feels the magic of the large, vigorous Italian landscape, and is impressed by the contrasts with an England in which 'everybody seems held tight and gripped, nothing is left free'. What he is moving towards – although it is sketched in rather than embodied in *Aaron's Rod* – is the possibility of throwing off English inhibition ('trussed with self-conscious string as tight as capons') and discovering a new life motive, the 'great dark power-urge' (pp. 238–9, 345).

In the closing pages of the novel Rawdon Lilly tells Aaron that what he must do is to give 'profound, profound obedience . . . to the incalculable power-urge'. The language Lawrence uses here suggests the struggle to make (as he sees it) an important distinction. Aaron must 'yield' and 'submit', but this must not be confused with 'subservience' or 'slavery': just as women must offer men 'a deep, unfathomable free submission', so men must 'in their souls *submit* to some greater soul than theirs . . . . You, too, have the need livingly to yield to a more heroic soul, to give yourself.' The *freedom* of such an act of submission is essential to the integrity of a man's 'single oneness'. Lawrence implies that 'one who is impelled' is no less free than 'one who urges', but, it has to be said, begs the question of how autonomy is to be maintained after one has submitted (pp. 346–7). The follower's sense that he is a free agent is uncomfortably akin to the illusion of independence common amongst members of any charismatic movement – the fond belief that they are acting spontaneously.[31] In *Aaron's Rod*, Lilly has already presented a strong case against mass movements precisely because they encourage such a delusion. That is, men who are individually 'craven and cringing' will become 'conceited in the mass . . . the mass-bullies, the individual Judases' (p. 120). The problem of dissociating individual followership from mass followership is a recurrent one in Lawrence's leadership novels. His hatred of 'the ghastly mob-sleep' (p. 145) is variously expressed, and the question of how a man is to follow the leader without joining the mass is never entirely resolved.

Lawrence is anxious also to distinguish the way in which authority is exerted by a bullying leader from natural lordship and mastery. What he wants, he argues, is the will-to-power, but not in the sense that Nietzsche means it: 'Not intellectual power. Not mental power. Not conscious will-power. Not even wisdom. But dark, living, fructifying power.' The negatives continue to pile up as Lilly works at clarifying the kind of 'power-urge' that *is* acceptable: 'never bully, never force from the conscious will. That's where Nietzsche was wrong' (pp. 345–6). The special quality of a power-urge that is unconscious of its aims and that does not coerce is in part conveyed through the musical metaphor that runs through the novel. Aaron's flute is capable of exerting this kind of influence over its hearers. Just as Lawrence cast himself sometimes as follower, sometimes as potential leader, so the followers in these novels are capable of exercising their own kind of power, whether as flautist, writer or goddess. When Aaron-Svengali plays for the Marchesa-Trilby, she enters into a trance-like state, singing 'at his bidding', then sitting dazed and silent, overcome by his 'magic'. Aaron's malehood, gratified, rises in mastery, so that he feels to the full his 'male super-power'. His 'male godliness, the male godhead' breaks out of 'locked' repression. But the Marchesa turns out to be a treacherous follower. Fearing him (he speculates), she seeks 'sacrilegious power' over his 'godlikeness', turning the tables on him – she becoming the priestess, Aaron changing from god to victim (pp. 298–306). Aaron is, by implication, better fitted to understanding the nature of 'life-submission', which would never make of the leader 'a mere instrument' for the follower's use. When Aaron loses his flute ('rod') in an anarchist bombing, he abandons his efforts to assert male mastery and turns instead to Lilly. The novel ends with him paying rapt attention to Lily's 'strange speech-music', which, like his own flute music, is free from rational meaning and conscious intention: 'It was more the sound value which entered his soul', and he 'understood, oh, so much more deeply than if he had listened with his head' (pp. 345–7).

Rawdon Lilly, though he does not have a political role, is given many of the qualities of a charismatic prophet, a born leader who has 'a certain belief in himself as a saviour' (p. 91). Lilly is a 'peculiar bird', a 'freak' and outsider who strikes Aaron as having no wish to compel others, leaving them to make their own choices and not seeking any connection, but at the same time 'maddening and fascinating' (no bully but a natural master, then). In what we see of him, it is mainly in conversation and domestic affairs that Lilly assumes priority, unaware, Aaron thinks, of the 'quiet predominance' he has over others (bearing himself with 'silent assurance' while he mashes potatoes and heats plates). In conversation, like Lawrence in his preaching mode, Lilly holds forth, 'the idol on the mountain top', denouncing the dead ideals of love, liberty, charity and brotherhood – 'all the whole beehive of ideals' that find political expression in socialism, public-spiritedness and equality of opportunity (pp. 290, 129). Lilly, like Lawrence, wants some alternative kind of power that is 'permanent and very efficacious', but has to confess, as he surveys the mass of people, that 'they are too many, and so what I think is ineffectual'. He reflects on his abhorrence of 'folks who teem by the billion' ('flea-bitten Asiatics') and his preference for the 'living pride' of the Aztecs and Red Indians, 'higher types' who 'breed slower'; he ponders his contempt for those who yield to the mob, the nation, Lloyd George and Northcliffe but would not submit to 'a bit of healthy individual authority' – that is, those who, in Lilly's own private sphere, 'resist me: my authority, or my influence, or just *me*' (pp. 118–19). The isolation of this 'superior being' and his lack of any larger political function makes it easier for Lawrence to dissociate him from the kinds of power of which he disapproves, allowing Lilly to be presented as a respecter of the 'holy individual' and not the preposterous megalomaniac he is sometimes accused of being. It also, however, by and large reduces the political dimension of *Aaron's Rod* to the level of drawing-room disputation, leaving the reader to deduce wider implications from the abstract and unconvincing sermonising of Lilly, who is trying, at the end of the novel, to persuade a sceptical Aaron to accept his views.

Aaron argues the case with Lilly, questioning the new mode of being that he describes, but in the pause at the end of their conversation – as he looks up into Lilly's 'dark and remote-seeming' face, 'like a Byzantine eikon' – he appears to move from conscious resistance to a request for direction. If he accepts the power motive 'in deep responsibility', Lilly says, his own soul will know to whom he should submit (pp. 345–7). Responsibility and direction, to which Lawrence recurs throughout the novel, are by no means straightforward problems. Aaron clearly has authorial approval when he rails against the government for undermining people's sense of responsibility for their own lives, a kind of benevolent bullying that destroys 'the man in a man' (p. 34). His actions in the novel are shaped by his realisation that he cannot give in to his desire to 'go on sleeping', but must 'get a new grip on his own bowels' and accept 'the horror of responsibility'. As Lilly tells him at the end, he always has to remember that the responsibility rests with his own lovely soul. But the question is, having freed oneself of the dead hand of the past, how to give useful direction to this 'new and responsible consciousness' (p. 183). The satirical parts of *Aaron's Rod* are often at the expense of the directionless lives of the modern Bohemians who toy intellectually with the notion of revolutionary purpose, talking 'rather vaguely' about such political issues as Labour and Bolshevism: there is Jim, for example, who is 'a red-hot revolutionary of a very ineffectual sort'; and Josephine, coming from the 'expensive comfort' of Bohemian circles but talking of how she would love it if the miners made a bloody revolution, so that she could go in front with a red flag, to which Clariss adds, 'We'd all Bolsh together' (pp. 73–7). Those involved in real 'bolshing', like the mob in a Communist procession in Milan, are viciously destructive as well as ineffectual. Wrought up to a pitch of intense excitement as a youth climbs up to remove a flag, the crowd moves towards anti-climax, imaged in the dejected climb down of the bold youth from his 'dangerous elevation' (p. 222). Aaron himself, just before this incident, has been worrying about the goal of his own personal revolution: 'He was breaking loose from one connection after another: and what for? . . . No – he was not moving *towards* anything: he was moving almost violently away from everything' (p. 214). Although Lilly offers what is perhaps a redemptive connection, he is much more given to preaching freedom from than movement towards: he finds it hard himself, he tells Aaron, 'to refrain from jumping: overboard or anywhere' (p. 126).

In the rapidly-written *Kangaroo*, Lawrence makes much more of an effort to connect the idea of submission to charismatic male power with actual political involvement. The Australian political scene is viewed from the perspective of Somers/Lawrence, a writer who is, rather improbably, courted by both left- and right-wing political groups. The Socialists are opposed by the fascistic Diggers, a secret movement led by 'Kangaroo' and characterised by an authoritarian, militantly nationalistic ideology. The inconclusiveness of Somers' Australian quest is a further manifestation of the difficulty that Lawrence himself had in imagining how his hopes for political transformation might function in a specific national context.

What Somers craves is akin to the relationship Lilly muses on at the end of *Aaron's Rod*: 'The mystery of innate, sacred priority. The other mystic relationship between men, which democracy and equality try to deny and obliterate . . . the joy of obedience and the sacred responsibility of authority.' When he first meets Kangaroo, he is ready to embrace him as 'some queer dark god', a 'wonder' whose eyes shine with 'a queer, holy light'.[32] As his early emotional responses to Kangaroo's potential power suggest, the godlike man is thought of as essentially indefinable – a mythic personage, rather than the leader of an actual political movement. It seems, in fact, that to act in any specific capacity is to diminish the all-important 'mystery' of the charismatic force itself. The leader affirms the 'sacredness and the mystery of life' and wants to offer himself, 'my heart of wisdom, strange warm cavern

87

where the voice of the oracle steams in from the unknown'. The difficulties lie in the fact that, as a man determined on action, he also offers his 'consciousness, which hears the voice' from the unknown, and his mind and will, dedicated to battling against obstacles and to sheltering mankind (p. 126). The beautiful voice and rapt face leave Somers spellbound, but when he frees himself from the enchantment, the hardening of sacred intuitions into a political shape is repellent to him. Consciousness, mind, and will are too much a part of the man; he slaves too hard at, and is too much enslaved to, 'the mental side of the business', organising debates which endlessly put for consideration questions of definition ('What is an Australian? . . . What is wrong with Soviet rule? Do we want a Statesman, or do we want a Leader? What kind of leader do we want?'). The men of his movement 'let him do the thinking', and his persistence in staying with what he can rationally articulate is, for Somers, a hopeless impediment (pp. 205–7). Like Somers, he rhapsodises on the unknown, 'the tangible unknown: that is the magic, the mystery, and the grandeur of love'. But, like other erring Lawrence characters (Gerald Crich, Hermione), Kangaroo is guilty of 'working everything from the spirit, from the head', and so is unable to countenance Somers' assertion that the ultimate sources of power lie somewhere beyond his comprehension:

> 'Enters us from the phallic self?' snapped Kangaroo sharply.
> 'Sacredly. The god you can never see or visualise, who stands dark on the threshold of the phallic me . . . who is just beyond the dark threshold of the lower self, my lower self . . .'
>
> (*Kangaroo*, pp. 150–1)

Kangaroo, who wearily and impatiently says 'I don't know what you mean', has, for all his magnetism, disqualified himself for the role of a political saviour. Whereas others (Buchan, for example) represent the charismatic leader as a profound danger to the maintenance of ordinary political life, Lawrence, with his extreme romantic perspective, represents all actual political life as a threat to the true, inner mystery of charismatic attraction. Somers dismisses his would-be leader as 'too human'. His demand, incomprehensible to Kangaroo, is for 'different gods . . . nearer the magic of the animal world' (p. 229).

The problematic nature of 'free submission' to an actual political leader becomes a central theme in *Kangaroo*. In the early stages of his acquaintance with Kangaroo, Somers longs to give himself up 'heart and soul and body' to the great leader 'and damn all consequences'. But he is perpetually in fear of all-consuming possession by the charismatic personality, a power imaged by his actually seizing hold of Somers, physically surrounding him 'like a great, sulky bear-god' (pp. 147–8). There had been, at the beginning of their relationship, a false promise held out of equality. Kangaroo declares that Somers is the one person in the world he can never command. In truth, however, most other images of their friendship deny the possibility of such equal alliance, not only the multitude of scenes in which Kangaroo forcibly grips Somers, clasps him, squeezes him too tightly, and coercively grasps his hand (it is never the other way around), but recurrent motifs of entrapment and spiritual possession, combined with the implication that the 'demon' which gives Somers his own identity will be exorcised. When Somers is in a compliant mood, he sends Kangaroo a wooden heart inscribed with a motto commending manly bravery: 'I send you my red heart (never mind that it is wood, the wood once lived and was the tree of life) . . . . And you may command me' (pp. 167–8). But this is a sentimental gesture: the heart sent is a 'Black Forest trifle' which is clearly too inconsiderable a trinket to bear the weight of the 'profound manliness' Somers temporarily attaches to it, and is, furthermore, suggestive of 'the Sacred Heart', to the dominance of which Lawrence attributes, in *Psychoanalysis and the Unconscious*, the tendency of contemporary man to give himself over to 'the devotional, self-outpouring of love, love which gives its all to the beloved'.[33] The gesture carries intimations of self-surrender, and, were his own heart to follow, Somers would be dispossessed of the most vital part of his being. After a particularly intense confrontation, Kangaroo is transformed for him into a Gothic monster, a grotesque spider of a man, 'a great Thing, a horror', devouring love coupled with a violent rage at being rejected, a gigantic apparition of imprisoning passion (pp. 234–5).

Lawrence can assert at one time that the 'absolute', if it is to be found, lies in the 'central, isolate self', and can, at another, proclaim with equal conviction that individualism is an illusion and that he is part of the great whole. Any notion of collectivism is offensive to the proud uniqueness of his own soul, but he nevertheless worries that his separateness is analogous to an ignominious retreat into a purely private life. The ambiguities of Lawrence's conception of the relationship of the inner self to the external world are not wholly resolved in *Kangaroo*, and a measure of his irresolution is the number of times and shifting vocabulary with which he returns to the dilemma during the course of the novel. With a passion both for separateness and for uniting with the whole, he seeks to square accounts with himself by emphasising that the quality of that with which he unites is of determining importance. The difference between cosmic and merely political merging is summed up in the contrasting fates of the wave and the fly. In the night of rhythmic swings, the retreating wave joins with the great sea, the 'mass' which is its source, as the oceanic, universal unconscious mind is the source of each individual mind. The idea of joining with the 'mass' of humanity, however, has quite different imagistic associations. In one of Lawrence's playfully extended metaphors, the balmy 'merging' of 'sympathetic humanity' is imagined as a pot of ointment into which an unfortunate fly (Somers) tumbles and, suffocating and gasping, crawls out, crying, 'Let me drag my isolate and absolute individual self out of this mess' (pp. 308–9). The contrast is also suggested by Lawrence's observation, in *Phoenix*, that, 'paradoxical as it may sound', the true individual only really exists when he is 'unconscious of his own individuality', and so becomes part of the 'living continuum'[34] – a state which can only be achieved if he pulls his self free from social and political merging, that is, from 'merging' within the old forms of thought, bankrupt modes of being, which are suffocating and life-denying. But the desire for militant, as opposed to merely impotent, isolation which Somers is capable of feeling becomes more urgent as the novel develops: he will seek isolate individuality in order to gather strength for a vision which will actually have transforming power. One of the main unresolved problems in *Kangaroo* is that Somers falls considerably short of imagining the nature of this mystic-vitalist transformation.

In spite of his own horror of the herd, Lawrence can only humanly locate transforming powers in the 'reversion to the pre-mental form of consciousness' characteristic of the masses. The breaking down of automatic, routinised political life cannot be accomplished without a welling up of primal and violent instincts in 'the dark red soul of the living flesh of humanity'. Ultimately, the only qualification he makes is that 'mindless vengeance' might 'degenerate into mobs' unless it is able to 'keep a spark of direction'. In Lawrence's political vision, the 'spark of direction' depends upon the notion of a great man having a 'vivid *rapport*' so all-embracing that he is able to achieve 'vertebral interplay' with the whole of mankind: with 'a deep, mindless current flashing and quivering through the family, the community, the nation, the continent, and even the world' (pp. 328–33). Lawrence's priest-rulers, having relieved the people of their burden of mental consciousness, would bring them into vital contact with 'the dragon of power at the heart of the cosmos', which could govern by 'the dark, passionate religiousness and inward sense of an inwelling magnificence, direct flow from an unknowable God' (p. 360).[35] Lawrence's conception of a priesthood in touch with the deep sources of power is only gestured towards in *Kangaroo*, in Somers' generalised reflections on the kind of authority which can mediate between the body of men and the flow of power, 'a culminating flow towards one individual, through circles of aristocracy towards one grand centre'. The essence of the 'new show' imagined by Somers is a recognition of innate differences between 'highness and lowness' and of the true majesty of 'the single soul that stands naked between dark God and the dark-blooded masses of men' (pp. 333–4). Lawrence's conception, however, is evidently not one which can be carried out by ordinary political leaders, the true 'mystery of lordship' not being available to someone as little willing as Kangaroo apparently is to shed his 'human' preconceptions.

In the Mexico of *The Plumed Serpent*, there is less to inhibit a reversion to primitive impulse, .and Lawrence is able to imagine a political religion that much more fully embodies the mystic-vitalist transformation which Kangaroo, with his 'nauseating benevolence', fails to provide. Mexico is useful to Lawrence both as a source of primitive myth and as the location of what he wants to see as an opposing way of life, the antithesis of an advanced Western world that denies the dark gods. The novel's potential convert is Kate Leslie, an Irish woman who, like Lawrence himself, is both fascinated and repelled by the 'huge serpent' of Mexico which seems to be her destiny. Kate vacillates, as do the other follower figures in these novels, over whether she will immerse herself in a new faith. As a woman, she finds submission a more natural activity than do Aaron and Somers (an aspect of the narrative more fully explored in the next chapter), but throughout the novel she experiences contradictory impulses, as can be seen at the outset simply in her response to the Mexican scene. At the end of the first chapter, she seeks respite in the corner of a cosmopolitan tea house, but this is obviously not a country in which she can simply forget by drinking tea and eating strawberry shortcake. Such civilised structures and rituals look hopelessly fragile alongside the 'cruel sacredness' of the stony hills and the roads 'deep in ancient dust'.[36] What Lawrence sees as the brutality and violence of Mexico are terrifying, but are also taken as evidence that here it is possible for a charismatic leader like Don Ramón to tap into ancient forces which are actually capable of breaking through smug, civilised forms. There is a double-edged image of Mexico pulling one down: this is, in one sense, the primitive pull of a country which (like Africa in *Heart of Darkness*) has a disintegrating effect on any man who lacks a rigid moral backbone; in another sense, however, it is a force which draws a man down to earth like the roots of a tree.

Lawrence's feeling that there might be a vast potential latent in the primitive Mexican scene is underscored by stress on the antagonism between these ancient forces and established Western cultural, political and religious institutions, which are completely devoid of magic and wonder. America is represented, for example, by a couple from the Mid-West – 'bloodless, acidulous' (*The Plumed Serpent*, p. 79). Americans are said to be a people in whom the God impulse has collapsed, and the soulless, mechanical automatism of the American way of life is thrown into relief by the strange, mysterious gentleness of the Mexican natives, 'between a scylla and a charybdis of violence' (pp. 126–7). England, like America, is 'safe and ready-made', and the construction of Englishness has been as dull and materialistic as her manufactures: 'I always think', Cipriano says, 'England has woven her soul into her fabrics' (pp. 240, 272). Mexico, on the other hand, is pictured as having a soul that has yet to be woven and, with its barbaric repudiation of the modern, it is supposed that this country at least has a chance of resisting the machine-made identities of England and America. In Kate's mind, the great weeds of white mental–spiritual life are contrasted with the 'new germ' of aboriginal blood-and-vertebrate consciousness. She herself, being Irish, to some extent escapes the limitations of 'our would-be fair-and-square world'. A residual capacity for Celtic mysticism separates her from the 'cog-wheel people' and brings her closer to what is imagined to be the potency of the 'sunwise', antediluvian Mexican world (pp. 451–3).

Chief amongst the well-meaning but unwelcome weeds of white mental-spiritual life are socialism and Christianity. Socialists have many of the same enemies as Lawrence (Capitalist, Church, Rich Woman, Mammon), and he therefore recurrently works to separate their ideas from his own. As in *Kangaroo*, socialism is shown to be capable of violently assailing disagreeable aspects of the political system and of generating institutional change, but not of creating a vital connectedness: it is part of 'the white man's Dead Sea consciousness', generating 'a whole forest of verbiage, new laws, new constitutions' (*The Plumed Serpent*, p. 97). To capture the abstract aridity of socialism, Lawrence uses Ribera's frescoes at the University, in which the Mexican Indians are incorporated into a purely intellectual construct. The frescoes show the Indians from an 'ideal, social point of view', as symbols in the script of modern socialism, a 'weary script' that depends on the strident caricature of its opponents and the tedious assertion of mechanical ideas (pp. 84–5). In socialist agitation, Lawrence implies, any original inspiration is routinised, forced into dead intellectual forms. Characters with some creative potential recognise how limited this is: Don Ramón, in particular, insists that he will not serve an idea, but instead will serve 'the God that gives me my manhood' (pp. 105–6).

Much more than in either *Aaron's Rod* or *Kangaroo*, the explicitly religious dimension of the charismatic movement is brought to the fore, with the cult aiming to rescue the 'god-stuff' that 'roars eternally' (p. 91) from the monopoly of the Christian Church. Here again, as well as building on the country's strong anti-clerical tradition, Lawrence uses the separateness of Mexican culture to reinforce his theme. The Church is shown to be irretrievably stamped with European ideals. Jesus was 'a stranger from over the seas', who was white and spoke with strange words: 'El Señor, El Christo del Mundo, is a *gringo*' (*The Plumed Serpent*, p. 260). Still worse, the 'real Christ' has now been replaced by 'the white Anti-Christ of charity, and socialism, and politics, and reform'. Carlota, the wife of Don Ramón, is devoted to the Church, and the conflict between husband and wife is used to establish the antithesis between the Church and the activities of the Quetzalcoatl cult. Embodying the deficiencies of Christianity, Carlota displays many of the qualities Lawrence most despises – charity ('that cruel kindness'), maternal possessiveness, loving 'with her *will*', self-righteous sanctity, 'irritating gentleness' (p. 245–7). The Church fosters emotional helplessness and the self-abasement of people who do not worship in any positive sense but let their souls sink into 'a sensual, almost victimised self-abandon to the god of death' and to 'the pretty white woman in a blue mantle' (pp. 311–12).

In Don Ramón's cult of the Quetzalcoatl, the white Christ and his doll-faced mother are to be replaced by a god from the ancient, barbaric world, rising with a potency that will sweep aside socialist pity and Christian gentleness. The religious element in Kangaroo's leadership is bound up with both Judaism and Christianity: as a Jew, he symbolises the encumbrance of ancient authority (Europe suffering under the 'weight of the Hand of the Lord, that old Jew, upon it'); as the 'new' Jew (Christ) he stands for a new kind of deadly fixity, the 'bee attitudes' of a benevolist ethic (*Kangaroo*, pp. 386, 312). The fictive religion of *The Plumed Serpent*, on the other hand, provides a source of mythic imagery much more in harmony with the kind of renewal that Lawrence had in mind. Whereas political manoeuvring and the social religion of socialism are only superficial, 'like washing the outside of the egg', the cult of the Quetzalcoatl is linked to fundamental images of generation and renewal – to getting inside the egg and 'growing into a new bird' (*The Plumed Serpent*, pp. 227–30). What is inside can neither be willed nor morally evaluated by conventional standards, any more than one can judge the 'dark fecundity' of a fountain that gushes in the 'invisible dark'. Rising in opposition to the God 'of one fixed purport', Quetzalcoatl is 'a confusion of contradictory gleams of meaning', a serpent of the middle-earth who can make a man 'master of up and down' – a myth which focuses some of Lawrence's most recurrently used images of natural power and harmony. Always troubled by the conventional connotations of familiar words, Lawrence finds the strange names of the Mexican gods linguistically fresh enough to be themselves like seeds, full of 'unexplored magic' and fertile sounds which, unlike the 'dead names' of Christianity, are capable of producing miraculous transformations (pp. 90–4, 265–6).

The nationalistic nature of the cult remains in some ways an awkward impediment, since the Mexicans do not strike Lawrence as altogether promising material – being, in his view, recalcitrant, resentful, lacking in energy, life-hating, destructive. This despair of the Mexican people is dissipated for Kate, however, when she thinks of the redemptive power of Don Ramón, who 'must be a great man', and so capable of picking up the 'old threads' that will re-establish a connection with the cosmos (pp. 171–2). It is less the Mexico she knows than the mysteriousness of an ancient land that will form the vital part of this connection, as the charismatic leader counters the contemporary unmagicking of experience by reaching back to the unknown gods. This involves, above all, a re-establishment of timeless natural rhythms. The modern ('jazzy') progressive rhythms must be supplanted by a leader who is able to 'set a new pulse beating'; the mechanical tick of the clock is to be replaced by the insistent blood-rhythm of the drum (pp. 137, 327). What the Mexican scene provides for Lawrence is the image of a public, political rhythm which, like the 'sound value' of Aaron's flute or Lilly's voice, enters the soul directly, without requiring conscious understanding. When the men of the cult gather, the drum (accompanied by a flute playing a savage melody) beats with 'a slow, regular thud, acting straight on the blood . . . like a spell' (p. 154). However disagreeable Lawrence may find them to be as a people, the Mexicans furnish the charismatic leader with an obligingly primitive emotional mass, susceptible not only to the spell of the drum but to the hypnotic power of the leader, whose speech rhythms closely follow the pulsing of the drum. The men who follow him form a wild chorus, fusing together and twitching involuntarily as he subdues them to the power of his will (pp. 234–5). It has to be said, however, that the Mexican people, when not directly under his sway, are suspected of not being entirely grateful for Ramón's guidance. Kate feels their latent grudging, which she attributes to a devilish animosity and a wish to foil and frustrate whoever is in power. Thus, although Don Ramón is able to awe his own people – his local congregation – into the 'soft mystery of living', his ultimate success in turning Mexico into a 'Quetzalcoatl country' seems less assured (pp. 440–1, 284–5). As in Buchan's case, the model of charismatic experience that is perhaps most in the author's mind is the nonconformist chapel – with drums rather than church bells but (except perhaps as a national religion) not really functioning in the political sphere at all.

The Plumed Serpent is strikingly different from Lawrence's earlier leadership novels in its much fuller representation of the kind of charismatic experience that attracted him: a transcendent experience, at once archaic and utopian, drawing on myths of ancient gods but imagining a future time when mankind might attain organic unity; making a regressive appeal to blood consciousness and irrational impulse; heavily dependent on the powerful male leader, on the selflessness of followers; rejecting the language of individual and political liberty – 'There is no such thing as liberty . . . . All we can do is to choose our master' (p. 105). In all of these respects, Lawrence's political philosophy could be said to overlap with Nazism's messianic creed, with its language of transcendence and its simultaneously backward-looking and utopian qualities. For Lawrence, however, these are elements in a redemptive vision that would seem, in the end, to have virtually no political content. To take an extreme counter-example, Hitler assimilated such elements to a movement designed to satisfy 'a whole spectrum of expectations and hopes – national, political, economic and social, cultural and even religious' and set great store by the state 'as a source of national cohesion and "positive" politics'.[37] For Lawrence, who only dreamed of a political role, the vision of immediate, visceral-spiritual charismatic experiences is wholly remote from any wider spectrum of popular or national expectations and hopes. Although the Quetzalcoatl cult is perceived by some (for example, by President Montes) as a potential political force, it is declared by Don Ramón to be beyond 'politics' in any mundane sense. Ramón, to the incomprehension of his ally, Cipriano, rejects the idea that he could hold high political office and maintains that he must 'stand in another world, and act in another world' – choosing to save his country's soul, rather than concerning himself with 'poverty and unenlightenment' (p. 227). Politics seems to him to taint and corrupt a man. What Ramón wants is a new spirit that is not contaminated by connection with any political party. He has a grandiose enough self-conception –

as First Man of the Quetzalcoatl, Saviour of Mexico, part of the world's Natural Aristocracy, bringer of organic unity – but all of this will have its existence in the Valley of the Soul, which has no truck with 'cities of commerce and industry', with socialists, fascists or 'national churches' (pp. 284–6). Lawrence's repeated efforts to distance his cult both from the national population and from all contact with actual political movements suggest the degree to which his political thinking, like Aaron's retreat from England, 'is not moving *towards* anything' but 'moving almost violently away from everything' – from a known political world that fails to satisfy a romantic desire for transcendence.

DEMONIC ENCHANTMENTS: THE MAGICIAN, MEPHISTO AND THE RISE OF FASCISM

When Lawrence, returning to Europe in 1925–26, saw Mussolini's fascism triumphant in Italy, his comments indicated distaste and some distress at the 'millions of laws' that secured fascist power. Though he continued to brood (as in *Apocalypse*) on the nature of power, he also began to express at least some doubts about the leadership principle ('On the whole I agree with you, the leader-cum-follower relationship is a bore . . .'); his stray derogatory comments on fascists during this period seem to suggest that he finds them to be, like bolshevists and socialists, possibly evil and certainly 'dreary and political'.[38] These, however, are mainly asides, the dawning, perhaps, of enough political truth to send Lawrence back to seeing future hope only in tender, sensitive relationships between men and women, but not (as a political insight) something he felt impelled to explore very deeply. We can exonerate Lawrence from the charge of having helped pave the way for fascist regimes, but we cannot really claim for him the political insight required to make him a cogent critic of totalitarianism.

For a thoughtful reckoning with the dangers and deceptions of charismatic, totalitarian political movements, we will obviously do better to turn to writers for whom the rise of fascism was a more central and far more deeply disturbing experience. Two of the most acute and best-known fictional representations of the fascist exploitation of charismatic powers are Thomas Mann's novella, *Mario and the Magician* (1930) and *Mephisto*, a novel written by his son, Klaus Mann, in 1936. What these texts have in common is a scathing demystification of charismatic attraction, and the creation of narratives which bring out the darker implications of the main metaphors of charismatic experience: mesmerism; the 'spell' of the theatre; the 'magical' display of godlike – or demonic – powers. The appeal of charismatic power depends heavily upon its ability to convey a sense of the authenticity of the emotional and religious experience shared with the audience. As J.P. Stern argues, even violence derives its sanction from the idea of authenticity – in Hitler's case, 'from the conveyed conviction that his every utterance is the expression of *this man's genuine feelings*'. As long as it seems to have this sort of authenticity, charismatic leadership will to some extent seem to be self-validating: ' "Here is my experience, here are my rock-like convictions . . ." Hitler is saying. "This is the self-validating source of my likes and hates, my scheme of values . . . ." ' To admit authenticity, then, is to acknowledge one of the major sources of such a leader's strength. However wary Buchan and Shaw are of the disruptive potential of charisma, they readily grant the sincerity of Laputa and St Joan, and it is above all this aura of sincerity which secures devotion: 'I am not [Hitler's hypothetical political message continues] a man to politick, or haggle with Fate. To my every decision my whole existence, and thus yours, is committed . . . . Therefore follow me.'[39] Lawrence, for whom authenticity (and hence the relationship of the private to the public sphere) is of paramount importance, goes to some lengths to establish that, for example, Don Ramón's private thoughts are of a piece with his public performances, showing him in the act of prayer, breaking the cords of the external world and spreading his 'soft, nourishing' spirit over his vital and peaceful inner world (pp. 205–6). But what if the powerful impression of sincerity is only a sham? Or what if the self that appears all of a piece is in reality 'tattered and torn and full of fears'? These are the questions posed by both Thomas and Klaus Mann, as their theatrical mountebanks give hypnotic performances to entertain (and, symbolically, impersonate) the leading figures in the rise of fascism.

Mario and the Magician, on the face of it a simple tale of how a hypnotist is shot dead by one of his subjects, was based on an experience that Mann had when he was on vacation with his family at Forte dei Marmi in Italy, in the late summer of 1926. The 'magician–artist', he said in a letter, 'was there and behaved exactly as I describe it', except that Mario ran away instead of shooting the magician. But this was, of course, also the period during which Mussolini, consolidating his power, was well on the way to achieving the 'complete fascistisation' of Italy, with crowds chanting 'Duce! Duce!', legends proliferating and 'the image of the Duce as benevolent Superman' looming ever more pervasively in the public mind.[40] The psychological details of the magician's seaside entertainment, his entranced audience and his abuse of his mysterious powers have thus inevitably been seen as a political parable, revealing the nature of the political seduction and mass suggestion of fascism – distilling it into the 'unholy and staggering experience' of the 'demoniac fires' of 'our tyrant', the diabolical Cavaliere Cipolla.[41] Mann himself described the message of the story as 'a warning against the rape [caused] by the dictatorial being who in the end was overcome and destroyed'. During the course of the thirties it became increasingly evident to him that the psychic demagogue and manipulator of the masses was as much of a danger in Germany as in Mussolini's Italy: 'When I wrote it I did not believe that Cipolla could be possible in Germany. It was a patriotic overestimate of my nation. The irritation with which critics already received the story should have told me where the trend was leading . . . .'[42] Mann saw the greatest cause for alarm in the temptation of the modern intelligentsia to abandon individuation and seek regression to mythic, unconscious depths. As in *Dr Faustus*, we see Mann's wariness of the political misuse of German Romanticism, with its appeal to the popular folk element, its celebration of the instinctive springs of being, its heightened emotionalism and its contempt for humanist morality. Mann saw, more clearly than many others, the destructive potential of the mass hypnotiser who possesses an apparently magical power to discover and manipulate people's irrational impulses and desires, and to use them to arouse a spirit of aggressive nationalism.

The atmosphere in *Mario and the Magician* is one of provincial nationalism. On the beach earlier in the day the narrator's family feels they are 'in the presence of a national ideal'; solemn phrases are dropped about Italy's greatness and dignity, and this seems to the narrator, as he explains it to his children, a sign of people 'passing through a certain stage, something rather like an illness, perhaps' (*Mario and the Magician*, p. 120). In the course of the story, they find that the magician, Cipolla, is capable of capitalising on this pervasive national 'illness': he is 'that dreadful being who seemed to incorporate, in so fateful and impressive a way, all the peculiar evilness of the situation as a whole' (pp. 137–8). A hunchback, appearing in a costume that suggests the charlatan and the mountebank, taking up a pretentious pose and arrogantly puffing smoke into the face of his audience, he has 'that curious, self-satisfied air so characteristic of the deformed'. In psychoanalytic terms, he is sometimes seen as the classic Freudian type of 'the underprivileged', compensating by means of his art for his vital emotional deprivations.[43] With his 'little physical defect', he has been forced to use his mental and spiritual qualities to conquer life, 'which after all only means conquering oneself' (pp. 126–31).

Cipolla is a Mephistophelean character, in some ways similar to Dr Krokowski in *The Magic Mountain*, a satanic tempter who sees to it 'that the nature of his powers should be clear beyond a doubt to even the least instructed person. He alluded to them, of course, in his talk . . . but only in vague, boastful, self-advertising phrases . . . .' His attitude to his audience is one of contempt. Claiming he wants only to serve, Cipolla manipulates and enslaves them: 'He pretended admiration for the powers of the people he questioned. But in all his compliments there was something fleering and derogatory . . . .' Mann's parable fixes our attention on the irrationality of charismatic attraction – the fascination exerted by this unlovely figure on an initially unwilling audience. All larger ideals are pointedly absent. The audience, though it manifests a certain reluctance to accept the magician, seems to lack any standard of virtue or reason by which to judge the performance, and concedes 'his possession of strange powers – strange whether for good or evil'. Even the narrator, who is a liberal and moral onlooker, is ambivalent, feeling, despite strong misgivings, the fascination of Cipolla's magic. In choosing not to leave when he has the chance, the narrator himself becomes Cipolla's accomplice, as much in thrall to the magician as anyone else. In fact, given his superior insight, he is actually guiltier in acquiescing than the rest of the audience. Pondering the question of why they did not choose to leave 'our lord and master' during intermission, the narrator says: 'I do not know why . . . I cannot excuse our staying, scarcely can I even understand it . . . . Our feelings for Cavaliere Cipolla were of a very mixed kind, but so were the feelings of the whole audience, if I mistake not, and nobody left' (*Mario and the Magician*, pp. 137–45).

The central image of *Mario and the Magician* is that of the hypnotic trance. Cipolla's performance has been advertised in a way that ignites contagious curiosity – as '*forzatore, illusionista, prestidigatore*' – and has promised 'a display of extraordinary phenomena of a mysterious and staggering kind'. His means of exerting psychic power over the audience is to enslave by speech, fascinating the crowd and blurring their judgement. Cipolla's voice is not a pleasant one, having a rather high, metallic quality, but it is powerfully effective. Mann makes it very clear how far this sinister magician is from being a heroic actor, not only in voice and appearance but in his own inaction. However, among people who highly value speech, what he says, although he has done nothing, is 'accepted as an achievement'. His power is in creating mysterious, even miraculous shows of obedience, which have the effect of gradually overcoming all resistance in the audience and of establishing his own 'calm superiority'. The most obvious physical sign of this capacity is his 'peculiar gaze', his possession of 'the strangest eyes', signalling his hypnotic power and his uncanny ability to bridge the gap between performer and audience. What he proposes to achieve is a division between 'the willing and the doing', with the audience becoming the instrument of his own will (pp. 128–41).

The members of the audience are under the sway of a strange compulsion, a force independent of the content of the programme, paralysing their resolve. In submitting to the repulsive and vulgar magician, they demonstrate how susceptible the human will can be to crude and frightening delusions. What Mann represents is a thoroughly malevolent force that appeals strongly to positive human emotions. So, for example, the pious Signora Angiolieri is enchanted by Cipolla, drawn out of her seat, 'whither he willed', with her pale face gleaming, 'moonstruck' (pp. 123–4). Hers is one of a series of grotesque and disturbing acts of surrender, as one by one the members of the audience are deprived of independent volition. When a young Italian challenges the magician, saying that he intends to exert his will to resist, he is told that his resistance will not alter the outcome: a master of rhetorical justifications, Cipolla tells his audience, 'Freedom exists, and also the will exists; but freedom of the will does not exist, for a will that aims at its own freedom aims at the unknown . . . . One must admit that he could not have chosen his words better, to trouble the waters and confuse the mind' (pp. 138–9). A stately, moustachioed colonel, unable to lift his arm after Cipolla tells him he cannot, struggles 'to regain his lost freedom of action'; a young man steels himself with 'heroic obstinacy' to resist – 'we were beholding a gallant effort to strike out and save the honour of the human race' – but ultimately dances as Cipolla wills him to, having not had any positive will to assert against him ('*not* willing is not a practicable state of mind . . .'). With this success, the magician's triumph reaches its height, the more so because his victim clearly finds it a pleasure not to struggle any more: 'Up there we could see his face as he "enjoyed" himself; it was clothed in a broad grin and the eyes were half-shut.' As in *Mephisto*, the dance, not willed but ecstatic, is a prime metaphor for charismatic immersion. After midnight, Cipolla controls virtually the entire audience, driving them like marionettes into an orgy of dissolute, abandoned dancing, a nightmarish somnambulism, 'a drunken abdication of the critical spirit which had so long resisted the spell of this man' (*Mario and the Magician*, pp. 147–51).

It is at this point of mass hysteria that Mario is finally called upon to participate and, as obedience is his calling, he finds it hard to resist 'a man so throned and crowned as Cipolla at that hour'. There is no brutality in the dreamy waiter, but the magician makes himself 'irresistible', leading Mario to 'an utter abandonment of the inmost soul, a public exposure of timid and deluded passion and rapture'. Forgetting that he cannot trust his ears and eyes, he breathes the name of his beloved 'from the very depths of his vanquished heart' and kisses Cipolla. Incipient violence has been present all evening, repeatedly suggested by the silver-handled riding whip which is Cipolla's trade-mark, his symbol of power. When Mario shoots him, it is an appropriate end to his domination and a liberation for the narrator, but also a dark foreshadowing of the capacity for violence on the part of those made to dance against their will by the charismatic leader (pp. 155–7).

Longer but slighter than his father's novella, Klaus Mann's *Mephisto* is based on the career of his brother-in-law, Gustav Gründgens (thinly disguised as Hendrik Höfgen), an actor who rose to a position of power and influence in the Third Reich. As a '*Schlüsselroman*' it includes portraits of many actors and political leaders of the time but, like *Mario and the Magician*, it uses charismatic stage performance and ecstatic dance as much more general metaphors. From the outset, there are strong suggestions of the violence underlying the 'ruse and pretence' of Hitler's Germany. A glittering assembly of dignitaries attending the birthday party of the prime minister, Hermann Göring, moves like marionettes, with 'something hidden in their eyes' and 'clouds of artificial fragrance' covering 'the stale, sweet stench of blood'. They admire one another and pay homage to 'the power which could give such a party', a power represented by the four central personalities present – Göring, the actress Lotte Lindenthal (Emmy Sonnemann), Goebbels and Höfgen/Gründgens – who are 'the four powers of this land . . . four actors'.[44]

The demonic Höfgen is a 'superb actor' who compels attention, gifted, distinguished and 'as careful as possible not to utter a single word of truth'. All eyes are fixed on him. Himself mesmerised by power, he in turn entrances the powerful, thus ensuring his own rise in the world of the theatre. He is capable, without an iota of sincerity, of simulating such inspiring enthusiasm that he charms all who hear him. Thinking 'this is real emotion', they sit spellbound by his enthusiasm, wearing expressions of religious solemnity (pp. 18, 36–7). Ordinary and undistinguished by day, he is transformed at night in the theatre, becoming a colourful, magical figure, irresistible when

101

he is behind the footlights. As a director, too, he undergoes a bizarre transformation, becoming a Dionysus who dances with bacchic frenzy: 'Strange grimaces passed over his white face; the gleaming eyes rolled in rapture; hoarse voluptuous cries broke from his lips' (p. 124). Höfgen begins his Berlin career with a small part in which he dances, to the amazement of Berlin audiences, making everyone marvel at the obsessive force with which he moves and at the ecstatic expression on his face. In *The Guilt*, his first large-scale Berlin success, he plays 'the most depraved of the depraved', winning great applause with a demonic expression that is seen as the incarnation of evil: 'Oh, how wonderfully wicked he is' (*Mephisto*, pp. 135–7). This enthralling performance is followed by his first film role, as the mysterious Black Devil. But his most important and impressive role is that of Mephistopheles, in which he is remarkable for his 'hypnotic jewel-like eyes', gliding across the stage 'with the grace of a dancer', a 'horribly elegant jester' who could plausibly transform himself into anything: 'The most improbable things could be believed of this Mephisto. He was strong – stronger even than God the Father', possessing a melancholy and cynical insight into the darkest secrets of the human heart (p. 152).

Höfgen's ascent as the devilish enchanter of the Berlin theatre coincides with Hitler's rise to power. In a chapter entitled 'The Pact with the Devil', Klaus Mann reflects on the 'foul lie' usurping power in the land, roaring 'in the congress halls, from the microphones, from the pages of newspapers, from the cinema screen'. He begins the process of charting the events after 'the man with the screaming voice' becomes chancellor of the Reich, to the astonishment of Höfgen and his progressive friends, who had so often ridiculed this 'blustering lout'. While Berlin is in 'an absolute delirium of enthusiasm for its new Nazi *Reichskanzler*', Höfgen decides to withdraw into 'enigmatic silence', but is ultimately unable to face life as an outlaw (pp. 155–8). His own plays and films having 'inspired the infamous, and at the same time infantile, cunning of the Nazis' (p. 159), he seeks reconciliation with the regime and, when *Faust* is again included in the repertory of the State Theatre, he contrives to again be given the role of Mephisto – 'this eternal, profoundly German role' – bewitching the prime minister with his 'blinding self-assertion of the spirit of evil, the pride of Satan in his hideous supremacy'. After the performance, when he goes to meet 'the demi-god' face-to-face, he concludes his Faustian bargain with the Third Reich: the prime minister 'in all his magnitude, his shining bulk', stretches out his hand to Höfgen, so that it looks like the sealing of a pact between the potentate and the actor – whereupon

Höfgen is surrounded by the 'enormous radiance' of power and is himself acknowledged as a great man (*Mephisto*, pp. 171–81).

From the outset, Mann plays on the popular perception of the German leaders as 'irreproachable gods'. The minister of propaganda (Goebbels), for example, the 'overlord of the spiritual life of millions', is an 'evil, solitary and cruel god' who casts a 'dreadful spell' on all around him (pp. 10–11); the prime minister's face is hidden by 'that mystic veil that has always hidden the faces of the prophets and the gods from the frightened gaze of mere mortals'; devotees of 'our Führer and Saviour' imagine themselves to be in heaven as they dance with joy, swept along by the frenzy: 'The magic of this situation was so potent that it enabled the young man to overlook many things he might otherwise have found disappointing.' The 'apotheosis' of Höfgen/Mephistopheles is thoroughly deserved, given that he is so manifestly appropriate an addition to the grotesque array of gods 'before whom a Godforsaken people writhe in a delirium of worship': 'he has its false honour, its hysteria, its cynicism and desire for devil worship . . . . The actor has approached the cluster of gods. Already he can bathe in their glamour . . .' (pp. 174–83). The affinities between the powers of the land and primitive 'dark gods' is a theme developed most explicitly in the 'deep and ingenious' pronouncements of the poet Benjamin Pelz, the representative of those intellectuals drawn to Nazism out of a readiness to support anything banned by respectable society – elevating violence and cruelty to virtues because they were opposed to society's humanitarian hypocrisy and to 'the dreary tyranny of reason and the bourgeois fetish concept of progress'. He adores National Socialism because it is going to obliterate completely the intolerable mechanised structure of civilisation, creating a new type of magical, warlike human being, and thus giving life 'a certain rhythm and charm'. It will awaken men from their torpor and lead them to rediscover 'the violent movement of the dance' – not marching forward, but 'reeling, staggering'. 'You lead the dance', Pelz raves, 'you subterranean potentates . . . . You cast a spell over us with your smiles and your marvellous eyes . . . . You would lead us under the earth into the depths, into the magic cavern where blood streams from the walls . . . where love, death and blood are mingled in orgiastic communion' (pp. 202–4, 235).

Ironically, the shrine at which Höfgen himself truly worships is that of the Princess Tebab, a dancer and black king's daughter with whom he has a sadomasochistic relationship. This complicated and secret affair with a 'fierce child of nature' is in fact the source of his strength, the Princess arousing him with a ritual of domination in which her face rears up 'like the awesome mask of a strange god, a god enthroned in a secret place in the deepest jungle and crying out for human sacrifice'. He imagines slaves dancing in a frenzy and sinking to the feet of 'the black god they love and worship with all their hearts, as men can only worship the one to whom they have sacrificed that which is beyond price – blood' (pp. 148, 52). Just as the true demonic nature of Führer-worship is hidden, so Höfgen must suppress all evidence of his relationship with this dark goddess as he rises in position and prestige in the Third Reich – a concealment rendered more ironic by the fact that the Princess in reality only acts the savage goddess and is a wholly human and benign figure in comparison to the genuinely dark gods of Nazi ideology, which are in truth the 'beasts' and 'devils' that Höfgen pronounces them to be before he is forced by ambition to abandon his opposition to fascism and militant nationalism. As he ascends to his position of power, he must also symbolically separate himself from his 'good angel', Barbara, who represents the liberal conscience he has to leave behind if he is to succeed in a society in which, as Barbara says, Nazi enthusiasm is 'the underworld crying out for power' (p. 119).

For all its flaws, Klaus Mann's novel is often a forceful satire of the pseudo-religious perversions and the mesmerising effect of charismatic performance in the rise of fascism. The career of Höfgen, juxtaposed with the destruction of those who oppose the regime, makes clear the difference between authentic belief and thraldom to theatrical illusion. At the end, having learned that one of Höfgen's oldest friends has died at the hands of Gestapo torturers for acting on his beliefs, Höfgen is seen envying those 'who could believe in something' and who could give their lives 'in the sweep and thunder of faith'. But at the same time we see the symbolic force of his panic-stricken declaration that 'I am absolutely indispensable! . . . The theatre needs me. Every regime needs the theatre! No regime can get along without me!' (pp. 260–1).

NOTES

1. Weber M. *Wirtschaft und Gesellschaft* 1922; in English, *Economy and society* 1968 vol. 1 pp. 241–4.
2. Conrad J. *Lord Jim* (1900) 1989 pp. 239–43 and 350–2; Conrad J. *Heart of darkness* (1902) 1973 pp. 87, 97.

3. Carlyle T. *On heroes* (1841) 1897 p. 11; Houghton W.E. *The Victorian frame of mind* 1985 p. 314; Pick *War machine* 1993 pp. 158–60.
4. Mitzman A. *The iron cage* 1985 pp. 184–89; Lindholm C. *Charisma* 1993 p. 27.
5. Le Bon G. *The crowd: a study of the popular mind* (1895). Ernest Benn 1952 p. 132 and Tarde G. *The laws of imitation* (1890). Henry Holt and Co, New York 1903 p. 198; and see Lindholm *Charisma* pp. 42–3 and 48–9.
6. Freud S. *Group psychology and the analysis of the ego* (1921) in *Civilization, society and religion* Penguin Freud Library 1991 vol. 12 pp. 101–5.
7. Lindholm *Charisma* pp. 41–3.
8. Held J. *The cult of power* 1983 p. 87.
9. Ludecke K. *I knew Hitler* Scribner's, New York 1937 p. 14, quoted by Lindholm *Charisma* p. 102; see also Lindholm p. 86 and Bullock A. *Hitler and Stalin* 1991 p. 393 on the role of charisma in the Soviet Union; Stern J. P. *Hitler* 1979 pp. 56–65.
10. Fest J. *Hitler* 1974 pp 326 and 517; Lindholm *Charisma* pp. 100–4.
11. Bullock *Hitler and Stalin* p. 411; Hitler quoted in Rauschning H. *The voice of destruction.* Putnam, New York 1940 p. 145; Lindholm *Charisma* p. 111; Hitler *Mein Kampf,* quoted by Fest *Hitler* p. 326.
12. Lawrence D.H., Democracy (*Phoenix* 1936). In *Selected essays* 1981 pp. 77–85.
13. Willner A.R. *Spellbinders* 1984 p. 62; Fussell P. *Abroad: British literary travelling between the Wars* Oxford University Press 1980 pp. 146–7.
14. Lawrence D.H., Nottingham and the Mining Country (written 1929; *The New Adelphi* 1930) and Dull London (written 1928; *Evening News* 3 September 1928) in *Selected essays* pp. 122–5; Russell B. *The autobiography of Bertrand Russell* George Allen & Unwin 1968 vol. 2 pp. 53–4.
15. Orwell G., The Lion and the Unicorn, in *The collected essays, journalism and letters* 1968 vol. 2 pp. 57–60.
16. Orwell G., Review of Burnt Norton, East Coker, The Dry Salvages by T.S. Eliot (*Poetry London* October-November 1942) in *Collected essays, journalism and letters* vol. 2 p. 240; Johnstone R. *The will to believe* 1984 pp. 1–36 and 134.
17. Daniell D. *The interpreter's house* 1975 pp. 61–3 and 131; and see Wisenthal J.L. *Shaw's sense of history* 1988 pp. 60–71.
18. Bracher K.D. *The age of ideologies* 1985 p. 122; and see, for example, Weber M., Major features of world religions (1915). In Robertson R. (ed) *Sociology of religion.* Penguin (1969) 1971 pp. 35ff, on chivalric as opposed to mystical interests.
19. Buchan J. *The African colony* quoted by Daniell *Interpreter's house* pp. 95–6.
20. Green M. *Dreams of adventure* 1980 pp. 149–50.
21. Buchan J. *Salute to adventurers* Nelson 1915 p. 113; and Buchan quoted by Sandison A. *The wheel of Empire* 1967 pp. 180 and 162.
22. Buchan J. *Prester John* (1910) 1956 pp. 71–3, 102–6, 141–66.
23. Buchan quoted by Green *Dreams of adventure* p. 164.
24. Buchan's Diagrammatic Chart of the Evolution of Parties within the Arena of Political Action since the Year 1845 (1911) quoted by Daniell

interpreter's house p. 90.
25. Beatrice Webb quoted by Holroyd M. *Shaw* 1991 vol. 3 pp. 113–14.
26. Holroyd *Shaw* vol. 2 pp. 286–7; vol. 3 pp. 280–1, 76.
27. Wisenthal *Shaw's sense of history* p. 69.
28. Shaw G.B. *Saint Joan* (1923) 1946 pp. 8, 19–21; and Wardle I., quoted by Holroyd *Shaw* vol. 3 p. 74.
29. Lawrence D.H. *Apocalypse* (1931) 1981 pp. 11–21.
30. Lawrence, Nottingham and the mining country, pp. 119–121; The State of Funk (written in 1928–29; *Assorted articles* 1930) in *Selected essays* p. 96.
31. Lindholm *Charisma* p. 41.
32. Lawrence D.H. *Kangaroo* (1923) 1981 pp 120–9, 143, 148.
33. Lawrence D.H. *Psychoanalysis and the unconscious* (1921–2) 1986 pp. 36–7.
34. Lawrence D.H., The novel and the feelings [The individual consciousness v. the social consciousness] in *Phoenix: the posthumous papers of D.H. Lawrence* ed and introduced McDonald E.D. Heinemann Ltd (1936) 1961 p. 761.
35. Hochman B. *Another ego* 1970 pp. 193–4 argues that these ideas began to crystallise in his correspondence with Russell, some important features of which are reflected in the dispute between Somers and Kangaroo.
36. Lawrence D.H. *The plumed serpent* (1926) 1990 pp. 129–30.
37. Stern J.P. *Hitler* 1979 pp. 96–7 and 103.
38. Lawrence quoted by Meyers J. *D.H. Lawrence and the experience of Italy* 1982 pp. 129–31.
39. Stern *Hitler* pp. 26–7.
40. Hibbert C. *Benito Mussolini* 1975 pp. 67–73.
41. Mann T. *Mario and the Magician* (1936) 1975 pp. 122–3 and 145–7.
42. Mann T., On myself, and letter to Bedrick Fucik (15 April 1932), quoted by Lesér E.H. *Thomas Mann's short fiction* 1989 pp. 193 and 197.
43. See Berendsohn W.E. *Thomas Mann* 1975 pp. 84–6.
44. Mann K. *Mephisto* (1936) 1983 pp. 4–9 and 17.

CHAPTER THREE

Sexual Dominance: Leaders and Lovers in Fiction Between the Wars

The psyche of the broad masses is accessible only to what is strong and uncompromising. Like a woman whose inner sensibilities are not so much under the sway of abstract reasoning, but are subject to a vague emotional longing for the strength that completes her being, and who would rather bow to a strong man than dominate a weakling – so the masses prefer a ruler to a supplicant and are filled with a stronger sense of mental security by a doctrine that brooks no rival than by liberal teaching which offers them a choice. They have very little idea of how to make such a choice and are prone to feel they have been abandoned. They feel little shame at being terrorised intellectually . . . . They see only the ruthless force and brutality of its utterances to which they always submit in the end.

(Hitler, *Mein Kampf*)

She had existed then . . . unconscious of the something that was lacking in her nature, and now she was alive at last . . . . Her eyes swept lingeringly around the camp with a very tender light in them. Everything she saw was connected with and bound up in the man who was lord of it all. She was very proud of him, proud of his hold over his wild turbulent followers, proud with the pride of the primeval woman in the dominant man ruling his fellow men by force and fear.

(E.M. Hull, *The Sheik*)[1]

At the end of *Mario and the Magician*, when Mario falls under Cipolla's power, he is entranced into thinking that the magician is his beloved. Taunting him, Cipolla says, 'I know what you are thinking: what does this Cipolla . . . know about love? Wrong, all wrong, he knows a lot. He has a wide and powerful understanding of its workings.' The 'moment of Mario's bliss', the kiss that confirms the magician's power, 'a monstrous moment, grotesque and thrilling', contains one of Thomas Mann's most disturbing insights into the nature of the demagogue's power, that is, the parallel between sexual attraction and romantic love on the one hand and charismatic attraction on the other. This need not imply the political exploitation of what would popularly be called 'sex appeal' or machismo. Charisma can, in some cultures, have an explicitly sexual dimension, as in the Indonesian belief in a link between sexuality and *sekti*, or supernatural power, evident in the view taken of Sukarno's sexual liaisons. In most Western countries, however, there is a less direct relationship between sexual and political potency, and careers can obviously be endangered or destroyed by sexual scandals. But even in Protestant and Puritan cultures, in which sex and politics do not mix publicly, there are deep connections. This is not just to say that a suggestion of charismatic sexuality can be an asset for a political leader; more fundamentally, what we are looking at is the pattern of dominance and subordination implied by the attribution of active male qualities to the charismatic leader and of self-effacing responsiveness to the passive female (or 'feminised') follower. This pattern is apparent in metaphoric and imaginative constructions, but is also not without basis in historical fact – that is, in the way women have often responded to strong male leadership. And, just as the phenomenon of totalitarianism has forced liberal humanist political thinkers to try to understand 'how it could happen', so historical examples of this interpenetration of sexuality and politics has posed a considerable problem of interpretation for feminists.[2]

Thus, for example, one key historical question, inseparable from our understanding of totalitarianism, is how to explain the responses of Nazi women to the male-dominated phenomenon of National Socialism. What is the relationship between fascism and sexuality? How was it that fascism as an ideology and charismatic fascist leaders held such an appeal for German women? This observed phenomenon is often seen in relation to wider questions about the application to political behaviour of the language of sexual conquest and romantic love. Does female submission actually provide a model for understanding mass behaviour? In asserting that the masses are 'like a woman', longing for 'the strength that completes her being', Hitler is only drawing on a way of conceptualising popular political movements that had been quite fully elaborated by crowd psychologists. The sexual stereotyping implicit in such analyses – 'the pride of the primeval woman in the dominant man' – is also, of course, at the heart of controversies over the nature of women's responses to the sado-masochistic sexual relationships represented in the popular fiction devoured so avidly from the twenties on. Those who wish there to be neither power relations in sex nor patriarchal patterns of sexual dominance and subordination in political life are, not surprisingly, distressed by the apparent persistence of this 'primeval' relationship between sex and power. In looking at real, theoretical or imaginative examples of the dominant male–submissive female model of behaviour, observers (then as now) were inclined to ask whether this is a reflection of a pervasive male ideology or a biologically ordained masochism – and hence whether, being culturally determined, the pattern can be changed or whether, being natural, 'Every model of morally or politically correct behaviour *will be subverted*, by nature's daemonic law.'[3] The implications for political life are not limited to the discussion of 'sexual politics'; as the concept of the 'female masses' makes clear, the sexual metaphor is used to capture in a more general way the submissiveness of the passive majority of the population to the 'strong man'. That is, 'femaleness' is just one of the sorts of powerlessness greatly exaggerated under totalitarian rule: 'It is', Arendt writes, 'as though mankind had divided itself between those who believe in human omnipotence (who think that everything is possible if one knows how to organise the masses for it) and those for whom powerlessness has become the major experience of their lives.'[4]

One of the most striking demonstrations of female submission to male power in our century was the ability of Hitler and Mussolini to secure the passionate adherence of women to a stridently masculine fascist ideology. Debate about the psychosexual determinants of mass politics was initiated in Germany in the twenties, and recent feminist critics have returned to these issues, arguing that it is important to understand 'the ways in which fascism, as an ideology, takes hold of and is fastened on to by women'.[5] Much more explicitly than other nationalist politicians of the time, Hitler demanded 'male triumph over the emancipated woman': he often reiterated that 'the Nazi Revolution will be an entirely male event'. Nazi misogyny was abundantly apparent, for example, in Alfred Rosenberg's *Myth of the Twentieth-Century*. Claudia Koonz's *Mothers in the Fatherland*, one of the best analyses of the role of women during the Second World War, addresses in great detail the question of why so many German women were devoted to a leader who proclaimed their subservience and bluntly told them that they should leave politics to their male betters. As Koonz says, in contrast to the egalitarian feminists, Nazi women turned towards a vision of an idyllic past, in which public space was dominated by strong men who were served by tender women and whose position was fixed by a mythical biological hierarchy. One of Hitler's followers, commenting on women's allegiance to the emphatically male political phenomenon of National Socialism, contrasted the aggressive female politician with the '*genuine* woman' who becomes a 'total woman' when, 'in her deepest feelings', she pays homage 'to the masculine principle of National Socialism'. As an American reporter wrote in the early thirties, women were from the beginning 'among the strongest pillars of Hitlerism', attending Nazi rallies in surprisingly large numbers: 'Hitler has a fascination for Germany's weaker sex which it will be the task of the psychologist to analyse.' In part, this is a response to the messianic dimension of Hitler's role. In describing their feelings for Hitler, women often used a heavily religious vocabulary, expressing their adoration and inner joy at seeing his 'righteous gaze', writing of his 'childlike smile of holy self-confidence', of conversion by a Heaven-sent crusader, a man whose picture they treasured 'like a shrine'. But equally, this can be seen as the replacement of one form of alienated desire by another – that is, as a transference of emotional attachment on the part of women whose lives had been church-centred for generations. One of the first to enquire into the psycho-sexual determinants of mass politics was Wilhelm Reich, in *The Mass Psychology of Fascism* (1946). Reich argues that the 'sadistic-narcissistic mysticism' of fascism relies (just as traditional religious mysticism does) on redirected sexuality, exploiting repression by providing substitute gratifications, as in the libidinous mechanisms of mass displays (pp. 31–2). The sexual chemistry in Hitler's appeal was very often stressed by those who witnessed women's adulation of him. Hitler's conception of the intrinsically feminine character of the masses had far-reaching effects on the planning of his public performances: 'Ask yourself', he said, 'what does a woman expect from a man? Clearness, decision, power, and action . . . . Like a woman, the masses fluctuate between extremes . . . . The Crowd is not only like a woman, but women constitute the most important element in an audience.' Fervent female supporters spread their enthusiasm by contagion to the rest of the assembly, and Hitler's own speaking techniques – clenching his fists and closing his eyes, 'surrendering to the spasms of his transposed sexuality' – were a calculated appeal to the audience's 'feminine' responsiveness. Characterised by rapid shifts of mood and range of emotional expression, Hitler was 'a virtuoso of ecstasy', evoking love by 'offering his followers participation in his own disintegrative, but controlled, aberactive frenzy'.[6] Mussolini was similarly adept at drawing women into the cause of fascism, a 'potent pope' who saw female support as a fundamental element in the consent needed for the seizure of power. Entering into a 'mystic marriage' with them, he brought Italian women on to the streets for the first time, structuring his rhetoric with female followers in mind and involving them in ceremonial displays, with 'salutes, rhythmic and bewitching cries, and a liturgy like that of the church'. As in German fascism, there was an imposition of sexual difference 'to an absurd degree', fascism taking as its point of departure the subordination of one sex to another. In Mussolini's virile propaganda, women belonged to the Fatherland and to the Blackshirts.[7]

The way in which fascist dictators conceived of their relationship to a mass audience was strongly influenced by the existing theoretical explanations of charismatic political leadership – that is, by the application of seduction and love imagery to crowd psychology and to the so-called mass mind. In this form of analysis, which crystallised in the 1890s, an existing model of male–female relationships was used to interpret the submission of large groups to the dominant leader, and thus the 'effeminate' crowd is characterised by passivity, obedience, adulation, loss of autonomy, dependency and complete identification. The assumption is that there is a natural tendency for these feminised followers to submit to domination by the active (male) leader, and that there is a natural connection between such submission and passionate, adulatory love for the 'dominant other'. This emotional bond, which is compulsive and inexplicable, impels the surrender of personal autonomy to the idolised patriarchal leader. It is a return to a state of dependency akin to that of childhood – a form of consciousness in which the boundaries of the self are blurred in a recapitulation of an infantile state of merger, a complete identification with the beloved object, which 'infects us with the significance of our *own* lives if we give in to it'. In the speculative history/anthropology of Freud's *Group Psychology*, there were from the first 'two kinds of psychologies, that of the individual members of the group and that of the father, chief, or leader', the argument being that the characteristics of group formations can be traced back to the primal horde, with the leader as 'the dreaded primal father' and the group still wishing 'to be governed by unrestricted force'.[8] The 'intense and degrading' love of follower for leader is seen by crowd psychologists as bestowed not on easy-going masters but on oppressive tyrants; it is, they maintain, exactly the leader's self-absorption (the apartness of the Nietzschean genius) that makes him attractive, since this gives him 'the obsessive power to escape imitation and to embody "the dream of command" in all its fateful and compelling glory'. It is often maintained that the actual experience of the crowd is dyadic and highly personal, that is, each person in the crowd experiences the relationship with the leader as 'immediate and compelling,' remembering, for example, the unforgettable, magical moment when Hitler looked into their eyes.[9]

111

Le Bon, one of the crowd psychologists who most influenced Hitler's demagogic methods, generally saw women, together with savages and children, as characterised by 'regressed' or unevolved states of consciousness, and used this paradigm of regression to interpret crowd behaviour. Crowd psychologists took for granted a developmental distance between female and male equivalent to that between child and adult, between primitive and civilised, irrational and rational. It was assumed that the regressed mentality of the female, emotionally charged, naturally suggestible and prey to intensely passionate but chaotic impulses, had to be channelled by the influence first of the father, then of the leader and lover.

Within this interpretive model, it is argued that the leader, like the lover, attracts by offering not only control but the possibility of rising above humdrum reality, of rebelling against the world as it is. By identifying with an 'active other' the woman/follower obtains an illusory participation in creative vitality (sometimes characterised as 'the abject love of the shapeless for the shaper'). In more positive terms, the contention is that transcendence of the mundane lies at the heart of the subversive power both of romantic fantasy and of charismatic political movements, making them oppositional and transformative. There are, then, in Western ideology, multiple parallels between romantic love and charisma – the overwhelming of the subject by magnetic charm, a sense of merger and fusion, loss of self experienced as exaltation rather than diminution, a feeling of transformation and revitalisation, and the apotheosis of the leader/beloved, who is seen as endowed with a special status and extraordinary powers.[10]

The British are by and large regarded by political scientists as less susceptible to this sort of 'passionate' charismatic attachment: 'they can admire and esteem but not adore'. Certainly much that was written during the thirties suggests that the fervent adulation of charismatic leaders was likely to seem, from a British perspective, something 'wholly alien from ourselves'. The nearest that Britain came to first-hand experience of the fascist demagogue was Sir Oswald Mosley, who, with his wavy black hair, hawk nose and disdainful mouth, had the good looks of 'the dark, passionate, Byronic gentleman-villain of the melodrama', and was said to give young ladies 'unaccountable palpitations'. A fellow MP, Ellen Wilkinson, said that his type 'is not that of the nice kind hero who rescues the girl at the point of torture, but the one who hisses, "At last . . . we meet."' He was, she said, 'The Sheik'. The British Union of Fascists, however, was estimated at its peak (1934) to have no more than 10,000 members in total, only about a quarter of whom were active. The spread of fascism in Britain was limited by several factors – arguably, for example, by 'British decency', which recoiled at fascist violence, and by the fact that parliamentary institutions were much more firmly established in Britain than they were elsewhere in Europe. It has also been argued that England was kept from fascism by the absence of substantial atomistic 'masses' ready for mobilisation by the fascist demagogue.[11]

But if the British 'masses' were not seen as promising material for political manipulation, they were nevertheless, as John Carey amply demonstrates in *Intellectuals and the Masses*, viewed by British intellectuals as no less contemptibly malleable than their continental counterparts – as the debased product of modern industrial civilisation, irretrievably low in their cultural tastes and easily controlled by the mass media. Regarded (like the crowd) as irrational, feminised and emotional, this undiscriminating collectivity was seen as all too receptive to regressive fantasies. One sign of the debased mass mind in Britain was undoubtedly taken to be the appearance of a vast new market for popular romantic fiction – for example, for the novels of Ethel M. Dell and E.M. Hull, which took readers by storm in the twenties. Ironically, like some of the more elitist of British writers (such as Wyndham Lewis and Lawrence), what the popular audience for romantic fiction manifested was a taste for fantasising at a distance about brutal, manly leaders who know how to master women and other inferiors.

The 'Sheik' who most stirred the British popular imagination was not Mosley but Ahmed, the hero of E.M. Hull's sensational erotic and sado-masochistic romance, which went through 108 editions in Britain alone between 1919 and 1923. It was snapped up so quickly that 'the demand for cheap editions could not be met'. In 1926, translated to the silent screen, it gave Rudolph Valentino his most famous role. Seen by 125 million viewers, it established Valentino's reputation as the 'love god', one of the first of the male film stars to become a sex symbol. Widely imitated, *The Sheik* itself was instrumental in creating a popular culture of female eroticism and in generating a huge appetite for romantic fiction in the interwar years, a large amount of it written not only for women but by women.[12] In comparison to actively supporting National Socialism – or even in comparison to fantasising about Nietzschean supermen – reading a desert romance is clearly not an overtly political act. But, even though contained at the level of pure (or impure) imaginative indulgence, the power of such a stereotype in popular fiction cannot be entirely separated from its power in the political sphere. The representation of male power and the imaginative identification with sexual submission are clearly political in a broad sense, structured around a strong binary sense of essential maleness and femaleness – man the actor, woman the acted upon. Part of the appeal of the popular romance is obviously transgressive (the representation of desires in excess of what is socially permissible), part akin to the spurious sense of power and freedom experienced by the charismatic follower who is 'vitalised' by submission to the forceful leader. In the literature of the interwar years, the political implications of romance formulas are, for example, evident enough if we look at Lawrence adapting the clichés of the desert romance in the political fantasy of *The Plumed Serpent*, or at Wyndham Lewis in *Revenge for Love* and Aldous Huxley in *Point Counter Point* satirising the way male political power feeds on sexual stereotyping. In all three novels, the relationship between private and public spheres of life is seen to be inextricably linked to a romantic pattern of male sexual dominance.

In more recent analyses of early twentieth-century 'mass culture', there are some striking similarities between the explanations offered for the enthusiastic response to Nazism and for the success of popular romance. The need for the kind of revitalisation apparently offered by both the imagined lover and the actual leader has been said to grow out of the anomie, alienation and ennui seen by many theorists to characterise modern society – with social complexity and personal isolation producing a fragmented self 'engaged in a convulsive search for pleasure and stimulation to compensate for a lost sense of vitality and meaning'. Thus the immense success of romantic novels during the interwar period has been attributed both to a general modern tendency to feel empty and alone and to the unsettling expansion of the feminine sphere, which left women exposed to complex influences and anxieties from which their comparatively sheltered experience had previously protected them. Similarly, the allegiance of German women to fascism has been seen in the context of the identity-threatening milieu of post-First World War Europe. So, for example, the Nazi psychologist, Anna Zuhlke, saw female emancipation as having deprived women of their sense of self by 'masculinising' the world and thus robbing them of the strong sense of identity which had traditionally given them inner security. Anxious women turned with relief to a simplifying call for 'more masculine men' and 'more feminine women', and reacted fiercely against the idea of the new woman.[13] Nazi women, who campaigned for moral purity and scorned anyone wasting their time reading best-sellers, would, of course, have had no truck with mass-produced romantic fiction. But by investing their desires in fascism they, too, can be seen to manifest a contradictory wish for passivity and action – gaining the satisfaction of identifying with a strong challenge to the existing state of society without any independent assumption of responsibility. However suspect we find generalisations about mass mentality to be, the possible comparisons between these two different forms of popular response do carry us towards some plausible generalisations about the psychological function of romantic fantasy. The romantic political world of fascism, like that of romantic fiction, appears to offer a more secure sense of self – the one politically assertive, the other sexually adventurous, but both combining this vicarious temerity with a reassurance of being at the same time more traditionally feminine. In both, a feeling of empowerment is paradoxically attained by unconditional submission to an unlimited force, and feminine identity is strengthened by the loss of self 'in the self of a potent object'.[14]

For progressive women writers, both the popular fictional and the fascist fantasies of biddable women and aggressive men were distasteful, potentially dangerous examples of puerile emotionalism. The intellectual contempt for mass tastes is as apparent in feminist responses as elsewhere. The crude energy of such phenomena is in itself seen as simultaneously amazing and distressing. Although Rebecca West, ridiculing Ethel M. Dell's immensely popular *Charles Rex*, pays a backhanded compliment to the 'demoniac vitality' of the bestseller, she ridicules its headlong pace as inspired by a Pegasus of ill-bred lustiness: in every line written about Charles Rex, 'one hears the thudding, thundering hooves of a certain steed at full gallop; of the true Tosh-horse'. Many other educated women, such as Virginia Woolf, Q.D. Leavis and Storm Jameson, decried the facile emotionalism and sensationalism of the romantic women's novelists. The objection to popular romance is in part, of course, that reading it is anything *but* a form of involvement in political life. As Vera Brittain protests, the reading of 'novels of escape' is of a piece with apathetic indifference to the political crises of the time, exemplifying what Wyndham Lewis called 'the supreme immorality of the desire to forget'.[15] But detractors also explicitly note the connection between 'the demand for light fiction' and the acceptance of a polarised conception of sexual difference – almost as much a snare for the girls who (to use Winifred Holtby's phrases) 'swing daily to their offices in suburban trains' as for the young women who don Blackshirts in the hope of distinguishing themselves from the 'bored, indifferent or neurotic leisured women' who seem to have given themselves up to decadence and lethargy.[16] In the final section of this chapter, I will look briefly at the way in which stereotypes of sexual difference and political dominance are challenged and rewritten in Virginia Woolf's *Three*

Guineas, Rebecca West's *Harriet Hume*, Katharine Burdekin's *Swastika Night* and Alexandra Kollontai's *A Great Love*. In such progressive and feminist texts, as in so much subsequent women's writing, one sees the preoccupation with both understanding and changing those aspects of the female response to male power which are sometimes characterised as passive and masochistic. They contest the assumption (implicit, for example, in the analyses of the 'feminine' crowd) that passivity and dependence are normal in females but abnormal in males, and write with the aim of refuting the proposition that true satisfaction, whether sexual or political, comes in 'the feeling of being the passive instrument of another person, of being stretched out supinely beneath him'.[17]

LAWLESS SHEIKS AND LIVING QUETZALCOATLS

In his survey of early twentieth-century bestsellers, Claud Cockburn introduces *The Sheik* with typical mischievousness:

> When a Washington girl, in a famous case, charged a man with rape, the Judge asked her, 'When did this rape occur?' 'When did it occur?' she cried. 'Why, Judge, it was rape, rape, rape all summer long.' The statement succinctly describes the theme of E.M. Hull's *The Sheik*. Week after week after week of fierce rape amid sights and scenes of Araby . . . . The public was flat on its back gasping for more in five languages . . . .[18]

Cockburn's brisk summary of the plot and popular reception of the prototypical desert romance conveys the reasons for its immense appeal and widespread influence, as well as for the disapproving eyebrows it raised. He also captures one of the main sources of feminist disparagement of *The Sheik*, in his implication that women's blithe acceptance of victimisation can be glimpsed in the spectacle of a sex-starved female audience identifying enthusiastically with the libidinous self-abasement of the heroine. Some more recent critics have argued that it is overly simple to see it just as an androcentric, phallic reflection of a male-dominated culture or as the backlash of a patriarchal society against the new freedoms acquired by women. Billie Melman, for example, writes that although it does juxtapose 'real', sensual, subdued femininity with modern independent womanhood, what it is really doing is celebrating a primitive, virile, priapic ideal of masculinity, and that the purchase of such books reflects both the increased spending power and leisure of the female audience and the need to grapple with changing ideas of womanhood. Alison Light, in *Forever England*, observes that having a heroine who is not punished, either morally or socially, and who is not stigmatised as a fallen woman or required to die once she is sullied, means that the novel is to some extent 'an affront to bourgeois morality'. Certainly, it exemplifies, as Light says, the need to find new vocabularies in which to speak of feminine sexual desires.[19] But whatever qualifications one makes, the success of the novel cannot be understood apart from the its sado-masochistic fantasy of 'rape, rape, rape all summer long'.

Perhaps more clearly than any other text of the period, *The Sheik* reveals the popular receptivity to the image of the sexually potent man of power, as opposed to the supposedly feminised, emasculated men of a decadent Western society. As a powerful, independent chief with devoted followers, Ahmed Ben Hassan is a genuine man of power, a superman figure standing 'outside the prescribed conventions' and obeying no law but his own (p. 258). Ceaselessly active, he possesses the energy typical of the charismatic leader, together with immense egoism, complete indifference to everything beyond his own will and a considerable flair for theatrical and aesthetic display: 'He demanded implicit obedience to his lightest whim with the unconscious tyranny of one who had always been accustomed to command' (pp. 93–4). He possesses, as do all other desert lovers of the time, the handsomest and cruellest face ever seen – a tall, strong-jawed, broad-shouldered figure to whom the heroine's gaze is 'instinctively' drawn – and is credited with abnormal strength which has, behind it, the lawlessness that allows free rein to his savage impulses. When he flings aside a cloak to reveal himself in the magnificence of his male power, he is more than likely to be compared with wild animals. As in Lawrence, the subconscious feelings of a heroine towards a man of power can be gauged by her reactions to the man's assertion of mastery over a horse. Diana Mayo, watching him break a colt (to which she is subsequently compared), finds that part of her ('illogically') wants to see him 'master the infuriated animal'; the horse is, like Diana herself, 'untamed', but, in the violent contest with the man, is first 'dazed' and then defeated. As she watches this 'hideous exhibition of brute strength and merciless cruelty', Diana is 'almost sick with horror', but also unable to turn away: 'her eyes clung fascinated to the battle that was going on'. The sheik seems similarly careless of human life, though he also, it is stressed, is capable of inspiring unfathomable devotion in those who serve him ('What was the power in him that compelled the devotion of his wild followers . . .?'). Increasingly, what Diana comes to recognise about him is the 'aliveness' of his sheer animality (pp. 101–5). In the same way, his 'wild tribesmen, with their primitive ways and savagery' become dear rather than disgusting to her, and inevitably come to represent the antithesis to civilised routine (the text repeatedly opposes civilised/natural, routinised/savage, false/genuine). The Sheik's 'haughty unconventionalism' is coupled with an antipathy to Englishness (pp. 144, 258–9). He turns out, in fact, to be half English and half Spanish (his Moorish blood filtered through the Spanish nobility), and this obviously, in the end, makes him a more acceptable husband for an English girl. But his anti-civilised credentials are manifest in the bad father (English) – good father (Arab) motif and in his emphatic preference for the desert life he has chosen, a life in which there is 'nothing effete or decadent' about the men with whom he surrounds himself (p. 277).

The positive role of Ahmed is clarified by his juxtaposition with the evil Sheik, whose fulfilment of the role of villain of course moves the plot along (and serves the purpose of temporarily removing Diana, to hasten Ahmed's recognition of his need for her), but which also acts to establish what (in a more academic context) might be called the good–evil eschatology that frees charismatic immersion from inwardly-directed aggression. The robber sheik, bloated, vicious, gross and unwieldy, is a caricature of Oriental depravity, a more primitive extreme that puts into perspective the acceptable primitivism of Ahmed. The contrasts are pointed. Reeking of sweat and grease, Ibrahaim Omair has the genuine 'pungent stench of the native', as opposed to the fastidious, spotless Ahmed (representative of the wholesome natural world); lolling his great bulk on a pile of tawdry (as opposed to opulent) cushions, he has a face that is ferocious (not 'fierce') and seamed with marks of vice (not brown and handsome); his blackened teeth are in a 'loose mouth' (not straight and strong); his eyes, bloodshot and inflamed, give looks of 'bestial evilness' (in contrast to dark eyes, flashing ardent, burning looks of passion); his actions – fumbling and 'hitching himself forward' – are the antithesis of Ahmed's tiger-like grace. It is quite different to be powerless in the grasp of this sheik than to be grasped by the finely shaped hands of Ahmed, and the implications are clear enough: it is protection against precisely such a dangerous abuse of power that is secured by faith in a strong, godlike leader.[20]

Diana Mayo serves to demonstrate the limitations of another contemporary sexual stereotype – in her case, of the dominant new woman.[21] She appears at the outset as a beautiful but masculinised orphaned girl, unkissed, untamed and heartless, her name (after the moon goddess, the virgin huntress) suggesting not only chastity but (like some of Lawrence's metaphoric associations of woman and moon) hard indifference and habitual repudiation. Born with the same 'cold nature' as her brother, she has been raised by him as a boy, given a Spartan upbringing which has made no allowances for sex or temperament. Diana seems debarred by her training from affection, shrinks from the thought of passion 'with the same fastidiousness as she did from actual physical uncleanliness' and rejects the 'fettered existence' of marriage. Known for her 'dauntless courage and obstinate determination', and preferring breeches and high boots to pretty dresses, she leads a life much closer to that of an adventure hero than a young lady, meeting danger and excitement in her travels with her brother (pp. 11–16, 28). Her 'dauntless aspect' calls to mind the qualities that Lawrence, in 'Cocksure Women and Hensure Men', associates with a 'really up-to-date', 'cocksure' woman – an image that is developed into an attack on the reversal of natural sex roles in the 'human farmyard', with timid and tremulous 'hensure men' dominated by the dangerous and devastating cocksureness of the modern woman, a creature tragically given to 'out-manning the man' in a way that leads to the loss of her 'lovely henny surety'. In *The Sheik*, as so often in Lawrence, the implicit argument is that, by moving a little closer to the original human farmyard, men and women can move into a 'truer' and more satisfying relationship with their natures, which for a woman consists of finding 'the real bliss of every female', denied to her by the modern world.[22]

From her first encounter with the Sheik, Diana finds her impersonation of the male adventure hero reduced to impotence. She is mocked by the 'real man' who, having surreptitiously loaded her revolver with blanks, laughs with mockery as she ineffectually discharges the gun in his face. Outridden and then swept from her saddle, Diana is literally carried away against her will. This is the first time a man has dared touch her, and the consequence is that she is suddenly reduced to helplessness. As the swift and powerful horse wheels suddenly, she loses all sense of time and direction. Like the later detail of the broken watch (for which she 'mechanically' looks), the abduction establishes separation from all of the settled routines of civilised life. Resistance to the physical strength of the Arab is impossible. His 'burning' eyes symbolically strip her of her boyish clothes, and the question he puts to her before he first rapes her is whether she is not 'woman enough'. The rape itself deprives her of all volition; power of action gone, she suffers a 'complete moral collapse' (pp. 56–9). This is in effect a systematic negation of all of the masculine qualities that have previously constituted Diana's identity.

She had thought she was brave and self-confident, but now realises she is craven; she cowers and cries, feeling unutterable contempt for herself. What she discovers is how superficial and how lacking in authenticity her previous sense of herself has been, and how readily its identifying marks are stripped from her by contact with a 'real man'. Recognising her true emptiness and absence of firm identity she becomes, temporarily, 'no one' (p. 87), a prelude to being recreated (as in charismatic immersion) by means of ecstatic adulation of the formative power of a natural leader who mesmerises and paralyses her with the fascination of his eye contact. Diana tries to regain her 'moral strength' by dressing as a boy again, but she has irrevocably passed through a gender transformation which is also a process of maturation. She is brought to recognise the reality of woman's role – 'the inferiority of her sex', as opposed to the hypothetical status she had possessed as an honorary boy. For the first time in her life she is 'of no account' and is 'forced to submit to everything to which her womanhood exposed her'. The 'ruthless violence done to her cold, sexless temperament' and the Arab's 'Oriental disregard of the woman subjugated' is shaking her 'to the very foundations of her being'. This is not, however, just an emptying of a previous identity, but a filling with emotion of which she had before been empty, and, as in Lawrence, the overpowering of the rational, daylight mind by primitive rhythms is represented by the beating of a savage drum, an 'irregular rhythm . . . hammering inside her own head' (pp. 89–92).

During and after Diana's one brief escape from her captor, she makes (like countless other heroines of romance) repeated efforts to understand the ambivalence of her feelings towards the man whom she simultaneously hates and admires. Her isolated, independent attempt to assert herself having ended, she feels relief at the thought of his protectiveness, a feeling of 'well-being and security . . . . Wrapped warmly in the cloak and held securely by his strong arm . . . .' It is a regressive image, with the heroine held and wrapped like an infant, followed by the recognition that she has, of course, loved him all along with a love of complete surrender: 'He was a brute, but she loved him, loved him for his very brutality and animal strength' (pp. 132–3). The whole centre of Diana's identity shifts as she submits herself so unreservedly to the hero that she is 'tamed thoroughly at last'. Now yielding her will 'absolutely', she gives way to the 'feminine weakness' she has despised, overthrowing all her 'preconceived notions': blind love turns her haughty expression to 'tender wistfulness' and brings her to his feet 'humbly obedient' (pp. 164, 192, 271).

Lawrence, in 'Surgery for the Novel – Or a Bomb', contemptuously dismisses *The Sheik*: 'The mass of the populace "find themselves" in the popular novels. But nowadays it's a funny sort of self they find. A sheik with a whip up his sleeve, and a heroine with weals on her back, but adored in the end, adored, the whip out of sight, but the weals still faintly visible.' In spite of his scorn, however, his own work of this period has some striking affinities with the desert romance. It is not only that he subscribes to the belief that sexual differences are biologically rather than socially determined, but that he uses many of the same fictional ingredients as the sensationalist romance, creating, in a remote and savage setting, a plot which revolves around the conflict between an adventurous, independent woman and a strong, dark leader of men.[23]

In *Fantasia of the Unconscious*, Lawrence rejects the notion that power relations between men might in some sense be sexual. Indeed, he insistently addresses this question, anxious, perhaps, to dissociate his views from any suggestion of a homosexual element: the craving of the heart for a new collective activity is 'not at all' like the sexual craving for woman; the purposiveness of men acting together is a 'commingling' and involves 'passionately obeying their soul-chosen leader or leaders' but must not be confused with 'a sex passion'. Connections between sexual passion and political power are there, however, in the form of the strong man's sexual dominance of the submissive woman. In the sexual romance of *The Sheik*, male political authority is at the root of sexual power (the Sheik is in part so attractive because he is a man of power); in *The Plumed Serpent,* sexual magnetism is one of the roots of political power. That is, the political dynamism of Don Ramón and Don Cipriano is underpinned by the sexual response of Kate and the other women in the novel. In comparison, say, to *Aaron's Rod* and *Kangaroo*, this aspect of the narrative of *The Plumed Serpent* enables Lawrence to establish more unequivocally the strength of the leader's mesmeric force, of the way in which he naturally compels obedience (in contrast to the rather unsatisfactory scenes in which a male hero – Aaron or Somers – responds in an 'attracted' way to a charismatic figure). More importantly, it becomes for Lawrence a way of assimilating the subordination of women to the male power theme of his leadership novels. As he explains at some length in *Fantasia of the Unconscious*, we are to see the male–female sexual relationship as secondary to male power relationships, existing in a separate and inferior sphere, though necessary to prevent the power relationship from becoming abstract and idealised (as it does when leaders – like Karl Marx or Woodrow Wilson - have loved ideas so exclusively that they have felt no 'hot blood-pulse of love for the working man' and have therefore been willing 'to abstract him away from his own blood and being'). Sexually satisfied, 'made new after the act of coition', the man will 'wish to make the world new'; he will be better able to fulfil his role as 'the pioneer of life, adventuring onward into the unknown', leaving behind the woman who 'for him exists only in the twilight, by the camp fire'. The power relations imagined in *Fantasia of the Unconscious* are thus founded on a fairly inflexible notion of sexual difference: 'pure maleness in a man, pure femaleness in a woman . . . . Women and men are dynamically different, in everything'; any apparent mutual understanding is always an illusion and, should you by mischance 'pervert woman into mentality', you will have a woman who appears to be good at 'manly tricks' but who will not be content until she is driven back into 'her own true mode' and forced to 'yield once more to the male leadership'. As Simone de Beauvoir says, while Lawrence's men incarnate transcendence, his women are dedicated to immanence: 'Not only does man play the active role in the sexual life, but he is active also in going beyond it; he is rooted in the sexual world, but he makes his escape from it; woman remains shut up in it.'[24]

Feminist critics have also (not without justification) seen an element of sexual revenge in many of Lawrence's novels and stories – in those narratives which offer up a 'new woman' to be broken and tamed, forced to admit the folly of aspiring to usurp male power. Such texts are perhaps more ambiguous than this might imply, given Lawrence's tendency to explore his own impulses to submit to a strong dark man: Anaïs Nin's comment that Lawrence often wrote '*as a woman* would write', Daleski's analysis of his strong feminine component and the comments of many other critics suggest a split in Lawrence's own make-up. But as Hilary Simpson observes, it is also important to note a marked post-First World War shift in Lawrence's view of women, reflecting the widespread reaction against feminist advances and the male anxieties generated in the twenties by radical changes in sexual ideology and by what was seen as a 'feminisation' of society.[25] In a narrative like that of *The Plumed Serpent*, though it expresses complex and to some extent contradictory desires, there are also unmistakable signs of a new insistence on sexual hierarchy and of an identification with the male to whom obeisance is made, who can make a woman (as Lawrence says in *Fantasia of the Unconscious*) 'yield her goal to yours, to make her, in her own soul, *believe* in your goal beyond . . .' (p. 192).

In contrast to Diana Mayo, Kate Leslie is no *ingénue* but a mature woman of nearly forty. Nevertheless, she is untouched by certain kinds of experience, and, though she is capable of resisting male power in more subtle ways, and of course is not subjected to any brutal physical assault, the tensions between 'new' and 'real' womanhood are very similar. Tough, independent and detached, Kate is full of 'handsome, ruthless female power', able to make a 'splendid show' in the outside world but 'second-rate' in comparison to a woman who knows 'the real secret of womanhood'. She has had lovers, two husbands and children, but still feels a sense of discontent, recognising intuitively, 'in her vague, woman's way', the limitations of Owen's sensation-seeking and trivial social round (bull-fights and tea-parties). Seeing the necessity of being 'born again', she is imaginative enough to feel wonder and mystery at the thought of the old gods, to catch 'contradictory gleams of meaning' without being overly worried by the contradictions. Kate's limitations and her positive capacities are both established by means of clear sexual and ancestral stereotyping. Whereas 'American' stands (as 'new woman' does) for traits that are aggressive, domineering and materialistic, Celtic connotes mystical, non-materialistic leanings, and 'real woman' signifies intuition and receptivity, like that of the 'hensure' woman who is sure 'without knowing anything about it'.[26] Qualified as she is by her Irish spirit to respond to the eternally roaring 'god-stuff', Kate is not limited by yearnings for 'fixed meanings' (*The Plumed Serpent*, pp. 90–1). The non-materialistic side to her nature is carefully established in the description of her attitude to her second marriage, to the Irish leader, Joachim: 'a woman like me *can* only love a man who is fighting to *change* the world, to make it freer, more alive', not a man like her first husband who, being content with the state of the world as it is, leaves you feeling 'so terribly sold' (pp. 103–4). As a *new* woman, however, she is associated more with America than with Ireland, and it is with respect to the freedom valued by American women that she is judged to be, paradoxically, most determined by social conditioning. So, for example, Cipriano says that she has been educated and thus 'compelled' to think only 'USA thoughts'. He classes her as American in all respects – thinking, having money, dressing. In fact, *most* women are much less free than they imagine themselves to be: 'Nearly all women are like that'; even if they are Mexican or Spanish-Mexican, they think like modern women, because 'USA thoughts' are the ones 'that go with the way they dress their hair' (p. 242). Kate is afraid of Cipriano, he maintains, because she knows he will not treat her as an American. Towards the end of the novel, as she ponders the value of her own sense of isolated individuality, she reflects on the unsatisfactory lives of modern women, and feels pity and repulsion as she summons up a Pope-like image of beauties grown old, changing from cats to grimalkins, 'greyish, avid, horrifying, prowling around looking for prey' (pp. 475–6).

To a considerable extent, however, Kate is also the carrier of some of the most characteristic Lawrentian themes. She is sometimes 'surprised at herself' when she suddenly speaks in Lawrentian phrases, using 'this language' of 'rich and alive' people wanting to 'breathe the Great Breath' and find 'the hidden greater thing'. The language with which Lawrence recurrently expresses his horror of the mechanical deadness of the modern world is also an important part of Kate's vocabulary. She exclaims inwardly over the 'dry-rot of the world's sterility', the unmagicking of modern experience, the 'horrible machine of the world', the degradation of sex, the 'cocoons of words' (pp. 137–45). Very much like Lawrence, she hates the common people, feeling uneasy from the start about 'the voice of mob authority' and the loathsome human species (not nearly as nice as bulls). Her thoughts are filled with Lawrentian images of the proud individual oppressed by the knowledge of the horrifying mass of humanity: the 'free *spirit*' of the outstanding individual risks being broken by the mongrel- or insect-like hordes of modern humanity (pp. 42–3, 170).

This '*spiritual* fear' is set alongside the quite different fear she feels in Mexico, 'the real heart-wrench of blood fear', the primitive terror of a civilised person's confrontation with the old life-modes and the 'old, broken impulse' that connects men with the mystery of the cosmos. Lawrence's antipathy to many aspects of Mexican life are echoed in Kate's 'Western' doubts about the viability of Mexico as a model of primitivist revitalisation. Many of the early scenes in the novel establish reasonable grounds for her nervousness of a country so beyond her civilised experience, and often so apparently inimical to any hope for spiritual regeneration. Her simultaneous fascination and repulsion are acted out in the dance in which a bare-breasted man draws her into the circle – reluctant but mesmerised by the 'soft barbaric nearness', so caught up (in spite of being made 'inflexible' and 'insulated' by her shoes) that she eventually feels her own desires to be 'gone in the ocean of the great desire', merged beyond the 'individualism of the body', absorbed into 'the great womanhood' (pp. 163–72). Ultimately, however, circumstances force on her the experience not just of festive merging but of complicity in Mexican violence, changing even more radically her feeling of separateness and immunity. The act of killing a man in defence of Ramón forms a bond between them, and establishes a kind of 'savage recognition' (p. 333). This deeper immersion in the savagery of male power is most explicit after the executions, when Kate is shocked and repelled to see that Ramón and Cipriano are capable of committing such violence, while at the same time finding something seductive in this barbarous knowledge: 'There was something dark and lustrous and fascinating to her in Cipriano, and in Ramón. The black, relentless power, even passion of the will in men!' (p. 422).

Ramón's wife, Doña Carlota, has already warned Kate against succumbing to the dubious attractions of these ferocious assertions of male power ('No, you must not be fascinated. No! No! It is not good.'). Lawrence uses the other female characters in the novel – most notably Ramón's two wives, Carlota and Teresa – to put into context the heroine's manner of acceding to male dominance, as well as to establish a range of female responses to male power, none of them without their own form of servility. Having worshipped Ramón, Carlota's love for him is 'now nearly all *will*'. She has settled into the role of gentle and sensitive victim, looking 'as if some secret enemy drained her blood', with Don Ramón setting himself, solid and unmoving, against her 'charitable quiver' of emotion – a conflict seen by Kate as the 'impassive male cruelty' of a changeless stone idol (pp. 191–3). Kate also, however, is astute enough to recognise the wrongheadedness in Carlota's own form of self-assertion, a combination of adoration and blind opposition which is a 'terrible burden' to Ramón, making his big heart swell with 'a suffocation of anger' (pp. 203–4). She refuses to allow him his separateness or male mystery, resenting the fact that he can sit 'secure within his own dark aura', so possessing a 'pure sensuality' which is 'hostile to her sort of purity' (p. 221). The images of their marriage are recurrent ones in Lawrence's work (in *Women in Love*, for example): pent-up manhood ('humiliated, goaded with insult inside him') is joined to the possessive wife/mother, whose very subservience is a way of laying claim to her husband – her 'property' – demanding intimacy, which 'means disgust'. Through Carlota, Lawrence argues his case that there are different kinds of womanhood and that, however womanly Carlota may seem, in a traditional sense, to be, she has not even approached her 'complete, final womanhood'. Carlota declares, 'Womanhood is always the same', but Ramón replies, 'Ah, no, it isn't! Neither is manhood' (*The Plumed Serpent*, pp. 246–7). Her defeat and humiliation are brought about when she vainly tries to stop the cult of the Quetzalcoatl taking over the church. It is the final confrontation between the rival faiths, between Ramón's 'exultance in power and life' and Carlota's devotion to the God of pity who makes women the thieves of virility and who has turned Carlota (as Cipriano says, comforting her on her death-bed) into a life-denying harpy – 'you

125

stale virgin, you spinster, you born widow, you impeccable wife, you just woman' (pp. 378–83).

The other main kind of womanhood presented in *The Plumed Serpent* is in fact very little criticised. Teresa is envied and despised by Kate as a 'harem type', and Kate, in turn, is seen by Teresa as a potential enemy who puts herself on equal terms with men. The 'harem trick' Teresa has mastered is simultaneously to make herself inconspicuous and to make Ramón into a 'full glory of a man', like a sultan or pasha. But this is, Lawrence implies, no superficial trick; it is the ancient mystery of female power, 'which consists in glorifying the blood-male'. From Kate's point of view, it is a degradation, the self-prostitution of a slave. Whereas Kate gives herself up to Cipriano 'just for moments', thus preserving the rest of her life as her own (a life imaged in the barren, civilised clutter of her room – the room of a woman who lived 'for her own self'), Teresa strikes her as infuriatingly servile. Yet ('yet' being one of the words most often used in defining Kate's divided views) the example of Teresa seems to persuade her that life's secret – 'the clue to all living' – lies in 'the vivid blood-relation between man and woman'. As she ponders her resentment of the relationship between Teresa and Ramón, the accumulation of positive Lawrentian vocabulary (making a man almighty and blood-glamorous, giving him a 'strange, heavy, lordly *aplomb*') strongly suggests that the sexual imbalance of which she disapproves is associated with the mastery of the world. The 'power of the world', which is dying in the blond, blue-eyed men, is 'going into the eyes of the dark men', and, contemplating this, she recognises both her own shortcomings (if she could have fanned the blood of Joachim he would not have died) and Teresa's strengths. This 'black little creature' is really 'neither significant nor humble', but possesses a 'strange old power to call up the blood in a man' (pp. 431–7). What Kate and Teresa have in common is a kind of ultimate faithfulness – a sense that it is better to stand behind really brave men than to push forward in the ranks of cheap and obtrusive women. But Kate's suspicion is nevertheless that her own female power is 'second-rate' in comparison to Teresa's 'deep passion of connection with Ramón'; her acquaintance with Teresa has made her see that well-dressed, beautiful European women who keep their souls 'for themselves, in a sort of purse' could be made, in spite of their money and class, to feel 'really nothing' by a look from Ramón (pp. 446–7).

Lawrence also uses Teresa to demonstrate the virtues of a protective male concern for the vulnerable female. He buttresses his assault on the new woman by the creation of more extreme examples of anti-feminist sentiment, the bogey-figures of the Catholic Church (which has the ability to exert its oppressive power 'especially over the women') and of Teresa's brothers, whose unpleasant male bullying is associated with the established structure of political power. The jeering brutishness of such men is calculated to put into perspective the sexual stereotyping of the Quetzalcoatl cult. Her brothers' unjustified taunts give Teresa a chance to assert some measure of independence and dignity in the face of humiliation, and, rather as in *The Sheik* (in which the unspeakable degradation threatened by the rival sheik dramatises Ahmed's role as guardian angel), Ramón is given a chance to 'save her sex from the insult' and thus to win her 'fierce reverence' (pp. 431–3). The barnyard political implications, as in 'Cocksure Women and Hensure Men', are perfectly apparent: 'When the chicken-hawk appears in the sky, loud are the cockerel's cries of alarm. Then the hens scuffle under the verandah, the cock ruffles his feathers on guard. The hens are numb with fear, they say: Alas, there is no health in us! How wonderful to be a cock so bold!' (p. 32).

In *The Plumed Serpent*, no less than in the desert romance, many of the key scenes centre on the clichéd contradictions in the female response to male cocksureness (he's a brute, but she loves him – and needs him to keep her from harm). For Kate, the process of learning not to disapprove depends upon her willingness to *un*learn her intellectual and judgemental skills. She must close her eyes and open her soul, getting rid of her 'prying, assertive self' and of 'the itching, prurient, *knowing*, imagining eye . . . the curse of Eve'. This intellectual mastery is a kind of 'cheap awareness', quite unlike the deep awareness that comes from giving way to the fascination emanating 'like a narcotic' from a man's hips and thighs, promising a potency that is 'like a great weight bearing the women down'. The contrast is closely akin to the differentiation, in *Fantasia of the Unconscious*, between 'a sensual way of beholding' (natural to the savage) and the faulty vision of a modern world that strains 'to see, see, see – everything . . . in one mode of objective curiosity' (*Fantasia of the Unconscious*, pp. 64–5). The abandonment of 'objective' sight allows the woman to surrender to the spell of phallic power. As in *The Sheik*, the heroine regresses, fearfully and wistfully looking on 'like a child' as the men open up a new world for her, in which 'the phallic wind' rushes through the dark and the men partake of the earth's 'volcanic violence'. In her marriage to Cipriano and, through him, her connection with Don Ramón (who is '*more* than life' to Cipriano), Kate accepts an absolute polarisation of maleness and femaleness. He is the old, supreme phallic mystery, 'the living firemaster', the assertive body with its storms of desire, a black fume of power, furious magnificence, limitless, unyielding, consummated, a god, a devil, a demon, undying Pan, 'this huge erection', a 'pliant column' swaying with power, emitting 'the dark rays of dangerous power'; she ('Poor Kate') is 'submission absolute', succumbing, 'perfect in her proneness', silent and helpless in her supreme passivity, her own pride dissolving, her will and 'her very self' gone so that she becomes 'elusive even to herself'. When the soldiers watch her, they see not the physical woman 'but the inaccessible, voluptuous mystery of man's physical consummation' (*The Plumed Serpent*, pp. 346–60). The instrumentality of the woman strikes Kate very forcibly, even as she accepts its wonder ('But where was the woman, in this terrible interchange of will?'). She is only the stone on which the man sharpens the knife of his volition, 'the sheath for his blade', 'the stone of rest to his potency', possessing no soul of her own: 'Alone, she was nothing. Only as the pure female corresponding to his pure male, did she signify' (pp. 422–4). So extreme is her self-abnegation that she abandons even the desire for female sexual satisfaction, orgasm becoming, like the man himself, one of 'the things that *are*, but are not known'. Living in mindless communion, she thinks how wonderful sex can be 'when men keep it powerful and sacred' (pp. 459–60, 473).

In political terms, the implication for the woman of such sexual submission is complete acquiescence in male political judgements. She may be ensconced as a goddess in the cult, but in this role as archetypal woman she is an object of 'intense, blind ambition', never ambitious on her own behalf, never the subject who acts and exercises power in the world. At the Quetzalcoatl ceremony, men stand (Ramón on a low throne), women crouch and cover their faces: 'Kate crouched down too', placing herself amongst 'the low dark shrubs of the crouching women', surrounded by 'a forest of erect, upthrusting men' (pp. 373–6). Just as Diana Mayo must accept the nature of the Sheik's absolute power over his people, so Kate feels bound to suspend her judgement of Cipriano's political violence: when she hears of the 'swift cruelty' of Cipriano and his soldiers, even of his execution of three helpless peons, she thinks, 'Why should I judge him? He is of the gods . . . . What do I care if he kills people' (pp. 429–30). As Lawrence argues in *Fantasia of the Unconscious*, the purposeful activity of building a world is an exclusively male activity; women (whose intervention in political life can only lead towards the kind of soft, charitable emotionalism that Lawrence abhors) should crouch by the camp fire.

Kate Leslie, struggling against her preconceptions as a new woman, inevitably finds that her rational faculties suggest many doubts about the role she has assumed. A sane scepticism is allowed to surface on several occasions, both about her own transformation and about the fate of the movement with which she has involved herself. In part (one would like to think) her doubts embody a lingering suspicion in Lawrence's own mind that there is something faintly absurd in Cipriano proclaiming himself the living Huitzilopochtli, with Kate as his goddess bride Malintzi. At least, Lawrence does not completely undermine her expression of a reluctance to be 'swallowed up' in her new identity and her vestigial mistrust of the 'high-flown bunk' of Ramón and Cipriano (*The Plumed Serpent*, pp. 408–9). In part, however, her resistance to the new life is due to the promptings of an 'old self' that is much too attached to a moribund European civilisation ('She belonged too much to the old world of Europe, she could not, could not make herself over so quickly.'). Her wish to flee seems, on balance, to be judged less an expression of healthy scepticism than a habitual and arid attachment to 'herself' (p. 458). As in *The Sheik*, the central question is whether the heroine can separate herself from the civilisation she knows and accept men 'as they naturally are', unlearning her role as a self-reliant new woman and being schooled in 'womanhood'. Should she stay or should she go? Kate forms plans to escape, asking herself 'how could she marry Cipriano, and give her body to this death?' (p. 283). But at the same time, she recognises the truth of Ramón's warning that she 'will find nothing in England'. This vacillation between identities – between the old Kate who belongs to an 'empty, dead house' and the unfamiliar woman within her who belongs to the new world – dominates much of the second half of the novel (pp. 348–52). In representing the conflict between Kate's two selves, Lawrence defines opposing qualities in such a way that we are left in no doubt which choice a truly daring woman will make – that is, paradoxically, she will choose the self that is 'not "free"' over the self that is 'curiously hard and "free"' – the former being sensitive, desirous, vulnerable and organically connected, the latter, finished, accomplished and immured in a past way of life. In the resolution of the conflict, as Kate appears to opt for Mexico, the remaining uncertainty is to do with the motives for her choice (pp. 465–8). Lawrence does not ask us to believe that (like the conventional heroine of a desert romance) she has been 'tamed thoroughly at last'; the shrewd and calculating new woman still harbours the belief that she can, if she stays, still keep 'myself to myself' without being discovered. Furthermore, responding to the promptings of her female ego, she wants to attribute her decision to male need – 'You won't let me go!' (p. 482). It thus remains, in the end, an open question whether the new woman will continue to engage in her customary intellectual deviousness and psychological power games or whether she will ultimately prove herself able to assume the identity of the 'true woman', confirming male power by unreservedly accepting her role as 'the Other'.[27]

SEX SYMBOLS SATIRISED: HUXLEY'S *POINT COUNTER POINT* AND LEWIS'S *REVENGE FOR LOVE*

The potential for living harmoniously in 'the communion of power' that seems to be held out at the end of *The Plumed Serpent* – with the two marriages signifying an actual or potential willingness of the women 'to serve a man in whom power lives' – is a reflection of what Simone de Beauvoir calls Lawrence's cosmic optimism, his belief in the restoration of human sexual and power relationships 'to the verity of Life'.[28] Lawrence's diagnosis of the ills of modern civilisation has much in common with the views expressed by such pessimistic contemporaries as Aldous Huxley and Wyndham Lewis, both of whom evince contempt for mass culture, believe parliamentary democracy to be bankrupt and see in strong leadership a possible remedy for conditions of crisis and collapse. When Lawrence reads their novels, however, he reels back in dismay at their apparent refusal to contemplate life-affirming alternatives. In *Point Counter Point*, he says, man is represented as being 'so nervously repulsive to man, so screamingly, nerve-rackingly repulsive!'. Although he expresses admiration for the truth and courage of Huxley's representation of the modern world, he reads the novel 'with a heart sinking through my boot-soles', much distressed by the complete absence of a sustaining vision. Huxley's is 'a sort of desperate courage of repulsion and repudiation', 'a *perverse* courage which makes the man accept the slow suicide of inertia and sterility'. This 'gruesome condition', resulting from the 'inward revulsion of man away from man, which follows on the collapse of the physical sympathetic flow', is to be seen also in the writings of Wyndham Lewis, who 'gives a display of the utterly repulsive effect people have on him'.[29]

Wyndham Lewis, for his part, includes Lawrence amongst the targets of his satire. There is, for example, the entertaining parody in *Snooty Baronet* of 'the gospel of Mithras according to St Lawrence', with Lawrence the Nature-crank 'all steamed-up over the Bull' and making Mithras in love with the Bull 'because he always put himself in the shoes of any god he got interested in'. Lawrentian primitivism is more fully dissected in *Paleface*, which identifies Lawrence as a follower of Bergson and Spengler and represents his praise of a more primitive kind of consciousness as 'an invitation of suicide addressed to the White Man', urging him to give up his 'White "consciousness"' and to 'Capitulate to the mystical communistic Pan of the Primitive Man! Be Savage!'[30] Huxley, much more gently and affectionately, praises Lawrence's great gifts as a writer and his 'immediate perception and artistic rendering of divine otherness', but sees his loyalty to 'the *daimon* which possessed him', however inescapable, as 'a very serious handicap': inhabiting 'a different universe from that of common men', Lawrence 'refused to write of the main activities of the contemporary world'.[31] Politically, both Lewis and Huxley have been, like Lawrence, accused of harbouring pro-fascist sympathies. This is particularly true of Lewis, of course, whose links with fascism (not repented until 1938) included his eccentric commendation of German Nazism in *Hitler* (1931), and who visited Sir Oswald Mosley often at his house in the thirties, applauding (in a 1937 article) Mosley's 'great insight and qualities as a leader'. Huxley, too, although his views had changed markedly by the mid thirties, earlier had good words to say about Mosley, expressing approval of his radical and vigorous plans for national renewal.[32] Even before they fully realised the true character of fascist leadership and the dangers it posed, however, it is clear that the sceptical, sardonic eye of the satirist would be unlikely to find cause for optimism in Lawrence's ideas about political salvation. The acerbic portraits of unattractive contemporary realities created in *Point Counter Point* and *Revenge for Love* are a world away from the Lawrentian vision of redemption achieved by a romantic cult of priapic–primitive leadership, and the function of the women characters in such satiric narratives differs accordingly. Lewis's contempt for women is well-known, and women are clearly not seen by either Huxley or Lewis as speaking for an alternative and superior set of values. Both novelists, however, use the woman defined as the Other (whether as innocent eye, victim or dupe) as a position from which to expose the treacheries and deceits of a masculinist ideology. The sexual dynamic of political life is revealed as cynical manipulation rather than confirmation of male power, and the satire brings into sharp focus the absurdity of political movements in which both sexes conform all too readily to the stereotypical roles of romantic male lead and gullible, vulnerable, heart-throbbing female.

The Western society that Huxley portrays is not unlike the fragmented, disintegrated contemporary scene from which Lawrence's characters repeatedly recoil in horror. Whereas *The Plumed Serpent*, however, views from a distance the mechanical sameness of USA thoughts and cogwheel men, Huxley, immersed in modern reality, emphasises the absence of intellectual consensus – embodied in the very form of a novel ('point counter point') in which characters express views that it would be almost impossible to reconcile. There is no central hero, or even anti-hero, but instead a range of characters, most of them fairly unmistakable portraits of Huxley's contemporaries, who alternately engage our interest, and occasionally (though perhaps not very often) our sympathy. Amongst the main characters are two with aspects of Huxley's own personality (Walter Bidlake and, more importantly, Philip Quarles); Everard Webley, the fascist leader who is a fictionalised version of Mosley; and Mark Rampion and his wife Mary (the proletarian son married to the lapsed aristocrat), who take most of their features from Lawrence and Frieda. During the time that they knew one another well (from a 1926 meeting in Florence until Lawrence's death in 1930), Huxley responded warmly to Lawrence's vitality, and, although Rampion is to some extent satirised as an inveterate theoriser (a boring gasbag, Lawrence complained), he is also, as a 'whole' human being, a foil for the false certainties of a large cast of unsatisfactory and one-sided people. In terms of political judgements, it is obviously not Lawrence's unguarded romanticism but his caustic dismissals of the contemporary scene that Huxley builds upon. Political life, Rampion says, is 'bound for hell': 'All, without exception. Lenin *and* Mussolini, MacDonald *and* Baldwin. All equally anxious to take us to hell and only squabbling about the means of taking us.'[33] This Lawrentian denunciation sums up the contributions of the novel's rival political extremists: Everard Webley (the Mosley figure) and Illidge (the Marxist assistant of Lord Edward Tantamount).

Webley, modelled on a man who based his popular appeal strongly on the emotions, is a study in political irrationalism. Huxley does not underplay the man's attractions. Webley is by no means a pure caricature and some of his views (for example, on rulership by the few) are not that remote from Huxley's own. But the core of the portrait is a vigorously satirical anatomy of the overbearing sexuality and inherent violence of the charismatic leader. In command of the British Freemen, who (like Mosley's British Union of Fascists) are much given to such activities as beating up the opposition and parading about in distinctive dress, Webley has 'a weakness for swords . . . his speeches were full of them, his house bristled with panoplies' (*Point*

Counter Point, p. 55). He collects not only old swords but firearms, coins, medals and other treasures, including emblems of great men of the past (Napoleon, Caesar, Alexander the Great) – embodiments of a 'schoolboyish ambition to ride about on a horse and chop people's heads off' (p. 275). He has considerable 'natural ferocity', is vain, touchy and lacking in a sense of humour. When he speaks at Hyde Park, dressed in green, wearing a sword and mounted on his white horse, Bucephalus, he is the very type of the demagogue, imagining himself as going to the people to wage a battle that can no longer be fought constitutionally. At the same time, however, Huxley conveys a strong sense of Webley's sheer magnetism and power, his capacity to attract and sway the masses. He possesses the kind of force which is always attractive, 'particularly if one lacks it oneself'; he is all 'rapidity and decision' (pp. 291, 299). We see him through the eyes of other characters, many of them hostile to him, but even his enemies testify to his energy and to the force and presence of his personality. He is a Robin Hood figure, the romantic villain, the 'pirate king'. 'You ought to play the part of Captain Hook in *Peter Pan*', Lady Edward says. 'Yes, really. You have the ideal face for a pirate king' (pp. 39–40). When he speaks, Huxley emphasises that it is not the content of what he says but a power inherent in the man himself that thrills audiences. Even Philip Quarles has to make a conscious intellectual effort not to be carried away by the spectacle: 'I felt as though there were a hole where my diaphragm should be; a kind of anxious tingling ran over my skin, the tears were very nearly at the surface of my eyes.' He is moving and convincing even to those who know that what he says is vague and meaningless. By analysing his reactions, Philip is able to conquer them, 'Or rather', he writes in his notebook, 'one part of me conquered.' But seeing Webley raises in him the question of whether the intellectual suppression of his emotions, of his gut responses, does not perhaps make him less of a whole man (pp. 344–6).

Philip's wife, Elinor, obviously finds herself considerably less capable than her husband of rationally resisting the dynamism of Webley's personality, and one of the main narrative lines of the novel involves the question of whether Elinor will remain loyal to Philip or seek companionship that is a little less purely intellectual in the arms of the dynamic fascist leader. The attraction is quite independent of any real sympathy for Webley's political views, and Huxley gives to Elinor (in comparison, say, to Kate Leslie) a much more unambiguous role as critic of the political implications of the leader's intentions. When she contemplates the abstract details of his political programme, Elinor realises that as far as she is concerned Webley might just as well be recommending insularity without nationalism as nationalism without insularity: they are just 'empty Words'. Her detachment from the male world of political decision-making is not just an example of woman's exclusion from public life; her fundamental doubts about the nature and value of political life are taken seriously, and her scepticism washes over the political programme of the British Freemen. Although Kate Leslie also raises questions about the real intentions behind the high-sounding male phrases, Elinor's misgivings carry more weight, particularly when she undercuts the rhetoric of liberty, justice and 'the best men shall rule' by voicing the suspicion that what the Freemen really stand for is the dictatorship and infallibility of Everard Webley (pp. 275–6).

In describing Elinor's near-seduction by Webley and her reactions to his public performance, Huxley establishes the essentially sexual and visceral kind of attraction exerted by the charismatic leader. With his 'fine' and 'disquieting' eyes and 'huge reserves of power', he contrasts strikingly with the aridity and detachment of Philip Quarles. Elinor's responses bring out the difference between an intellectual and an emotional (and regressive) response to charismatic leadership. Webley's arrogant assurance that he will be master and impose his will first strikes her as absurd, but this is 'the protest of her critical intellect against her feelings'. Her feelings had been 'strangely moved' by his 'vibrating latencies of power and passion' (pp. 278–80). When she sees him at a political rally, she realises that it is 'childish' to have been so moved by the sight of him on his white horse, but nevertheless responds with intense emotion to his 'penetrating' and passionate speech, however long-winded or vulgar the actual content might be, and the symptoms of her response are clearly sexual – blood rushes to her cheeks, she turns away in confusion and, not daring to look at him, begins to cry 'for no reason' (pp. 342–3). She is 'carried away', at this stage metaphorically, though Webley's sexual pursuit of her also does draw her physically away from her marriage to Philip. The images associated with the relationship are of an inner warmth and intoxication. However ridiculous, ranting or melodramatic the sense of his words, she feels an irrational desire 'to exult'. As in *The Sheik* and *The Plumed Serpent*, the powerful male challenges the woman to live more fully: 'you're afraid . . . you've been half dead all these years' (p. 279).

What Webley offers is primitive, dangerous and exciting, but also disturbingly violent. As he tempts Elinor, his voice makes her flesh quiver with 'obscure and violent exultations', as though she hears him directly with her body (vibrating 'at her very midriff'), even though she rationally knows that the love he talks of is just brief violence 'in the intervals of business', and that he despises women and resents them because they waste a man's energies. In all his encounters with Elinor, we have an impression of great physical force and potential destructiveness. His entry to a house is compared to the burst of an exploding bomb: 'There was a rush of feet on the stairs; the house shook. The door of the drawing-room burst open . . .' (pp. 277–80). At first, as she contemplates having an affair with him, though she is thrilled by the power that seems to radiate from him, the spontaneous habits of her body and her instinctive self rebel. When Everard does 'carry her away' to the country, though he has no horse on which to abduct her, he terrifies her with the 'furiousness' of his driving. His speed gives him a sense of 'power and superiority': although Webley scarcely impresses her as a beauty-lover, he is magnificent as a 'power-lover', and his 'violent impetuosity' as a driver is the last we see of him before he is shot (pp. 346–7). Webley's own capacity for violence and the violence of his end are, like speeding motor cars, far more a part of the real contemporary world than the semi-mythical violence of Don Ramón and Don Cipriano, and he is judged accordingly.

Wyndham Lewis, in *Revenge for Love*, creates a Lawrentian primitive who looks as though he should be both violent and powerful, but in fact is neither. Victor Stamp's name and clichéd good looks mark him out for the role of the bold leader, and the plot turns on Victor being mistaken for an actual man of power. But Lewis's technique is to separate out the attributes of the political strong man, and, by fragmenting them, expose their absurdity. Victor's heroic appearance, used, manipulated and betrayed by those around him, is seen alongside other types of political personality: the fashionable agitator, the thug, the obsequious 'genius', the bogus magician. The women, similarly, represent distinctly different kinds of female submissiveness and, through their relationships with the various heroes *manqués*, Lewis develops a wide-ranging satire of the interpenetration of sexuality and politics.

Wild man, 'Kipling Man', Hollywood sex symbol and chauvinistic Blackshirt commingle in the character of Victor Stamp. His actual origins – a 'wild Australian' – equip him to play 'the big rough boy', contemptuous of 'word-slingers', characterised himself by animal will and energy. His own sentiments seem to belong to 'the simple life', 'the elemental things in life', the 'great open spaces'. There is, however, a gap between appearance and capacity for action: 'Victor slept. In sleep he was heroic . . . .' He is symbol rather than substance:

'Some men are symbols', and Victor, as Margot reflects, has 'some title to be considered as a Man with a capital letter – as the Kipling Man, for instance', or at least 'the Kipling Man – 1930 American model'. Such men were perhaps 'semi-extinct' and out of place in the modern world, but it does give Margot a sense that he is 'something' rather than 'nothing' ('she *could* love a *symbol*').[34] The similarities between Victor and the equally insubstantial Hollywood sex symbol are quite explicit. A Clark Gable look-alike, he is Margot's 'private screen star', a 'great passion' whom she hovers over 'in her ecstasy of lovesickness'. Her passion for Victor is also linked to a vague (more aesthetic than political) preference for Blackshirts. Her genteel, quietist spirit finds politics 'very gross material' to pronounce upon, but her private cult of Victor includes politics to the extent that she has seen a Blackshirt bearing a distant resemblance to Victor – with the same jaw, the same atlantean shoulders and the same indefinable 'something' (*Revenge for Love*, pp. 70–6). But although he has the 'figure' of a leader, Victor is really a victim and a 'have-not'. An extended comparison between Victor and Germany, which is regarded as 'a particularly good joke – both against Victor and against Germany', represents Victor as a Great Power, but one that is impoverished and mutilated; he is like the Third Reich in being 'very nationalist. His nation is Victor! And he suffers from a permanent sense of injury' (pp. 272–4).

Margot is in some ways the very type of the subservient female, the submissive lover, gentle, painfully uncertain, her 'dully-beating heart' sending out 'waves of apprehension'. She feels herself to be a 'frail contraption' of no practical use, lacking both money and talents, having only love to offer. Margot has created herself in the fragile image of the utterly devoted woman who hopes, in turn, to be idolised and cosseted – 'poised upon her Dresden China pedestal, exquisite, impassive as a mannequin, she belonged to a "period" – of her own manufacture' (pp. 69–70, 75). She is the embodiment of the private life, dreading and disliking 'all these false politics, of the sham underdogs', with a predatory Party 'athirst for power' advertising the injustices endured by a 'pukka underdog' like Victor (pp. 163–4). Limited though she is, and however vulnerable the romantic self-image that governs her own life, Margot is given a degree of credibility as an outsider who witnesses the clichés and posturings of contemporary political life. She has the sound intuition that these political poseurs threaten her private existence – 'her precarious nest' (p. 181). At O'Hara's party, upper-class Reds straddle dogmatically above Victor and Margot, threatening to trample them, looking down on them, a 'dangerous crowd of shadows' hovering over them (pp. 174–6). Her reflections on the people at the gathering provide a central image of the sham political life led by those avid to see Percy Hardcaster. A world away from the painfully established sincerity of Lawrence's would-be revolutionaries, Lewis's upper classes, talking sedition, are less like human beings than 'big portentous wax-dolls, mysteriously doped with some impenetrable nonsense . . . wound up with wicked fingers' (p. 165).

These political charlatans symbolically impersonate the proletariat by forging Victor's signature and involving him as the supposed 'boss of the outfit' in an expedition into Spain to smuggle machine guns. Here again, Margot, detached from male power games, sees things more clearly than Victor. But his false optimism, engendered by handsomeness and by his being a 'godlike antipodean beauty', makes it impossible for her to warn him of dangers (pp. 294–5). The involvement of Margot and Victor in the gun-running fiasco reveals the romantic hero and heroine – the strong man with the square jaw and the delicate, doting woman – to be pawns manipulated by forces they cannot understand. In the surreal events of the final part of the novel, their sense of self disintegrates as they encounter both unconscious truths and political realities. The true nature of the woman's slavish devotion to a world of male power surfaces in Margot's bizarre encounter with a crowd-pleasing dwarf. The scene provides a grotesque analogue for the female response to the public performance of the demagogue, as well as exhibiting the psychological defects of Victor and Margot on a public and politically symbolic stage. The dwarf, with his swelled head and earsplitting howl, swaggering as if he owns the whole earth, strongly suggests the 'feminine', childish, comic Hitler described by Lewis in *The Hitler Cult*.[35] In picking Margot as a mock-mother figure, the dwarf becomes the disturbing emblem of the monstrosity born of weakness that masquerades as strength (of Victor's inferiority complex and Margot's submissive passion). In this 'preposterous exhibition' of '*a public orphan*', the dwarf is 'free to insult or to hector, having paid the price of extreme deformity', and Margot finds herself 'to her horror' responding, feeling she is holding the 'infant' in her arms. She is led to think what it would be like if she and Victor were to give birth, 'out of their misery', to such an infant, a 'crooked monstrosity' which 'bellowed incessantly', and knows instinctively that she would love it even more because of its ugliness. The effect of this vision on Margot is traumatic. Becoming 'unconscious' of the rest of the company, she pushes down her rational self and allows this 'evil madonna' to come grinning to the surface, bringing the 'submerged tenth' of her character into action (*Revenge for Love*, pp. 295–305).

Towards the end of the novel, we are increasingly aware of the extent to which Margot and Victor are engaged in desperate play-acting, whilst those with real power alternately deride and exploit them. The 'brutal invasion of the external plane by the internal plane' makes their stereotypical male–female roles seem more and more automaton-like and futile – Victor as 'he-man' narrowing his eyes and squaring his jaw, Margot despairingly playing the part of 'the opposite number to the masterful male' (or, as Mateu sees it, the part of the 'dirty little fascist doll') in an effort to save Victor's life. In the end, Margot is as helpless as Mateu's image implies – dedicated to a man whose primitive male potency is swallowed up by the mindless mechanism of the motor car. Margot detests this 'muscular machine', carrying her forward by means of 'unceasing explosions', whereas Victor, of course, identifies himself as closely with this 'horrible machine' as Ahmed identified with his horses – 'But men will be men', Margot sighs (pp. 324–5).

Bearing much more responsibility for the final débâcle – though scarcely a successful man of power – Percy Hardcaster is active in the behind-the-scenes efforts to manipulate the doomed 'strong man'. Physically the antithesis of the romantic hero, Percy has the political ambitions and pretensions that Victor lacks. This 'big fat English kid of forty, in the Revolution game', with his flushed, corpulent face – and with 'a frown like a fretful pram-pushed protagonist of the nursery' – is from the beginning seen as a caricature of imperious male power in relation to the self-abasement of the charitable female – in the first instance, of a determinedly helpful nun (pp. 23, 189). With his 'upright cynicism' Percy turns this and the other events of his Spanish Civil War experience into 'atrocity propaganda' for politically fashionable English drawing rooms (p. 375). Having acquired a wooden leg in the service of the cause, he becomes a red patriarch, reclining in his invalid magnificence and pointing his artificial limb at 'an impressive grouping of salon reds' which is cowed and almost frightened by this 'man-of-action' (pp. 148–50). Those who surround him are heavily satirised versions of other self-romanticising aspects of male power – Tristram Phipps, whose 'genius' expresses itself in talking revolution with young chaps from Oxford in a flat above the sewers; the elemental Jack Cruze, a 'natural' force who stands for male violence and thuggery; Abershaw, described as a conjurer but in truth only a master of a 'manipulative deftness' in politics that amounts to trickery and deceit; Sean O'Hara, another performer and magician, whose dark, hairy body comes 'bang out of the repertory of a sagaman – where the physical assumes a symbolic importance' (pp. 95–6, 166, 133).

It is through the women, however, that the false posturing of Hardcaster and the other male characters is revealed. The sexual dimension of their power is more inherently absurd than the stereotypical romance of Victor and Margot. So, for example, Sean O'Hara's wife Eileen romanticises, in Lawrentian fashion, the vitality of Ireland's primitive culture. Though Sean in fact tries to impersonate an Englishman, Eileen yearns to identify with the 'romantically provoked', 'beautiful shootings' of Ireland, even though she has her romantic images trampled underfoot as Sean works to readjust romance and reality (pp. 134–5). She sees him as importing the melodramatic politics of the Fenian into humdrum surroundings, though what he actually embodies is the capacity for political treachery essential in a thief and an informer.

More centrally, Lewis develops the role of Tristram's wife Gillian, representative of modern women intellectuals who can 'talk Red politics with the best', but nonetheless wholly at the mercy of male humbug (p. 108). Although woman as an outsider (Margot) can act as an innocent eye, seeing through male pretence, Lewis does not credit women in general with any special insight – and, in a world of deceit, the new woman, priding herself on her superior insights, is in fact most likely of all to be taken in and, if disenchanted, unceremoniously discarded. Involved with both primitive violence (Jack Cruze) and parlour charisma (Percy Hardcaster), Gillian is 'the Aphrodite of the Sewers' (p. 116). There is a grotesque and comic account of Jack's efforts to woo Gillian with the equipment of the male chauvinist swine, sticking out 'his muzzle of cave-man indigo' and giving her a kiss imaged in such a way that it becomes a parody of sexual violence: the 'scarlet pout' of her mouth is like 'something split open'; Jack pushes his mouth into the 'wet cut' (pp. 119–20). It is a relationship that (we are explicitly reminded) mocks Lawrentian clichés, with Gillian, who knowingly plays the 'little innocent girl' attracting the satyr, the 'pagan soul', who crows like a rooster (pp. 200–2). Gillian's flirtation with Percy is stimulated by left-wing chic and hero worship rather than primitive physicality – and it is here, most of all, that we see she is as vulnerable as any Lawrentian new woman to delusions of perspicacity. Pressed against Percy's 'sick leg', Gillian responds in the stock female way to a tale of male heroic action and suffering – a tear standing in her eye, indulging her feelings of 'lofty horror' and 'proud indignation' as she gazes sternly 'at this man who had been broken upon the Spanish rack in the interests of *étâtisme* and Dictatorship' (pp. 148–52). Percy, hot and short of breath, is so out of his element in his amorous role that he is decidedly nonplussed when Gillian engages him in suggestive 'Jackish dialogue'. It is Percy's feeling that he is being 'drawn into the Jack-business in spite of himself' that precipitates the revelations which completely demolish the 'Percy' to whom Gillian imagines herself to be attracted. As he dismantles every detail of the propagandistic narrative he has given to her and his other admirers, he turns into 'something else', no longer the hero of the barricades. What Gillian is caught out in is not only a romantic misjudgement but an ideological inconsistency. As Percy impresses upon her, heroism itself is a bourgeois notion with no place in the Communist world view: ' "But do you get worked up about heroes!" he protested, in a tone of heavy mock-astonishment. "I thought you were a Communist." ... "You make Communism seem very dull", Gillian yawned . . . .' But even if she accepts that there is no place in the Communist vocabulary for the 'showy and cheap' sentiments of the hero-worshipper, Gillian is left with a problem of identity – ' "But who are *you*?" ' (pp. 203–10).

Lewis is not only ridiculing the inconsistencies of salon revolutionaries but is exposing both the indispensability and the essential hollowness of the charismatic figure. However 'superior' she may seem, Gillian's commitment to the cause contains (under its 'false bottom') a wish to be ravished by the dynamic heroic male. She has been 'kissing *ideas*', and her desires will not be fulfilled by a fat man without a heroic exploit to his name. Percy has 'debunked [Gillian's] little romance' by forcing upon her the shocking recognition that she has 'slobbered over this wounded *hero* of a little bricklayer'. Gillian ends by recognising the dishonesty of the politics she has embraced in her longing for a grander and more exciting form of public life. But she is unable to tell her husband the truth about what happened to 'his little god', or to explain why she has turned out to be 'barren soil' for 'the words of wisdom of the infallible Percy Hardcaster': romantic political delusions are powerful and persistent (pp. 211–14, 226–31).

UNSUBMISSIVE WOMEN

Virginia Woolf, too, satirises political delusions, but the focus of her attack and the kind of imagery she deploys are determined by her prioritising of feminist issues. Bewildered kitchen maid, transfixed rabbit and invisible outsider – in the final section of Woolf's *Three Guineas*, these are three of the central images of the woman in relation to patriarchal power structures. Asking men to 'look from our angle', Woolf considers the implications of each image: the submission, separation and silence of the maid, representing women as an underclass; the complete immobilisation of the fascinated rabbit, exposed to the full 'illumination' of male power; the self-effacement and isolation of the female outsider who is anxious neither to arouse male antagonism nor to fall under the spell of male power. These themes – subservience, obedience and exclusion – recur, as they are bound to do, in the writings of Woolf and the other women of the time who are looking seriously, whether in fiction or non-fiction, at the question of how women can do anything other than submit to what plainly seems, in the mid thirties, the disaster-bound male domination of the political world. This is a period, however, when interest in feminist issues had considerably diminished, and militant women are therefore less numerous than one might expect. As one leading feminist of the time wrote: 'Modern young women know amazingly little of what life was like before the war, and show a strong hostility to the word "feminism" and all which they imagine it to connote.'[36] Woolf thus writes not only to rebuke men but to rally women, embedding her discussion of the threat of fascism within a vigorously feminist analysis of the position of women. The indirectness of her response to the international crisis reflects a belief at the heart of her view of fascist aggression and dictatorship: that is, that political tyranny and the subjugation of women are rooted in the same barbaric maleness; domestic bullying, the patriarchal organisation of society and the more violent forms of political oppression are all, she argues, manifestations of masculine assumptions and values.

Similar challenges had been issued at the time of the First World War. The suffragist Helena Swanwick, for example, maintains (in *Women and War*) that 'Prussianism' – a name invented by the British for the doctrines of a hated enemy – is in truth 'the very doctrine with which our British Anti-Suffragists have made us very familiar during the past ten years'. Her contention is that one can legitimately label as 'Prussian' all states organised on a militarist basis and dominated by male conceptions of honour, glory and adventurous combat. Other pacifist and feminist writers of the First World War period, such as Mary Sargant Florence and Catherine Marshall, also stress the close connection between militarism and the oppression of women. It is arguments such as these that Woolf extends in her more wide-ranging polemic.[37]

Three Guineas is in the form of an answer to three letters requesting subscriptions to aid with the rebuilding of a women's college, to support a society for assisting professional women in obtaining employment, and to help prevent war. The third section addresses most directly the question of women's role in the preservation of peace and the protection of culture and of intellectual liberty. It opens with the suggestion that for men to ask the advice and support of women in such matters is analogous to the Duke of Devonshire stepping down into the kitchen and asking the maid who is peeling potatoes to construe a difficult passage in Pindar: 'would not Mary be surprised and run screaming to Louisa the cook, "Lawks, Louie, Master must be mad!"' We are meant to see, to begin with, the sheer improbability of the master, in the normal course of events, 'descending' to ask Mary's views on anything other than potatoes (any more than Ahmed or Don Ramón would have turned to their respective women for advice on how to run political affairs). Mary's astonishment at being consulted is a comic reflection of women's disbelief that they could have anything of value to contribute – 'we who have been shut out from the universities ... we who are, in fact, members ... of the ignorantsia'. The imagined scene fixes our attention on Mary in her kitchen as woman in her separate sphere, under the guardianship of entrenched male power, here with the addition of strong class and educational differences 'below stairs', reinforcing the impression that those confined to such a sphere would be incapable of making judgements about matters of importance to their male masters.[38]

Earlier in *Three Guineas*, Woolf cites the accusations of C.E.M. Joad and H.G. Wells that women are apathetic and indifferent. Joad, she says, has accused young women of being more politically apathetic than at any time during the last half-century, and has suggested that if they are unwilling to give their time and money to the cause of peace they should 'give up the pretence of playing with public affairs and return to private life'; Wells has charged that 'There has been no perceptible woman's movement to resist the practical obliteration of their freedom by Fascists or Nazis.' To counter such arguments, Woolf produces a detailed case not only for recognising women's complete subordination and disadvantages in terms of position and salary in the work place but for acknowledging how widespread is the male view that the proper place of women is either in domestic service or 'in decent homes' (a contention supported by three extracts from the *Daily Telegraph*). There is in these quotations, she writes, 'the egg of the very same worm that we know under other names in other countries' – in embryonic form, the fascist dictator who believes that he has the God-given right to tell others what to do. Juxtaposed with the *Daily Telegraph* pieces is a German pronouncement about the natural rightness of separate spheres – 'the world of men and the world of women'. The views of a male-dominated English society all too closely echo the Nazi wish to attain 'the most holy thing in the world, the woman as maid and servant'.[39] Woolf moves towards the conclusion that the fascist threat is equally 'here among us', and that a woman's obligation to fight fascist oppression should lead her, in the first instance, to fight patriarchal oppression in England itself, 'to crush him in our own country' before attempting to crush him abroad. As she develops her argument, however, what she most forcefully establishes is the continuing exclusion of women from all of the rights and privileges which would give them any real power within the society. In reality, the distance is still as great between the woman's sphere and the world of male power as between the kitchen and the dukedom.

The political contribution of women seems to be confined to the role of the adoring audience for male ceremonies – the sort of thing Vera Brittain has in mind when she writes of the glamour and magic of war delirium which, while it lasts, has more compelling power than any other emotion; or that Ruskin presumably had in mind when he pictured women as war's audience and catalyst ('all women like to hear of [men] fighting . . . . This is a fixed instinct in the fine race of them.').[40] The figure of 'Man' as 'the quintessence of virility', eyes glazed and braced in a martial pose, 'tightly cased in a uniform', adorned with medals and other 'mystic symbols', carrying a sword – 'in German and Italian Führer or Duce; in our own language Tyrant or Dictator' – is evoked by Woolf to demonstrate the inseparable connection between the tyrannies and servilities of private and public worlds (*Three Guineas*, pp. 162–3). The patriarch, dictating to the women of his own country, coalesces in the mind's eye with the image of the dictator imposing his will on all who are weaker. But more than this, recognising the nature of this composite enemy is essential if people are not to be 'passive spectators doomed to unresisting obedience', rather than people capable of changing the oppressive figure, both in the public and the private spheres (pp. 130–2). As in *The Plumed Serpent* or the desert romance, the key question is whether the woman will submit or resist, but in Woolf, of course, it is the methods of resistance rather than the joy of submission that she wishes to teach. How is woman to escape the role of unresisting obedience? Clearly, it is 'not by joining your society but by remaining outside' (p. 164).

143

The implicit question is whether women can act politically without either angering men or succumbing to their political assumptions. Is it possible to avoid arousing male anxieties about the female challenge to their domination? Woolf suggests that women's resistance must go ahead quietly and secretly, since it is tactless to criticise your 'master'. With his ear to the ground, an observer such as Wells might believe 'that a movement is going forward, not altogether imperceptibly, among educated men's daughters, against the Nazi and the Fascist': there is a gulf between the sexes, a gulf 'of silence . . . inspired by fear', and those who are economically dependent have reason to be cautious (pp. 137–8). For women to raise awkward questions about their status, or to assert themselves, is to arouse primitive male fears: 'powerful and subconscious motives' raise the hackles of the 'old savage', of the patriarch who craves the siren, of 'dominance craving for submission'. These are 'ancient and obscure emotions' which are responsible for the limitation of freedom both in the private house and the public world (pp. 147–8). At the same time, however, women must be wary of complicity. Woolf vividly represents the danger of being put under the spell of male power, of being made part of the system that produces violence and oppression. To 'join your society', whether literally or metaphorically, is to 'merge our identity in yours; follow and repeat and score still deeper the old worn ruts'. Woolf sees in public life a magnification of the most oppressive human impulses. The conglomeration into societies releases all that is most selfish, most violent and least rational; it inflates, in place of private brother, a monstrous male. This public male is loud-voiced and hard-fisted, penning human beings within arbitrary boundaries, decorating himself like a savage, going through mystic rites and enjoying 'dubious pleasures of power and dominion', his women passively adoring him whilst confining their own influence to the private sphere of the house. From this it is evident, Woolf argues, that women should not join with men, so merging their identities with them, but should remain as a society of Outsiders. For such outsiders, indifference is the proper response to an instinct for martial glory and patriotic pride. Women, she argues, are debarred by their sex from understanding the satisfaction that fighting provides for men. They may well have a romantic notion of their country's superiority and indulge in 'patriotic' emotions, but if the intelligent women Woolf addresses use their reason to grasp how little they, as women, will benefit from national success, they will realise that they should absent themselves from all political demonstrations and military displays (pp. 120–6).

The argument of *Three Guineas* rests very heavily on Virginia Woolf's conception of the relationship between private and public life, and it is here, not surprisingly, that she seems most in danger of reaching a familiar impasse. One of the main feminist objections to fascism, as we have seen, is to the way it consigns women to a separate sphere, excluding them from the realms of power. As Winifred Holtby says in an article of the mid thirties, Mosley's declarations concerning sexual difference ('we want men who are men and women who are women') are 'characteristic of that Fascist inclination to dream of an eclectic Olympus of virile he-men . . . separated sharply from all lower forms of being'.[41] And yet, as Woolf implies, women want to be able to assert private and personal values against political ones – inevitably raising the question of whether this can be done without conforming to male stereotype (women as women) and without paying the price of powerlessness. Addressing the same question that Woolf confronts in *Three Guineas*, Vera Brittain (in 'Can the Women of the World Stop War?') similarly expresses the view 'that a civilisation in which military values prevail is always hostile to women's interests'; she argues that the 'new element' of women in politics might stand some chance of resisting the male impulse to revert to primitive impulse, and exhorts the 'inert mass of lethargic womanhood' to stop absorbing themselves so completely in their own domestic affairs and to accept 'the moral obligation to be intelligent'; unlike Woolf, however, she urges women both to support peace organisations and to use 'the ordinary machinery of politics' to resist the movement towards war.[42] In the contrast between Brittain's call for political activism and Woolf's more separatist arguments, we see a conflict that has obviously not been resolved in subsequent feminist debate, with those who want to diminish the distance between politics and feminism seeing a danger that emphasis on the intuitive and emotional in the female character and on the gap between 'your methods' and 'ours' will simply confirm male stereotypes; that, in distancing themselves from conventional political life, women are actually playing into the hands of the masculine ideology they castigate. Certainly, in the context of so anxious a time, it was not easy for the self-declared outsider to convince her critics that what she proposed constituted responsible involvement in the most pressing public issues. Q.D. Leavis, for example, in a well-known review, accuses Woolf of being unacquainted with the realities of life, of 'not living in the contemporary world', of trying 'to make a weapon of feminine inconsequence'. Even very favourable reviews, like that of Theodora Bosanquet, while finding revolutionary force and prophetic vision in

145

the book, are inclined to the view that 'the world may have to wait a long time' for the fulfilment of the prophecy.[43] And even Woolf herself, in a footnote, seems to accede to the view that the necessary changes in 'hereditary constitution' and in the conception of manhood and womanhood may, in Huxley's phrase, be 'an affair of millennia, not of decades' (*Three Guineas*, p. 205).

The long perspectives thrown open by such speculations find natural fictional expression in fantasies of biological mutation, either utopian or dystopian. Thus Rebecca West, for example, plays with the question of whether women, as outsiders, can affect the course of political life in the whimsical fantasy of *Harriet Hume*, in which an idealised intuitive woman has been gifted with a kind of second sight, enabling her to act as the conscience of a man of power. The man on whom she exercises her remarkable skill is Arnold Condorex, the embodiment of vigorous male power, as forceful as a 'great horse' galloping unstoppably. Men follow him because of his 'proud disposition to accept vast challenges'; his advancement is 'sacred' to him and he thinks of his own face as being like a marble bust, his 'official' body having become 'somewhat dead' in thick ceremonial clothes.[44] Looking, in his rigidity, like a Japanese representation of a great warrior, he is emblematic of the desire to form links with a well-ordered society. A charismatic figure who can sway large meetings, Condorex has a voice that soars with serene confidence. Beneath the gentleman's dress and rhetoric, however, there is scheming and betrayal, and it is this hidden side of the man that can be seen by Harriet Hume. Harriet possesses a rival power, though one which she exercises only in the private sphere. Being, by a 'miracle of thought', able to see into the mind of Condorex, she can penetrate his hypocrisy and disguise – and has at least the potential power to shame and reform him, to modify his political methods by means of a non-rational female faculty (pp. 32, 57). As well as being, in more ordinary human terms, the woman Condorex sacrifices to his political career, Harriet symbolises the moral qualities he rejected to pursue his ambitions – his conscience and 'some principle' that she seems to embody. Perhaps, he thinks, she stands for love, truth, justice or poetry (p. 93). There is an implicit contrast between Harriet and those women who listen spellbound to Condorex the public orator. What she hears is the politician's 'inner speech': ' "It is a very odd thing", he thought, "but she looks as if she were listening to some sound I cannot hear" ' (p. 151). The reversal of the conventional power relationship does not require Harriet to take on a masculine role, but only (while looking perfectly submissive) to be 'vigilant' through the exercise of this very feminine gift. In the end, however, these reversals confirm a female power which has little positive force in the real political world, and Harriet herself recognises that she has been living in a sphere of life in which the compromises of actual power are not demanded of her: ' "I may have been innocent, but I was also impotent." ' She has not been able to establish her heightened understanding 'as the accepted order of life', and therefore ' "I should be churlish if I blamed those who have the power I lacked, and went out into the world, and did what they could . . . to govern it" ' (pp. 266–8). Her innocence has been impotence and smugness, whereas his overbearing masculinity and inner betrayals have at least been part of an effort to achieve something in the world.

It would have to be said, I think, that not only Harriet's fey talent but the whole of West's gentle and fanciful tale seems remote (as deliberately remote, perhaps, as any fairy-story) from the actualities of political life between the wars. The later, much darker fantasy of Katharine Burdekin's *Swastika Night*, on the other hand, imagines a mutation that projects the very worst possibilities for women that fascist oppression might be seen to hold. This future-world transformation is again an accentuation (rather than a diminishment) of sexual difference, in this instance an ultimate biological response to the suppression and humiliation of women. Burdekin's dystopian narrative is in fact a plot virtually *without* women, almost all of the females of the species having disappeared completely from human social–political life, becoming as invisible and subhuman in reality as they previously were in the masculinist ideology of Nazi Germany. Sustained by an entirely male religion which venerates Hitler as a godlike figure, the future world enshrines as its chief values phallic pride, courage, brutality, bloodshed, ruthlessness and other soldierly and heroic virtues. Like *Three Guineas*, *Swastika Night* makes clear the connection between private and public conduct, with 'female' values disregarded and women reduced to their reproductive roles in both the domestic and the political spheres. Unlike Woolf, however, Burdekin to a considerable extent dissociates Britain from the unbalanced patriarchal thinking that animates Nazism. Whereas the English are, by nature, 'sturdy heretics' who 'are hard to move to dubiously moral courses by spiritual pressure', the German character, she suggests, seems given to moral cowardice and spiritual panic; also, the British Empire was the result of little more than restless roving, whereas German imperialism had at its core an ethos of conquest and virile militarism which assumed the inferiority of both women and subject races. It is the abandonment of the liberal humanist ideals of independent judgement and individuality which has made possible the true, unspoken nature of this extreme example of a male-dominated political system.[45]

The narrative centres on the struggles of the archetypal Englishman, Alfred, and of an honourable German Knight, von Hess, to discover the truth behind the propaganda of a Nazi future world. Amongst the most important of the questions they confront concerns the original motive for the 'Reduction of Women'. Von Hess suggests that the power of choice and rejection is too considerable a right for a thoroughgoing masculinist regime to tolerate. Considerable influence is attributed to 'von Weid's book', which Burdekin based on the early twentieth-century writings of Otto Weininger, who, in *Sex and Character* (1903), provided one of the best-known schemes of sexual dualism – man as the active shaper of the formless nothingness of woman, man as subject, woman as object, man as reason and activity, woman as emotion and passivity. Under the influence of von Weid, German males 'wanted *all* women to be at their will like the women of a conquered nation'; the Women's Worship teaches 'humility, blind obedience and submission to men' (pp. 79–81). In the world of *Swastika Night*, masculine power thus becomes equivalent to legally sanctioned rape. Motherhood itself comes to be a privilege conferred by male power, with women reminded of 'the Lord Hitler's supreme condescension in allowing them still to bear men's sons and have that amount of contact with the Holy Mystery of Maleness . . .' (pp. 8–9). With women denied all control of their own lives, their reproductive powers and their offspring, their total loss of self-respect produces a form of reverse eugenics – in the first instance, a physical degeneration of women (who are no longer 'as beautiful and desirable as boys') and ultimately a drastic fall in the number of female births (pp. 11–12). Burdekin's satire differs from the other anti-totalitarian dystopias of the period in its focus on totalitarianism as a wholly masculine cult of power. But, like the other dystopian novelists, she creates her future world by extrapolating the psychological effects of an all-encompassing power structure, with those affected largely unaware of the transformations imposed by a monolithic system: 'they were no more *conscious* of boredom or imprisonment or humiliation than cows in a field' (p. 158).

Burdekin is one of those who most forcefully makes the case for understanding the possible extent of women's complicity in their own 'reduction', with future-world women submitting, she implies, just as German women did in the thirties by giving themselves over to the male-dominated ideal of Nazism: when Hitler wanted to impose a new pattern of living on women, 'they were wildly enthusiastic about him and everything he did' (p. 110). Women are judged an easily hypnotised audience, and female passivity and acquiescence in male-dominated decision-making are construed by men as a willing acceptance of female subjugation: 'Women will always be exactly what men want them to be . . . they are only a reflection of men' (p. 70). The analogy with domestic life is strongly underlined. Women's acceptance of the fanatical theories of von Weid is seen as just one further example of female obedience to male wishes: once convinced that utter self-abasement was what men wanted, women threw themselves into it with enthusiasm, rejoicing in their hideous uniforms and pulling out their front teeth. Burdekin's own line of argument is that if women are to be something other than 'an incarnate desire to please men', the acceptance of difference must not entail acceptance of inferiority. Unless each thing believes itself the best form, it is a 'crime against life', such as was committed in prehistorical 'tribal darkness'. Women only live according to 'an imposed pattern' if 'they are not *themselves*'; they have sacrificed their identities in their acceptance of men's idea of their inferiority, and 'the pliancy of woman is the tragedy of the human race' (pp. 106–9).

The emphasis in Woolf and Burdekin on the connections between patriarchy and fascism draws attention to the very explicit sexual assumptions of fascist ideology. Many looked to socialism to provide a system under which a belief in equality would end patriarchy and erase the divisions between the sexes. This possibility seemed to be strengthened by such things as Lenin's decree affirming women's right to self-determination in economic, social and sexual matters. Writing in 1949, Simone de Beauvoir could still hope that, even though a change in women's economic situation was not in itself enough to transform her place in society, this factor 'has been and remains the basic factor in her evolution', and such a change might be obtained were the promises of the Soviet Revolution to be fulfilled. In fact, though, Communism ultimately proved no less oppressive, and it became clear that the extreme Left had by no means achieved an end to the oppression of women. De Beauvoir, for example, writing more than two decades after the publication of *The Second Sex*, recognised that she had been wrong in thinking 'that the problems of women would resolve themselves automatically in the context of socialist development.'[46] One of the main prophets of the Soviet 'sexual revolution' was Alexandra Kollontai, who tried to combat the hypocritical double standard and the inequalities of 'bourgeois' sexual ethics. She was opposed, as well, to 'the vulgar "communist" notions of sex, unadorned by emotions', championing instead a new sexual morality of 'comradeship, equality, work, collectivism, communal living and child care'.[47] She met, however, with much opposition, both personal and political, and, denounced as bourgeois and decadent by a Soviet regime that was moving instead towards reconstruction of the traditional family ideal, Kollontai left Russia in 1922. In the following year, she published *A Great Love*, which builds its story around Lenin's affair with Inessa Armand, who was, like Kollontai, one of the leading radical voices in Bolshevik discussions of sexual politics. Kollontai's novel explores the connections between personal and public life and the position of women in the revolution – the subordination of their needs to those of the men in the movement, no matter how they struggled to integrate sexual and revolutionary politics.

Set in the period before the revolution, when Lenin and other exiled Bolsheviks were living in France, *A Great Love* begins by asking its readers to see the relevance of its story to the 'new world' that has now dawned in Russia. The Lenin figure, Senya, is worshipped by the young and ardent Natasha, with feelings of reverence 'like pagan people experienced when worshipping *their* idols'. But this is no woman absorbed wholly in the personal life; she is herself a dedicated intellectual, writing an 'ambitious book' and capable of being 'completely carried away by her work'. Before their affair, Senya's effect on her has been to stimulate her belief in herself – to urge her on to new heights of political commitment, 'striding up a steep mountain path'. As their relationship develops, however, his disparaging references to her work for the Party ('They'll manage very nicely without you.') bring home to her the strength of male prejudice.[48] He dismisses her problems as trivial, and she feels 'constantly undermined by him' (*A Great Love*, pp. 50–3). His emphasis on his own needs and disregard of hers fills her with self-doubt. Like many a lady intellectual, she begins to suspect that he might not want her for her mind alone. What if he had only pretended to take her intellect seriously and to value her political work because she was 'his woman' and his property? Even though he theoretically wants – and repeatedly reassures her of – 'complete equality between us', he seems constitutionally incapable of seeing her as an integrated human being. He sees her only 'in profile, never head-on as a whole person, as she really was'. When she tries to make him understand her sense of humiliation, she meets only insensitive complacency and incomprehension (pp. 128, 63).

Ingrained masculine responses, however, only account for some of the difficulty faced by the would-be independent woman. 'She was, as always, considering his needs first': Natasha's own impulse to sacrifice herself to Senya's needs as the great figure of power in revolutionary circles in itself goes some way towards explaining why he attaches 'absolutely no importance at all to her work' (pp. 32–4). In one sense, Natasha is locked in combat with another woman. Anyuta, Senya's wife, who tries desperately to control her husband by awakening guilt and pity (repeatedly attempting suicide) corresponds, like Carlota in *The Plumed Serpent*, to the traditional image of the devoted wife, unable to 'stand alone in the world', and so dedicated to her private, domestic role that she fails to see the importance of her husband's Party work – 'Natasha understood this, of course, which was why she was always so self-effacing' (*A Great Love*, p. 49). Natasha's selfless determination to protect Senya and sustain him in his difficult role leads her to throw herself into the task of being 'his consolation, his ray of hope, his one and only joy'. But when she goes secretly to 'G'ville' to be with him and is forced to hide her presence, her stay in the hotel becomes 'a kind of voluntary incarceration', and she begins to feel the cost of regarding him as a 'pasha' and 'surrendering her name and identity when she went incognito to meet him'. It is at this stage that she realises how far her own position – imprisoned, silenced and secretly aggrieved – is becoming indistinguishable from that of a long-suffering wife. Senya indeed exclaims that she reminds him of Anyuta, and she herself begins 'to understand something of what Anyuta must have been feeling, and what made her act so hysterically'. Even their rooms at the hotel, chosen by Natasha, image the wholly traditional inequality that their relationship has settled into – Senya's the brighter, more spacious room, Natasha's 'a little dog-kennel of a room', in which she endlessly waits for Senya to 'burst in' unexpectedly (pp. 92–4, 78). The end of the affair, with the independent woman refusing any longer to act as a prop for the 'spoilt' man of power and instead throwing herself into her own work, is represented as a lesson to insensitive men, but is clearly also intended to stiffen women's resolve to define their own political identities – not, as in Woolf, by taking up the role of invisible outsiders but by becoming an individual voice within the male-dominated world of the revolutionary movement: 'Now she belonged body and soul to her work. Long, long ago she had felt a great love, but that love had ebbed away. Semyon Semyonovich, in his heedless, male stupidity, had destroyed it' (pp. 133–4).

The woman in love, as de Beauvoir says, 'will try to rise above her situation as inessential object by fully accepting it'; the independent woman, by being productive and active, will try to regain her transcendence and affirm 'her status as subject'.[49] Kollontai, in

A Great Love, delicately and touchingly explores this problematic transition from object to subject. As is apparent from her own exile and the suppression of her voice in Stalinist Russia, the energetic self-assertion of the female subject is by no means assured of success. Lenin reportedly said of Kollontai's marriage to a young sailor, 'I will not vouch for the reliability or endurance of women whose love affairs are intertwined with politics.'[50] For quite different reasons, of course, Kollontai herself was fully aware of the formidable difficulties created by the intertwining of sexuality and politics.

NOTES

1. Hitler *Mein Kampf* trans Murphy J. Hurst and Blackett 1939 p. 48; Hull E.M. *The Sheik* (1919) 1921 p. 181.
2. Mann T. *Mario and the magician* (1936) 1975 pp 565–6; Willner A.R. *The spellbinders* 1984 pp. 131–3.
3. See, for example, Brownmiller S. *Against our will: men, women and rape.* Bantam Books, New York 1976 and Helene Deutsch *The psychology of women* (2 vols.). Grune and Stratton, New York 1944–45, both discussed by Modleski T. *Loving with a vengeance* 1990 pp. 29–38; Paglia C. *Sexual personae* 1992 p. 2.
4. Reich W. *The mass psychology of fascism* (1946) 1991 p. 32; Arendt H. *The origins of totalitarianism* (1951) 1967 p. xxix.
5. Caplan J. Introduction to female sexuality in Fascist ideology. *Feminist Review* 1 1979: 60.
6. Koonz C. *Mothers in the Fatherland* 1988 pp. 53–67; Hitler, speaking to an old comrade, Ernst Hanfstängl, quoted by Koonz p. 66; Lindholm C. *Charisma* 1993 pp. 103–6.
7. Macciocchi M. Female sexuality in Fascist ideology. *Feminist Review* 1 pp. 67–82; see also Millett K. *Sexual politics* 1985 pp. 158ff.
8. Freud S. *Group psychology and the analysis of the ego* (1921). In *Civilization, society and religion* Penguin Freud Library 1991 vol. 12 pp. 154–60.
9. Lindholm *Charisma* pp. 46–7.
10. *Ibid.* pp. 44–7 and 183–7.
11. Willner *The spellbinders* p. 41; Warner R. *The cult of power* (1947) 1969 pp. 15–16; Ellen Wilkinson, *Peeps at politicians* (1930) pp. 38–40, quoted by Skidelsky R. *Oswald Mosley* 1981 pp. 163–4; and see Skidelsky pp. 331–3.
12. Melman B. *Women and the popular imagination in the twenties* 1988 pp. 46 and 90–1; Carey J. *The intellectuals and the masses* 1992 passim.
13. Lindholm *Charisma* pp. 80–3; Melman *Women and the popular imagination* p. 8; and Koonz *Mothers in the Fatherland* pp. 75–6.
14. Lindholm *Charisma* p. 59.

15. West R. *The strange necessity* (1928) 1987 p. 320; Light A. *Forever England* 1991 pp. 160–2; Brittain V., While we remember (11 November 1932), in Brittain and Holtby *Testament of a generation* 1985 p. 211.
16. Holtby W., The wearer and the shoe (31 January 1930) and Shall I order a black blouse? (4 May 1934) in *Testament of a generation* pp. 65 and 170–1.
17. Robinson M.N. *The power of sexual surrender* (1959) p. 158, quoted by Millett *Sexual politics* p. 206.
18. Cockburn C. *Bestseller* 1972 p. 129.
19. Melman *Women and the popular imagination* pp. 102–3; Light *Forever England* pp. 175–6.
20. Lindholm, *Charisma* pp. 101, 206–25.
21. It is, however, only partly true to say – as Melman (*Women and the popular imagination* p. 90) does – that Diana is 'politically emancipated, economically independent and sexually uninhibited'. In spite of her 'masculine' independence, she is the very image of sexual repression.
22. Lawrence D.H., Cocksure women and hensure men (written 1928; *The Forum* January 1929), in *Selected essays* 1981 pp. 31–4.
23. Lawrence D.H., Surgery for the novel – or a bomb (*Vogue* 20 July 1928) in *Selected literary criticism* 1955 p. 116; others who have touched on the similarities between *The Sheikh* and *The Plumed Serpent* include Hilary Simpson, in *D.H. Lawrence and feminism* 1982, and Kate Millett, in *Sexual politics*.
24. Lawrence D.H. *Fantasia of the unconscious* (1921–22) 1986 pp. 108–10, 115, 187–93; de Beauvoir S. *The second sex* (1949) 1988 p. 249.
25. See, for example, Millett *Sexual politics* pp. 283–93 on *The plumed serpent* and The woman who rode away; Simpson H. *D.H. Lawrence and feminism* pp. 13–17.
26. Lawrence D.H. *The plumed serpent* (1926) 1990 pp. 73–4 and 446–7; Cocksure women, in *Selected essays* p. 31.
27. See de Beauvoir *Second sex* p. 254.
28. Lawrence, Blessed are the powerful, in *Reflections on the death of a porcupine* 1988 p. 327; de Beauvoir *Second sex* p. 245.
29. Lawrence D.H., letters to Huxley, October 1928 and to Ottoline Morrell, 5 February 1929, in *Selected literary criticism* pp. 146–7; and Lawrence D.H., Preface to *Bottom dogs*, in *Selected literary criticism* pp. 411–12.
30. Lewis W. *Snooty Baronet* 1932 pp. 91–9; Lewis W. *Paleface* 1929 pp. 174–97.
31. Huxley A. *The olive tree* 1947 pp. 208–32.
32. Huxley A. Greater and lesser London (October 1931) in *The hidden Huxley* 1994 p. 91; and see Bradshaw's Introduction pp. xvii-xix; Meyers J. *The enemy* 1980 pp. 191–2.
33. Huxley A. *Point counter point* (1928) 1994 p. 301; Huxley *The olive tree* pp. 203 and 233–7.
34. Lewis W. *Revenge for love* (1937) 1982 pp. 78–81, 184 and 358–9.
35. Lewis W. *The Hitler cult* 1939 pp. 78–9.
36. Strachey R. *Our freedom and its results* (1936), quoted in Marder H. *Feminism and art* 1968 p. 29 (and see pp. 26–30).

37. Swanwick H.M. *Women and war* (nd); Florence M.S., Marshall C. and Ogden C.K. *Militarism versus feminism*. *Writings on women and war* (1915); both quoted in Pick D. *War machine* 1993 pp. 149–51.
38. Woolf V. *Three guineas* (1938) 1986 pp. 98–101. .
39. Feder G., Die Deutsche Frau im dritten Reich (4 April 1932), quoted by Millett *Sexual politics* p. 163.
40. Brittain V., Why not a real peace crusade? (1934), in *Testament of a generation* p. 220; Ruskin J., War (1865), in *The crown of wild olive* quoted by Pick *War machine* p. 70.
41. Holtby W., Black words for women only (24 March 1934), in *Testament of a generation* p. 84.
42. See, for example, Toril Moi writing on Cixous, *Sexual/textual politics* 1993 pp. 123f; Brittain V., Can the women of the world stop the war? (February 1934), in *Testament of a generation* pp. 217–19.
43. Leavis Q.D. *Scrutiny* review of *Three guineas*, and Bosanquet T. *Time and Tide* review of *Three guineas*, in Majumdar R. and McLaurin (eds) *Virginia Woolf: The critical heritage* 1975 pp. 409–19 and 403.
44. West R. *Harriet Hume* (1928) 1980 pp. 79–94 and 112–16.
45. Burdekin K. *Swastika night* (1937) 1985 pp. 6, 79–80, 113–14, 134–5.
46. De Beauvoir *Second sex* pp. 733–4; Millett *Sexual politics* pp. 168ff; de Beauvoir S. *Simone de Beauvoir today. Conversations with Alice Schwartzer 1972–1982* (1984) quoted by Toril Moi *Sexual/textual politics* pp. 91–2.
47. Held J. *The cult of power* 1983 pp. 80, 87.
48. Kollontai A. *A great love* (1923) 1991 pp. 55, 33–9.
49. De Beauvoir *Second sex* pp. 653, 689.
50. Miller J. *Women writing about men* 1986 p. 138.

CHAPTER FOUR

Violence: The Thirties Thriller and 'The Gathering Storm'

You begin with the relations between Might and Right . . . . But, for the term 'might', I would substitute a tougher and more telling word: 'violence' . . . . Conflicts of interest between man and man are resolved, in principle, by the recourse to violence. It is the same in the animal kingdom, from which man cannot claim exclusion . . . . Very soon physical force was implemented, then replaced, by the use of various adjuncts . . . . Now, for the first time, with the coming of weapons, superior brains began to oust brute force, but the object of the conflict remained the same: one party was to be constrained, by the injury done him or the impairment of his strength, to retract a claim or a refusal. This end is most effectively gained when the opponent is definitely put out of action – in other words, is killed.

(Sigmund Freud, *Why War?*, September 1932)

Violence has often been equated with power: it is the ultimate kind of power, its essence, its most flagrant manifestation. Hobbes declared that 'covenants, without swords, are but words', Hegel that the state and war are structurally inseparable, Mao that power grows out of the barrel of a gun. Political theorists have repeatedly defined violence or 'naked power' as the final arbiter. In the main, however, it is a conclusion most reluctantly reached. As Freud wrote in his famous 'open letter' to Einstein, 'war runs most emphatically counter to the psychic disposition imposed on us by culture; we are therefore bound to resent war, to find it utterly intolerable'. It was only after the First World War that Freud had come to see human destructiveness as a primary phenomenon of life. As a humanist and pacifist, he tried, at the end of *Why War?*, to find some way of avoiding the implications of his own theories, which equated power with violence and explained violence in terms of an innate 'destructive instinct'. The concluding paragraphs expressed a hope that the development of civilisation might eventually achieve a constitutional repression of aggressive instincts. In the thirties, however, this looked like a slender basis for optimism. As Wyndham Lewis wrote in 1939, Hitler 'forces *us* to be *Kampfnaturen*'. Continental political developments led many to pose the question that Einstein put to Freud: was it possible that all efforts to find ways of 'delivering mankind from the menace of war' were doomed to 'lamentable breakdown'?[1]

The revulsion against violence combined with a recognition that 'the principle of force (i.e. war) was once more to come into its own'[2] is the central dilemma represented in the thrillers written before or just after Britain's entry into the Second World War. The most important thriller writers of the period – Graham Greene, Eric Ambler, Geoffrey Household – in many ways transformed the genre, and the 'seriousness' with which they are credited is most clearly manifested in their preoccupation with understanding the sources of violence, the relationship between violence and power and the nature of the opposition between civilised restraint and violent action. Whereas, in the 'sensational' thrillers of earlier and later periods, violence is very much taken for granted, their novels focus our attention on the humanistic doubts, uncertainties and moral contradictions created by the pressure to act violently. These are often narratives of reluctant aggression, constructed around the deferral or avoidance of violent action: an ordinarily human, non-heroic protagonist, a representative of normal, civilised decencies, is initiated into a violent world and confronted with the alternatives of engagement or retreat. In those plots which move towards a partially optimistic resolution, political responsibility is figured in an individual action which either, as in Household's *Rogue Male*, establishes a basis for justified violence or, as in Ambler's early thrillers, temporarily 'ends war'. In the darker thrillers of the period, in particular those of Graham Greene, anxieties are less easily allayed: the conventional moral reassurances of the thriller as a genre are more fully subverted, liberal humanist values are undermined and 'alien' violence flourishes in the midst of the 'civilised normality' of England itself.

In their narratives of reluctant engagement and in their explorations of the boundaries between civilised restraint and violent action, the thrillers of the late thirties and early forties mirror national misgivings about transforming Britain into a country capable of meeting continental violence. There was a well-established pre-First World War tradition of opposition to war and to militarism, but the war itself was regarded as the major catastrophe of modern times – 'the plunge of civilisation into this abyss of blood and darkness' – and was taken to epitomise all of the evils to be avoided in the future. The memory of the First World War greatly strengthened both pacifist feeling and the determination to keep Britain out of continental conflicts. Although it was also seen as a tragic culmination of late nineteenth-century developments, the war was primarily apprehended as an absolute experiential divide, what Rilke called 'the unnatural and terrible wall of the war', an event which so altered the perception of warfare itself that future wars became, for many, unthinkable. At the same time, the First World War had created the conditions which bred conflict – destabilising political systems, undermining economic viability and, by destroying nineteenth-century autocracies, preparing the way for twentieth-century dictatorships, with their ideological predisposition to violence. As the thirties drew to a close, the Wilsonian vision of a world 'made fit and safe to live in', assuring protection against 'force and selfish aggression', appeared to be an increasingly remote ideal. Conflict, brutality and the glorification of violence were at the heart of a fascist ideology which explicitly rejected traditional social values and the ethical codes associated with liberal humanism and democracy.[3]

In most British eyes, the phenomenon of fascism was foreign in every sense, the product of an utterly different society – of the aggression and professional militarism stereotypically associated with Germany as a nation, which was constructed as the embodiment of all that was non-English. The sense of English separateness is something that has very often been articulated. Although analyses of origins differ, the summarising judgement of a recent influential study of English individualism succinctly captures this belief in absolute difference and independence: 'it is not possible to find a time when an Englishman did not stand alone'.[4] But in the thirties, any reassuring sense of immunity was shadowed by a fear that to 'come together' with Germany in open conflict – to 'join battle' – would, as such language implies, diminish the gap imagined to separate the two countries. Perceived differences would be eroded. Orwell, as we have seen, anatomises, in 'Wells, Hitler and the World State', the habits of mind springing from 'the sheltered conditions of English life', leading her liberal humanist intellectuals to dissociate themselves – to the point of incomprehension – from the repellent, 'anachronistic' emotions aroused by fascist militarism. The difficulty was clear: 'Before you can even talk of world reconstruction, or even peace, you have got to eliminate Hitler, which means bringing into being a dynamic not necessarily the same as that of the Nazis, but probably quite as unacceptable to "enlightened" . . . people.'[5] The encounter with fascism, seen as a clash between humanity and brutality, raised the fundamental question of how 'humanity' was to stand against 'brutality' without itself being brutalised. Again and again, the political essays of the late thirties return to this immobilising contradiction. E.M. Forster, for example, wrote in 'The 1939 State':

> Intelligent and sensitive people are having a particularly humiliating time just now. Looking at the international scene, they see . . . that if Fascism wins we are done for, and that we must become Fascist to win. There seems no escape from this hideous dilemma and those who face it most honestly often go jumpy. They are vexed by messages from contradictory worlds, so that whatever they do appears to them a betrayal of something good; they feel that nothing is worth attempting, they drop their hands, break off in the middle with a shriek . . . . Their grasp on reality paralyses them.[6]

This 'hideous dilemma', with its humiliations, contradictions, betrayals and paralysis, is at the heart of the anti-fascist thriller. The development of the thriller has often been linked to the decline of Empire,[7] but in fact, in the late thirties and early forties, the usual perception was not of lost strength or of irreversible decline, but of a great world power which had an obligation to act on the international stage in a way which at least appeared to be consistent with the virtues of magnanimity and fair-mindedness. The crises of conscience represented by Greene, Ambler and Household reflect a national preoccupation with the problem of 'virtuous' action, represented either in general terms or in relation to the issues of disarmament, pacifism and conciliation, as opposed to rearmament and war.[8] Popular feeling against the use of military force was strong, with the anti-appeasers only gradually gaining ground towards the end of the decade. The non-militant Left, in particular, faced a moral quandary: an idealistic abhorrence of war and criticism of the British Government's decision to speed up rearmament were mingled with extreme ideological hostility to fascism and calls for action against it. Many vacillated between a commitment to halting fascism and a belief in the moral rightness of pacifism.[9] The contradictions and tensions besetting the Left are especially evident in the thrillers of Eric Ambler, but the novels that Graham Greene wrote during this period, though less partisan, are equally preoccupied with the moral perplexities of the English liberal response to mounting violence and cruelty. By the end of the decade, both Ambler and Greene can be seen to have moved, with the nation, towards war, creating characters who ultimately do respond with violence to the dangers posed by fascist aggression.

In the formulaic, sensational thrillers of, say, Sapper' (Herman McNeile) in the twenties and early thirties, or of Ian Fleming in the fifties and sixties, international tensions and ideological conflicts are embodied in elementary oppositions between Good and Evil – in contraries which lack the potential for conversion or change.[10] Although serious thrillers do not altogether avoid oversimplification, Manichean oppositions are at least in part replaced by distinctions which must *necessarily* break down if the contest of the thriller is to take place at all. E.M. Forster imaged liberal humanist values set against violent aggression as 'no stronger than a flower, battered beneath a military jackboot',[11] and his metaphoric pairing suggests some of the opposed terms which are most important in the construction of the serious thriller: vulnerable/tough; passive/active; non–aggressive/aggressive; powerless/powerful. The attributes of fascist aggression tend to remain fixed and antithetical to 'the good', but many anxiously doubted that it was possible, in combating the forces of what they saw as an evil and devious enemy, to rely on nothing more than fitness, skill, gallantry and honourable fighting ('the real, highest, honestest business of every son of man').[12] The fear is that, if he is to engage in action, the hero (or anti-hero) must take on at least some of the qualities of his adversaries, and the process of transformation is in itself traumatic, forcing the unwilling protagonist to traverse the shifting, uncertain terrain between the contradictory worlds of humanity and brutality.

The tension generated by the serious thriller almost invariably involves anxiety about loss of humanity. The protagonist's survival is threatened, but the threat is equally to his sense of human identity, defined both in terms of his own 'psychic disposition' and in terms of his connections with the culture which formed him – a culture of which he has become, by chance, the defender. Beyond mere self-preservation, his defensive aggression is an effort to avert the breaking up of cultural continuity. The 'salvation' towards which the plot of the thriller moves above all entails the rescue of a cherished culture from the threatened destruction of its traditions and core of values. Violent engagement in itself, however, disrupts the continuities which are being defended. Boundaries have been crossed, innocence lost: 'It was extraordinary how the whole world could alter after a single violent act.'[13] The protagonist is separated from his society, often classed as an outlaw and pursued by 'normality' as well as by the enemy.

In this alienated state, the protagonist comes to represent the feared schism in Englishness itself. Both structurally and in its recurrent patterns of imagery, the thriller expresses this sense of being divided from oneself, of paradoxically becoming what one is not. The structure commonly involves a peace-loving Englishman plucked from normality (his ordinary round of activities) by men who embody foreign violence. For most of the story he is himself non-violent, but the plot (both in a narrative and a political sense) will not release him until he has discovered a minimal capacity for effective action or has, in more pessimistic variations, suffered humiliation and defeat or death. This decent chap with a constitutional intolerance for war suddenly finds that essential elements in his identity are being distorted and that he is becoming a different person. The transforming effects of violence are metaphorically represented by processes which crucially alter a man's sense of himself – for example, by disease, rebirth and regression. He may be infected by contact with malignant aggression, undergo a process of rebirth into a violent world or suffer reduction to a level below that of civilised humanity. Beneath such casual phrases there are often complex assumptions about the nature of violence – evident as well in the way that psychologists and other academic commentators employ biological metaphors and organic explanations in their discussions of human violence. So, for example, a reliance on metaphors of disease can be intended to present violence as malignancy or abnormality springing from sadistic perversion or collective psychosis, or as a contamination of innate goodness. In contrast, the comparisons drawn in instinctivist explanations, which represent violence as stemming from our animal natures, are frequently brought into play in support of the argument that human violence is ultimately ungovernable, a lamentable but inevitable relapse into innate patterns of behaviour. Such images may also, of course, be used to extol violence, as in the romantic nihilist's assertion of kinship with sharks and tigers 'of well-known cruelty'. Even in their less extreme form, theories of our inborn animal aggression can, as Freud saw, serve as 'a biological justification for all those vile, pernicious propensities which we now are combating'.[14]

In the thriller as well, if less systematically, deployment of organic metaphors is closely related to the writer's underlying conception of violence and power. The polarised Good and Evil of the sensational thriller are commonly related to an opposition between natural and unnatural (psychopathic) violence and, even in the serious thriller, conventional imagery connoting psychological abnormality is retained to distinguish fascist violence (sadistic, brutal) from what Erich Fromm categorises as 'benign aggression'. The 'naturalness' of defensive aggression can, as in Household, be established by emphasising connections with the animal kingdom; conversely, the underplaying of man's animal aggression and the separation of the machinery of war from 'natural' destructive impulses, as in the early novels of Eric Ambler, can spring from an optimistic vision of power without violence. The comparative pessimism of Greene's thrillers is reflected in his use of disease imagery not just to delineate an alien psychopathology but to create an atmosphere in which the infection of violence has spread to those who had formerly thought themselves immune. Belief in a fundamental and universal aggressive capacity, in comparison to which English decency is merely superficial, can be established by a narrative that moves towards a meeting with primitive forces, as the protagonist is driven back by contemporary political circumstances to encounter destructiveness as a basic element in the human psyche. Thus, the recurrent metaphor of a birth into violence can imply a continuity of political violence with what is inborn and instinctual, with rebirth signifying the emergence of a new self able to engage in combat without the inhibitions and moral constraints of the overly civilised Englishman. The imagery of rebirth can also, however, be developed to suggest a transformation which amounts to innocent helplessness, complete disorientation in a hostile landscape and the inadequacy of humanistic preconceptions – as, for example, in Greene's image of the 'blind eyes' of the Spanish volunteers at the end of *Lawless Roads*, 'now beginning to open, like those of new-born children opening on the lunar landscape of the human struggle'; or in Arthur Rowe's childlike emergence, at the end of *Ministry of Fear*, into a world where there was 'all this talk of a man called Hitler . . . cruelty and meaninglessness . . . as if one had been sent on a journey with the wrong map'.[15]

HOUSEHOLD'S *ROGUE MALE*: 'A BEAST IN ITS DEN'

One of the simplest, most memorable narratives of 'the English dilemma' and of rebirth into a capacity for violence is Geoffrey Household's *Rogue Male*, in which descent to an animal level is integrally linked to the question of whether violence is an offence against natural law or an inevitable part of it. Published in 1939, *Rogue Male* is the first-person narrative of an unnamed 'sportsman'. At the beginning of the novel, he is stalking 'the biggest game on earth', the leader of a foreign power, who, though unidentified, is generally taken to be Hitler.[16] The narrator's hesitation at the crucial moment means that he is caught before he fires his shot. Having learned the secrets of endurance by spending his formative years at an English public school, he survives torture and escapes, only to realise that he is now an outlaw in his own country, hunted by agents of the enemy power and literally forced to go to ground.

The hero as metaphoric hunter is a familiar figure in the formulaic thriller: Sapper's Bulldog Drummond, for example, treats the hunting of villains as a particularly satisfying form of sport, entirely in keeping with natural morality. His novels progress towards a final hunt in which Drummond engages in a fight to the finish with his most despicable adversary.[17] In *Rogue Male*, the 'moral innocence' of the hunt, which implicitly makes killing acceptable, is called into question by the literalisation of the metaphor. The narrator is an *actual* hunter, and the question that he poses on the opening page of the novel is whether his sporting stalk of a great man can be seen as innocent of criminal intent. It is a question which involves definitions both of national ethics and of the human species itself. The stereotypical associations of sportsmanship are quite explicitly linked to the Englishness of the narrator: he is carrying a Bond Street rifle, not an assassin's weapon; given his English reticence about enquiring too closely into motives, he has not thought deeply about what he intends to do, but has simply embarked on the stalk in a spirit of adventure; there has been no cold-blooded planning and there is no hint of professional militarism; he is acting in the great British tradition of the chivalrous and high-minded amateur whose main concern is to obey the rules of the game. He describes the prey he hunts as a splendid specimen, 'a lone and magnificent male . . . a particularly fine head' (*Rogue Male*, pp. 15–16). The assumed opposition – the humanity of the hunter set against the animality of the prey – is in part what the narrator has failed to look into: his moment of hesitation is to do with a confrontation with the actual humanity of his victim, who is presented in decidedly human form, wearing a waistcoat and winding up a watch. The sportsman is, as he later observes, 'An embodiment of that myth of foreigners, the English gentleman, the gentle Englishman. I will not kill' (p. 129).[18] The remainder of the narrative, recorded in a journal in which he attempts to make his behaviour intelligible to himself, is an adventure of a wholly different kind, leading him ultimately to redefine his concept of human and animal and to reconsider his understanding of what Englishness excludes. This is achieved by going through a process of reduction, becoming, it seems to him, less than English and even less than human.

The plot calls these conventional distinctions into question by forcing the narrator to see himself defined as 'other'. Once he has become a hunted man, he can neither telephone nor enter his club. As much as anything, his own inner sense of guilt excludes him, given that he has begun to think of himself as a potential murderer, capable of killing in cold blood rather than self-defence. As the tensions of his predicament increase, the narrator becomes aware of the absurd incongruity between his capacity for aggression and the 'damned silly punctilious courtesy' that he knows he would show even to his most deadly enemy should he find himself in the same living-room. The inhibitions of the English gentleman make him preoccupied both with self-control and with the notion that the arch-villain may also be a reasonable man: a man who plays chess may, after all, be made to see sense. Echoing the delusion embodied in the Munich Agreement that a 'method of consultation' could be devised which would avert war with Hitler's Germany, the narrator says that he 'was obsessed with the idea of talking, not killing' (pp. 132, 137). Before he can come to understand himself as a man who will ultimately resort to violence, the narrator must also come to some understanding of how much he himself has repressed. One of the things he has repressed is a distinct reason for action, revenge for the death of the woman he loved, but this is only part of a long process of coming to terms with the non-rational in his nature.

The landscape in *Rogue Male* associated with the narrator's love – a hidden cleft in the Dorset downs – becomes the womb from which he ultimately re-emerges, psychologically equipped to face a world at war. From the very beginning of the pursuit, he experiences a loss of human status and identity, reduced by his captors to a mud-caked wreck who can only move forward on his belly, leaving a reptilian trail of slime and blood. This diminishment of his sense of self is carried much further, however, when he buries himself in the secret valley he had originally discovered in the regression of love. He burrows into the unmapped lane to escape his pursuers, and this Crusoe-like existence dominates the last half of the novel. As he sheds his social self in his lonely retreat, he begins to identify with the nameless and formless mass of 'the outlawed, the persecuted, the damned' (p. 30), but the erosion of his identity is more radical than this. An outlaw for whom national borders have suddenly become almost impossible to cross, he instead finds himself crossing the border of his species, until he himself becomes a 'rogue male'. He is, to begin with, morbidly anxious to assure himself that he is 'losing none of [his] humanity' (p. 108), but, as he perfects his burrow and works to obliterate all traces of himself, he finds that regression is inevitable. He inspects his face in the mirror, seeking a comforting image of his spiritual attributes, but sees only 'eyes fouled with earth . . . hair and beard dripping with blood-red earth'. He realises that he has even begun to think as an animal: 'Living as a beast, I had become a beast' (pp. 118, 135).

Compelled to recognise that 'man cannot claim exclusion' from the animal kingdom, the narrator gradually comes to terms with the implications of being at war. Conceiving of himself as 'the mandarin . . . the civilised, scrupulous sportsman', he has been consigned to the role of passive sufferer, immured in a 'temporary grave' which he compares to a dugout at Ypres; having seen himself more clearly, demoralisation is at an end and he can pass to a spiritual offensive (p. 154). To move from passivity to action is to accept the necessity of violence: at first, he writes, he just lies still underground, wanting no violence; by the end, however, his plans are directed towards 'a swift and deadly break-through into the lane', and he is 'at last able to admit that all [his] schemes for escaping without violence were impossible'. Symbolically, his weapon of escape is a bow fashioned by using the skin of a dead wild cat who has been his only companion: 'I realised that in his body was power' (pp. 161–2). In the tense scenes which culminate in the narrator killing his pursuer, Household explores in some detail the complex relationship with the enemy implied by a final recourse to violence. Quive-Smith, the enemy agent who has stalked him to his lair, is a blend of psychoanalyst and Nazi ideologue. The narrator reflects, 'if I killed him I could foresee nothing but murder on my conscience . . . . Psychologically I was at his mercy. My mind cowered' (pp. 141–2). As Quive-Smith tries to persuade the still-immobilised hero to sign a confession, amounting to a declaration of officially sanctioned aggressive aims, his inquisitorial techniques force the narrator's recognition of his true motives and intentions. However, as he moves towards realising his own capacity for aggression, he is still haunted by the problem of distinguishing himself from the enemy, and in this, although he readily dissociates himself from the 'usual morality play' of the English government, he must still cling uncertainly to the distinction between defensive and malignant aggression (p. 147). Quive-Smith, though a brave and clever man, is 'without – I was going to write ethics. But God knows what right I have to claim any! I have neither cruelty nor ambition, I think; but that is the only difference between Quive-Smith and myself' (p. 139). Once his pursuer is dead, and the narrator 'reluctantly, belatedly, but finally' takes on 'the mentality of war', he actually travels on Quive-Smith's passport, the passport photo being a 'near enough' resemblance. The last moral choice faced by the narrator, that of dealing with Quive-Smith's craven henchman, presents itself in terms of resemblance and contrast: like

Quive-Smith, he sees the need to dispose of the man, but whereas the Nazi agent would have pushed Muller overboard the night before reaching port, the narrator decides to push him over in reach of land (pp. 180–6).

Rogue Male ends with a resolution of notable clarity. The narrator gains a restored sense of his humanity, integrated with a capacity for violence but free from the taint of sadism or cruelty. He is poised in moral confidence to enter the crusade for national salvation: 'My escape was over; my purpose decided; my conscience limpid. I was at war' (p. 190). If we think of it in the context of the actual conflict to come, the narrator's emergence into the bright sunlight of the moral high ground could leave Household open to the charge of oversimplification and martial cliché. In contrast to the sensational thriller, however, the final readiness for violence has been hard-won, the narrator's painful journey from passivity forming the basis for a quite different sort of narrative to that founded on the unthinking, enthusiastic resort to violence characteristic of Bulldog Drummond or, in the postwar thriller, James Bond, who has, in his later cinema career, come to be the best-known exponent of the technological fix, with technological cleverness helping him to achieve the spectacular destruction of diabolical cunning. Whereas Household's hero agonises over morally assimilating the 'body power' of the animal, Drummond's and Bond's complete adaptation to war and killing is underscored by the way that images of natural, animal vitality are routinely assimilated to images of mechanical efficiency: both are 'perfect fighting machine(s)'; Drummond has a fist 'like a pile driver', Bond a right hand with a perfect 'cutting edge'. This fusion of metaphors for destructive force – of animality with mechanism – is, of course, often to be found in twentieth-century glorifications of violent action. Its mirror-image can be seen, for example, in Marinetti's futurist manifesto, in which machines are conceived of as living forces, animal-like, sleek, deep-chested, sniffing, pawing – a rhetorical blending which can be taken to suggest Marinetti's affinities with Hitler and Mussolini. In his second *Futurist Manifesto*, Marinetti sets speed ('the intuitive synthesis of every force in movement') against the 'new evil' of 'slowness which is associated with the analysis of every stagnant prudence . . . . passive and pacifistic'. The phrases he uses here can readily be applied to the contrasts between the sensational and the serious thriller. In *Rogue Male*, as we have seen, instead of a rapid 'synthesis' of forces, there is prolonged 'stagnation'. The moment of hesitation which causes the narrator's initial assassination attempt to fail must be relived in slow motion. The main substance of the novel becomes an act of extended analysis, the long process of introspection which the hero must undergo before he can choose his path of action.[19]

ERIC AMBLER AND THE 'INFERNAL MACHINE'

In the prewar thrillers of Eric Ambler, the shift of emphasis to doubt about employing violence is even more marked, as is the structuring of the narrative around inconclusive events during a protracted period of hesitation. Ambler and Greene are generally regarded as the writers most responsible for the mutation in the thriller genre in the late thirties and early forties.[20] Ambler's first thriller of the thirties, *The Dark Frontier* (1936), prepares the way for this transformation by parodying the type of the thoughtlessly violent hero. When his car overturns, a methodical, cautious professor of physics (possessor of superior technical knowledge but too ineffectual to succeed in conflict) suffers a blow to the head which miraculously overturns his identity. The man who emerges from the accident is the superhuman thriller hero, Conway Carruthers. Like Drummond and Bond, the literary model for the professor's new identity combines the qualities of animal and machine into a single, flawlessly competent implement of power, with steely eyes and voice.[21] The professorial half of his dual personality lingers on to cause hesitation at key moments when the conventional hero should act, but in contrast to the dual identities of some of the more famous superheroes who sprang into action from the late thirties on (an ineffectual nonentity like Clark Kent, say, or a model of civilised restraint like Bruce Wayne), this is not a case of deliberate transformation. The professor has no conscious control over his alter ego and can will him neither to materialise nor to vanish, suggesting, perhaps, a much wider breach between 'normality' and aggression.

Ambler's satire of 'the perfect fighting machine' is centrally related to his role as the most deliberately left-wing of the thirties thriller writers. Ambler described his political views in the thirties as non-communist (he had not 'joined THE PARTY'), but 'theoretically' socialist; as anti-fascist, but less inclined to be 'pro something'. As a statement of personal commitment, this is on the inconclusive side, but in the novels themselves the full lure of left-wing political faith is more consistently evident. By his own account, his intention when he first tried his hand at the genre was not only to 'intellectualise' it but to shift its political perspective from right to left wing: 'Sapper was writing solid right wing. He was an outright fascist. He even had his heroes dressed in black shirts. Buchan was an establishment figure . . . . I decided to turn that upside down and make the heroes left wing and popular front figures.'[22] It is a little misleading to say that the heroes, or antiheroes, of these early Ambler novels are themselves left-wing, although they do often form close links with figures who are clearly to be identified with the political Left (for example, the idealistic Russian agent Zaleshoff, who appears in both *Cause for Alarm* and *Uncommon Danger*). What is true is that his left-wing perspective accounts for comprehensive alterations in the basic elements of the thriller, as well as for some fairly direct statements of the illusions that afflicted the Left in the late thirties – for example, the belief that fascism could be fought by pacifism, communism and the critique of democracy.[23] The peace-loving communist Zaleshoff argues that the violence of power politics is only an effect of the capitalistic system and sees violence as the temporary product of unfavourable social or economic conditions, rather than biologically constitutive of human nature: 'Human nature is part of the economic system it works in. Change your system and you change your man.' There is a tacit rejection of the view that there are irresolvable internal conflicts within man's nature and a tendency to see technology and armaments as in themselves the cause of conflict. Human nature can be separated from destructive impulses, power from violence. This vision of a utopian transformation is evident, for example, in Ambler's creation of plots which centre on the production and proliferation of armaments, with a hero who is often involved in their production but who has no 'natural' relation to violence and may not even recognise the implications of what he is impersonally producing – who thinks of a gun as no more than 'a series of mathematical expressions'.[24] Although, during the course of the novel, the hero moves from detachment to involvement, his transformation entails no new contact with a repressed inner nature or a latent animality, and does not lead him to emerge into the 'competence' of violent action. In the novels written before 1940, Ambler's plot resolutions offer salvation in the form of conflict averted: weapons of destruction are dismantled, 'explosive' documents are destroyed, and war is thereby rendered less likely.

Ambler represents the creation of weapons less as an extension of natural physical force than as a separate phenomenon, a sophisticated war machine which is primarily the product of financial greed.

His prewar thrillers were written at the beginning of the period which was to see large-scale mechanisation of destruction, with its attendant separation of the 'harmful product' from all sense of personal involvement and responsibility.[25] Ambler saw ahead (in *The Dark Frontier*) the spectre of modern large-scale destructiveness, but he also saw hope in the possibility of separating the machinery of destruction from the innately human. His early thrillers establish the grounds for such a separation through images of both the production and the function of armaments. An avaricious and desiccated capitalism produces the armaments. The men in control are not intrinsically violent, but merely profiting from the generation of conflict. 'Big Business' is run by 'gentlemen who would, in all probability, hesitate before they swatted a fly'. The armaments are actually used by men who are themselves the creation of capitalism, and the cause of violent acts is related to the ultimate economic function of maintaining conflict: 'When Saridza ordered that Captain to beat you with a *Totschläger* until you gave him some photographs, it was to increase the income of what he called his principals in London.'[26] The 'dirty work' is controlled by a complex business structure, a vicious circle in which the proliferation of arms itself generates conflict, and conflict creates greater demand for armaments.

The villain Saridza and his henchman are thus reduced to necessary instruments, and Saridza is simply allowed to walk away at the end. In the resolution of this and Ambler's other early plots, it is seen as far less important to rid the world of 'evil' individuals than it is in the sensational thriller. The main objective is instead to preserve peace by breaking the vicious circle of conflict and arms production, either by eliminating armaments or by thwarting the capitalistic 'manipulation of public opinion by means of incidents, rumours or scandals'. *Uncommon Danger*, for example, ends with the physical destruction of stolen B2 mobilisation instructions which would have been used to create fear and suspicion of Russia. The documents are themselves represented as implements of destruction – 'fifteen pieces of chemically-coated paper more dangerous than the most powerful high explosive, the deadliest poison gas' (pp. 121, 138–9). *The Dark Frontier* centres on the creation of what is supposedly the first atomic bomb, and the objective pursued by Conway Carruthers is the complete elimination of this immensely destructive capacity, together with the knowledge that created it.

In writers like Sapper and John Buchan, the pacifists are men isolated from normal humanity: in Sapper's *The Final Count* (1926), the representative pacifist is a scientist driven to madness by the realisation that his unworldly idealism has served the cause of monstrous villainy; in Buchan's *Mr Standfast* (1919), pacifism is identified with a neurotic with 'ladylike nerves' who finally confesses that he would give everything he has to be the kind of 'great violent high-handed fellow' he sees Richard Hannay to be; he longs to serve as 'an ordinary cog in the wheel' rather than remaining 'a confounded outsider who finds fault with the machinery'.[27] In Ambler, however, human normality and unity are served by the central assault on the 'violent machine'. The nuclear disarmament theme of *The Dark Frontier* is echoed on both the personal and the political levels in the closing pages of the novel: again, a despicably villainous character is spared, and the gun of the hero is flung into the shadows, at which point he reverts from the literary stereotype of Conway Carruthers to a normal middle-aged man; and the country is put into the hands of the Ixanian Peasant Government, which, in the interests of unity and prosperity, immediately disbands its armed forces and establishes friendly relations with all its neighbours (pp. 218, 138–9). The alternative hope is that fascist aggressors will turn against one another – with hindsight, perhaps, an example of what Orwell saw as the British tendency to underrate the danger and hope that 'evil ... will somehow destroy itself'. In *Cause for Alarm*, the plot involves a scheme for creating suspicion between the potential aggressors by giving the Germans information on secret Italian aerodromes. Its 'Epilogue' imagines an Axis weakened by distrust, and the last sentence affirms the alliance of the European democracies with Russia, acting as 'an irresistible force for peace. But ...' (pp. 214, 319–20).

The open-ended 'But ...', the last word of *Cause for Alarm*, succinctly expresses the doubt about peaceful solutions which always haunts Ambler's more optimistic vision of power without arms and of neighbourly co-operation. The ideal is darkened by ever more insistent images of specifically fascist violence, and Ambler himself seems to share some of his heroes' bewilderment at this alien phenomenon. It has been argued that Ambler demystifies English innocence,[28] and this is true to the extent that he represents capitalism as international, and therefore as a force responsible for creating violence and evil which can as easily be located in England as anywhere else. In his detailed representation of contemporary European politics, however, Ambler often focuses on the energy and brutality of fascist militarism, and in doing so establishes the impression of a force which is very far from being the mere creature of vaguely conceived capitalist greed, ultimately to be eradicated by reforms in present conditions. The Rome–Berlin axis, 'one of the most effective principles of European power-politics that has ever been stated', is characterised in terms which emphasise its autonomous power to shape events (*Cause for Alarm* p. 128).[29] It cannot be explained by a simple model of economic causation. Continental political violence, which is viewed as a distinctly un-English political phenomenon, is seen as rooted in primeval instinct and pathological states of mind; it is associated with sadistic violence, manifest in scenes of systematic torture. Ambler's most extended exploration of the causes of violence – innate as opposed to conditioned – is *The Mask of Dimitrios* (1939), in which the objective is to understand the mind of an international political criminal and assassin who is the embodiment of foreign violence. Conflicting explanations are unresolved: he could simply be classed as evil ('if there were such a thing as evil'), he is the product of 'Bad Business', of 'the European jungle', of 'the *Stock Exchange Year Book* and Hitler's *Mein Kampf*', of a 'might is right' ethic, of 'chaos and anarchy'. The possible causes listed are never brought together in a coherent explanation, and the ultimate impression is one of worried perplexity in the face of a phenomenon so complex as to be beyond both comprehension and solution: 'can one explain Dimitrios or must one turn away disgusted and defeated?'[30] The story of Dimitrios is mediated through the mind of Latimer, who has a theoretical knowledge of Nazi thought and a fiction-writer's expertise in criminal behaviour, but who emphasises that he dreads violence. He has in fact taken to writing detective stories as a refuge from his academic exposure to the philosophy of Alfred Rosenberg, one of the leading ideologues of National Socialism, and at the end of the novel, after his brief and traumatic encounter with European politics, he again turns to the consolatory form of the country house murder, with its soluble puzzles and antiseptic corpses, contained within the secure confines of 'an English country village. . . . The time? Summer; with cricket matches on the village green . . .' (p. 268).

Orwell judged that the English mind was particularly unsuited either to grasping or to dealing with the more 'primitive' sources of continental violence: 'The energy that actually shapes the world springs from emotions – racial pride, leader-worship, religious belief, love of war – which liberal intellectuals mechanically write off as anachronisms, and which they have usually destroyed so completely in themselves as to have lost all power of action.' This combination of innocence and ineffectuality is what most consistently characterises Ambler's protagonists. He himself identified his primary theme as the loss of innocence, and the innocence he portrays depends upon the possession of some very 'English' qualities, separating his characters from the world of violent action which they struggle to comprehend.[31] Thrillers are sometimes classified according to whether their heroes are professionals or amateurs, but Ambler's central figures do not even attain the status of competent amateur achieved by, say, Buchan's Hannay. Whereas Hannay is a man of action whose soldierly skills enable him to improvise successfully when he is caught up in dangerous missions, Ambler's restrained central figures have partial knowledge but no competence in the wider world of action. Teachers, writers or engineers, they are invariably intelligent, cautious, unemotional and completely unprepared for their encounters with 'unknown men with murderous "psychologies" and fire-arms in their pockets'.[32]

In the characterisations of his engineers, Ambler's demystification of English innocence is to some extent in evidence. Their inability to 'connect' with the machinery of mass destruction they help to produce is a hypocritical form of detachment. Marlow, for example, the hero of *Cause for Alarm*, protests that he is only an agent for selling machine tools: 'I did not create the situation. The responsibility for it is not mine' (p. 100). In *Journey into Fear* as well, we are left in no doubt that there is an element of self-deception in the reluctance of the English to dirty their hands by involvement in European politics: English hands are already dirty, and there is something culpably blind about the national illusion of detachment, something immature about such failures to connect. At the same time, the qualities of character with which this detachment is associated remain as very positive values. Non-violence, reasonableness, a sense of proportion, decency and dispassionate understanding all stand in implicit opposition to the brutal, uncivilised, malignant aggression associated with the Berlin axis, and Ambler's early thrillers embody all of the anxiety of the time about how the honourable, if often weak and self-deceived, English ethos can effectively deal with a force so antithetical. The plots of his early novels repeatedly move towards the question of whether his heroes, having been shaken out of their sense of immunity, will be required to implicate themselves further by meeting violence with violence.

Aside from the parodic figure of Conway Carruthers, none of the heroes in Ambler's first five novels (1936–39) resorts to direct physical violence. They are, however, forced to confront the implications of an involvement with violence, and must 'mature' sufficiently to make complex moral choices in the real political world. Separated from their own society by having crossed the Channel, they enter a liminal time of transition. One enduring myth of the First World War is that it was a one-way passage in the psychological life of the nation – a vortex, threshold, origin or midwife to history[33] – and, in the thirties, the coming war was similarly prefigured as a time of national transformation, imagined, at an individual level, as a rite of passage. The tension of Ambler's plots lies in the potential danger for his heroes of being suspended between roles, metaphorically awaiting a rebirth. In *Uncommon Danger*, Kenton becomes a hunted man when he is wrongly suspected of murder and escapes clad in what he later discovers to be the bloodstained overcoat of the actual murderer. The process of initiation gradually takes him towards the possibility of becoming a murderer himself. He is first given an unloaded gun; then, after imprisonment in the womb- (or tomb-) like enclosure of a vulcanising tank, he bursts free and finally, 'gingerly', takes hold of a loaded gun. He does not, however, use it: as Zaleshoff recognises, it would have 'worried' Kenton to kill Saridza (pp. 244, 254). In the course of his ordeal, Kenton realises that his sympathies have shifted to Zaleshoff, and in that Zaleshoff is seen by Ambler as representing a 'mature' political choice, Kenton can be said to have been changed by his experience, although he himself is still the kind of man who could only back up an ultimatum by 'writ[ing] to the *Times* about it' (p. 229).

The choices of the hero are often thrown into relief by a process of framing him between characters who represent different kinds of peaceful resolution – the one ineffectual (madness or total withdrawal), the other a strong but morally principled and largely non-violent commitment to a left-wing cause. In *Cause for Alarm*, for example, a mathematician called Professor Beronelli embodies an extremity of withdrawal from the violent upheavals of European politics. Fleeing the reality of a world dominated by fascism he has locked himself in an utterly private world of madness, obsessed with the conviction that he has mathematically proven the possibility of perpetual motion in a manuscript covered 'with childish pencil scribblings' (p. 299). This image of ultimate regression and retreat from a harsh encounter with politics is very explicitly set against the robust engagement represented by Zaleshoff, who again appears in the narrative as a figure able to intervene effectively in turbulent political affairs without himself becoming brutal, the personification of justified force as opposed to sadistic violence. The physical descriptions of the Russian agent repeatedly (in fact, repetitively) suggest animal force and destructive energy, but do not ever imply that his power is used malignantly. He looks like a prize-fighter, explodes and snarls a lot, and thrusts his jaw forward like a battering-ram, but is essentially compassionate and goodhumoured. Poised between reclusiveness and robustness, Marlow, like Kenton, struggles through partial initiation. Charged with espionage and hunted by the Italian secret police, he is no longer a 'composed Englishman' but is forced to confront the 'naked realities' of the mess he is in (pp. 208, 214). As the adventure reaches its climax, he and Zaleshoff hide in a 'nest' of naval gun shells, packed in what the Russian describes as egg boxes. Having fallen asleep in this symbolic hatchery, they are awoken by the flash of a captor's torch, an awakening in which Marlow sees 'a dream of fear changed suddenly into the reality' (pp. 235–7). Once again, however, as in *Uncommon Danger*, this birth into a new consciousness of a violent world does not produce an effective man of action. It is Zaleshoff who supplies the strength and competence to meet the crisis, keeping violence to a minimum but nevertheless going beyond what Marlow feels comfortable with. Marlow has still to be babied: 'He was treating me, I thought, like a child. And I was feeling sorry for the man he had clubbed' (*Cause for Alarm*, p. 248). At the end, Marlow has written an article hopeful about peace, but he has also taken a job as a production engineer at one of the branch factories of the many-tentacled arms manufacturer, Cator & Bliss, with the clear implication that his personal capacity for shaping political affairs is restricted, as Kenton's is, to small contributions to verbal debate.

The inconclusive initiations in Ambler's prewar novels can perhaps be said to reflect the English sense of impotence and reluctance on the eve of war. *Journey into Fear* (1940) was the last novel he published before spending six years in the British Army. Written after the Nazi–Soviet pact, and set during the 'phoney war' of early 1940, it recasts the basic materials of his earlier thrillers, projecting a new and darker sense of violent engagement as unavoidable. The hero, Graham, is again an engineer employed by Cator & Bliss, but (in contrast to Marlow) without any disapprobation. With 'the world await[ing] a bloody spring', the European conflict is played out in miniature on board a ship from which there is no escape (p. 10). Armaments now promise salvation rather than destruction – essential equipment for the survival of Britain and her allies. The objective is to get Graham back to his job with Cator & Bliss, in order that the Turkish navy can be re-equipped on schedule. There is still a gesture in the direction of the economic causation of violence, but these ideas are now put into the mouth of a French socialist who is given some of the traits of the heroic Zaleshoff (looking defiant, sticking his jaw out and putting forward a strong line about capitalists being the real war criminals) but who is also henpecked and personally ineffectual. In contrast to Zaleshoff, the Frenchman is not made a spokesman for pacifist principles, but for justified aggression. The pacifist case is only put in a distorted, duplicitous form by the sinister villain Moeller, who mocks sacrifice of life in the interests of one's country in order to tempt Graham into betrayal.

Like Ambler's other engineers, Graham must, during the course of his journey, re-examine his impersonal relationship to the machinery of destruction. In his case, however, there is no surrogate hero to do the dirty work for him, and his survival depends upon his possession of and competence in handling a revolver. The national recognition that there was no alternative but armed combat is represented in Graham's existential confrontation with imminent death. The discontinuity from normal life is complete: his wife, house and friends 'had ceased to exist. He was a man alone, transported into a strange land with death for its frontiers' (*Journey into Fear*, p. 132). Under such circumstances, to lack a revolver leaves one 'as defenceless as a tethered goat in a jungle' (p. 59). The ship, ironically meant to provide a passage home to the ordinary world, provides instead a transit into a regressive world of violence. Repeated metaphors of animality, throw-backs, running naked and the primeval swamp establish violence as latent in the subconscious, but without the sense of a source of strength discovered (in contrast, for example, to *Rogue Male*). To make this liminal voyage is to enter 'the world beyond the door . . . the world in which you recognised the ape beneath the velvet' (*Journey into Fear*, p. 194). The climax is reached when Graham himself throws civilised restraint aside and, his own aggressive impulses finally released in a blind fury, kills the villain. The novel ends with a reminder of the fear of aerial bombardment. Though Graham turns away and goes back to his beer and sandwiches, the border between peace and war has been irrevocably crossed. As Greene wrote in *Lawless Roads*, 'life was never going to be quite the same again' (p. 23).

GRAHAM GREENE: 'THE HOUSE INFECTED'

The 'world beyond the door' is far more insistently present and much nearer home in the work of Graham Greene. In the 'Prologue' to *Lawless Roads*, Greene describes a symbolic door of his childhood, a green baize door at Berkhamsted School, beyond which was the alien ground of another country: across the border 'one was aware of fear and hate, a kind of lawlessness – appalling cruelties could be practised without a second thought' (pp. 13–14). The image of violence, cruelty and evil just across the way from a croquet lawn is part of an implicit refusal to see England as blessed with a special immunity. In contrast to Ambler, Greene sets his best thrillers of the period in England – an England in which the home-fire virtues often flicker fitfully, but never without sinister shadows. To use one of Greene's recurrent metaphors, the house of English innocence, of the non-violent civilised ideal, is infected and there is no saving vision, either of naturally powerful animal aggression or of power untainted with violence.

Greene's boyhood experience of dormitorial hell led him, he said, to turn to religion – 'And so faith came to me' – and his dark conviction that evil and violence are close at hand, combined with his turn to religious rather than political salvation, makes the tone of his work far more pessimistic than that of Household or Ambler. Although his Catholicism is little in evidence before the publication of *Brighton Rock* (1938), his rejection of an optimistic political faith means that his novels consistently blur or subvert the distinctions of political rhetoric. Greene recognised the attractions of communism, but, in spite of the four undergraduate weeks he spent playing at being a party member, he generally presented himself as no more than vaguely liberal-left and theoretically anti-capitalist in his political views. Like Ambler, he developed his novels around the theme of lost innocence, but in Greene's work innocence is most often blighted from the start, and, at least within the realm of secular political life, there is no innocent or ideal future to be conjured from 'what we are'.[34] Although Ambler's personal commitment to left-wing politics was not, evidently, especially strong, it was a dominant influence on the shape of his fictions. The importance of left-wing grounds for hope in his early thrillers can perhaps be measured by the marked changes in his fiction at the beginning of the war, in *Journey into Fear*, and in a post-war novel like *Judgement on Deltchev* (1951), in which his disillusionment with Russia is manifest.[35] In Greene's work, there is no corresponding watershed because the sense of disillusionment is there from the outset. What does to some extent change with Britain's entry into the Second World War is the directness of Greene's response to contemporary political conflict. In *Confidential Agent* (1939), written after the Munich Agreement, when 'trenches were being dug on London commons' and the approach of war seemed certain,[36] and in *Ministry of Fear* (1943), written in the midst of the war, fascism is, not surprisingly, represented as the primary source of malignant violence, engaged in an unequal contest with an opponent weakened by civilised scruples. Even in these novels, however, those who embody the civilised norm are themselves contaminated by the disease of violence and are not imagined as ever being free of its effects.

Greene's simultaneous affection for and subversion of a core of humanistic values is most clearly evident in *England Made Me* (1935). Like *Brighton Rock*, *England Made Me* is closely related to the thrillers that Greene wrote during this period. Although both novels have been complicated and modified in ways that lift them out of Greene's category of 'entertainments', they strongly echo the more popular genre, both structurally and in terms of their handling of the central themes of violence and power. The novel opens, as does Ambler's *Dark Frontier*, with an unheroic protagonist walking through a door to a meeting which will draw him away from familiar surroundings, to an alien country, to danger and violence in the world beyond the door. The differences between these central figures, however, are striking, and are not only due to the contrasts between the 'thriller proper' and a 'proper novel'. Instead of Ambler's scholarly innocent, Greene gives us the 'depraved innocence' of Anthony Farrant, looking no more mature than a schoolboy, but shifty, scheming and deceitful. The unheroic hero of *England Made Me*, drawn into involvement with corrupt foreign forces and obliged to decide whether he, too, is capable of engaging in this violent world, is an absurdly diminished hunter figure. He takes on a man-of-action role for which he is constitutionally unsuited, suffering as he does, both actually and metaphorically, from the weak chest of the English: 'his chest was an imposing facade hiding a congenital weakness'.[37] He boasts of his prowess in shooting, but in reality has no credentials other than his ability to win prizes in funfair shooting galleries. The big game he hunts is a toy tiger, appropriately, since he has not even mastered the 'game' of violence at the level of a genuine hunt. A flawed version of the child-Englishman encountering adult-continental brutality, he carries 'his corner of England' with him, feeling perpetually like an exile 'longing for the tea urn' (pp. 74, 120). He carries with him also, as English as the tea urn, the virtue of moderation in all things: 'he was dishonest, but he was not dishonest enough' (p. 11).

The cosily English virtues are imaged in the shabby domesticity of Anthony's childhood home. 'The old honesties and the old dusty poverties of Mornington Crescent' convey a nostalgic sense of security, but also a sense of powerlessness in the face of the violence and chaos of the modern world. The threadbare decency of English values is tested against the ruthless power of monopoly capitalism, personified in Erik Krogh, a Swedish financier who has built around himself an enclosed world of steel and glass that effectively dehumanises him. Krogh is far less caricatured than, say, Ambler's Mr Joseph Baltergehn of the Pan-Eurasian Petroleum Co., who also does business in modernist architectural isolation, but he is equally representative of the power commanded by men who themselves live 'padded' lives, insulated from the violence done on their behalf. Anthony is taken across the border into Krogh's dangerous territory by his twin sister, Kate, who works for Krogh and is his mistress. Hoping to improve Anthony's future prospects, she gets him taken on, incongruously, as Krogh's personal guard. Kate is represented throughout as a mother substitute, making anxious, maternal efforts to ensure his rebirth into contemporary reality: 'she was like a dark tunnel connecting two landscapes'. As she tries to explain to Anthony her alliance with 'this crooked day, this inhumanity,' she thinks to herself, 'a child inside would be no closer than we've been', and as she tries to persuade him to move from the past to the future, she warns him, 'Dear Anthony, you're newly hatched compared with [Krogh]' (pp. 138–45). Juxtaposed with Kate, there is a much more conventional female figure, a representative of the kind of normality which, in the less complex world of the thriller, would stand for the society which must be defended – the life of England secure from foreign conflict. Loo, a simple girl from Coventry, is picked up by Anthony in Sweden, and, after a brief assignation, they agree to meet again at a café in Coventry High Street, 'on the same side as Woolworth's . . . at tea-time' (p. 179). Like Anthony, Loo is a flawed innocent, an almost-virgin, longing for freedom with respectability, as old-fashioned as Anthony himself. The tackiness of this badly made-up, cheaply pretentious embodiment of the ideal does not lessen the pathos of Anthony's failure to return to it. It is dry land to a man who 'had always feared the water', and who, in the end, is drowned (pp. 115–19).

Anthony's death at the hands of Krogh's henchman poignantly suggests the vulnerability of the old ethos. He is, as Kate says, 'too innocent to live': he imagines he can exert pressure on Krogh by threatening to give information to the press; he refuses to act violently on Krogh's behalf. Greene implies that, for all their *naïveté* and inadequacy, the virtues of his 'dusty righteous antecedents' should not be undervalued (pp. 186, 139). Questioned about why he is throwing up his job with Krogh, Anthony reflects that he is suspended between the two roles which justify violence, revolutionary and patriotic – 'not young enough to believe in a juster world, not old enough for the country, the king, the trenches to mean anything at all'. His moral conscience instead consists almost entirely of his commitment to restraint – the things he 'won't do' (p. 180). In this, Anthony is obviously not unlike the cautious, prudential heroes of Ambler's thrillers, except that he is not allowed the escape route of 'peace with honour'. There is no virtuously forceful ally on hand with the strength to secure a partial victory or attain some temporary limitation of the sphere of violent action. Anthony's only helper is the seedy journalist Minty, and in this instance the pen is emphatically not mightier than the sword. His redemption instead lies only in his dogged refusal to enter the fray. When he declines to remove by force a bothersome workman, Krogh says, 'I pay you, don't I? Go and throw him out', and Anthony replies, 'I'm damned if I will' (p. 173). *England Made Me* is a pessimistic novel, but Anthony's resistance to being 'damned' by involvement in violence is perhaps a kind of salvation for him.

In Greene's next two novels, *Gun for Sale* (1936) and *Brighton Rock* (1938), the central male figures in effect choose damnation. Greene explores the resort to violence by those who are powerless without it and who are, literally and symbolically, homeless, occupying a position on the margins of society which has left them untouched by residual English decencies. In *Gun for Sale*, although there is no direct encounter with the violence of fascism, the alien nature of Raven intrudes like a harbinger of war. Whilst acknowledging his debt to Buchan, Greene said that the act of writing a thriller brought home to him the inappropriateness of Buchan's ethos to the moral climate of the late thirties, in which the upright, gentlemanly amateur would find himself completely at a loss ('It was no longer a Buchan world.'). Accordingly, in *Gun for Sale*, he rewrites some of the basic conventions of the thriller, inverting the positive values generally attached to the dominant male character by making Raven someone who acts not to save his country but out of revenge for life's dirty tricks. Raven, who is both hunted and hunter, needs no initiation into the world of violence because he has been born to it: 'He had been made by hatred; it had constituted him into this smoky murderous figure . . . hunted and ugly.' His father was hanged, his mother committed suicide; 'he was made in this image . . . he didn't want to be unmade'. The scene of his mother's suicide is a threshold he crossed at the age of six and the memory of it is now a 'closed door'. When Raven himself dies, the moment of his death is metaphorically associated with his own birth into violence: 'It was as if he had to deliver this pain as a woman delivers a child.'[38]

The reversals of the novel are deliberately designed to call into question the conventional moral dichotomies of the thriller. So, for example, the immaturity often associated with ineffectual innocence is here linked to the unyielding sense of grievance that motivates the 'wounded' characters of Raven and later, in *Brighton Rock*, Pinkie, to whom Raven is explicitly compared in Greene's *Ways of Escape*: 'The Pinkies are the real Peter Pans – doomed to be juvenile for a lifetime.' In contrast, say, to Ambler's immature heroes, Raven and Pinkie seem beyond the possibility of growth or change. Set in implacable opposition to the moral majority, their own self-definition involves a reversal of the conventional same/other polarity, with a hypocritical 'respectable' society as the 'other' which motivates their violence: 'The world is full of Others who wear the masks of Success, of a Happy Family' (*Ways of Escape*, pp. 56–7). This fixity goes with other traits which are often concentrated in the villains of the formula thriller as identifying features – for example, in Raven's case, his livid hare-lip, his ugliness, the resentment expressed in his 'bitter screwed-up figure', his inner coldness, his failed sexuality (p. 5).[39] Even Raven's name suggests a being stripped of full human identity: from the perspective of normal society, he is the wholly Other.

Raven's violent role is attributed both to his distorted nature and to the distortions of the social system (although, by ironically giving the same background to the pacifist War Minister who is assassinated, Greene implicitly questions the influence of social conditioning). Men of power see Raven as an abomination, but, like violence itself, a useful one. As in *England Made Me* and in Ambler's novels, instruments of violence are represented as being necessary to capitalist exploitation, and this dependence on violence is imaged in the manipulation both of large-scale armaments and of the individual. Just as they regard violence as a means to an end, those who employ Raven as an assassin regard him as purely instrumental. When he meets with them in their prosperous surroundings, so naked an implement of violence seems out of place: he is a 'gun for sale' and, like the automatic he failed to leave behind at the scene of the assassination, he is 'dark and thin and made for destruction' (*Gun for Sale*, p. 13). As in Ambler's prewar novels, there is a strong emphasis on the connection between violence and the profit motive, though without the optimistic implication that an abolition of monopoly capitalism would secure a non-violent world. Greene complicates the sort of commercial transactions Ambler represents by building up a kinship of violence, and a shared psychopathology. Sir Marcus, the armament manufacturer who employs Raven, is equally separated from normal society – an orphaned outsider, unable to 'realise' others, devoid of pleasures, experiencing no vivid emotion except venomousness. Both Raven and Sir Marcus act as inhabitants of a destabilised world – the unsettled world of those who have crossed the boundary into the territory of violence, 'betrayed by the lawless', their revenges 'stretching into an endless vista of time' (pp. 29, 112).

Gun for Sale is a thriller which takes place wholly in England, but, despite this, it intensifies the fear of destabilising, disruptive violence more often figured in individual adventures on the continent. Greene praised Buchan for realising the 'dramatic value of adventure in familiar surroundings', thus demonstrating 'how thin is the protection of civilisation'.[40] The abnormal, isolated characters who bring murder into the middle of England are men for whom 'there's always been a war' and, from his point of view, Raven's murder of the idealistic War Minister at the beginning of the novel simply promises to extend this natural state to the rest of society (p. 47). The shootings at the end of the novel presage war. Although in fact serving to bring about a resolution in which war is averted, they are imagistically associated with barbed wire, trenches and holocaust. Characters feel they are entering strange countries lying beyond 'the edge of civilisation' (p. 163).

The atmosphere of impending war creates the context for a sustained exploration of the varieties and justifications of violent acts. Greene is careful to avoid the implication that violence only belongs to those on the outside of English society. The plot which connects the assassination at the beginning of the novel with the killings at the end draws in characters who represent other types of aggressive behaviour. Two of the minor characters are used, for example, as would-be embodiments of the aggressive masculine ideal of the sensational thriller and adventure story. Major Calkin's spirits lift when he contemplates the prospect of imminent war, though his uniformed swagger is only that of a 'small plump bullying henpecked profiteer' (p. 114); Buddy Fergusson, a medical student who hopes for 'war and death' to save him from 'the confinements, the provincial practice', is, in terms of his self-image, a Bulldog Drummond in the making, inflating his chest and making his biceps swell, reflecting with satisfaction on his 'superior physical strength', and looking forward 'with pleasure and excitement to war' – to being 'the daredevil of the trenches'. But, encountering 'genuine war' when Raven forces him to strip at gunpoint, his conception of himself is reduced from splendidly potent animality ('the town bull') to the naked, shivering human animal with no natural defences (pp. 146–8).

Defencelessness is, of course, a quality commonly associated with female characters. Greene develops the role of the threatened woman in the character of Anne, a policeman's fiancée held hostage by Raven. Given the absence of a normative hero, she is in a sense the protagonist, and her role can be interpreted as a strongly positive embodiment of the normal human warmth which must be missing or suppressed in those who act violently. Her apparent friendship for Raven momentarily seems to suggest a redeeming possibility for a man who has lived excluded from the human community, but he seems, ultimately, too terrifying a form of life for even her generous compassion to include. When they hide together in a freezing goods-yard shed, their refuge is ironically compared to home – for Anne, a home bare of all warm, human associations; for Raven, a reminder of the violent home that has made him what he is. As they talk, Anne is exposed to the full truth about the violent acts Raven has committed and comes to 'see' his ugliness vividly, even though he is invisible to her in the confessional dark. Her own identity is transformed by what she hears. Her revulsion against Raven is a humane response to the horror of his brutal assassination of the old Socialist; at the same time, however, this initiation into Raven's dark knowledge extinguishes her human pity for him. He is now 'just a wild animal who had to be dealt with carefully and then destroyed' (p. 132). When Anne leaves the shed, she dons Raven's coat and hat to act as a decoy. This is the thriller's stock reliance on disguise and mistaken identity, but also more than that. The irony of Anne's new knowledge of violence is that, in disowning and combating it, she has taken on some of the qualities of Raven himself. A portion of her warm humanity has been numbed in the cold of the shed: later on, she cries 'without tears . . . as if those ducts were frozen'; she becomes hardened, duplicitous and finally, though indirectly, is herself responsible for violence. Her betrayal of Raven leads directly to his death, and the realisation of what she has done lingers on for Anne as 'a shade of disquiet'. The end of the novel is in many respects that of a conventionally optimistic thriller, not unlike Ambler's early plot resolutions: the heroine is reunited with Mather, her policeman fiancée; her information about the assassination averts war. But her success seems to her to contain failure and, although Raven is a 'fading spectre' whom she soon forgets, the closing pages of the novel are haunted by the shadow of this human sacrifice. The defence of humanity has been accomplished at the cost of a loss of humanity. Anne and Mather journey home through a darkening landscape which has won only a temporary reprieve from war, and the last sentence of the novel offers a resolution laden with irony: ' "Oh", she said with a sigh of unshadowed happiness, "we're home" ' (pp. 184–6).

In the thriller – as in political propaganda – woman and home are icons to be defended against alien violence and aggression. The threat to British womanhood stirs Bulldog Drummond to uncompromising revenge; Ambler's protagonists are trying to regain home and all that it represents, often returning to wives or fiancées innocent of Continental violence but potentially vulnerable to it, emblematic of the normality which has been threatened. Other thriller writers have, from time to time, given female characters a more active role, but even then, the woman's involvement in violent action is not allowed to undermine fundamentally her function as a repository of civilised order and restraint. If women exert power in a male-dominated world, it is without recourse to violence. Thus, for example, the role of Buchan's Mary Lamington (eventually Hannay's wife) is an active one – involving a deep entanglement with the villain in *Mr Standfast* and a key role in *The Three Hostages*. The latter, published in 1924, opens with post-First World War peace defined by Mary and home, and with Hannay feeling peculiarly happy and contented in a patch of England which is his own; it nears its climax in an extraordinary scene in which Mary, briefly transformed into a figure resembling Joan of Arc, accomplishes the humiliation of the villain, Dominick Medina. Radiating command, unrecognisable to Hannay, 'a figure of motherhood and pity rather than awe . . . a stranger', Mary creates terror in Medina by threatening him with the 'elixir of death' contained in 'a little oddly-shaped green bottle' that she draws out of her black silk reticule. Medina is humbled by this apotheosis of sanctified motherhood: she is a stern goddess who obtains the release of the child he has hypnotised and returns him safe to his 'little house'. The sinister green bottle turns out to have contained no more than eau-de-cologne.[41] A rather more credible mobilisation of the non-violent female is to be found in Nicholas Blake's (C. Day Lewis's) *The Smiler with the Knife* (1939), another of the left-wing thrillers that brings its protagonist face to face with the menace of fascist (or crypto-fascist) conspiracy. Georgia Strangeways is, like Mary Lamington, a brave and resourceful young woman, thrown by crisis into the role of heroine, and forced to cope far more single-handedly than Mary does. She feels she is becoming an 'arbiter of life and death' and that she can deal without compunction with the dangers which threaten her. In the end, however, intrepid though she may be, Georgia is, after all, only a woman. She faints at the final moment of crisis and doesn't actually see the men disarm the thugs who are about to kill her; the nightmare interlude over, Georgia and her husband can return to their normal life of domestic harmony and to a comically handled obligation to maintain their hedges.[42]

In many thrillers, then, whatever the variations, this cluster of images constitutes a strong 'natural' antithesis to violent action, as well as the most emotive rationale for defensive aggression, which is conventionally represented as necessary to territorial defence (home), as a response to threatened violation (woman), and as a protection of future generations (the child). Greene's ironising of these central icons is one of the means by which he persistently suggests the inadequacy of all secular ideals. The tattiness of the Farrant childhood home, Loo's tawdry version of English womanhood, Anne's desperate efforts to exclude the shadow of Raven's 'home' as she returns to her own home and to her alliance with the 'heavy humourless rectitude' of Mather – all of these work to undermine the justifying vision of the standards implicit in our 'common humanity'. In *Brighton Rock*, Greene carries much further the process of ironising this overly simple conception of virtue. His shift in psychological and moral perspective has the effect of debunking all of the moral assumptions underlying the action of the conventional thriller. Its subversion of formulaic patterns is the more disturbing because the familiar surroundings into which danger intrudes, the thin layer of civilisation which is to be protected, has been so thoroughly devalued.

Brighton Rock cannot be classified as a thriller, but Greene's original intention was to produce a detective story and, in its finished form, the novel remains closely allied to Greene's 'entertainments'. In fact, given its focus on the future it is more nearly related to the thriller than to the mystery story. In religious terms, the quest for salvation is the theme of what Greene himself called his 'too obvious and open' metaphysical reflections on good and evil.[43] In secular terms, this quest takes the form of Ida Arnold's determination to save Rose from Pinkie, which becomes a more overpowering obsession than the conviction of Hale's murderer. Ida's zeal for protecting innocence from violence and for ensuring that right will triumph has much in common with the thriller hero's or heroine's defence of civilisation. In *Brighton Rock*, however, Ida's crusade is seen through the diminishing glass of eternal salvation, and she becomes a caricature of the iconic female figures who, in Buchan or Ambler, bravely uphold beleaguered humanistic morality. In her ample bosom, gathered with comic fullness, are all of the conventional virtues. Law-abiding, jolly, healthy, honest, kindly, 'of the people', she sees herself as the epitome of common humanity. Human nature, she philosophises, is like the centre of Brighton Rock, 'bite it all the way down, you'll still read Brighton'. Her own capacity for compassion and comprehension is described, like seaside candy or inexpensive perfume, as saccharine and mass-produced. Greene repeatedly reminds us of the limitations of her homely heart, with its good nature and cheeriness, its 'sound old-fashioned hallmarked goods . . . nothing nasty, nothing shady, nothing you'd be ashamed to own, nothing mysterious'. Violence is one of those things she would be most ashamed to own, a darkness that is alien to her.[44]

But however non-violent she is, Ida is a born hunter. As the climax of the novel approaches, her gusto for the chase parodies the swaggering moral certainty and individual assertion of the thriller's conquering hero: 'The world was a good place if you didn't weaken; she was like the chariot in a triumph – behind her were all the big battalions – right's right, an eye for an eye, when you want to do a thing well, do it yourself' (p. 221). She has been associated throughout with the ethic of fair play, and her enjoyment of the hunt is manifest in her good sportswoman's laugh and in the excitement she feels at vigorously 'doing right' (p. 112). The case in *Brighton Rock* against this ethic is aimed not only at its shallowness and banality, but on the contradictions shadowing the sportsmanlike English ideal of firm but fair-minded resistance to wrongdoing. The charge is essentially that the ethic fosters its own kind of brutality and only hypocritically dissociates itself from the violence it opposes. Ida's virtue is merciless: she is a 'terrible woman' who 'act(s) for the best', transfigured at the end 'like a figurehead of Victory', her responsibility for violent death unacknowledged (p. 244).

The home to which Ida returns is the emblem of her spiritual impoverishment, softening her 'great warm heart' with its reminders of the 'multitude of popular sayings' that have given give her the illusion of understanding the world in which she's been meddling (pp. 244–5). The ironic darkening of home is repeated for all of the major characters in *Brighton Rock*. Pinkie, who bridles at what he thinks of as Rose's repellent domesticity, recognises his exclusion from everything that home represents. Although he at times thinks nostalgically of making peace and going home, he resists both spiritual Heaven and the 'haven' that Rose wants to offer him. The heavy irony of the end of the novel is in part secured by the use of the word 'home' in Pinkie's gramophone message: 'God damn you, you little bitch, why can't you go back home for ever and let me be?' (p. 177). Ida, completing her mission to protect Rose's innocence, takes her at the end to a parental home now devoid of meaning for her, offering no consolation, no salvation. Against the continuity associated with home, *Brighton Rock* sets the continuity of violence which breeds violence: 'there wasn't any end to what he had begun' (p. 106). Both 'right' (Ida) and 'good' (Rose) are hopelessly compromised in their efforts to secure the peaceful virtues of domestic harmony against the raw power and violence which reign absolute in Pinkie's territory. Rose's simple goodness, reaching out to embrace its opposite, does not save it, but is united with it: she carries at the end the offspring of Pinkie's violent hatred. Rose fears 'the horror of the complete circle' of a return home and looks towards what can be salvaged from the room she shared with Pinkie – as she moves towards her discovery of the message which will confirm the 'complete circle' of hate (p. 247).

The circle of the thriller's quest (home regained) is, in *Brighton Rock*, the circle of sin, the blighted child as the guarantee of the future. Pinkie, the child-man, voices the theologically-grounded conviction that there is no innocence. In his own ambiguous nature childhood coalesces with extreme old age – his skin smooth and fair, his eyes as heartless as 'an old man's in which human feeling has died' (p. 8). He is 'dead' not only to feeling but to the possibility of change; his growth as a character consists only of his progress towards power based on a capacity for violence. Pinkie is often referred to as the hero of *Brighton Rock*, and he does in a sense combine aspects of both hero and villain. Engaged in a power struggle with a 'greater villain', Colleoni, 'the Boy' must pass through the pain of initiation, which marks him with a scar that women, to his disgust, will take 'as a mark of manhood, of potency' (p. 110). His 'graduation in pain' is presented as analogous to the movement from a boy's game to a more fully 'mature' exercise of his power over others. Seeing himself as a full-grown man, he is 'filled with awe at his own powers', the only one in the mob who knows how to act (pp. 167–9). Pinkie's viciousness can be viewed as the consequence of social injustice and exploitation,[45] but Greene's theological vision requires a conception of evil which goes far beyond a socially conditioned corruption of values. In contrast to the serious thriller, with its tendency to reject the polarities of good and evil, *Brighton Rock* reinstates these fundamental categories, together with the sensational thriller's melodramatic representation of the irremediable malignancy of evil. Pinkie is marked not just by the scars of his initiation into a world of adult violence but by the cluster of physical and psychological traits which conventionally distinguish the born villain: he is fixed for us as a character by his stunted, dehumanised physical appearance, his sexual abnormality, and his inability to connect with others; he is associated with images of diseased, pathological violence, with 'secret venom' in his veins (p. 105); his minutely detailed sadism is linked to his distorted sexuality, as we witness him, for example, pulling the legs off a leather-jacket to the refrain of 'She loves me . . . she loves me not . . . .' Pinkie is the very embodiment of the innate sadism that seeks out 'the finest of all sensations, the infliction of pain' (pp. 95, 102).

There is a sense in which *Brighton Rock* can be judged to be, in its heightened vocabulary, faithful to the violent realities of the thirties. Orwell argued that those who described Hitler as Antichrist, 'or alternatively, the Holy Ghost', were perhaps nearest to understanding the times they were living through. Angus Wilson, writing in praise of *Brighton Rock*, saw Greene as conveying the magnitude of what was at stake: 'It was 1938. A time when we all needed . . . to realise, and more important to feel, something deeper than just right and wrong . . . .'[46] Greene gestures repeatedly towards the graver political traumas of the decade. The power Pinkie aspires to is that wielded by Colleoni, head of 'the great racket', whose expansive gestures 'map . . . out the World as Mr Colleoni visualised it'. He looks 'as a man might look who owned the whole world', including police, Parliament and the machinery for determining right and wrong (pp. 63–5). Pinkie, challenging his entrenched power, is imaged as 'a young dictator' of unlimited ambition (p. 109). He visualises ahead of him not only the suite at the Cosmopolitan and the gold cigar-lighter but 'busts of great men and the sound of cheering', with Colleoni himself bowing before his conquest: 'His breast ached with the effort to enclose the whole world' (pp. 132–5).

Magnification of the scale of these gangland ambitions, then, encourages comparison with political events of the thirties; it doesn't, however, force Greene to confront the issue of violence, or of good and evil, in terms of actual political decision-making. Pressure towards a politically responsible development of the theme is relieved by the fact that Pinkie is *not* a would-be dictator set to 'massacre a world' (p. 175). The confinement of the theatre of action in effect frees Greene from the thriller-writer's need to relate his vision of the world to actual political choices and judgements. This containment, of course, often involves ironising Pinkie's 'unbounded' ambition, catching his naïve self-aggrandisement and his delusions about the scope of his 'achievement': he makes plans as complicated as those for Waterloo 'on a brass bedstead among the crumbs of sausage roll' (p. 112). But the restriction of his realm of power has other implications. The geographical limiting of Pinkie's territory allows Greene to invest this territory with its primary spiritual significance. It becomes a 'region of the mind',[47] a territory of mortal sin, foreign to the other, more normative characters. It is analogous to the foreign territory of the thriller, 'a place of accidents and unexplained events', its coded communications unintelligible to those who are too suddenly engulfed by it. As in the thriller, we are brought to see a contrast between academic knowledge of this territory and actual residence in it: Cubitt, for example, is 'like a professor describing to a stranger some place he had only read about in books' (p. 185). The knowledge imparted to inhabitants of this territory, however, pertains not to time but to eternity. The 'annihilating eternity' (p. 21) that touches Pinkie's vision of the world radically alters our moral perspectives. The choices which so often account for the prolonged central hesitation of the serious thriller – the choice of whether to act violently or to reject violence, the choice of sides, the choice of engagement or retreat – are still centrally important in *Brighton Rock*, with all of the main characters involved in just such moral decisions. These decisions, however, are not to be humanly but divinely judged. Greene's emphasis on the magnitude of the moral issues involved has, then, two quite different effects: by insisting that we think in terms of good and evil, rather than merely right and wrong, he affirms the seriousness of what is at stake; at the same time, by focusing his attention on the theological implications of these distinctions, he renders insignificant anything but the issue of eternal salvation. Seen from this paradoxical perspective, good and evil are actually kindred – the 'glory of man' lying in his 'capacity for damnation' as much as in his salvation.[48] The shift away from secular salvation and from the realm of human power to God's mysterious and arbitrary power not only exposes the clichéd nature of conventional morality but diminishes the importance of the choices involved in political action and judgement.

Greene's pessimistic vision of the inadequacy of all secular hopes and solutions was, as Angus Wilson said, a salutary reminder that the 'decent, sensible, no-nonsense' world of Ida was 'not going to be enough'. However, in terms of the political crisis of the late thirties, neither was Greene's Catholicism, which can in a way be seen as a personal 'exit', a means of escape from the spectre of chaos and barbarism, and arguably one which (with its paradoxical alliance of good and evil) leaves little point in fighting the evils of fascism.[49] With war looming, although Greene continued to write 'as a Catholic' – for example, in *The Power and the Glory* – he also turned more directly towards the consideration of the political dilemmas of contemporary Europe. As he wrote in *Ways of Escape*, all that was personal ultimately receded in the face of a national anxiety about the inexorable drift towards engagement with continental political violence: living under the shadow of the rise of Hitler, 'It was impossible in those days not to be committed' as 'the enormous battlefield was prepared around us'. *Confidential Agent* was the first of Greene's novels to confront explicitly the dangers of fascist aggression. The Spanish Civil War, Greene said, 'furnished the background, but it was the Munich Agreement which provided the urgency' – urgency in a personal financial sense, but also, perhaps, in the sense of pressing home the implications of involvement in the war which was now 'undoubtedly' to come.[50]

Greene's objective was to convert contemporary conflicts into 'something legendary'[51] rather than to deal explicitly with the threat posed by fascism or Nazism, and accordingly, he calls his rival agents D and L, and makes no references to Spain. The effect, however, is in fact to create a thriller which reflects distinctly English anxieties and preoccupations as the country moved into the Second World War: one character's struggle against the forces of fascism is used to presage the impending confrontation with violent aggression in Europe at large; if we don't necessarily identify the protagonist as Spanish, we do tend to associate him with qualities thought of as decidedly English – a gentle and civilised man 'pushed around' by the pressures of political violence. In contrast to the central male characters of *Gun for Sale* and *Brighton Rock*, D is a man who 'by nature' belongs on the civilised side of the green baize door, and with Greene's shift of focus from theology to political morality, the civilised man's humanistic responses are revalued and invested with a sense of fundamental rightness. Ideologically, D suffers from a lack of certainty about what constitutes the good that he is protecting. As a professor of Romance literature, he ponders the heroes of the Song of Roland, united to their fellows by a common belief, in contrast to his own allegiance to a side which has 'so many varieties of economic materialism, so many initial letters' (*Confidential Agent*, p. 56). What *does* still unite, however, is a humanistic core of values – compassion, a preference for non-violence and basic human decency, values compromised but not cancelled out by the acceptance of commonly shared guilt. As Arthur Rowe reflects in *Ministry of Fear*, 'Wasn't it better to take part even in the crimes of people you loved, if it was necessary hate as they did, and if that were the end of everything suffer damnation with them, rather than be saved alone?' (p. 132).

The dilemmas faced by the principled man as he moves from impotent passivity to reluctant aggression are central to Greene's theme. D's initiation into violence had taken place when he was buried alive in a cellar, an experience of total powerlessness which permanently altered his sense of the probable and the permissible: 'you couldn't be buried in a bombed house for fifty-six hours and emerge incredulous of violence' (*Confidential Agent*, p. 32). Eventually,

D and his companion, Rose Cullen, feel themselves propelled into a repugnant course of action: 'They had both been pushed around, and they were both revolting against the passive past with a violence which didn't belong to them' (p. 145). Like the protagonists of Household and Ambler, they have had to confront the implications of their own passivity. To reject violence is to be powerless; the choice *not* to be passive marks the central turning point in the plot, reversing the direction of the pursuit. This commitment to action is an 'admission' of violence in two senses: it implicitly acknowledges that one *can* act violently, and it gives access to something perceived as alien, to 'a violence which didn't really belong to them'.

For D, a weapon is no natural adjunct: 'The hand which held the gun shook with the impending horror' (p. 140). Going on the offensive means a complete break with the graspable order of his passive past – 'the blind shot . . . in the bathroom of a strange woman's basement flat. How was it possible for anyone to plan his life or regard the future with anything but apprehension?' (p. 156). Alongside this image of the world of violence as an unknowable territory is the counter image of a stable territory, England itself, which would *seem* to exclude the possibility of violence. As in his earlier novels, Greene both ironises and views nostalgically the English sense of immunity from violence – of being able to indulge without fear 'the eccentricities of a country which had known civil peace for two hundred and fifty years' (p. 196). Running like a refrain through the novel are phrases suggesting that in England violence seems tasteless and improbable. When a young girl who has helped D is murdered, he thinks of her as having become 'by the act of death . . . naturalised in his own land . . . . His territory was death' (p. 128). The journeys by ship at the beginning and end of *Confidential Agent* reinforce our sense of Britain's actual vulnerability, an island surrounded by death. The ship on which D travels to England is itself metaphorically a territory of death, with its deck 'like a map marked with trenches, impossible positions, salients, deaths' (p. 10); his departure from England seems to him and to Rose a voyage into death. Ironically juxtaposed with these voyages is the hotel in which D stays before he leaves the country – a quintessentially English 'cruise on land', offering organised games and keep-fit opportunities coupled with an illusion of complete security – 'no seasickness'. It is from this 'haven' that the British law tactfully and unobtrusively organises D's departure, in the hope of leaving Britain free from 'his infection . . . from embarrassment, from the dangerous disclosure' (pp. 195, 203).

In *Confidential Agent*, the imagery of disease is predominantly that of infection, suggesting a state in which men or, by extension, countries, succumb to disorders not 'natural' to them. D himself has been so thoroughly contaminated that it seems as though violence has become a part of him: 'He had indeed brought the war with him: the infection was working already' (p. 21). He finds that he is 'like a typhoid carrier . . . responsible for the deaths of strangers', and feels guilt at having carried his disease into another country (p. 99). Physically, what is striking about D is that, as he realises when a passport officer compares his face to his photograph, he has been totally transformed by the violence he has experienced, though he has not been changed enough to transform his essential nature or for him to become proficient himself in acts of violence. When he shoots at Mr K, he hits the mirror, only technically committing murder when the man drops dead anyway. In contrast, the one 'true' murder in the novel is the work of the Manageress, who, like Raven and Pinkie, is portrayed as a biological abomination, not merely a carrier of infection but a horrifying apparition with no control, her head 'swelled up like a blister', threatening to gouge out eyeballs with her 'thick decisive thumb' (pp. 73–4).

In D's hesitant confrontation with danger and in his final defeat, Greene encapsulates British anxiety on the eve of war. His mission having failed, D is 'powerless' – that is, he returns home without the power (coal) essential for his side to continue. His own half-hearted aggression (in contrast to the heartless sadism of the naturally vicious Manageress) would seem to give him a poor chance of survival. War has changed everything for him and accomplished nothing. Nonetheless, he has had no choice but to engage in it. He is not, as the pacifists are, out of touch with reality, but he has been forced to recognise his ineptitude in an age of violence: 'He might be a good judge, but he would never make an executioner' (p. 142).

Ministry of Fear, Greene's last novel of the war years, is his most searching representation of the emergence of the ordinary individual into a world in which violence seems inescapable. The location of the action in England again reinforces a sense of total discontinuity between the stability of 'Englishness', associated with 'the profound natural common experiences of men' (p. 178), and the bewildering speed and abnormality of violent intrusion. *Ministry of Fear* overlays domestic with alien violence. Arthur Rowe, who carries a burden of guilt for the mercy killing of his sick wife, is very deliberately established as a character who is *not* 'innocent' in the way that, say, Ambler's technocrats and teachers are. Rowe's action has separated him not only from domestic normality but from the rest of ordinary society.

Unlike Raven and Pinkie, he is not outcast because of distorted natural propensities but simply because the effect of the killing and of the concomitant guilt has been to isolate him, consigning him to a world in which he is 'an exile' from 'the old peaceful places' (p. 47).

Rowe's private shame is set in the context of Britain during the Blitz, and his nostalgia for 'the old peaceful places' has considerable resonance. Greene said himself that while he wrote *Ministry of Fear* he had vividly in mind his own experiences of London during the Blitz, and 'a little of the love crept, I think, into the book'.[52] The main dichotomy that he establishes is between, on the one hand, a regretful involvement in violence, motivated by love and mindful of suffering, and, on the other, the malignant aggression associated with fascism. Britain's involvement in the war is figured in Rowe's anxiety and guilt over what he had, after all, done for the best of motives. Rowe reflects, 'It wasn't only evil men who did these things. Courage smashes a cathedral, endurance lets a city starve, pity kills . . . we are trapped and betrayed by our virtues' (p. 74). The 'evil men', however, are characterised by very different reflections: Hilfe, for example, the German spy, is nihilistic, devoid of feeling, utterly ruthless: 'The maximum of terror for the minimum time directed against the fewest objects' (p. 201). Hilfe's beauty, unmarked by grief or pity, embodies the barefaced, triumphal violence associated with fascism itself. He lectures Rowe on the differences between old-fashioned murder and the 'respectable' murders unashamedly committed for position or power: 'Nobody will refuse to meet you if the position's high enough. Think of how many of your statesmen have shaken hands with Hitler' (p. 47).

As the unsuspecting Rowe gets caught up in the complex web of murder, deceit and spying, explosions and 'massacres' bring about further changes in his identity, allowing him in effect to experience the opposing alternatives of passive withdrawal and heroic engagement. The first crucial transformation takes place half-way through the novel when Rowe agrees to deliver a suitcase to a room in a hotel in which you can lose yourself – a labyrinthine wilderness of darkness and danger in the heart of London. The blast from a bomb in the suitcase leaves Rowe with amnesia and a new identity, recovering in a shell-shock clinic which restrains all violence, taking it to be a form of madness. Like Professor Beronelli in Ambler's *Cause for Alarm*, he lives in a mental isolation that wholly detaches him from the events of his time: ' "It seems so strange", she said. "All these terrible years since 1933 – you've just read about them, that's all"' (p. 116). In the 'madhouse' of Europe, the clinic seems to be an 'arcady' in which Rowe feels the inexplicable happiness of someone 'relieved suddenly of some terrible responsibility' (p. 111). He is 'The Happy Man' and fears regaining his memory. Paradoxically, however, it is precisely this regression which ultimately makes Rowe capable of acting. Before his amnesia, he has been tortured by self-judgement. He doesn't, Hilfe's sister tells him, have the 'right marks' to be one of the 'bad people', because he worries too much 'about what's over and done' (p. 100). Relieved of his worries, Rowe is in a psychological state much closer to that of his boyhood, when he 'thought life was much simpler – and grander'. As he begins to regain his adult self, Rowe feels 'the horror of returning life': 'memories struggled to get out like a child out of its mother's body' (pp. 162, 148). Whilst the process is still incomplete, however, he seems for a time in touch with 'the untried courage and the chivalry of adolescence' and is able to embark on violent action in a spirit of adventure, 'drunk' with a sense of exhilaration, and, like Hilfe, untouched by pity: 'He didn't understand suffering because he had forgotten that he had ever suffered.' Hilfe himself tells Rowe that he turned out to be an unexpectedly dangerous opponent after he lost his memory, having thus so painlessly acquired 'illusions of grandeur, heroism, self-sacrifice, patriotism . . .' (pp. 176, 205).

At the end of the novel, when Rowe is again 'a whole man', his wholeness contains all of the tensions and contradictions of English involvement in violence. The icons of civilised gentleness and normality are present but in altered, fragile form. He returns home in the knowledge that it is not really his home, but irretrievably changed – it was impossible to retreat, closing the door 'as if one has never been away'. He is at war and, knowing not to expect peace, he has joined the 'permanent staff' of the 'Ministry of Fear'. The woman he loves, Hilfe's sister, her face 'despairing as a child's', must be protected (pp. 220–1). This is necessary, however, not because she is innocent but because, craving the unclouded happiness of the arcadian interlude, she wants to protect Rowe from the knowledge of his own original guilt; she longs for him to remain 'innocent' of it, ignorant of the full truth about his past. Rowe must therefore, in turn, protect her from the knowledge that her brother has, just before his death, told all. Hilfe has given Rowe wholeness at the cost of guilt and secrecy. The future, in which Rowe and Hilfe's sister must each speak as though the other is innocent of troubling knowledge, is a form of civilised connivance. In broader terms, the implication is that any resort to killing, however noble the motive, runs so far 'counter to the psychic disposition imposed on us by culture' that it must not be 'admitted' as part of the harmonious communality that is the embodiment of the humanistic ideal. *Ministry of Fear,* more forcefully than any other thriller of the period, expresses the anxiety that the recourse to violence will in itself 'ruin' what is defended: earlier, when Rowe contemplates London in ruins, he says that what frightens him is 'how I came to terms with it before my memory went . . . . God knows what kind of ruin I am myself. Perhaps I *am* a murderer?' (p. 163).

NOTES

1. Freud S. *Why war?*: the translation used here is that of the pamphlet published by the League of Nations in 1933; a slightly different translation is available in Freud S. *Civilization, society and religion* Penguin Freud Library 1991 vol. 12 pp. 343–62; Fromm E. *The anatomy of human destructiveness* 1990 pp. 581–9; Lewis W. *The Hitler cult* 1939 pp. 6–7.
2. Freud *Why war?*
3. Lee S.J. *The European dictatorships* 1987 pp. 2–6 and 15–16; President Wilson's Fourteen Points (8 January 1918), quoted by Lee p. 6; Pick D. *War machine* 1993 pp. 190–3 (quoting the letters of Henry James and Rainer Maria Rilke).
4. Macfarlane A. *The origins of English individualism* Basil Blackwell 1978 p. 196.
5. Orwell G., Wells, Hitler and the world state (1941), in *Collected essays* 1968 p. 161. Worries over the problem of distinguishing the antagonists can also be clearly seen during the First World War, for example, in Norman Angell's pamphlet *The Prussian in our midst* (1915). See Pick *War machine* pp. 150–1.
6. Forster E.M., The 1939 state, in *The New Statesman* (10 June 1939) p. 888.
7. See, for example, the discussions of historical background in Palmer J. *Thrillers* 1978 and Denning M. *Cover stories* 1987.
8. For the British government, the key issue in the interwar period was the manner in which British influence was to be exerted. There were, of course, those who had a romantic fascination with violence, but this was far from being the dominant mood of the country. See Kennedy P. *The realities behind diplomacy* 1985 pp. 223–4 and 241.
9. Bracher K.D. *The age of ideologies* 1985 pp. 151–3; Kennedy *The realities behind diplomacy* p. 247; Graves R. and Hodge A. *The long weekend* (1940) 1988 p. 455.
10. Eco U. *The role of the reader: explorations in the semiotics of texts* (1979). Hutchinson 1985 pp. 162–3.
11. Forster E.M. *Two cheers for democracy* 1951 p. 65.
12. Hughes T. *Tom Brown's schooldays*, quoted by Girouard M. *The return to Camelot* 1981 p. 281.
13. Greene G. *The confidential agent* (1939) 1971 p. 121.

14. See, for example, Arendt H. *On violence* 1969 pp. 73–6 and Fromm E. *Anatomy of human destructiveness* 1990 pp. 37–46 on biological metaphors and organic explanations; Isidore de Lautréamont *Lay of Maldoror* (1927) quoted by Lewis W. *The diabolical principle* 1931 pp. 49–52; Freud *Why war?* p. 46.
15. Greene G. *Lawless roads* (1939) 1982 p. 223; Greene G. *Ministry of Fear* (1943) 1979 p. 163.
16. Household G. *Rogue male* (1939) 1989 pp. 7–8.
17. See Bloom C. (ed) *Twentieth-century suspense* 1990 pp. 58–62.
18. See Girouard *The return to Camelot* Chapter 15.
19. McNeile H.C. *'Sapper': the best short stories* (1920–37) 1986 pp. 184 and 199–200; Fleming I. *Goldfinger* Coronet Books 1993 pp. 9–10; Eco *Role of the reader* p. 145 notes that after Casino Royale, Bond 'is to abandon the treacherous life of moral meditation' and so 'ceases to be a subject for psychiatry and remains at the most . . . a magnificent machine'. Marinetti F.T. *Futurist manifesto* (1916), quoted and discussed by Fromm *Anatomy of human destructiveness* pp. 458–9.
20. See Denning *Cover stories* pp. 59–65 and 92–3 (on the links with le Carré and Deighton).
21. Ambler E. *The dark frontier* (1936) 1988 pp. 28–31 and 171–2.
22. Hopkins J., An interview with Eric Ambler, in *Journal of Popular Culture* **9** (2): 286–7.
23. See Bracher *Age of ideologies* pp. 151–3 on the 'great misjudgement' of the thirties.
24. Ambler E. *Cause for alarm* (1938) 1988 pp. 304–5; Ambler E. *Journey into fear* (1936) 1988 p. 107.
25. Fromm *Anatomy of human destructiveness* pp. 459–63.
26. Ambler E. *Uncommon danger* (1941) 1988 p. 121; see also Fromm *Anatomy of human destructiveness* p. 262 and Denning *Cover stories* p. 74 on the figurability of capitalism in this period.
27. Bloom *Twentieth-century suspense* pp. 63–4; Buchan J. *Mr Standfast* (1919) 1988 pp. 234–5.
28. See, for example, Denning *Cover stories* pp. 67–80.
29. For example (p. 128), 'It *changed* Austria . . . . It *made* England . . .' (my italics).
30. Ambler E. *The mask of Dimitrios* (1939) 1988 pp. 225 and 267.
31. *Orwell, Wells, Hitler and the world state* p. 162; Interview with Ambler, *Journal of popular culture* **9** (2): 287.
32. Ambler *Uncommon danger* p. 43.
33. Pick *War machine* pp. 257–8.
34. Greene G. *Journey without maps* (1936) 1980 p. 20; and see Johnstone R. *The will to believe* 1984 p. 70.
35. Ambler's other novels have been less directly political in content. See Cawelti J.G. *The spy story* 1987 pp. 108–9.
36. Greene G. *Ways of escape* 1981 pp. 67–8.
37. Greene G. *England made me* (1935) 1977 pp. 9–11 and 115.
38. Greene *Ways of Escape* p. 54; Greene G. *A gun for sale* (1936) 1979 pp. 66, 49 and 170.
39. See Eco *Role of the reader* p. 151, on the negative values gathered in the figure of the Bond villain.

40. Greene G., The last Buchan, in *Collected essays* The Bodley Head 1969 p. 223.
41. Buchan J. *The three hostages* (1924) 1988 pp. 7 and 346–9.
42. Blake N. *The smiler with the knife* (1939) 1985 pp. 105–6 and 273–84.
43. See Todorov's definition of the thriller *vis à vis* the detective story, discussed in Bloom C (ed) Spy thrillers 1990 pp. 53–4; Greene *Ways of escape* pp. 58–60.
44. Greene G. *Brighton rock* (1938) 1971 pp. 32, 198, 77 and 72.
45. See, for example, the arguments of Couto M. *Graham Greene* 1988 pp. 58–61.
46. Orwell, Wells, Hitler and the world state p. 162; Angus Wilson, Greene: Four Score Years and Then, *The Times* (7 September 1984).
47. Greene *Ways of escape* p. 58.
48. Greene's use of this quotation from T.S. Eliot in an essay of 1938 is discussed by Adamson J. *Dangerous edge* 1990 p. 40.
49. Wilson A., quoted by Adamson *Dangerous edge* 41–2; and Karl F., Graham Greene's Demonical heroes, in Bloom H. (ed) *Graham Greene* 1987 pp. 47–57.
50. Greene *Ways of escape* pp. 29 and 67–8.
51. Ibid. p. 68.
52. Ibid. pp. 78–9.

CHAPTER FIVE

Law: The Liberal Critique and the Totalitarian Nightmare

'You think that Kamenev may not confess?' asked Stalin, his eyes slyly screwed up.

'I don't know', Mironov answered. 'He doesn't yield to persuasion.'

'You don't know?' inquired Stalin with marked surprise, staring at Mironov. 'Do you know how much our state weighs, with all the factories, machines, the army, with all the armaments and the navy?'

Mironov and all those present looked at Stalin with surprise.

'Think it over and tell me', demanded Stalin. Mironov smiled, believing that Stalin was getting ready to crack a joke. But Stalin did not intend to jest. He looked at Mironov quite in earnest. 'I am asking you, how much does all that weigh?' insisted he.

Mironov was confused. He waited, still hoping Stalin would turn everything into a joke, but Stalin kept staring at him and waited for an answer. Mironov shrugged his shoulders and, like a schoolboy undergoing an examination, said in an irresolute voice, 'Nobody can know that, Yosif Vissarionovich. It is in the realm of astronomical figures.'

'Well, and can one man withstand the pressure of that astronomical weight?' asked Stalin sternly.

'No', answered Mironov.

'Now then, don't tell me any more that Kamenev, or this or that prisoner, is able to withstand that pressure. Don't come to report to me', said Stalin to Mironov, 'until you have in this briefcase the confession of Kamenev!'[1]

The Moscow show trials that accompanied Stalin's purges of the thirties were in essential respects not trials at all. They were unsupported by the moral authority of natural law; there was no proof of guilt, no effort to produce evidence, no separation between judge and prosecution; the actors in the proceedings played prearranged parts, carefully stage-managed to give the illusion of legitimacy. Stalin's grotesque literalisation of the colossal 'weight' of the state expresses with brutal clarity the powerlessness of the accused individual. The Russian state appropriated the name of the law by ostentatiously observing certain legal forms. Stalin aimed not just to eliminate his old opponents but to destroy them morally and politically, and to accomplish this he organised the show trials with such formality, with such 'perfect legal artifice', that many observers were persuaded that the verdicts reached were right and just.[2] In his legitimisation of terror, of concentration camps and mass executions, we see the extent to which legal forms in themselves can be taken to imply the substance of a proper and ethical enquiry. The subjective, inner space of the individual conscience is shut inside the external space and pretended objectivity of legal procedure: the official form of Mironov's briefcase will contain a 'confession', with its implications of intimate knowledge, private revelations and troubled conscience; the purported narrative of the inward moral life of the individual, rewritten in conformity with the requirements of the state, will sustain the public sham of the show trials. What Yevgeny Zamyatin, in *We*, calls the 'little valise' of the individual conscience becomes, under totalitarianism, an incomprehensible repository of 'extraneous impedimenta'.[3]

The perversion of justice in Stalinist Russia, as in Nazi Germany, provides liberal theorists with their most compelling evidence of what the 'negative virtue' of justice is meant to *prevent*. Nazi derision of the law was more open, but in spite of Hitler's contempt for the legal profession, German lawyers were remarkably ready to 'provide the rationale of their own debasement'. Hitler discovered early on that the merely formal gesture of acknowledging the law gave him the licence to destroy its substance. The Party's legal machinery abandoned positivist law, cut through the legal technicalities of abstract law and completely jettisoned both the notion of equality before the law and the rules governing factual evidence. This was done under a pretence of returning to 'natural justice' – in practice, for National Socialism, a very subjective notion, which often meant retroactive laws personally formulated by Hitler, applied to legalise the lawlessness of the Party's consolidation of power, providing a 'legitimate' framework for such measures as the execution of communists and Jews and creating 'a bombed and flattened moral landscape' in which there were no boundaries and no limits to the exercise of power.[4] The underlying assumption was that the law had no substance except as the means for furthering the German national community. The starting point of legislation was not individual freedom but 'the weal of the whole', allowing the legal profession to avoid the dilemma between justice and morality simply by declaring that 'natural law' was to be identified with the concept of 'sound national feeling'. Individual conscience was completely obliterated by reference to the will of the state: 'There is no authority and ultimate source of law other than the conscience of the Nation itself', and, since the Führer was the keeper of the nation's conscience, his word was law. The law was 'personalised' not just in the sense that it was an expression of the will of the leader but also in the sense of being willing to go much further in supplying a narrative of the inner character of the individual in the supposed interests of the public good; courts presumed to judge the individual conscience with extraordinary comprehensiveness, and punishment depended not just on the gravity of the 'crime' but on the psychological type to which the defender was said to belong, as well as on the national political circumstances under which the offence was committed. Such a system created 'the myth of a law that is uniquely capable of identifying and justly evaluating the authentic subjectivity of the offender, that which he "really" is'.[5] In Nazi as in Soviet regimes, then, all civilised rules regarding the administration of justice were violated with brutality and cynicism. In both cases, a spurious objectivity was secured by an apparent maintenance of legal forms, covering what in actuality was an abandonment of all procedural guarantees, of any notion of fairness or justice and of all formal safeguards for the individual.

The Russian and Nazi revolutions are, Stuart Hampshire argues, 'the two most important sources of evidence for moral philosophy in our time', their abuses of power clarifying the values contained in the concept of justice.[6] Amongst the key elements in a Western concept of justice discarded by totalitarianism is the historical individualistic basis of the law. The liberal idea of natural justice is grounded in the idea of individual responsibility and individuality itself, as opposed to the stress, under totalitarianism, on collectivity and community.[7] Strictly speaking, there is no such thing as justice 'within' an individual, since justice concerns only relations between an individual and other individuals (or between the individual and the state). But we nevertheless think of there being a spirit of conscientiousness in all forms of moral action – implied by the Platonic idea of 'justice in the soul' or, in religious terms, by the Judaeo-Christian belief in the value of the individual soul and the authority of conscience, notions which brought fully into consciousness the aspect of justice concerned with individual rights.[8] These values are summarised, for example, in the lectures given by Ernest Barker at the University of Cambridge in the thirties. Barker defines the state as an association which exists for, in and even 'as' the law, in the sense that it is a regularly enforced system of rules (procedural justice) which are given value by an underlying conception of what is good or moral (substantial justice). Procedural justice entails the careful, unbiased weighing of arguments on both sides of a case; substantial justice is what we have in mind if we say that the value of a law resides in some inherent quality that we recognise as 'just'. When we enquire into the 'controlling idea of the right and the just', we are asking, in Barker's phrase, what is the source of the law's 'justifying grace and obliging power':

> The course of the argument has led to the conclusion that the idea of justice, which is the impersonal source of law, is an idea which itself has its source in ethics and ethical principles. But the foundation of ethics, and the source of all ethical principles, is the value and worth of the individual personality. The moral world is a world of individual persons, each intrinsically valuable . . . .[9]

There are, of course, numerous critics of Western values who dismiss the whole liberal conception of the relationship between the individual and the law as imprisoning, reactionary and parochial. Perhaps the best known recent critique has been that of Foucault, who talks about the walls of confinement enclosing the 'negative' of the bourgeois dream of a 'moral city', within which there is 'a sort of sovereignty of good' – the underside of this dream being the forceful imposition of the 'republic of the good . . . on all those suspected of belonging to evil', and a conviction that 'the laws of the state and the laws of the heart' are identical. The Marxist critique of the liberal 'myth' uses the idea of inherent contradictions to mount a sweeping assault on a rule of law idiom which is said to conceal actual violence and arbitrariness under the potent fiction of a rule-governed society. So Merleau-Ponty, for example, attacking *Darkness at Noon* (in an effort to draw attention away from rather more serious inconsistencies in the totalitarian manipulation of justice), represents the commitment to 'truth, law and individual consciousness' as simply the justification for suppression.[10]

Liberal theorists themselves, whilst arguing strongly against this wholesale undermining of the ideal, have gone some way in probing the contradictions and suppressions which in practice can weaken the Western concept of justice. For those within the tradition, the two main sources of disquiet about the liberal ideal are the negative terms in which the rule of law is conceived (it prohibits, condemns, punishes); and the nature of the relationship between, on the one hand, the intrinsic value of individual personalities and individual moral thought, and, on the other, the legal association of the state. With the decline of the influence of religion, what remains of the 'sacred' in Western secular government is in the framework itself, especially the constitutional framework of law. But loss of faith in the notion of transcendental justice has left Western governments with the problem of providing alternative sources of meaning, of filling spiritual lacunae: without the sacred dimension of authority, only the sword remains. The secular-libertarian model of government is neither heroic nor glamorous, and, in the absence of traditional religiously enshrined values, its guardians face the question of what can continue to hold the system together. The negativity of the ideal can mean that the law itself becomes a source of guilt, particularly since (as its opponents observe) it must ultimately rely on the violence it is designed to prevent. It is this sort of difficulty that is addressed, for example, in Bertrand Russell's *Roads to Freedom* (1918), which attempts to account for the fact that government and law in their very essence consist of restrictions on freedom, even though paradoxically freedom is the greatest good. More recently, Stuart Hampshire, in *Innocence and Experience* (1989), has considered the implications of the fact that we think of justice as a restraint on human desires for dominance or for a disproportionate share of rewards: it is 'a denial of pleonexia', and thus, when justice must be enforced, the scene is one of frustrated ambition rather than immediate harmony; 'a barrier is erected, an impossibility declared'.[11]

The potential opposition between individual conscience and the will of the state can never be simply resolved, and the dual matrix of legal code and moral code, of external and internal worlds, will inevitably generate conflicts. Although the concept of justice is ultimately derived from ethics, it is not a rule of the inward but of the outward life, and this is the source of many of the apparent contradictions which bedevil the ideal. An uneasy awareness of the paradoxes and difficulties arising from the conflict between individual and state is arguably an essential aspect of the Western attitude to the law; under a totalitarian regime, on the other hand, this sense of conflict is 'officially' eliminated by an ideology which discounts at the outset the claims of the individual and the basis of legal justification in individual rights.

The individual conscience has itself been traditionally imaged in terms of legal metaphors. Even if there is no such thing as 'justice *within* an individual', we frequently adopt the vocabulary of the courtroom to describe our inner deliberations, and the process by which we regulate and censure our own conduct is often conceived in terms of a legal space, presided over by conscience upon a judgement-seat: we value, as Sterne says, our 'sacred COURT', within which we want to be assured that 'INTEREST stood always unconcerned whilst the cause was in hearing, – and that passion never got into the judgement-seat, and pronounced sentence instead of reason . . . .' Men can be found guilty

– 'convicted' – by judicial procedure or by 'their owne conscience',[12] the virtue of justice in a legal sense depending on the ultimate *coincidence* of these two kinds of conviction. The public institutions of the law are justified, as we have seen, by arguing their foundation in the inner moral world of the individual.

In popular fiction, the paradigm of this dual matrix is the denouement of the crime drama. Whether this takes place in the courtroom or elsewhere, it involves a communal space in which individual guilt is narrated and made manifest. The paradigm is sketched by Auden in *The Dyer's Hand*: before the crime, the society must appear innocent, with no need of law and no distance or contradiction between individual will and general laws; Nature, too, reflects the innocence of the human inhabitants, and is the Edenic 'Great Good Place'; the loss of innocence through the murderer's commission of a crime creates a situation in which 'the individual and the law become opposed to one another', an opposition only to be resolved once guilt is uncovered and innocence is restored. What happens in the courtroom or analogous space is the reconstruction of the events in question, of the circumstances of the criminal act, plus allowable speculation about the intention of the individual 'in whose mind the fact is considered as having a place'.[13] The idealised crime drama very often reaches its climax in a scene which constructs *within* the communal space (in film often by means of flashback) a dramatisation of events which can only be fully known first-hand by the guilty person, whose extreme reaction (of fear or anger) acts as a confirmation that the deliberations which *should* have taken place in the malefactor's conscience have now been made known and judged. In the courtroom dramas of Erle Stanley Gardner, for example, Perry Mason (in 1933) takes his audience back to the fatal night, repeatedly demanding of the criminal who is about to be exposed, 'And isn't it a fact . . .?', until the spectators see him first visibly worried, then turning 'a few shades whiter', until, with the climactic accusation ('And isn't it a fact that . . . you crashed a club down on his head and caved in his skull?'), 'the agonised face' of the guilty man clinches 'the silent verdict of the court-room'.[14] A hidden truth is made present in the courtroom, and the law 'rests its case' on the identity of the inner space of conscience and the external space of public judgement, confirmed (in the ideal courtroom drama) when the final legal narrative coincides in every particular with the narrative previously available only to the 'inner courtroom' of the guilty conscience. This identity serves to demonstrate the basis of the proceedings in natural law; it is their 'substantial' justification.

In dramas of this kind, we are generally not allowed to involve ourselves too closely with, or to know too much about, the inner life of the guilty person: the lack of sympathetic identification or more complex knowledge allows the reassuring conviction that guilt has been located in an 'other' whose action has only temporarily breached the solidarity of the 'innocent' community. Guilt is often externalised and given an objective reality by means of the 'least likely person' convention, which allows us sufficient information about the criminal to confirm his guilt, but not enough to complicate or render ambiguous his motives and behaviour or to generate in the audience a sense of kinship with him. It is the conventional assumption of communal rectitude and a guilty 'other' that gives point to a sardonic reversal of the genre like J.B. Priestley's *An Inspector Calls* (1946), in which the conscience-like inspector reveals the hidden guilts of an entire family, every member of which was feeling 'so confident, so pleased with ourselves until he began asking us questions'. The inquisitor is mysteriously able to control the deliberations in five separate 'inner courtrooms', turning the communal bond of innocence to a bond of guilt: 'You see, we have to share something. If there's nothing else, we'll have to share our guilt.'[15]

The smug expectations of 'respectable' society about the functioning of criminal justice are challenged in Priestley's play by the creation of an 'inspector' who is not in reality a representative of the law – and who may in a sense only exist in the inner moral space of those who are questioned. On the other hand, doubts about the foundation or functioning of the legal process can be expressed by a sharp separation of the inner space of conscience from the outer space of the law, creating a central struggle between the private moral world and its (false) public counterpart. Tensions are brought out by emphasising the existence of more than one narrative: the socially constructed story of an action officially disapproved of threatens to displace the genuine story of the accused, which contains a quite different truth and meaning; or the revelation of 'who done it' is replaced by a revelation of the meaning of an action in the consciousness of the accused. In Mauriac's *Thérèse Desqueyroux* (1927), for example, some of the attributes of the crime novel are combined with the use of flashback not to establish guilt but to explore Thérèse's effort to judge herself, creating an acute sense of separation between her search for 'the secret springs of actions now fulfilled' and the wasted body and painted face seen and judged by those around her (Bernard realises 'what a fool he had been not, at any cost, to have kept that terrible figure out of sight').[16] In critiques of liberal justice, misgivings about the functioning of legal institutions are often expressed in images of absence and separation. During the interwar years, before the shadow of totalitarian abuses of power altered all perspectives, it is images such as these that trouble the liberal conscience in its confrontation with the actual functioning of Western justice: so, for example, Forster's *Passage to India* (1924) and Greene's *It's a Battlefield* (1934) both centre on the absence of more positive justifying ideals and on the separation of the accused individual from the society which constructs the codes of judgement.

In the darker narratives which work to expose totalitarian abuses of power, fear is created by the strong sense of entrapment and enclosure, attendant both on literal imprisonment and on the containment of 'personal space' within 'official space' (like the confession in the briefcase, a spurious identity imposed by the requirements of the system). The violation of the individual conscience is literally and metaphorically represented by the invasion of private space, by the motif of confined official interiors and by the claustrophobic dream-space of the nightmare, in which the most overwhelming sensation is the loss of individual will and motion. The conflicts represented tend to involve a separation of the private from the legally defined individual (who is seen as less than fully human and hence outside the 'universe of obligation').[17] The extent of this separation is emphasised by bringing before us, as readers, the 'full being' of the accused, not the 'partial person' who turns out to be the culprit in the classic crime story, but someone whose private individuality is much more fully available to us. The process of inquisition and trial thus comes to be seen as the betrayal of an ideal – of the ideal of autonomous individual moral vision, as opposed to submission of identity and sense of self to the defining power of the law and to an antagonist's narrative of one's inner moral life.

This undermining of separate identity (a troublesome issue for the liberal mind even where justice is perceived to be functioning in a comparatively 'just' fashion) is most alarmingly apparent in a judicial system which, having removed the basis of the law in individual ethics, is supported in its methods by a belief that 'To tell the truth and to act out of conscience are nothing but alibis of a false morality.'[18] Under such a system, the individual only exists in so far as he is defined by the state. There is a collapsing of the space between the individual and the state – a forced assimilation of the space of the individual conscience to the officially defined codes and preconceptions of the state, with a consequent sense of helplessness so acute that only the panic and paralysis of nightmare seem adequate to describe it.

In the second half of this chapter, we will discuss in some depth Koestler's *Darkness at Noon*, which gives a first-hand account of the horrors following on an elimination of all individual moral space. It is one of the books that did the most to bring Stalinist atrocities to public attention. Koestler revealed the monstrous pseudo-legalism of the Stalinist purges in such devastating detail that many English readers were disinclined to credit some aspects of his account as anything *other* than fiction. After reading *Darkness at Noon*, Forster wrote to Koestler, praising the novel for having 'gripped and held' him, but adding that Rubashov's Diary, though a damning indictment of Stalinism, was 'I suppose an exaggeration, for the Russians couldn't have fought as they have if they had so little to fight for'.[19] For someone as committed as Forster to the classic liberal assumptions about that value of the individual conscience and the sanctity of private experience, it is almost inconceivable that there could be a functioning political system which 'leaves no space for private life and . . . destroys man's capacity for experience and thought just as certainly as his capacity for action'. This phrase, from Hannah Arendt's *Origins of Totalitarianism*, is part of her analysis of the way in which totalitarianism's brutal extension of the area of legal authority eradicates the boundaries of the ethical private self and succeeds in dominating and terrorising human beings from within. Totalitarian government, she writes,

> . . . substitutes for the boundaries and channels of communication between individual men a band of iron which holds them so tightly together that it is as though their plurality had disappeared into One Man of gigantic dimensions. To abolish the fences of laws between men – as tyranny does – means to take away man's liberties and destroy freedom as a living political reality; for the space between men as it is hedged by laws, is the living space of freedom.[20]

THE CRITIQUE OF LIBERAL JUSTICE: *A PASSAGE TO INDIA* AND *IT'S A BATTLEFIELD*

When Ernest Barker published his Cambridge lectures in 1951, he printed the preamble to the Constitution of India at the beginning of the book, 'moved to quote it', he said, by his pride in the thought that India had begun its independent life 'by subscribing to the principles of political tradition which we in the West call Western, but which are now something more than Western'.[21] In *A Passage to India*,

Forster confronts the limitations of the liberal ideal as it manifested itself in pre-independence India; the Western legal system is seen in the context of the varieties of inward experience contained within 'the real India'. The legal proceedings against Aziz and the theme of justice constitute only part of a complex pattern. Nevertheless, some of the widest themes of the novel are focused in the central event of the trial: adherence to legal forms in the public realm of the law is judged by its ability to protect the individual personality; political necessity is measured against moral conscience; officially constructed narrative and proof from circumstantial evidence are related to the most wide-ranging reflections on order and chaos; the effectiveness of the law in achieving the general ordering of society is tested by the 'muddle' of India, and its claims to embody liberal values are set alongside the more positive private virtues. Substantial justice seems to have been for Forster a 'misty abstraction', elusive in itself, and difficult to embody adequately in institutional form, the 'good' being more easily located in the individual moral personality than in judicial or ethical systems. Forster's tendency to 'float above' actual political and social problems is reflected in the fact that he winces at the 'rough engine' of the law and is troubled by its negativity in comparison with the other elements of social morality 'which we regard as going beyond mere justice'.[22] Such qualities (love, generosity, charity) are embodied in the absent heart, the positive ingredient of social morality which cannot be enjoined by the negative system of justice, and without which justice can degenerate into the partial and unsatisfactory unity of solidarity. Forster's reservations about the limitations of justice as it is constituted and practised are metaphorically expressed by a series of absences: the absent god (only a mockery), the absent fact (that is, the emptiness of the cave in which the legally investigated event is supposed to have occurred), the absent individual conscience. Even if the form or procedure of the law is in essential respects hollow, however, he does not dismiss out of hand the necessity of such forms and procedures. It is characteristic of the balance of *Passage to India* that there is an underlying affirmation of the virtues of form itself (as in procedural justice), however far short this may fall of the justifying ideals which give such potency to the liberal version of the rule of law. He considers what the ideal *does* embody that might conceivably have some species-wide value – procedural justice as an indispensable, if minimal, protection, one of the reasonable forms of civilised life that function to keep things going.

Forster's respect for the forms of procedural justice and for the qualities of character which enable a man to administer the law well is of a piece with his respect for decent, civilised norms of behaviour in all contexts. Legal processes are so closely bound up with the widest themes of *A Passage to India* because they are the very embodiment of everything we do to keep natural disorder at bay (the creation of ordered space within which discriminations can be made, clear identification of boundaries, imposition of regular processes, construction of coherent narratives). It is an inherent part of his belief that the forms which 'contain', in the sense of inhibiting direct, emotional retribution, are not to be lightly discarded.[23] Even characters who are, by Forster's standards, humanly deficient, can play their part in serving an elementary procedural concept of justice. McBryde, the District Superintendent of Police, although predisposed to believe in the criminality of all natives, is constrained both by his background and by the nature of the system itself, treating Aziz with a courteous punctiliousness as he discusses bail, visiting regulations and the separation of powers ('I am not your judge'). The Collector, when his impulse is to flog every native in sight, is restrained by his determination to remain 'scrupulously fair'.[24] Forster acknowledges the fundamental importance of 'the flimsy framework of the court' (p. 224), the basic structure of a legal system which can dam up the flow of destructive emotions and which forces the Collector to keep reminding himself that Aziz is innocent until proven guilty, even though the effort fatigues him. Ronny Heaslop, in spite of the impoverishment of his personality, 'doesn't come out badly' (p. 239) because the demands of the system he serves actually lend a kind of impartiality and restraint to his behaviour which are often absent in the behaviour of those who have less respect for the processes of law. Whilst exposing Ronny's complacency and self-satisfaction, Forster makes apparent the integrity he brings to the task of trying to judge evidence fairly – of 'trying to decide which of two untrue accounts was the less untrue' (p. 50). At the climax of the trial, when Adela withdraws the charge against Aziz, what sustains her in her recantation is a 'hard prosaic' commitment to giving an accurate account of what has happened and to seeing that justice is actually served (pp. 223–4). Forster, then, has arranged the events of the novel so that the law in many respects *is* seen to operate with the kind of impersonality that gives it a virtue 'more than Western'. The community which has imported the system rages when it is seen to be in crucial respects beyond their personal control: 'that [Das] should be judge over an English girl had convulsed the station with wrath' (p. 191). It would appear that it is a system which, passed on to other cultures, can function as an honourable (even if inevitably flawed) method of achieving a standard of decency. The integrity necessary for the system to operate is repeatedly shown to be present in Das, who is courteous, intelligent, honest, impartial in his attention to evidence and determined to conduct the trial in as firm and fair a way as possible.

Fielding, too, recognises the modest virtues of orderly procedure. Forster's gentle mockery of the impoverishment of his honest but limited empiricism and practicality does not diminish our respect for Fielding's principled effort to sustain the ordinary decencies of public conduct. Civilised life as we know it would be ill-protected if men dispensed with the prosaic forms of this bounded world. In a novel which is always 'looking beyond', some of the more transcendent visions serve to clarify the strengths of the liberal's down-to-earth commitment to fair adjudication, and regular, reasonable forms. The banal, rationally defined space in which such deliberations take place is implicitly contrasted with the impractical idealism of other perspectives. When Aziz sits in Fielding's room, it becomes in his imagination an ideal space within which he can see himself dispensing justice. He indulges in a nostalgic vision of a vanished past in which benevolent clerks and officials sat in harmony on carpets, handing out rupees from a bottomless purse. He dreams of a generosity and tenderness that are almost boundless: in this idyllic world, there would be no adverse judgement, no one would be punished, banquets would be given and there would be feasting and happiness 'till peace comes'. The ladies approve, and we, as readers, warm to the expansive nature of Aziz, but Forster's firm authorial voice reminds us of the utter unworkability of the ideal: it is 'the tenderness of one incapable of administration, and unable to grasp that if the poor criminal is let off he will again rob the poor widow' (p. 70). It is not entirely viable to have so exalted a conception of Justice; it lacks both painstaking commitment to rationally defensible, well-established procedures and a willingness to accept the law's negativity and to contemplate punishments as well as rewards. In the end, it is merely rhetorical, consisting only of 'words' and a set of mental conventions. Alongside this soaring rhetoric of capitalised abstractions, Fielding's circumscribed ethic seems threadbare, 'too definite and bleak' (p. 108). Without it, however, substantial justice is difficult to secure. The waywardness of Aziz, charming though it is, could not construct the foundations of a just society. We see, for example, his casualness about objective truth – 'Incurably inaccurate, he already thought that this was what had occurred.' And we see also his panic in the crisis, in contrast to Fielding's sensible, well-ordered approach, restrained and attentive to detail – 'Put your hat straight and take my arm. I'll see you through' (pp. 156, 159).

But if procedural justice is necessary, Forster implies, it is by no means sufficient. Substantial justice – the capitalised Justice of Aziz's vision – is an ideal which all too often seems to elude the socially bound proceedings of actual civilised institutions. These larger issues of substantial justice are at the heart of the question of the British role in India. The territorial nature of the conflict, with the British simultaneously occupying Indian space and perpetually excluding the Indians from superior British space, is both metaphorically and actually present in the legal conflict. Actual events, like Fielding's forced departure from the club, are reflected in the images of the space and boundaries in terms of which people think: 'at a time like this there's no room for – well – personal views. The man who doesn't toe the line is lost' (p. 168). Within the courtroom, the British intention of asserting moral superiority (and thus forcing the immediate conviction of Aziz) is comically captured in their ascent *en masse* to the elevated platform. The European party has sought to establish its dominance of the space of the courtroom by securing the platform which confers authority, and Das, if he is to serve justice, must assert himself to secure their climb down. In spite of Das's effort to ensure impartial control of the trial, 'English justice' is inevitably equated with the imperial presumption of the British (p. 218). The trial brings to the fore the question of whether the values inherent in the British rule of law are invariably embedded in a particular way of life. When the Indians ask Fielding 'how is England justified in holding India?' they expect an answer couched in terms of Justice and Morality. Instead, Fielding shuffles; his honesty will not allow him to claim the high moral ground by invoking idea of 'good', and this reticence would seem to be shared throughout by Forster himself, as is evident in his suspicion of the justifying ideal of substantial justice (p. 108). The representation of the role of the British in India in terms of the enforcement of a Western system of justice focuses our attention on the rationale behind British administration. We are led to see the absurd disjunction between the legal and the actual, the incongruity of a tiny enclave trying to contain within its administrative boundaries the whole of India. The 'why' of the British in India, which is, on one level, a specifically political question about the justification of Empire, is also, on a deeper level, a question about both the origins and the substantial content of the Western ideal of justice.

Ernest Barker, enquiring into the possible origins of the 'total notion of justice', suggests that (aside from the Marxist concept of positive law, which simply has its source in the fact of economic strength) there are three main sources, all closely related to one another: religion, nature and ethics. These can be described, respectively, as rules of right expressed by God and 'above and behind all man-made law'; as 'the natural order of things'; and as 'the moral standard of the community', that is, a standard which satisfies 'the demands of the general moral conscience'.[25] All three of these justifications are of fundamental importance to the thematic structure of *A Passage to India*. What we see, in effect, are crucial recognitions of the absence of these main sustaining elements: the lack of divine sanction, the vulnerability of natural law to 'nature' in a wider sense, and the impossibility of an ethical sanction which does not imply an unacceptable assimilation of the individual to the system that claims jurisdiction over him.

The role of the English in India, Ronny says, is to 'do justice and keep the peace'. He speaks, his mother suggests, like a would-be god, and raises the question of whether British rule is a response to an Indian need – 'India likes gods' – or purely an assertion of British arrogance – 'Englishmen like posing as gods' (p. 49). The idea that human law must derive its authority from conformity with divine law, though lightly handled, is ultimately related to Forster's deeper themes, reflecting a religious sense which, although it involves no expression of positive belief, yearns towards something beyond the limitations of political life. The religious dimension of English justice is an easy target for satire, and the 'sacred COURT' administered by the English in India is only ironically represented as enshrining an ideal of godlike potency. Turton, for example, at the time when the collective zeal for revenge seems to be concentrated in his person, is 'revealed' to Fielding 'like a god in a shrine' (p. 160). Having set the scene for the courtroom proceedings, Forster again ironically gestures towards the divinity traditionally associated with the origins of the idea of justice, placing opposite the small, cultivated assistant magistrate the large symbolic figure of the punkah wallah, a man wholly lacking the power of either class or enlightened intellect but nevertheless an ideal of physical perfection who appears as 'a male fate, a winnower of souls' – a figure of such godlike indifference that the presumption of little human 'gods' is humbled, and the question 'by what right' echoes in Adela's mind. The punkah wallah seems to embody some higher judgement than the merely human orderings (orderings which, in social terms, relegate him to the status of untouchable). Adela fancies that he controls the proceedings, and his presence rebukes the narrowness of her perceptions, the 'brand of opinions' which justifies the trial and 'the suburban Jehovah who sanctified them' (p. 212).

'Jehovah' suggests the relation of the Jews to their God, represented in the Old Testament as 'a continuing negotiation within the law', justice being for the Jews 'the central moral concept'.[26] In Godbole's Hindu festival, we have, on the other hand, the antithesis of Jehovah the law-giver: the elusive Hindu God is everywhere and nowhere, and in those who worship him we see the 'sacred bewilderment' of the human spirit trying 'by a desperate contortion to ravish the unknown' (pp. 279–83).

The artificial space within which human justice is administered comes to seem flimsy and insubstantial juxtaposed with the vast mysteriousness of the country supposedly contained by the system. The chaotic diversity of India, which is, like Godbole's ceremony, 'a frustration of reason and form', does not seem very likely to furnish a pattern of 'the natural order of things'. The substantial idea of natural justice represents an appeal to 'human nature', and the usual attribute of human nature chosen as the basis for this is reason, or rationality: 'It is because we are rational beings that we recognise natural law' (by this argument, for example, animals, being without reason, are not judged to be bound by natural law). Throughout *A Passage to India*, Forster places his characters in circumstances which erode their confidence in reasonable judgement and problematise any sense of a correspondence between positive law and the judgements arrived at when characters are isolated from the regular practices which constitute convention.[27]

When the Europeans venture out, leaving behind the suburban sanctities of the civil station, the natural world they encounter is emphatically not one which lends support to human orderings. In the darkness on the Marabar road, the Nawab Bahadur's car swerves into a tree. Adela is convinced that the cause was a large animal which 'rushed up out of the dark'; Mrs Moore, hearing the account of the accident, murmurs, 'A ghost'. It is only when we rejoin the Nawab Bahadur, waiting for the repair of his car, that we learn that, in his own mind, the Marabar road has in effect been the scene of a 'retrial', the animal dark collaborating with the spirit of a drunken man who had, many years ago, been killed by the Nawab Bahadur's car: he had been judged innocent 'before God and the Law', but a judgement which emanates from a quite different source than either divine or humanly rational sanctions was now asserting itself (pp. 96–7).

As is characteristic of Forster, the incident of the Nawab Bahadur's car is presented in a tone of light social comedy. But it has resonance beyond the incidental humour. The ghost is an 'unspeakable form' – a secret which, like the silence and echoes of the Marabar caves, is something inexpressible. This pre-linguistic, non-rational sense of retribution is not limited or put to rest by the formal adjudication of the legal codes, by compensation, or other forms of official appeasement. The ghost suggests the collapse of 'frail cherished distinctions'. Instead of distinctions, there is an absence of difference, an insurrection of the dead that makes visible something of which there can be no adequate representation. Space is usurped by something immaterial, an intrusion of non-signification. As in the linguistic jumble of Godbole's festival, the articulated codes of the community are undermined. The body of civilised conventions (legal process, compensation, even double compensation) is powerless against such an unpleasant manifestation, emerging from the undifferentiated Indian landscape to assail a vehicle that more properly belongs to an advanced European culture. The human passengers seem to be interlopers in a mysterious world that obeys quite different laws from those written in statute books.[28]

In an even more extreme form, the Marabar caves negate human efforts to order and judge rationally, to weigh evidence, to discriminate between values – negate, that is, all the bases of our sense of natural law. The caves are the most disturbing of the spaces set against the ordered space of the courtroom, and together these spaces constitute the ironic centre of the novel, with a non-event in the meaningless cave-space constructed as a crime by the English community and given judicial meaning. The 'echo' breaks down all of the empirical and moral distinctions (true/false, right/wrong, innocent/guilty, lofty/vile) on which human judgement depends. The obliteration of coherent sound is a return to a pre-linguistic universe which in no sense acts to confirm human orderings and oppositions: when Mrs Moore exits from her cave, she looks for the 'villain' who had struck her face, only to find that it was 'a poor little baby'; for Adela, the echo is an assault on her capacity for reasoned thought, interfering with 'the natural honesty of her mind', and intervening whenever she tried to 'think the incident out' (pp. 145–6, 190). The echo renders both of them unfit for the trial – Adela in her inability to supply a true, rational narrative, Mrs Moore in her indifference to the rationale of the whole proceedings, to the determination of guilt and innocence. What for Adela is a crisis about the determination of fact is for Mrs Moore a crisis of moral meaning. The echo is not insurmountable – not the 'last word' – but the experience is enough to shake severely any serene confidence in our powers to discern what is 'naturally' good and true. The caves are 'a central place in the novel' – a space of utter nullification through which all the characters must pass, rendering insecure our sense of any natural basis for the 'orderly hopes' and 'reasonable forms' of humanity (pp. 206, 275).[29]

Legal processes, as we have seen, are perceived by Forster as a fundamental safeguard, but at the same time he takes quite full account of the ways in which the law can itself become an instrument and a reflection of the communal 'madness' released by the caves. The law forestalls the excesses of a raging tribal revenge, but also serves to convert the cultural prejudices of the community into a more organised form. Both religious and natural justifications most readily resolve themselves into ethics – the moral standard of the community. It is the community which provides the space, the cultural forms and the language (the 'high-sounding words') which express the substance of the ideal of justice (p. 203). This is the aspect of substantial justice that Forster most centrally and critically represents. He develops throughout the motif of artificial constructs – the small, bounded enclave which claims to administer a universally valid system of justice, which it is assumed will be manifest in the trial. Instead, however, this controlling enclave is increasingly isolated by the proceedings. The sense of unity the English have comes not from a genuinely unifying vision of justice but from the partisan togetherness generated within the community in power. It is founded on a suppression of individuality which is clearly, for Forster, the most disturbing aspect of cohesion around an ideal of justice. Barker cautions that in framing a concept of substantial law based on ethics, one must think in terms of satisfying 'the demands of the general moral conscience', rather than 'some single "broken arc" of value called by the name of "solidarity" or by some other such name'. What *A Passage to India* forcefully illustrates is how difficult it is to maintain a *general* notion of moral conscience in the face of the 'solidarity' of a dominant community; and how far such solidarity also invalidates the proposition that 'the moral world is a world of individual persons'.[30]

The apparent exclusion of the full human personality from the process of administering justice is taken by Forster to suggest a separation between ethical principles and the idea of justice as it is conceived of by the 'social' or 'group' personality. Forster's oft-quoted declaration that 'temperamentally, I am an individualist' - that he would always 'favour the individual at the expense of the community' – has clear implications for his conception of substantial justice.[31] In *A Passage to India*, as the trial gets underway, the European characters cease to function as individuals and take on a collective identity, an identity in part defined by an increased, often hysterical, insistence on the boundary between communities: 'All over Chandrapore that day the Europeans were putting aside their normal personalities and sinking themselves in their community.' The crime that has supposedly been committed is diagnosed as a failure to keep the English and the Indians sufficiently separate. Forster's punning commentary emphasises that, in abandoning all claim to coherent reasoning, they have moved further than ever from the capacity to form human connections: 'the power of putting two and two together was annihilated' (p. 162). This separation, most acute at the time of the trial, is apparent, of course, from the beginning of the novel, not only in the physical boundaries drawn between the strongholds of the English and the undifferentiated Indian landscape but in the casual comments of both communities. The Indians, discussing the possibility of forming social connections with the English, observe that it is only a matter of time until the English in India are all 'exactly alike' (p. 13). Though the conclusions reached may be too sweeping, Forster shows us the core of truth in the observation every time we witness and judge the behaviour of the English – as when Ronny, for example, fails to hear Professor Godbole's remarks, not because of intentional rudeness but because 'the only link he could be conscious of with an Indian was the official', never the individual (p. 75).

The effects of the trial, of course, are both to strengthen the boundaries and to impose upon everyone the requirement of solidarity, unifying the expression worn by all English faces at Chandrapore. Immediately before the climb up to the caves, Adela expresses the fear that by marrying Ronny she will inevitably become an Anglo-Indian. And however much she hopes to avoid 'the mentality', she is already detecting signs of change in herself, as she becomes less willing to express very directly attitudes which would offend the Anglo-Indian community. Her hopes are expressed with the timid, rather colourless rationality characteristic of Adela; as we have said, her own experience of the caves is one which completely undermines, for a time, her powers of reasoned apprehension, and her worst fears are thus speedily confirmed. There is a sense in which Adela herself is 'on trial'. This is partly a matter of her haunting feeling of personal guilt ('She felt that it was her crime'), an aspect of the confrontation which is explicitly taken account of by Fielding when he and Adela are trying to get to the truth of what actually happened, and he summarises their grounds for agreeing 'that he is not a villain and that you are not one' (pp. 190, 235). More fundamentally, however, what she is guilty of, until the climax of the trial, is precisely her inability to continue functioning as a moral individual – as one capable of making individual judgements of guilt or innocence. The dry and sensible girl, who is 'not pukka' and is 'the last person in Chandrapore wrongfully to accuse an Indian', has not been truly incorporated into the English community, but she has been 'caught' by it (pp. 176–7).

Adela is not a person for her compatriots. It is not her character but her public position as 'the English girl' who has been wronged to which they respond. They are unsure what to call her – 'Miss Quested, Adela, what d'ye call yourself . . .' (p. 207). Indeed, both Adela and Aziz in a sense lose their individual identities, their names remaining unspoken by the English community ('she, like Aziz, was always referred to by a periphrasis'). She was simply 'a victim', Aziz 'the prisoner', 'the person in question', the 'defence' (pp. 179–82). Aziz recognises at the outset that Adela's accusation means that he will lose his 'name', in the sense of his reputation, but the repetition of the motif of lost or avoided names creates a much wider impression of the way in which the communal recourse to legal action erodes 'the source of all ethical principles . . . the value and worth of the individual personality'. It is only as Adela begins to move towards a recognition that she may be in error that she begins to pronounce his name: 'Aziz . . . have I made a mistake?' (p. 197). At the trial itself, actually seeing him in person for the first time since the expedition to the caves again leads her to reflect on the possibility that she may be wrong. In the wake of the trial, Adela feels completely isolated from the community, both literally and metaphorically unable to 'join them' again, since from their point of view she is now 'emptied, valueless'. To a moral individual, however (to Fielding), she has at last become 'a real person' (pp. 225, 238).

Within the courtroom, Adela relives her individual experience of the cave space, and, as she is transported back, the proceedings collapse. The suppression of individual identity by communal solidarity has created two key absences: the absence of narrative, that is, the absence of the truth of what happened in the caves; and the absence of 'heart'. The narrative that sustains the accusation against Aziz is built up largely on the basis of circumstantial evidence. It is based, as McBryde says, on the 'logic of evidence', the flight of Miss Quested and her 'terrible state', the field-glasses in Aziz's pocket, the newly broken strap, the jammed eye-piece (pp. 164–5). In general terms, the function of circumstantial evidence is to reveal the truth about people who have something to hide, about those 'who do things unseen'. The construction of the prosecution's narrative is in fact often taken to be confirmed by silence on the part of the accused.[32] What happens in the caves is 'unspeakable' in the deepest sense: it is ultimately mysterious, unknowable, absent as an event; no character in the novel will ever able to 'tell' what it was that happened ('It will never be known'). Over this void, characters attempt to construct a narrative which will make sense – or which, in the case of the English community, will create within this empty space the basis for a legal demonstration of their own rectitude. They are seeking to establish a discursive construction of facts that will play an important part in confirming the solidarity of their community and that will achieve a fit with the stock of socially constructed narratives which mirror their own sense of the power relations of British India. The privilege assumed by the English community is that of narrating the thoughts of others (of both Adela and Aziz), and is a striking demonstration of the way in which legal narratives can represent 'a threat to private being'. In part, this is manifested in the novel through the motif of violations of individual personality – for example, the invasion of privacy and the misconstruction of evidence, forcing another narrative on someone else (as in McBryde's search through Aziz's belongings). The narrative of the prosecution bespeaks a presumption of guilt and a theory about inferior character types ('All unfortunate natives are criminals at heart.'). The expectations of the audience to whom the stories are told are also a powerful factor, and Fielding rightly surmises that Adela's 'own story' might be quite different if told to someone who actually believes in Aziz rather than to 'people who disbelieve in Indians' (pp. 164–7).[33]

The determination of truth by legal means seems a hopeless task, until Adela's moment of vision sweeps away the carefully managed representation of 'fact' and she becomes, from the European point of view, a 'broken machine' (p. 224). Her vision of the truth allows her to recapture her ability to distinguish and to see clearly, and thus to supplant the constructed narrative by 'direct access'. In effect, she makes present the space of her own experience of the cave within the courtroom. Such flashbacks in crime fiction often function to reveal a hidden narrative, the guilty secret of the criminal. The experience of the caves, however, is a blankness, not to be filled even by honest empirical enquiry. What is revealed is vacancy and absence of narrative. Watching in her vision for Aziz, Adela fails to locate him. Even Fielding, committed as he is to getting at the truth of the matter, is ultimately defeated by the silence at the heart of the story: Adela's vision disappears when she tries to interpret it.

Through the experience of the Marabar caves, characters are led to confront all that the law cannot include and the ways in which justice alone is insufficient; they discover that (to borrow Foucault's phrase) 'the laws of the state and the laws of the heart' are *not* the same. Adela's saving vision is a non-rational, intuitive moment that emerges inexplicably, not by the standard methods of legal enquiry. And there are other forces at work that are even less amenable to rational explanation. In Adela's case, whilst her action comes from the heart, it does not include the heart – 'cold justice and honesty' being more in her nature than passion or generosity (p. 238). But beyond her honourable recantation and beyond the legal framework of the court, Forster places the 'magic' of Mrs Moore's transcendentally benign influence. In comparison to Esmiss Esmoor, the procedures of the law can only appear negative – 'In vain the Magistrate threatened and expelled' (p. 219). Equally, as Fielding says, 'Love is of no value as a witness' (p. 240). But, although Forster finds the impracticality of his spiritual–intuitive characters in some ways as worrying as the aridity of the legal process, the absent Mrs Moore's ability to stir people's feelings even after her death gives some measure of the superior power of love. Stuart Hampshire writes that 'whether it is applied to individuals or to institutions or to policies' justice is 'negative, in comparison with love and friendship, or courage, or intelligence'.[34] Although, in *A Passage to India*, the forms of procedural justice have protected a wrongly accused man from a gross injustice, the imaginative picture of human relations that informs substantial justice remains problematic in comparison to such virtues as these. The reason that substantial justice seems for Forster to be a rather unsatisfactory, misty abstraction is in large part to do with its external nature. Barker summarises it in this way: justice 'is not a rule of the inward life, but a rule of the outward life', though this rule of the outward life of relations 'is vitally and intimately connected with the inward moral life: it is a condition, or set of conditions, needed and designed for the free movement of that life'. The metaphor he uses is that of a fence around a house, law being 'the best and highest set of conditions, set round the house and forming, as it were, a fence for its protection, which has to be ... firmly established, before moral action can find a free space for its play'.[35] In *A Passage to India*, we see what Forster takes to be both the strengths and the limitations of the fence of justice: its formal procedures, in so far as they are impartially observed, do protect individuals in essential ways, but this rule of the outward life fails to satisfy man in his search for some more positive human qualities to set against the chaos of the vast landscape beyond the fenced terrain – and here, it is the qualities of the inward life and not the rule of the outward to which Forster turns.

In *A Passage to India*, then, the courtroom drama is at the centre of an action which makes us aware of the distance between interior space, or private being, and the public space within which legal judgements hold sway. Graham Greene's representation of the limitations of the liberal legal system, *It's a Battlefield* (1934), is set in the post-trial period, after Jim Drover has been convicted of killing a policeman at a political meeting. Like Forster, though more harshly, Greene conveys a sense of unease about possible abuses of the legal machinery and about the law's negativity. He focuses on characters who are not, in terms of the central legal conflict, the main combatants, that is, he does not make us well-acquainted with either the accused or the prosecution. The effect of this is to throw into sharper relief the separation of private and public spheres and the extent to which each is absent to the other. Public institutions are hidden from the private gaze; seeing the isolation and ultimate unknowability of the accused individual, we recognise his alienation from the remote and incomprehensible legal system.

As in *A Passage to India*, there is an absence at the heart of the narrative. In Greene's novel, the absent centre of the novel is the accused man himself. Just as we cannot ever really discover what took place in the Marabar caves, we cannot look into the mind of the man who has been condemned to death for the crime of murder. Drover, locked away in prison, is invisible except when glimpsed briefly through a peep hole or through a glass: 'they spied on him through a little window the size of a postcard in the cell door'. What we see, instead of Drover the man, is the legal construction of the individual, and the helplessness of anyone who is caught up in and defined by the system of 'law and order'. The officials who come to view him through the window in his cell door see an anonymous-looking man wearing 'grey loose unaccustomed clothes', sitting as though waiting for someone to paint his portrait: ' "I suppose he's a type", the secretary murmured . . . .' Outside his cell, Drover appears as a name printed in 'great letters' on a poster, a signifier of his publicly constructed identity, which bears no relation to the man who cut bread and stirred tea at the breakfast table.[36] The effect of Drover's trial and unsuccessful appeal is to remove his full humanity from the perception of others – and thus to make him 'other'. This loss of individual identity is most apparent in the heavily caricatured speech of Mr Surrogate, who represents Drover's impending death as a blow to the capitalist system, a martyrdom in the communist cause and a symbol of the coming of age of the Party. Surrogate's response is the mirror image of the legally sanctioned communal solidarity we have seen in *A Passage to India*. His reaction is based on the premise that the proceedings are *un*just manifestations of the capitalist ethic and, in opposition, he formulates a counter abstraction, as dependent as any other theoretically-based solidarity on the exclusion of the full human personality: he resents the intrusion of Drover as an individual, requiring him only as a Comrade, a sacrifice whose fate will help to confirm the reality of 'the lovely abstractions of Communism' (*It's a Battlefield*, p. 44).

One of the dominant images of Greene's novel is that of surrogation – in official and legal usage, the process whereby someone acts in place of another who is absent or dead. At no stage is the accused man able to represent himself. It is as though the real man, virtually invisible to us as readers, as well as to those around him, can be present only in a series of distorted and partial representations. This is obvious enough in the trial itself, during which the story of the accused has to be interpreted in terms appropriate to legal discourse, in a way that allows it to be 'categorised easily within the legal statutes that apply to the case'.[37] In Court his case is disputed by 'three white wigs' and 'silk robes', dehumanised, pantomime figures, disinterested not in the sense that they are unbiased but in the sense of a 'complete lack of interest', with the two counsel nodding, exchanging compliments and finally going off together arm in arm for lunch. Although counsel for the defence argues 'with great skill on the question of motive' (that is, that Drover killed the policeman because he thought the man was going to hit his wife), this is not taken as grounds for setting aside the conviction (pp. 59–60). Outside the courtroom as well, in the post-trial period most directly represented in the novel, 'the murderer' has ceased to exist as his own man, with Mr Surrogate's substitution of his theoretical version of a Comrade for the real Drover as only the most extreme example of this false advocacy. Drover's brother Conrad, for example, takes the place of the condemned man in more than one sense. He believes that his official role should be to act on his brother's behalf to obtain a reprieve, but the kind of action he contemplates springs from a more complex feeling that he has in a way become his brother. He has slept with his brother's wife, and in doing so thinks that, just as a cannibal takes on the qualities of the enemy he eats, he has become 'something of the same man': 'For an instant last night he had been his brother, he became capable of killing a man.' But rather than taking on Jim's simple strength, Conrad instead takes on his guilt and isolation. As readers, we are given an extended analysis of Conrad's tortured conscience, as he contemplates the fact of adultery and the possibility of murder. Conrad's self-examination is revealed to us instead of Jim Drover's absent, unknowable moral being, and the revelation serves to press home the degree to which a man's conscience is formed by the social and legal system to which he belongs. Ignored and unrecognised,

Conrad is untouched by 'the approach of authority', but is nevertheless himself subject to external conceptions of guilt. His inner self is defined by labels not of his own devising but taken from others who have made the rules under which he suffers: 'it was unfair that they should leave him so alone and yet make the rules which governed him. It was as if a man marooned must still order his life according to the regulations of his ship' (pp. 159–60). In dramatising the conflict between private judgements and official legal verdicts, Greene locates one of the central ironies in the often illusory nature of individual autonomy. Having internalised the codes of his society, Conrad 'convicts' himself, 'as if he were a judge, aware of his own secret sin, who must still sit there and condemn'. This inward process of adjudication paradoxically both joins him to his society and separates him from it. Conrad is ultimately as isolated as his brother, and his final action (attempted murder ending in his own accidental death) is, to official eyes, 'incomprehensible' (pp. 172, 198).

Throughout the novel, the ideal of justice is put at issue by the inability of the judicial system to 'comprehend' and take proper account of the motives and intentions behind individual actions, even when these actions are founded on moral assumptions formed 'according to the regulations of the ship'. The Assistant Commissioner, in whose 'thin bureaucratic body' Conrad sees the whole of the legal system personified ('justice with a file of papers'), feels as though he is 'fighting in a fog', unable to extract meaning from the contradictory Drover reports. Although he is in many ways shown to be an honourable man, the Assistant Commissioner's inability to transcend his official role is a constant theme (pp. 161, 166). He is a 'mercenary', only upholding 'a system in which he had no interest because he was paid to uphold it'; he has no 'abstract reasons', and is only occasionally given conviction by the sight of 'some brutality'. He dreams, however, of an organisation that he could serve for higher reasons than pay, 'because of its inherent justice' (pp. 129–30). Although he reflects with relief that, as things stand, justice is not really his business (like Pilate, washing his hands) he is, 'in his secret life', deeply troubled by the deficiencies of official justice: 'In private life one could not leave justice to the Home Secretary, to Parliament, to His Majesty's Judges; possibly to God, but the Assistant Commissioner was not fully satisfied of His existence' (p. 162).

Conrad ironically believes that he can personally affect the whole machinery of justice by focusing his hatred and revenge on the individual figure of the Assistant Commissioner. The unmoving rusty trigger of the gun with which he has been supplied and the blanks with

which it has been (without his knowledge) loaded suggest the extent
of his powerlessness, but he is equally disabled by his thoroughgoing
misconception of the system itself. If the individual conscience is
invisible to the official eye, both the official machinery of the law
and the ideal of justice are equally unavailable to the inspection of
the private individual. Its workings seem impenetrable even to men
experienced in interpreting public life: Conder, the journalist, reflects
on the 'incomprehensibility of those who judged and pardoned,
rewarded and punished' (p. 39). To the insignificant private person,
like Conrad and Drover's wife, those who 'pull the wires' of the
system are as invisible and insulated as Drover in his cell. They are
'confident cultured faces' who are part of another world: 'One could
not appeal to them for justice; justice to them was another word for
prison' (pp. 64–5). The remote inscrutability of those who incarcerate
in the name of justice is matched by the mysteriousness of justice itself.
None of the characters in the novel is able to define its meaning. Those
who demand justice, Conder cynically observes, speak as if 'justice
were a pound of tea, as if it existed anywhere . . .' (p. 103).

A cynical despair of locating worldly justice is set against various
manifestations of religious faith, though these are not yet for Greene
a solid enough presence to stand against the inadequate secular system.
In a later book like *The Power and the Glory* (1940), Greene establishes
a much sharper dichotomy between legal (or pseudo-legal) judgement
and religious judgement. There, the secular categories of crime and
punishment are defined by a corrupt and inflexible system, wholly
subservient to the humanly deadening power of abstract political zeal;
the religious categories of sinfulness and expiation, on the other hand,
spring from a faith so dogged and, in spite of everything, resilient that
it is capable of transcending all that a repressive state can inflict on it.
In secular terms, Greene's priest is tried, found guilty and sentenced
to death at a trial at which he is not present. What preoccupies him,
however, is not earthly but divine justice: when he says, 'I just want
justice, that's all', he is reflecting not on his impending sentence but on
the imminent prospect of damnation. The main focus of the narrative
is the priest's inner compulsion towards confession. Tormented by
guilt and, in the end, denied the ritual of absolution, he convicts
himself of carnal sin, of being a bad priest, of pride, drunkenness
and despair – of a multitude of failures accumulating in secret until
'one day they would choke up, he supposed, altogether the source
of grace'. Although he makes his biographical 'confession' to the
Lieutenant who has pursued and captured him, it is not in the hope
of changing anything. Whereas the Lieutenant is willing to 'make a

massacre' in order to 'begin the world again', the priest knows that he has already 'made his own world', and from this acceptance gains both fellowship ('a sense of companionship which he had never experienced in the old days') and an intense commitment to understanding and evaluating the choices he has made. He has the ability to move with painful honesty through his own moral world even when he is in a jail cell so crowded that he can barely squat. Although he fears death, the rigour of his self-examination rises entirely above the power of secular judgement.[38]

In *It's a Battlefield*, on the other hand, we listen in passing to meditations on faith, but observe nothing with the transcendent quality of the whiskey priest's spiritual integrity. Neither the vague, old-fashioned faith of Caroline Bury nor the temporary spiritual uplift experienced by Jules Briton seems to provide any adequate alternative, and, at the end of the novel, Greene holds in ironic balance the consequences of secular and divine justice, each in its way apparently productive of undeserved misery. Unaccountable human justice grants a reprieve for Drover, but circumstances are such that the outcome seems worse than the death penalty: there is the prospect of an eighteen-year sentence, condemning his wife to years of waiting, with Conrad – her 'one comfort' – dead (the final blow having been his shock at a misapprehension of what has occurred); Drover himself attempts suicide to escape 'the misery of too protracted a life'. The prison chaplain resigns because he cannot any longer stand the arbitrariness and incomprehensibility of human justice, but concedes that divine justice may be equally unfathomable (pp. 199–201).

Neither *A Passage to India* nor *It's a Battlefield* represents a systematically unjust society. As Conder observes, although he is occasionally flushed with revolutionary fervour by the knowledge that incomprehensible decisions are made on the basis of whim, prejudice and favouritism, 'he knew well enough that it was not systematic enough to be called injustice' (p. 39). The ideal of substantial justice is shown to be elusive, and the problem of connecting the moral world of the individual with the official domain of the law is foregrounded by both writers. Equally, however, in both novels, basic procedural justice does actually operate to prevent gross miscarriages: flawed though the system is, Aziz in the end is acquitted; the legal battle over Drover's case is unaccountable and unsatisfactory, the motives behind the reprieve suspect, but he is not in fact hanged. The abuses and insensitivity of legal institutions are abundantly apparent: in both texts, there is a humanistic discontent with the displacement of individual moral being, and the liberal dream of justice is represented as an elusive one, not readily defined in terms of its originating ideals. By the late thirties, however, the hypocrisy and muddle that bedevil the basic concept of justice had paled into insignificance by comparison with totalitarian perversions of judicial forms, abuses far more disturbing than the shortcomings of the liberal ideal.

THE TOTALITARIAN NIGHTMARE: *TRIAL OF A JUDGE* AND *DARKNESS AT NOON*

There is obviously an essential difference between an ideal of justice which is elusive and one which has altogether disappeared. As Rubashov discovers in *Darkness at Noon*, powerlessness has 'as many grades as power'.[39] Indeed justice is, in a sense, an ideal which is most clearly perceived in its absence: 'Of all the moral concepts', Stuart Hampshire writes, 'it is particularly the concept of justice that cannot be fully understood without a consideration of the forces of destruction to which the virtue of justice, both in private and in public life, is meant to be an obstruction.' Since justice is a negative virtue, 'one has to ask . . . what it prevents rather than what it engenders'. Both Nazism and communism, in their different ways, utterly rejected and overturned liberal ideals of justice – rejected, as Merleau-Ponty said in his attack on *Darkness at Noon*, 'the idea of locking ourselves within the judicial dream of liberalism'.[40]

Nazism, as we have seen, had as its explicit aim the elimination of everything traditionally implied by the concept of justice – balanced adjudication, rational legal procedures, the impartial review of evidence – thus opening up 'an infinite moral space . . . for natural violence and domination', for an exercise of power without limit, requiring no justification and admitting no restraint.[41] Marxists also explicitly denounced bourgeois notions of justice and the rule of law – Lenin, for example, declaring that the dictatorship of the proletariat meant 'power based directly on force and unrestricted by any laws', Lukács that legal order must be rejected as one of the means which 'mystify' consciousness of 'the world historical mission'. The Russian Revolution retained a rhetoric of justice, but, in contrast to 'bourgeois justice', this was based on the argument that 'revolutionary justice adopts the future'. In this form of 'ultra-consequentialism', a remote 'end-in-view' (as opposed to actual objective consequences) is taken to justify any act. It is taken to overthrow completely the idea that truth and meaning can be determined by the individual conscience.[42]

These two competing assaults on liberal notions of justice are dramatised in Stephen Spender's *Trial of a Judge* (1938), in which a 'kind, gentle, just' judge[43] is forced to confront the totalitarian alternatives. The schematic nature of the play is generally taken to be its main limitation, but this also means that important issues are foregrounded in an unusually thoroughgoing way. The drama centres around the sentences of death passed on the 'blacks' (fascists), who have murdered Petra (thinking him a Jew), and on the 'reds' (communists), who have been convicted of carrying firearms, which is punishable by death under a new law. The government is pressuring the judge to reprieve the black prisoners, whilst the judge thinks the President of the State should reprieve the three red prisoners he has just had to sentence to death. Each side supports its cause by developing its own vision of national unity – visions which are in both cases premised on a dismissal of liberal justice as dishonest and weak: 'when liberal justice whines of violence', one of the fascists proclaims, 'Power flies to those with the right of might.' The blacks rise against liberal laws 'for the sake of an indivisible nation / Embossed beneath one iron will' (pp. 29–30). The reds, who see the 'justice' of the judge as the hypocritical mask of the old order, are no less willing to kill anyone who opposes them and to refer all judgements to the 'tall perspectives of future years' (pp. 59, 71). Both sides reject what Merleau-Ponty called 'the judicial dream of liberalism', and it is significant that the play opens with a dream sequence in the mind of the judge, during which he addresses a chorus which faces him, 'as much the accusers as the accused', in a scene supposed to be staged so that it 'vaguely recalls the arrangement of the Court' (pp. 13–14). The judge examines his own conscience and indulges a wish for 'absolute justice' – for an ideal above political enmities and expediency, the justice 'once delineated by an inner eye'. The main conflict in the play centres on the struggle of the liberal judge to come to terms with a world in which such a concept of justice is 'buried' and 'bound' (pp. 30, 46).

The conflicting spaces of Spender's play are what the judge calls the court of his mind, the actual Palace of Justice ('The Small Scene'), and the wider political and social world ('The Large Scene'), which is represented by the crowd outside of the Palace of Justice. As the play moves towards this larger scene, the focus is increasingly on the extent to which the law can be above the specific demands of political expediency. Even in the first act, the outer space is imagined as encroaching on the inner, with the black chorus, for example, intruding so strongly on the judge's dream that they finally come, at the end of the scene, to stand between the judge and the audience. The abstract ideal of justice which, for the judge, 'speaks to my own conscience', finds its physical equivalent in the 'white square room' of the Palace of Justice, but the judge is reminded with increasing brutality that outside, with 'all the world in crisis', there is a demand for 'sacrifices of opinion': 'We are trampled beneath a brutal present / Far realer than our life-long dream' (pp. 42–8). By the end, private space has become coterminous with public: 'I have become / The centre of that clamorous drum / To which I listened all my life . . .' (p. 108). Images of interment and incarceration establish the 'necessary' subjugation of the inner courtroom of conscience to the political forum: 'I here bury my own will and cancel / My mystical hand and unbiased sight'; murder will flourish 'above that soil where the law is buried' (pp. 48, 57). The judge himself, in the dream-vision of Hummeldorf (a minister of the Government), is 'tied to a stake . . . . My feet chained to a pillar / In a stone cell under ground'. The play ends in actual cells, a 'living tomb', and with the suspicion that, if one descends to using 'their methods', 'our truth' becomes 'the prisoner of necessity' (pp. 84, 100–3).

The apparent intention of Spender's play was to vindicate the call of the 'reds' for strong transforming action, uninhibited by the weak scruples of liberal justice, and there is no question that the communist side is presented in a far better light than are the fascists, whose bestial brutality – 'we stamped on him / And kicked his face' (p. 17) – is evident from the start. As has often been observed, however, the position of the liberal judge himself is so forcefully stated that the intended message is undermined: Louis MacNeice, who records the objections of fellow-communists to Spender's evident belief in abstract justice, says that the moral was 'sabotaged' by Spender's 'unconscious integrity'. A contemporary reviewer concluded that 'The only moral I could find was that Stephen Spender ought not to be a Communist.'[44]

The inner tensions evident in *Trial of a Judge* suggest, of course, that Spender's left-wing political views, like those of many other fellow-travelling intellectuals of the thirties, are of the kind that leave him vulnerable to the charge that he subscribed, in Wyndham Lewis' phrase, to 'the *salon* communism that looks so hypocritical to the outsider'.[45] The too-glib transition from the judge's eloquent plea to the final choruses of the red prisoners, hymning the prospect of peace and freedom flowing from 'the necessary killing hatred' (p. 103), suggests that there is an uncertain grasp of the realities of the system on which future promises depend. Spender's equivocations to some extent lend support to the arguments Orwell puts forward in reviewing Koestler's *Darkness at Noon*. Orwell's contention is that all of the outstanding works of literature dealing with totalitarianism are being produced by continental Europeans; it is impossible, he says, for the English to write adequately about totalitarianism because they have not experienced it from the inside. Therefore, although they might hold opinions on, say, the show trials, they are unable to see that such proceedings are 'an unspeakable horror'; similarly, English disapproval of Nazi outrages strikes Orwell as 'an unreal thing'. Detached observers, they are unable to imagine themselves as the victims.[46]

And unquestionably, it is continental literature that produced the most powerful and telling images of the actual experience of totalitarian injustice. What the writer acquires from such an experience, Czeslaw Milosz argues in *The Captive Mind* (1951–52), is a direct and concrete knowledge of a system in which 'there is no boundary between man and society', in which everyone is kept under 'minute scrutiny', indoctrinated in ways of thinking which render him 'helpless' and 'paralysed', with 'the crushing might of the state . . . hurled against any man who refuses to accept the New Faith'. In the opening dream sequence of *Trial of a Judge*, Spender conveys the impression of an autonomous space, into which external events and pressures intrude (ultimately with fatal results), but within which the individual conscience can exercise independent judgement with a degree of integrity and dignity – as Milosz says, a space where inner commands can be supported by 'a belief in an order of values that exists beyond the changeability of human affairs'.[47] It is this inner space that is violated by the total perversion of justice. Images of the dissolution of boundaries between inner and outer worlds, paralysis and crushing weight recur in many accounts of Nazism and of the Stalin era. The invasion of private space and deprivation of individual free will are often assimilated in the metaphor of nightmare, which is so ubiquitous as to lose, when used in passing, some of its capacity to communicate real terror. When the image is more fully realised, however, it can acquire something of the force inherent in the pathological definition of the phenomenon of nightmare as described by Ernest Jones (who himself might be said to apply to the psychological phenomenon the language of political oppression): the sufferer is subject, Jones writes, to agonising, incomprehensible dread, great oppression and helpless paralysis; he experiences difficult respiration and 'a total privation of voluntary motion'; he reaches 'a pitch of unutterable despair' and feels

225

as though he is caught in the coils of a horrid monster or crushed under the weight of a 'mighty stone . . . laid upon his breast'; he 'never feels himself a free agent', but 'remains an unresisting victim for malice to work its will upon', as though 'his whole being is locked up' and he is 'arrested and tortured by the pangs of suffocation produced by the pressure to which he is exposed; or he loses his way in a narrow labyrinth, and gets involved in its contracted and inextricable mazes'.[48]

Perhaps the most famous nightmare of justice perverted is Kafka's *The Trial* (written in 1914), in which, for the hapless Joseph K., private space is entirely eliminated by the arbitrary, incomprehensible decisions of the Court. The processes of the Court are wholly inscrutable: at the very end, K. asks, 'Where was the Judge whom he had never seen? Where was the High Court, to which he had never penetrated?' Legal formality is an endlessly repeated ritual that never progresses, with 'ceremonial interviews, one after another', and 'responses like a litany'. Were a man to try to meet the 'unknown accusation' of the Court, the whole of his life would have to be 'passed in review, down to the smallest actions and accidents', though such a review is pointless, given that the Court, once a charge has been brought, never alters its conviction. There are no limits or boundaries to the Court's powers of intrusion. As the Court painter explains to K., 'everything belongs to the Court'. K. wonders whether there might not be some way of circumventing the Court and living completely outside its jurisdiction, but his bondage is total. Whether he is wandering in the labyrinthine corridors of the law or trying to carry on with his life, the effect of his 'trial' is inescapable. As in a nightmare, disorientation and suffocation combine to enforce the sense of helpless entrapment. The painter, for example, with his inherited Court connections, seems to have grown to accept an atmosphere which makes K. long to fling open a window: 'The feeling of being desperately cut off from the fresh air made his head swim.' Ultimately his detention by this capricious authority is alarmingly physical, as two men, formal but inexorable, march K. from his lodgings, winding their arms round his at full length, 'holding his hands in a methodical, practised, irresistible grip', with K. walking 'rigidly between them . . . interlocked in a unity . . . such as can be formed almost by lifeless elements alone', so that 'he suddenly realised the futility of resistance'.[49] Many readings of *The Trial* focus on only the metaphysical or psychological aspects of the novel – the exploration of the inner state of guilt, sin and suffering, or of a state of deep neurosis (the law as the Father, justice as repressed guilt). Others, most notably J.P. Stern, have argued persuasively that, without denying these dimensions of the narrative, it is possible to take seriously the social and political meanings of a novel which was, after all, written by a man who had spent several years practising as a lawyer, and to see it both as a response to the mechanisms of power as Kafka saw them operate in late nineteenth- and early twentieth-century Europe and as an anticipation of totalitarianism. As Stern says, Kafka is not a prophet, but the age to which he belongs in Germany culminates in the rule of National Socialism, and, with hindsight, we can see that the rule and circumstances which made totalitarianism possible are continuous with the inhumanities of the age in which Kafka himself lived: 'his status as a Jew is symbolic of the powerlessness and conformism of humane and liberal beliefs everywhere'.[50]

One reason for the divergent readings of *The Trial* is that the lack of distinction or separation between private and public space enables us to read it either as a primarily psychological or spiritual account of inner guilt (with the Court itself as metaphoric) or as a representation of external political and legal realities, an exposure of actual abuses of the power of the law. In Koestler's *Darkness at Noon* (1940), there is no such doubt as to its contemporary political relevance. It so clearly refers to events during the period of Stalin's show trials that it has been judged, amongst other things, on the basis of its historical accuracy. Thus Merleau-Ponty, for example, criticised it for not giving a sufficiently faithful picture of the trial of Nikolai Bukharin, arguing that 'there is a drama in the Moscow Trials but one which Koestler is far from giving a true presentation'.[51] At the same time, there has been a tendency in England to regard the book less highly because of the very direct nature of the political content – to dismiss it as literature because it *is* 'one of the essential documents of the political life of our time' or because, as Orwell said, it is not simply a story of imaginary adventures but 'a political book, founded on history and offering an interpretation of disputed events'.[52] Orwell's was one of the more favourable reviews, and the reception of Koestler's novel is in some ways analogous to the English response to Orwell's *Nineteen Eighty-Four*.[53] In France, on the other hand, Koestler's novel – published there in 1946 as *Le Zéro et l'Infini* – was a *succès de scandale* and sold over 400,000 copies. From the point of view of a French audience, the novel addressed some of the most contentious political issues in a postwar France which was seeing the extension of Communist Party influence, and it fuelled a fierce debate. The best-known contribution to this debate was Merleau-Ponty's *Humanism and Terror* (1947), a polemic prompted by the way in which Koestler brought to the fore difficult questions about the show trials and the nature of revolutionary communism. *Darkness at Noon*, then, in France in particular, was at the centre of a controversy over the framing of Soviet laws to allow Stalin 'legally' to apply brutal pressures to his political opponents, over the preference for and the use made of confession and the question of how confessions were obtained. Analysis of the process of breaking down those under arrest broadened to take in such issues as the opposition between the individual conscience and totalitarian pressure, and the relationship between the use of confessions and Stalin's determination to obtain complicity as well as submission.[54]

Elements of a political debate still arguably give Koestler's novel too much of the feeling of theoretical political disputation, but it nevertheless draws considerable strength from its central images of the way in which an individual conscience can be (to borrow Jones's description of nightmare) 'overpowered by resistless and unmitigable pressure'.[55] As in *The Trial*, the action of *Darkness at Noon* begins with an official invasion of a private room. There is first the nightmarish dreaming of Rubashov, and a terrifying confusion between nightmare and reality. The worst part of Rubashov's dream is his fear that his awakening could be the 'real dream' (p. 11), and this confusion of waking and sleeping, elsewhere as well, captures the horror of losing a grasp on commonplace, ordered reality. It also emphasises at the outset the affinities Koestler wants to establish between the opposing brands of totalitarianism (since the fascist officials of the dream merge into the reality of an arrest under a communist regime). Koestler's own initial motives in committing himself to the communist cause were at least in part, as for so many others in the thirties, to do with a feeling that it was the front line of defence against fascism.[56] Part of his disavowal of communism involves, therefore, an insistence on the similarities created by each system's total abandonment of the liberal ideals of justice and individual rights: 'He was in his own country, but it had become an enemy country' (p. 118). At the very end, as he is executed, Rubashov's last thought is a question that again registers the existence of indistinguishable extremes: 'what insignia did the figure wear on the sleeves and shoulder-straps of its uniform – and in whose name did it raise the dark pistol barrel?' (p. 211). The use of the machinery of the law by both fascists and communists to crush opposition is literalised in images of great weight that recall Stalin's sinister enquiry: 'can one man withstand the pressure of that astronomical weight?' The Praetorian guards of the German Dictatorship – 'overgrown', 'breathing heavily', carrying 'grotesquely big pistols' – who haunt Rubashov's opening nightmares are replicated in the 'uniformed giant' with a 'brutal face and hoarse voice' who orders the 'leadenly tired' Rubashov to follow him to his interrogation. Those who do not come to terms with the 'new generation' will be 'crushed; there was no other alternative' (pp. 10–11, 146–9). Gletkin, his interrogator, who seems to have become indistinguishable from 'No. 1', is also described in terms of oppressive weight, and uses methods which involve 'complete physical crushing of the accused': 'He again bent his whole body towards Hare-lip, as though he wanted to crush him with his weight across the space between them' (pp. 170, 160). The pressure is not directly physical (torture, Gletkin tells Rubashov, is forbidden by the Soviet criminal code), but the incubus-like physical presence of the interrogator seems in itself to compel complete submission: 'Massive and expressionless, he sat there, the brutal embodiment of the State' (p. 183). 'Hammered mercilessly' into Rubashov's skull is the message that it is impossible to stand against a country that 'covers a sixth of the world and contains a tenth of the world's population' (p. 188). The inner world of the individual has no defence against power of such magnitude. The two thousand men locked in the beehive of cells fill the silence of the prison only with 'their *inaudible* breath, their *invisible* dreams, the *stifled* gasping of their fears and desires', and, Rubashov reflects, 'If history were a matter of calculation, how much did the sum of two thousand nightmares weigh, the pressure of two-thousandfold helpless craving?' (p. 146, my italics).

The utter powerlessness of the prisoners is embodied in the paralysis of nightmare. Rubashov's dream of arrest is one of 'tormenting helplessness' in which he vainly tries to put his arm into the sleeve of his dressing-gown 'until a kind of paralysis descends on him: he cannot move, although everything depends on his getting the sleeve on in time' (p. 11). As Rubashov's ordeal goes on, one of the most insidious threats to his moral being is a final acceptance of immobility and impotence. To capitulate brings a feeling of relief: 'The consciousness of his complete defeat filled him with a kind of relief; the obligation to continue the fight, the burden of responsibility were taken from him; the drowsiness of before returned.' The attractions of sleep are not simply a consequence of the exhaustion of a man deprived of rest, but a longing for the ultimate irresponsibility of death itself. The most persistent temptation during the indistinguishable days and nights consists 'of the single word written on the cemetery of the defeated: Sleep' (pp. 168–72).

The frequently-experienced nightmare sensation of being unable to cry out[57] is in the end replaced by the 'peaceful' silence of final resignation – an acceptance of the pointlessness of all speech. Earlier, however, it is a motif used to suggest both the official silencing of dissident voices and the 'replacement' of a person's own voice by that of his political masters. Koestler explores different kinds of silence: the fearful silence, the politic silence, the silence of the martyr, and ultimately the silence of innermost being, of the final recesses of an individual who no longer has the capacity to affect anything in the external world. Even in the context of the rule of law, those who rely on normal public language are generally at a disadvantage in comparison to those familiar with the formal language of the legal system, and the silence of the accused can be construed as an admission of guilt.[58] Under totalitarianism, the disjunction between the formal requirement and the inner voice is far more radical, and involves the explicit elimination of the private, personal voice of conscience. The duty of the revolutionary is seen as the stifling of any debate in the court of conscience: 'When the accursed inner voice speaks to you, hold your hands over your ears'; at the same time, the inner self is in effect occupied by the thoughts and words of others. 'My way of thinking', Ivanov says, 'and of arguing is your own, and you are afraid of the echo in your own head' (pp. 121–5). Rubashov is more than once presented with the alternatives of remaining silent or speaking the words that the party expects. Variations on the phrase 'Rubashov was silent' recur throughout – his silence implying a degree of resistance, but also an inability to speak in his own voice. When, in a period before his arrest and interrogation, the official line is that his silence will be interpreted as a confession of guilt, he speaks the required words – the 'declaration of loyalty' to the Party – in a disavowal which 'finishes' his mistress, Arlova (p. 75). In his diary, Rubashov reflects on the alternatives available to the dissident: short of organising a *coup d'état* (or the 'noble gesture' of dying 'with a moving swansong on your lips'), the only choices are 'mute despair' ('to die in silence') or to suppress one's own convictions and speak in the voice of the Party, to 'act according to the text-book', making a 'public disavowal of one's conviction'. When he ultimately chooses dishonourable speech to silence, what he is left with, for the brief time before his execution, is another kind of silence – the silence of metaphysical musing ('In death the metaphysical became real'). Having given up all possibility of acting as a public being, he has become 'a man who had lost his shadow, released from every bond'; he is also now, of course, a man whose social-political self has been definitively constructed for him during the course of his trial, and so he exists in a way as two entirely separate entities: the public Rubashov, and the unknowable, nameless inner man, of whom the state makes no further demands – except, of course, for the sacrifice of his life. What is left is an inner being mystically joined (by the 'oceanic sense') to the rest of humanity, but at the same time intensely aware of its own isolation, of the 'grammatical fiction' of the first person singular, an introspective self that exists in 'blessed quietness'. In the end, the grammatical fiction is the only reality; the rest (the politically constructed man) is fiction (pp. 199–203, 138).

The closing pages of *Darkness at Noon* are an affirmation of faith in the persistence of an inner sense of self even after the public sphere has appropriated the whole of a man's external social identity, and so are a refutation of the 'faith' described much earlier in Rubashov's diary – that is, the theoretical basis of 'revolutionary ethics', a creed, as Rubashov says, that admits 'no private sphere, not even inside a man's skull'. The dramatic tension of Koestler's novel arises out of the systematic violation of this inner space by those for whom 'personality does not matter' and who have no room for 'subjective good faith'. The explicit, abstract debates of the novel define the nature of those who demand 'that the individual should in every way be subordinated and sacrificed to the community', and who thus stand at the opposite pole to a 'Christian and humane' conception of ethics which declares the individual to be sacrosanct (pp. 83–4, 128). Rubashov's own past betrayals are represented as being due to the fact that 'merely personal disgust' is dismissed by the Party as a part of bourgeois morality (p. 104). The duty of the revolutionary is represented by his first interrogator, Ivanov, as a series of repressions – of sympathy, disgust, despair, repentance, atonement – all belonging to a view of the world 'as a sort of metaphysical brothel for emotions'. The choice is represented as one between mankind and ' "man" in the singular'. To follow 'Gandhi's inner voice' or 'one's own conscience' is to 'abandon mankind' (pp. 124–5, 202). Gletkin himself, Rubashov's second interrogator, is presented as the very image of the human being emptied of all personality. In contrast to the extraordinary expressiveness of the personality of the prisoner in cell No. 402 (never seen, only tapping messages, but full of human emotions, excitable, volatile), Koestler creates the completely null Gletkin, stiff and stony, a physical and vocal image of the draining of all personal substance, with his colourless voice and expressionless eyes, in his 'correct position' behind the desk (p. 154).

So extreme is the dehumanisation of Gletkin that he seems to represent a complete severance from the world of nature, and hence also, of course, from all 'natural' sources of justice. The break with the old liberal ethos of honour and 'hypocritical decency' is imaged in the Gletkins of the world having been born without umbilical cords. The law applied in *Darkness at Noon* thus has no connection with the natural order of things. These 'new Neanderthalers' slaughter and desecrate, transgressing 'against every law and tradition of the jungle' (pp. 183–4). Throughout the novel other natural absences go with the denial of the individual basis of justice. The natural images with which the Party is associated are indifferent and inhuman – a narrow path with thin air; a river following the 'law of her being', oblivious to motives and conscience, the only crime being to 'swerve from the course' (p. 65). For those who do swerve, there is the ultimate separation from all natural life in the prison cells, the all too literal and sharply physical reminders of the precariousness of individual identity under such a regime. On Rubashov's first entry into the prison, he observes the number and spy-hole juxtaposed with the individual name of the prisoner. It is impossible to see behind anyone else's window. The cells are the means justified by the ends, but, in more senses than one, they come to be identified with the ends themselves. For Gletkin, Rubashov thinks, everything is justified 'with the principle that the bastion must be preserved. But what did it look like inside? No, one cannot build Paradise with concrete' (p. 205).

The Party, with its spurious objectivity, has constructed a legal system without any 'just' substance, invoking the name of the law (arresting Rubashov for having 'conspired against law and order') to create a form of systematic terror that at last becomes an end in itself (p. 25). It seems clear that, for Stalin, the purges were not, ultimately, the price to be paid for a remote political end, but were rather the actual objective, psychologically reducing his ever-present fear of conspiracy and assassination, satisfying his desire for revenge, silencing all dissent. But continuity with revolutionary tradition was also maintained, particularly in the rhetoric of consequentialism which so often served to confirm Party infallibility and justify suppression of all suspected of oppositionism, including those Stalin called 'the silent ones' – anyone in whom 'there were still traces of an independent attitude'. In *Darkness at Noon*, as characters reflect on possible explanations for the Terror, Koestler takes account both of the paranoia and vengeful brutality of one man (with No. 1 making all who preceded him look like 'dilettantes in tyranny') and of the Party doctrines which facilitated such actions 'in the name of the law' (pp. 142–3, 13). As Rubashov says, 'Acting consequentially in the interests of the coming generations, we have laid such terrible privations on the present one that its average length of life is shortened by a quarter' (p. 129). For Rubashov himself, the most terrible privation (short of death) is the gradual elimination of his own inner ability to distinguish any more between guilt and innocence. His 'admissions' are at first only of guilt in holding oppositional views, following sentimental impulses, placing man above the idea of mankind and rating the question of guilt and innocence above that of political utility. Eventually, however, as the 'solemn ceremony' continues, he relinquishes the idea that an injustice was being done to him and accepts Gletkin's rules, ceasing to differentiate between a crime which had been committed and one which he merely 'should' have committed, given his beliefs. With this inner capitulation, except for 'rare moments of clearheadedness', his conception of his own guilt becomes inseparable from that of Gletkin (pp. 166, 179). The establishment of such total control over the prisoner's mind is, as Alan Bullock says, not something achieved by casual brutality but by techniques acquired in 'centuries of experience in breaking down the resistance and identity of human beings'. The reason Koestler's novel fired such controversy, and arguably the main source of its fictional staying power, is its very detailed exploration of the process by which individual psychic space is eliminated within a system which, as Grigori Pyatakov declared in 1928,

> . . . is based on the principle of coercion which doesn't recognise any limitations or inhibitions . . . . This principle of boundless coercion is the absence of any limitation whatsoever – moral, political, even physical . . . .
>
> A true Bolshevik has submerged his personality in the collectivity of the Party . . . . In order to become one with this great Party, he would fuse himself with it, abandon his own personality, so that there was no particle left inside him which did not belong to the Party.[59]

NOTES

1. Orlov A. *The secret history of Stalin's crimes* (1954) pp. 129–30, quoted by Conquest R. *The great terror* 1971 p. 144. Conquest and Alan Bullock both defend Orlov as a reliable source: see Chapter 13 in Conquest; and Bullock A. *Hitler and Stalin* 1991 p. 1110.
2. Sypnowich C.E. *The concept of socialist law* 1990 pp. 46–50; Conquest *The great terror* pp. 207–10.
3. Zamyatin Y. *We* (1920) 1983 pp. 71–2.
4. Hampshire S. *Innocence and experience* 1992 pp. 68–9.
5. Stern's discussion of 'the spirit of National Socialist law' (in Stern J.P. *Hitler* 1979 pp. 116–29) provides one of the best summaries of abuses of justice in Nazi Germany.

6. Hampshire *Innocence and experience* pp. 66–9.
7. See Apter D. *The politics of modernization* 1967 pp. 274–5.
8. Raphael D.D. *Problems of political philosophy* 1970 pp. 169–70.
9. Barker E. *Principles of social and political theory* (1951) 1967 pp. 89, 97–103 and 123.
10. Foucault M. *The Foucault reader* 1987 pp. 138–9 (and pp. 62–3); see also Merleau-Ponty M. *Humanism and terror* (1947) 1969 pp. xxiii–xxiv, Harden I., Lewis N. *The noble lie* 1988 pp. 31–4 and 46–1, and (for general discussion of opposing sides) Apter *Politics of modernization* p. 292.
11. *Ibid.* pp. 290–1 and 304–11; Hampshire *Innocence and experience* pp. 71–2.
12. Stern L. *Tristram Shandy* (1759–67), Penguin 1978 p. 143; *John* viii.9, quoted by *Shorter Oxford English Dictionary* p. 388.
13. Auden W.H. *The dyer's hand* (1963) 1987 pp. 150–1; Bentham J., quoted by Welsh A. *Strong representations* 1992 pp. 37–8.
14. Gardner E.S. *The case of the sulky girl* (1933), Consul Books 1962 pp. 183–7.
15. Priestley J.B. *An inspector calls* (1946), in *Time and the Conways and other plays* Penguin 1969 pp. 184–5; and see Cawelti J.G. *Adventure, mystery and romance* 1976 pp. 90–2.
16. Mauriac F. *Thérèse* (1927–28), Penguin 1959 pp. 23 and 102.
17. See Pick D. *War machine* 1993 p. 187.
18. Merleau-Ponty *Humanism and terror* pp. 103–4.
19. Forster E.M., letter (9 December 1941) in *Selected letters* 1985 vol. 2 p. 198.
20. Arendt H. *The origins of totalitarianism* (1951) 1967 pp. 474 and 325; and see Raphael *Problems of political philosophy* p. 166 on the restriction of the area of legal authority in a democratic society, with the intention of leaving as much room as possible for individual liberty.
21. Barker *Principles of social and political theory* p. vi.
22. Forster E.M., letter (15 Feb 1940) in *Selected letters* p. 173; and see Raphael, *Problems in political philosophy* p. 166.
23. See Hampshire *Innocence and experience* p. 63 on the central importance of reasonable procedure.
24. Forster E.M. *A Passage to India* (1924) 1964 pp. 164 and 179–80.
25. Barker *Principles of social and political theory* p. 103.
26. Hampshire *Innocence and experience* p. 70.
27. See Scruton R. *A dictionary of political thought* (1982), Pan Books 1983 pp. 316–18.
28. Beer G., Ghosts, *Essays in Criticism* **28**: 260, quoted by Jackson R., *Fantasy: the literature of subversion* Methuen 1981 p. 69; Punter D. *The literature of terror: a history of Gothic fictions from 1765 to the present day* Longman 1980 pp. 320–31.
29. Furbank P.N., Haskell, F.J.H., An interview with E.M. Forster, in *E.M. Forster, A passage to India: A casebook* (1970), ed Bradbury M., Macmillan 1975 p. 28.
30. Barker *Principles of social and political theory* pp. 117 and 123.
31. Forster E.M. *Two cheers for democracy* 1951 pp. 70–3.
32. Welsh *Strong representations* pp. 29 and 97–9.

33. Jackson B.S. *Law, fact and narrative coherence* 1988 pp. 62ff; and Welsh *Strong representations* p. 40.
34. Hampshire *Innocence and experience* p. 68.
35. Barker *Principles of social and political theory* pp. 167–8 and 119.
36. Greene G. *It's a battlefield* (1934) 1980 pp. 20–1 and 30–1.
37. Bennett W.L. and Feldman M.S., *Reconstructing reality in the courtroom* Rutgers University Press, New Brunswick 1981 p. 10.
38. Greene G. *The power and the glory* (1940) 1971 pp. 194–205, 58–60, 148 and 128.
39. Koestler A. *Darkness at noon* (1940) 1964 p. 171.
40. Hampshire *Innocence and experience* p. 68; Lukes S. *Marxism and morality* 1990 p. 137.
41. Hampshire *Innocence and experience* pp. 67–9.
42. Lenin V.I., Speech at the First Congress of Economic Councils (26 May 1918), and Lukács G., Bernstein's triumph: notes on the essays written in honour of Karl Kautsky's seventieth birthday (1924), quoted by Lukes *Marxism and morality* pp. 106 and 115; Merleau-Ponty *Humanism and terror* pp. 28–9; see also Lukes *Marxism and morality* pp. 134–7.
43. Spender S. *Trial of a judge* 1938 p. 93.
44. MacNeice L. *The strings are false: an unfinished autobiography* (1965) and 'K.A.', review in *New Verse* (Summer 1938), quoted in Weatherhead A.K. *Stephen Spender and the thirties* 1975 p. 174.
45. Lewis W., First aid for the unorthodox, *London Mercury* **32** (May 1935): 31, quoted in Weatherhead *Stephen Spender* p. 42.
46. Orwell G., Arthur Koestler (1944) in *Collected essays* (1946–53) 1975 pp. 236–7.
47. Milosz C. *The captive mind* (1953) 1985 pp. ix–x and 217–21; the Author's Note records that the book was written in Paris in 1951–52, when most French intellectuals 'placed their hopes in a new world in the East, ruled by a leader of incomparable wisdom and virtue – Stalin'.
48. Jones E. *On the nightmare* (1931), Liveright Publishing Co, New York 1951 pp. 16–20.
49. Kafka F. *The trial* (1925) 1992 pp. 250–1, 196, 142–3, 166–7 and 246–7.
50. See Stern J.P., The law of *The trial*, in Kuna F (ed) *On Kafka* Paul Elek 1976 pp. 24–7 and Heller E. *Kafka* 1974 pp. 103–6; Dodd W.J. *Kafka and Dostoyevsky* 1992 pp. 132–4; and see also Stern *Hitler* pp. 59–60 and 127–9.
51. Merleau-Ponty *Humanism and terror* p. 62.
52. Harris H. (ed) *Astride the two cultures: Arthur Koestler at 70*, Random House, New York 1976 p. 119; Orwell G., Arthur Koestler (1944), *Collected essays* p. 243.
53. See Forster *Two cheers* p. 75; and see Harris *Astride the two cultures* pp. 149ff on Orwell and Koestler.
54. See Conquest *The great terror* pp. 128–9, 207–10 and 378–9.
55. Jones *On the nightmare* p. 17.
56. See Levene M. *Arthur Koestler* 1984 pp. 10–16.
57. Jones *On the nightmare* p. 23.
58. See, for example, Jackson *Law, fact and narrative coherence* pp. 64–5.
59. Bullock *Hitler and Stalin* pp. 562–70; and Pyatakov G., in a conversation with Valentinov N. (1928), quoted by Bullock pp. 564–5.

CHAPTER SIX

Technopower: 'Leviathan on Wheels' in Dystopian Science Fiction

I protest that if some great Power would agree to make me always think what is true and do what is right, on condition of being turned into a sort of clock and wound up every morning before I got out of bed, I should instantly close with the offer. The only freedom I care about is the freedom to do right; the freedom to do wrong I am ready to part with on the cheapest terms to any one who will take it of me.

(T.H. Huxley, 'On Descartes' "Discourse on Method"'; address delivered in 1870)

We all ... have read as school-children that greatest of all the monuments of ancient literature which have come down to us: *Time-Tables of All the Railroads*. But place even that classic side by side with The Tables of Hourly Commandments and you will see, side by side, graphite and diamond .... Who can help but catch his breath as he thunders and races headlong through the pages of the *Time-Tables*? The Tables of Hourly Commandments, however, really does transform each one of us into the six-wheeled steel hero of a great poem. Each morning, with six-wheeled precision, at the very same minute and the very same second we, in our millions, arise as one. At the very same hour we mono-millionedly begin work – and, when we finish it, we do so mono-millionedly.

(Yevgeny Zamyatin, *We*, 1920)[1]

It is absurd, of course, to think of the vigorous and combative T.H. Huxley happily transformed into an obedient clockwork automaton, and the very incongruity of his hypothetical bargain calls to mind some of the more obvious sources of unease about the mechanical model of human behaviour. Theoretical models of this kind strongly influenced progressive scientific minds from the time that Descartes' *Discourse* compared organic behaviour to the motions of a clock. Grandfather of Aldous Huxley, tutor of H.G. Wells, T.H. Huxley supplies us with an image of man regularised into virtue which recurs in innumerable twentieth-century future-worlds. In the clock-time dystopian extrapolation of human development, the idea of the clockwork man is a recurrent anxiety, embodying all the horrors latent in the prospect of carefully designed human perfection: surrender of individual choice to external control (being 'turned into' something and 'wound up' by 'some great Power'), constant adherence to an inflexible standard of well-ordered conduct and right thinking, an immutable ideal achieved at the cost of human vitality and dynamism. Aldous Huxley said of utopians that they were meditating not on man but on 'a monster of rationality and virtue', filling their future worlds with creatures radically unlike human beings.[2] Fear of such 'monstrosity', which is felt to reside in a willed severance from what is natural, has engendered much pessimism about the direction of human progress in a technological society. Mechanistic metaphors in themselves can be taken to imply a rational design contrived to achieve wholly predictable and limited objectives, and thus to imply a creation that lacks all organic capacity to seize opportunities, resist external pressures, choose freely or act creatively. In the late thirties, in a book suppressed by the Nazis, Friedrich Georg Juenger asks what most clearly distinguishes 'that leitmotiv of technology', the striving for perfection. The answer he gives is one echoed by countless others: technological progress is synonymous with an increase in all kinds of automatons, of the clocks and other machines which have, since their invention, both fascinated men and horrified them, threatening to penetrate organic life and evoking ideas of deathly stasis, 'akin to the awareness of a lifeless, mechanically self-repeating time such as clockwork measures'.[3]

The vision of entire societies of human automatons, functioning 'mono-millionedly' with 'six-wheeled precision', has haunted the twentieth-century political imagination. Those looking back on previous centuries have also, of course, been able to discern much earlier connections between total political control and mechanistic ways of thinking. Foucault, for example, in *Discipline and Punish*, analyses the eighteenth-century political implications of thinking in terms of Man-the-Machine and observes that the links between the materialist reduction of the 'intelligible body' and the technico-political manipulation of the 'useful body' are evident in such things as the military disciplines which produce economical and efficient movement, achieving the kind of meticulous control which imposes docility and utility. Foucault also notes the obsession of Frederick II with clockwork automatons, and implies, as Louis Mumford does, that a princely delight in such toys was no accident. Automatons, Mumford says, perfectly embodied 'the royal demand for unconditional obedience, absolute order, push-button control', and the successful functioning of automatons 'gave point to Descartes' question: May not living organisms be satisfactorily explained, and so governed, as if they were machines?' Mechanomorphism is thus often seen as related from its inception to a desire for progress towards a regimented political order. The kind of political principles that could facilitate such mechanical regulation of human actions were perhaps most forcefully articulated in Hobbes's *Leviathan*, which both enjoins absolute submission to the all-powerful state and conceives of the human heart as a spring, the nerves as strings, the joints as wheels and life itself as 'nothing but a motion of the Limbs'. The components of 'Leviathan on wheels' – armies, bureaucracies, factories and ultimately educational and communications systems – can all, from this perspective, be characterised as predictable, standardised, rigidly organised and centrally controlled.[4]

In the first half of the twentieth century, two major transformations led people to view with increasing alarm the prospect of political power joined to technological resourcefulness: that is, the emergence of totalitarianism and the unprecedented growth of technology, together with new methods for the efficient exploitation of advanced technologies. Optimism about the march of technology had waned dramatically after the First World War. Although some of the champions of technological progress (for example, J.B.S. Haldane and Hugo Gernsback) still proclaimed its possibilities, an increasing number of sceptics cast doubt on the hopes of technological advancement, calling into question man's ability to control either its destructive powers or its potential for fulfilling hedonistic desires. From the thirties on, anxieties about technological development were intensified by the emergence of totalitarian regimes, and the future-world vision of technological instrumentality at the service of political absolutism became the staple theme of dystopian literature.[5]

Both fascist and communist dictatorships seemed to provide ample grounds for extrapolating a dystopian future-world in which the autonomous individual would be transformed into an obedient cog in the great machine of state. Twentieth-century totalitarianism has involved far more thoroughgoing control of all functions of society than, say, seventeenth- or eighteenth-century absolute monarchs could have dreamt of achieving. Goebbels, describing the total revolution of Nazism, declared that it encompassed 'every aspect of public life' and 'replaced individuality with collective racial consciousness and the individual with the community'. The Nazis aimed for the creation of organisations 'in which every individual's entire life can take place', and for the disappearance of all free space within which the individual belongs to himself, for the replacement of personal happiness by collective happiness.[6] The future-world vision of technology at the service of totalitarianism seemed to many to be an all too probable projection of a contemporary reality in which thoroughly modern technological competence was the tool of atavistic political regimes. Both Russian and German police states vastly extended their power by technological means. Forced nationalisation under the aegis of the Stalinist police state produced the kind of technological advance once predicted as the future of Tsarist Russia – 'Genghis Khan with a telegraph'. In Germany, in spite of a primitivist mystique that was ultimately detrimental to technological development, Nazism built its power on a technology which was already so highly advanced that Germany itself was sometimes figured as a mechanism – with Sir Walter Raleigh, for example, declaring in 1918 that Germany was 'a carefully built, smooth-running machine, with powerful engines' (and only one fault, 'that any fool can drive it'). British horror of what was seen, under fascism, as a combination of barbarism and advanced technology was perhaps most famously expressed in Churchill's wartime speech, 'Their finest hour' (18 June 1940), in which he warns that failure in the Battle of Britain will mean that the whole world 'will sink into the abyss of a new Dark Age made more sinister, and perhaps more protracted, by the lights of a perverted science'.[7]

Another source of danger could be seen in the development of ever-more efficient methods of capitalist production, particularly under the influence of the theories of management science expounded by F.W. Taylor in *The Principles of Scientific Management* (1911). Taylor saw the possibility of rationalising mass production by applying social engineering techniques, enhancing human efficiency by the elimination of waste time and motion. In the following decades, such theories came to be a central element in Western technological advance, as developed countries (the United States in particular, of course) looked forward not only to economic growth and improving material standards provided by technological innovation and 'scientific management' but also to a future in which national destiny would be underwritten by (or indeed fused with) an ever-expanding 'technocomplex'. Such thinking is attacked in a number of anti-capitalist dystopias, but other dystopian projections often incorporate strong elements of both totalitarianism and consumer capitalism – combining, on the one hand, enforced conformity to a collectivist system, organised mass emotion, complete state control of all means of communication and the total elimination of free speech and free association with, on the other, a vision of ever-increasing industrial organisation, specialisation, and the brutal exploitation of assembly lines served by a dehumanised workforce. Yevgeny Zamyatin, for example, was influenced in writing *We* both by his experience of regimented industrial society in the West and by his exposure to the collectivist mystique of Russia. In his essays, too, a Wellsian London ('the present-day city, with its uncrowned king, the machine') merges with the image of a world in which there is 'no tsar, but the slaves remain', with men 'living in an epoch of suppression of the individual in the name of the masses'.[8]

Zamyatin's phrases suggest a twofold explanation of the development of a tyrannical techno-political order. The old absolute monarch, the tsar, is no more, but the modern individual is suppressed both by the 'uncrowned' machine king and by the political leaders who claim authority 'in the name of the masses'. One of the issues which has most divided twentieth-century commentators on technology and society has been the question of whether or not technology is truly 'king'. Many have maintained that technology is no more than a super-efficient servant which enables the powerful to achieve their aims. Amongst other things, this line of argument suggests that it is not technological values themselves which endanger mankind but the subordination of technology to the demands of power politics or big business: 'The sorcerer's powers are in the hands of a vain and foolish apprentice and disaster threatens.'[9]

If the machine is king, however, it is a different problem, and those who conceive of things in this way are more likely to flee to intellectual Luddism. One of the most strikingly recurrent elements in dystopia is the machine that develops a will of its own. The robot in Čapek's *R.U.R.* that declares, 'I want to be master over people'[10] is one of innumerable science fiction projections of the fear that technology itself will become the main determining force in political life – a fear already given expression in late Victorian England, with Ruskin, Carlyle and others lamenting the nexus of technology, industry and 'progress' and representing machinery and the machine mentality as leading to the inevitable running down of the system. Some of the most dire and fatalistic twentieth-century dystopian visions have been based on the assumption that technological change will be the dominant factor in the shape of the future, with politics strictly subordinate or ultimately even eliminated. Oswald Spengler, for example, one of the most influential purveyors of doom-laden prophecies, sees man's destiny forced on him by 'machine-technics': 'As once the microcosm Man against Nature, so now the microcosm Machine is revolting against Nordic Man. The lord of the World is becoming the slave of the Machine, which is forcing him – forcing us all, whether we are aware of it or not – to follow its course.' Machines can seem to be invested with autonomous force because they are semi-automatic in operation, driven by independent sources of power and designed not by those who operate them but by a remote technological elite.[11] Pushing this image further, critics of the machine age think of a future shaped by technological imperatives: that is, the mechanisation of work will inevitably produce the mechanisation of human organisation, not only in the form of the disciplined routine of the factory but in the form of complex social and political structures, causing a greater concentration of power, with all its attendant effects.[12] As Bertrand Russell writes in *Icarus*: 'Science has not only brought about the need of large organisations, but also the technical possibility of their existence.' It provides all of the devices – power stations, railways, telegraphs, telephones, modern methods of printing, broadcasting – which make control from the centre and uniformity of opinion possible. Russell himself, though he takes very full account of the capacity of technique to *change* the world, also stresses that the growth of democracy, as opposed to submission to fanatical creeds, will determine whether technology is applied for good or ill.[13] Others, however, subscribe to a much more thoroughgoing technological determinism and envision a future in which the worship of speed, order and technological efficiency inevitably leads to a new totalitarianism founded on technical necessity. Science and technology, like the rebellious robot, are imagined as having a will of their own. Orwell suggests that the process of mechanisation has come to be seen as 'a huge glittering vehicle whirling us we are not certain where'; Juenger imagines a wholly autonomous inhuman force infiltrating the government and usurping the functions of the state, producing automatism and rigid organisation. Organisation in itself is a hostile entity. It 'seizes man whenever he enters the field of technical progress .... To use a familiar technical term that describes it well: "It plugs man in."' Many later writers have similarly personified technique, seeing a convergence on man to produce an 'operational totalitarianism' so all-encompassing that 'no longer is any part of man free and independent of these techniques'.[14]

The extremity of the case against technology and of dystopian literary resistance to the momentum of technological advance can partly be seen as reactions against the scientific and technological messianism of the many writers who optimistically celebrated the solving power of technical change – just as the pessimistic visions of totalitarian closure are a dark reflection of the political messianism of monistic political faiths. The expectation of beneficent technological progress was expressed from the late nineteenth century on in a variety of prophetic tales fetishising technology – for example, in such mechanised utopias as Bellamy's *Looking Backward*, Fuller's *A.D. 2000*, Thomas's *The Crystal Button* (all published between 1888 and 1891) and, perhaps most notoriously, Gernsback's slightly later development of his literary genre of 'scientifiction', as in his utopian romance *Ralph 124C 41+*, which promotes the marvellous potential of the technology of the twenty-seventh century. A more seriously influential contributor to modern utopianism was, of course, H.G. Wells. Although many of Wells' early stories and novels were pessimistic – indeed, warned of the disasters that improperly controlled scientific development might bring – he became most strongly identified with the super-scientific utopia of gleaming machines and a benevolent world state. Described by Mumford as the quintessential utopia, Wells's *Modern Utopia* (1905) projects a world in which the ideal of a scientifically planned welfare state has been realised.[15] Science, again personified, is 'a too competent servant', abused, under contemporary circumstances, by her 'wrangling underbred masters'; a glimpse of the utopian alternative, however, teaches us that science is in fact a being who could, if properly respected, teach mankind the way ahead:

> The plain message physical science has for the world at large is this, that were our political and social and moral devices only as well contrived to their ends as a linotype machine, an antiseptic operating plant, or an electric tram-car, there need now at the present moment be no appreciable toil in the world, and only the smallest fraction of the pain, the fear, and the anxiety that now makes human life so doubtful in its value.[16]

The application of mechanical metaphors to moral improvement recalls T.H. Huxley's clockwork compact, as does the objective of the Wellsian world state, that is, the rational attainment of universal peace and virtue.

At their most optimistic those who believed in the transforming power of technology saw this 'newest mode of government' as moving mankind away from muddle, pain, injustice and barbarity. In comparison, the negativity of the law seemed a disabling liability, and technology appeared to possess a much greater potential for harmonising, reconciling and restraining – offering a more creative way of resolving the tensions we have discussed in earlier chapters, arising from man's primitive needs for dominance and submission, his aggression and violence. Not only the 'technological fix' but increased psychological understanding seemed to promise a release from the older sources of conflict and discontent.[17]

The idea of an all-solving power, however, in itself inspires unease. In contrast, say, to heroic myths of origin, the myth of the technological utopia suggests not beginnings but endings – a perfectly achieved goal, an end to division, an end to unhappiness and, consequently, an end to all further need for originating action. The most obvious reasons for rejecting utopian idealism are to do with this sense of loss and closure – loss, among other things, of the kind of struggles and challenges that have traditionally tested human virtue. George Kateb, in *Utopia and its Enemies*, talks of what he calls the Puritan side of anti-utopianism, an expression of the fear that any reduction of the gap between precept and inclination would diminish not just difficulty but all sense of real virtue, which requires exertion and depends on the tension between alternative courses – on the possibilities of choice embodied, for example, in narratives of heroic action.

This fear of human diminishment also arises from the dualistic opposition of hero and bureaucrat. It is thought that, if there is a trend towards increased rationalisation and bureaucratisation of society, there will be concomitantly less space for individualism and for intellectual and moral heroism. This conception of change in the modern world is very apparent, for example, in Weber's analysis of the rule of bureaucratic life ideals. The code of the bureaucratic official, like that of the sober man of business, centres not on 'being' but on 'function' – a Nietzschean formulation implying a fundamental opposition between a philosophy of authentic, spontaneous human expression and a rational-calculator paradigm of human life, between energetically heroic Nietzschean man and the instrumental rationality of economic maximisers. Oppositions such as these reflect the greatly increased (post-First World War) scepticism about the idea of progress, undermining the older unilinear view of the rationalisation of life and of the prospect of continuing cultural and moral improvement – a scepticism evident, for example, in Spengler's *Decline of the West*.[18]

The strategy of the dystopia is to assail the simple clarity of this unilinear view by means of ironic reversals or inversions. Thus instead of obedient machines, we see the triumph of mechanism, with a dehumanised mankind serving the machine rather than machines serving to liberate man from labour; instead of universal harmony there is mass conformity; instead of unending progress, eternal stasis, stagnation and an end to human enterprise. The utopia, as Zamyatin says, has no, or almost no, plot dynamics.[19] The dystopian writer, who fuses satiric with science fiction fantasy, sets in motion a plot in which an unplanned (and fully human) intrusion disturbs the equilibrium of the too-stable future-world. We tend to read this dystopian plot both as satire and as extrapolation: that is, such plots satirise, by extension and exaggeration, the dangerous tendencies evident in early twentieth-century technological and political developments; but also, because of the strong temporal dimension (in contrast to the purely spatial nature of a satire such as *Gulliver's Travels*, for example), the conventional dystopian plot is seen as in some sense predictive, so that it has made sense for the writers themselves to debate the real merits of their forecasting powers. Huxley, for example, argues in 1974 that Orwell's magnified projection of totalitarian tendencies has lost some of its 'gruesome verisimilitude' in light of recent developments, whereas his own nightmare of total organisation 'has emerged from the safe, remote future and is now awaiting us, just around the next corner'.[20] This element of extrapolation, particularly if it prompts a literal-minded consideration of the writer's predictive powers, has complicated the popular judgement of futuristic fantasies (this was evident, for example, in many of the essays on Orwell-as-prophet published in 1984). Judged as satire, however, dystopian fiction is capable of effectively drawing attention to the limitations and dangers inherent in monistic patterns of thought, with polarised oppositions acting as the exaggerations of caricature rather than as speculations about the actual shape of the future. As so often in satire, the central theme is the disappearance of the heroic, and the core of positive values expressed almost invariably contains strongly traditional elements. Underpinning the standard dystopian satire, we see, in essence, the forms of romantic reaction analysed by Mumford, that is, belief in nature and the primitive, in the value of the isolated individual and in the ethos of adventure.[21] These three forms of reaction are apparent (respectively) in the key oppositions examined in the remainder of this chapter – between man and machine, individual and mass, energy and entropy.

In British dystopian fiction – in particular that of Forster, Huxley and Orwell - the defence of diversity, individualism and natural vitality has elements of a specifically English nostalgia. The oppressive absolutes of foreign models of perfection (American consumer capitalism, continental totalitarianism) are imposed on a recognisably English landscape which provides strong reminders of a more personal, more open, small-scale, disorderly past. The all-devouring homogeneity of technocracy is invariably seen as lacking any such rootedness – 'rootedness', as Gabriel Marcel writes, being 'a grafting on to the local scene, a local individuality of custom, which . . . technical progress tends to forbid'. This sort of contrast is central, for example, to Rex Warner's *Aerodrome* (1941), in which the familiar meadows and the old-fashioned life of the English village are taken over by the rigidly organised, efficient aerodrome, which boasts 'the most powerful machines that have been invented by man' and provides training which cuts the airman off from 'the mass of men'.[22] But specifically English elements in dystopian fiction are obviously far less striking than the sense of shared, cross-cultural anxieties. Fear of anonymous technocracy and of the totalitarian misuse of scientific power has been a very widespread phenomenon, and British writers must therefore be seen in the context of American, Russian and Eastern European dystopian fiction, including the large amount of mainstream science fiction which has incorporated the stock themes of the mechanistic utopia gone wrong and of revolution against an oppressive totalitarian superstate.[23] Although there is not space here for any very thorough analysis, the discussion will take in two of the most influential of continental dystopian writers, the Czech, Karel Čapek, and the exiled Russian, Yevgeny Zamyatin; as well as Williamson and Vonnegut, who typify the development of these ideas in American science fiction writing of the late forties and early fifties. It is also useful to see dystopian fiction in relation to the innumerable social–political analyses and prophecies that have, since the twenties, considered the implications of mechanisation, technological progress and mass society – for example, Haldane's *Daedalus*, Russell's *Icarus*, Juenger's *The Failure of Technology*, Marcel's *Man Against Mass Society*, Mumford's *Technics and Civilization*, Adorno and Horkheimer's *Dialectic of Enlightenment*, Marcuse's *One-Dimensional Man*, Kateb's *Utopia and its Enemies*. Like fictional visions of the future, these discussions often focus on imagined contradictions in the perfected technological paradise, embodied in such oxymoronic phrases as 'living machines', 'ruthless benevolence' or 'final change'. Their most recurrent metaphors are central as well to dystopian visions – for example:

> the mechanisation of humanity ('Technical thinking, imbued with an unlimited drive for power, acts imperiously and recklessly . . . it promotes and expands organisation in all directions, and engulfs unorganised life wherever it finds it . . . . In the end . . . this thinking leads to the human robot, the functionary without a will of his own . . .');
> mass culture as a rigid mould ('Culture now impresses the same stamp on everything. Films, radio and magazines make up a system which is uniform as a whole and in every part. Even the aesthetic activities of

political opposites are one in their enthusiastic obedience to the rhythm of the iron system.');
and regression to Eden ('A society in which moral choices ceased to be made would be a society permeated by sluggishness and indolence, and possessed of a *vegetable* quality; it would be a return to an Edenic state, and as such would be no mere return, but a regression.').[24]

MAN/MACHINE

E.M. Forster's long short story, 'The Machine Stops' (1909), is amongst the earliest reactions against the vision of a technologically perfected future world. In his own later preface to his stories (1947), he describes it as 'a counterblast to one of the heavens of H.G. Wells', and it is clearly in many respects a reply to *A Modern Utopia*. Forster's dystopia is explicit in its technological determinism. The events of the story, he says, were attributed by some future-world inhabitants to the Central Committee, but in fact those in power had only yielded 'to some invincible pressure, which came no one knew whither'. This state of affairs had been labelled as progress, and no one was prepared to admit that the Machine was out of hand.[25] Forster's case against the lordship of the machine is one that was to be repeatedly echoed in later dystopias.

His tale is set in an environment cut off from nature, an underground world state whose citizens almost never emerge from their tiny, cell-like, windowless rooms. Vashti, the hero's mother, is introduced to us as unwholesome and unnatural, a 'swaddled lump of flesh' with a fungus-white face, terrified by the prospect of venturing on to the surface of the earth. Forster's semi-mystical, romantic feeling for the beauties of the English landscape prepares us for an end in which the city is rent apart, giving those imprisoned in it one final glimpse of an untainted sky. Disaster has followed inevitably on a loss of human control over the Machine, which has been served efficiently but with decreased intelligence by workers who only know their own specialised duties, so that there was no one in the world who understood 'the monster as a whole' ('The Machine Stops', pp. 137–8). When the machine begins to break down, there is no one who can remedy its defects, and the inhabitants become increasingly helpless: Vashti, though equipped with all the elaborate instructions supplied in the Book of the Machine, is reduced to striking ever more desperately at the buttons with her bleeding hands. Man is in the end 'strangled in the garments that he had woven'. The image of 'beautiful naked man' covered in the garment of the machine implies a paradise sacrificed in the process of human submission to something artificial and external. Having lost the ability to shed the 'garment of subserviency' at will, man has committed 'the sin against the body'. Those living in the city have surrendered their humanity. They are able to communicate with one another only through the speaking-tubes of the Machine and to live only through their contact with the buttons and switches that move, bathe, feed, entertain, warm, cool and cure them. As part this process, there is a mechanical–human reversal. The Machine itself has taken on human and even godlike qualities, becoming a vast surrogate body, its wires acting as enormous eyes and ears and nerve-centres. Man, 'who had once made god in his image', has now created a machine to be his god. Although the underground city-dwellers think of themselves as completely secularised, they end by worshipping the Machine in an officially established religion of 'undenominational Materialism' (pp. 141–5). The Machine, which is 'the only thing that really lives' below the surface of the earth, ultimately develops in its own way. Our initial impression of the interpenetration of man and machine – of the ceaseless hum of the Machine coursing through the human bloodstream – is underscored by a grim reversal, with mankind itself imagined as the blood that sustains the Machine: 'The Machine proceeds – but not to our goal. We only exist as the blood corpuscles that course through its arteries' (p. 131).

In Forster's story we can see in condensed form four of the elements which have most consistently characterised the dystopian case against the machine state: severance from nature; utter dependence on a force which cannot be completely grasped or controlled; men themselves mechanised – the horror of reduction to inorganicism; and, in a complementary reversal which confirms man's diminished status, machines taking on human qualities and acquiring mastery over men, challenging the optimistic vision of human lordship over technology. The utopian enthusiasm for the machine is 'peculiarly offensive to literary men in the twentieth century'[26] – an anti-machine reaction which is epitomised by Forster. Dystopian fantasies are almost invariably nostalgic, with the extrapolation of present fears into a future world intensifying the longing for a past already gone. As in Victorian denunciations of the machine, the body and landscape are viewed as either wholly pure or wholly impure. Narratives are invested with pathos and horror by the extremity of the presentation, and the fears themselves are expressed in images of entrapment, coalescence and undifferentiation – suggesting an assault on human form and human difference by a power which breaks down the integrity of the individual human character.[27]

The romantic theme of man's alienation from nature is predictably expressed through images of architectural enclosure and imprisonment, and of a consequent separation from the earth – the earth itself often having been destroyed by mechanisation, as when the demented machines of *La Révolte des machines* (a filmscript of the early twenties) run amok, wrecking fields, crops and trees. The architecture of the city is presented as conterminous with the machine and with its attendant power structure. The urban landscapes of science fiction dystopias are places in which, as in Mumford's image of the baroque city, mechanical order and inflexible control are 'written all over' the design of the buildings: the destruction of organic complexity brings mechanisation and total control, leading to the creation of structures designed according to a predetermined plan by engineer-architects who serve an autocratic authority.[28] Foucault, in his discussion of 'Space, Knowledge, and Power', similarly maintains that, during the seventeenth and eighteenth centuries, cities were perceived as the models for governmental rationality, a premise generating a series of utopian schemes in which 'the model of the city became the matrix for the regulations that apply to the whole state'. Foucault's argument is that the way in which the city – tight, efficient, bounded – acts as a metaphor for the well-regulated state inevitably changes with the birth of new technologies that 'escape the domain of architects'; technologies which facilitate communication and speed are likely to alter the way in which we think about space, so that our conceptions are no longer 'modelled on the police state of the urbanisation of the territory' (pp. 241–4). But whatever the actual changes in the relations of space and power, what is striking in the conventional dystopian projection is the extent to which power is still conceived spatially, embodied in enclosed, rigid urban structures. Speed of transport and rapid communications serve only to connect these mechanised units, and so are not imagined as fundamentally altering the metaphoric import of urban space. In the dystopia, the city *is* the territory.

Wells himself, in his more pessimistic scientific romances, imagines the city as the huge and terrifying embodiment of an oppressive power structure. The Utopian town buildings of *A Modern Utopia* are the realisation of 'the dream of structures, lighter and bolder than stone or brick can yield' (p. xxi); but together with this kind of Utopian rebuilding of the city his work contains darker counter-images, projections of existing abuses of power on to the architecture of the technological super-city. In contrast to Forster, Wells is no technological determinist. He sees technology itself as inherently good and capable of fulfilling its potential under the guidance of a benevolent intelligentsia; it can also, however, be perverted by bad masters, under whose control the 'lightness' of the dream city can be replaced by the oppressive weight of the totalitarian nightmare city (p. 243). In *The Sleeper Awakes*, the Sleeper, coming to consciousness after over two centuries of suspended animation, finds the new city overwhelming. There are 'Titanic buildings', 'mighty cantilevers', and a 'tracery of translucent material' that shuts out the sky. The intricate architecture has a certain delicacy, just as the political world has its subtle, cunning councillors at the pinnacle of the power structure. But the dominant impression is of a maze of 'inhumanly vast metallic structures': girders, wheels, beams, turret projections – like the vertiginous, brutal vaults of Piranesi's 'Carceri', dwarfing the tiny human figures trapped within.[29] The gigantic buildings of the city are correlated, the Sleeper is sure, with a 'gigantic discontent' felt by the machine-minders and machine-feeders, who inhabit crowded vaults and subterranean aisles, crushed beneath the complexity and vast weight of massive pillars and cross archings (pp. 64, 219). From the perspective of the underclass, 'Every city now is a prison', and the multitudes of workers suffer from a new tyranny of the cities, which was only just beginning when Graham went to sleep at the end of the nineteenth century. When this process started, half of the world's population still lived freely in the countryside: 'The cities had still to devour them' (pp. 178–9). Now there is city beyond city, and anyone rash enough to try to live in the countryside would be an isolated savage with no proper clothing, food, medical care, company or recreation (pp. 144–5). Wells does not take the romantic view, as expressed in 'The Machine Stops', that there is an inherent virtue in nature and that man tampers with the natural world at his peril. Thus, in contrast to the conventional dystopian vision, his pessimistic tales do not allow characters to draw any strength from nature in their resistance to the power structures of the city. In his later *Story of the Days to Come*, we again see a roofed-in city – a 'magnificent prison' – and a largely depopulated countryside. A young couple tries to escape a plunge to what are literally the lower depths of this towering twenty-second-century city in which the buildings have merged together, leaving the rich elevated in their sumptuous hotels of the upper stories while the industrial poor dwell below. Although the would-be escapers briefly experience the glory of the sunset and stars in a world with no walls or ceilings, their 'exile' is short-lived. Natural disorder and danger, combined with the policing of the countryside by the city powers, make them retreat to the city, having realised that 'the world is too civilised. Ours is the age of cities. More of this will kill us.'[30]

Stereotypically, the dystopian opposition between the city and the surrounding wilderness involves a strong central focus on the question of whether it is possible either to destroy or to live beyond the bounds of the repressive super-city. Science fiction's romantic polarisation of the organic–rural and the mechanical–urban tends to generate plots in which there is no middle ground; there is such a wholesale rejection of 'the urbanisation of the territory' that the only option, other than giving in, is to renounce urban life altogether, either seeking an escape route or trying to break down the walls which hold nature at bay. Zamyatin's *We*, Huxley's *Brave New World*, and Orwell's *Nineteen Eighty-Four* are all narratives which move out into a more natural, more primitive environment *en route* to the hero's final death or submission to the powers that control the city. Of the three, Orwell attaches least importance to the natural world: it is a glimpsed Arcadian past, briefly visible when Winston and Julia have their tryst in the clearing in the wood, an idealised pastoral setting for a gesture of disrobing 'by which a whole civilisation seemed to be annihilated'.[31] We know by the end of the scene that the emphasis here is on 'seemed': as the lovers part, we are told that they never went back, and the room over Mr Charrington's shop turns out to be inside rather than outside the boundaries of the all-powerful totalitarian state, even though it belongs architecturally to an older, freer past.

Having rejected the idea that technology could provide a gleamingly efficient future, Orwell reserves his use of futuristic architecture for symbolising power maintained as an end in itself, divorced from any socially beneficial function. Totalitarian efficiency is seen as strictly limited to policing its territory: within the ramshackle fabric of the older city power is maintained by the all-seeing telescreen which, like Bentham's panopticon, functions to provide continuous and anonymous surveillance by an invisible guardian, so that the 'inmate ... must behave as if surveillance were perpetual and total'.[32] The use of electronics obviates the need for an architecturally perfected power mechanism and allows Orwell to create a divided scene (reminiscent of the hierarchical skyscrapers of *The Sleeper Awakes*) in which four huge ministry buildings contemptuously dominate a decaying cityscape. The architectural incongruity establishes both the unresponsiveness of totalitarian power and its failure to provide a utopian future for the cities it controls – the imaginary future looked forward to by people in the early twentieth century in a rich, orderly antiseptic world of glass, steel and snow-white concrete. Orwell, who tends to see totalitarianism rather than technology as the determining factor, uses Goldstein's book to suggest that technology *could* have been used to achieve such utopian improvements, but that the machine threatened to equalise the distribution of security and leisure, and would thus have undermined the position of the privileged caste.

Zamyatin and Huxley both create centres of power which approximate much more closely to the gleaming, tightly bounded utopian super-city in which technology has provided its mass-produced satisfactions even if only in the form of food which is a derivation of naphtha. They are also alike in attaching more structural importance to the division between organic complexity and the self-enclosed city. At the end of *We*, although the narrator capitulates, there is a degree of optimism in the fact that a revolution is still in progress against The One State, aiming to demolish the glass wall separating natural vitality from the mathematically rational, artificially maintained, totally controlled city in which all people ('numbers') live in glass rooms in full sight of one another, watched over by the Guardians, timed by controllers, recorded by street membranes. The rooms that Zamyatin does value – like the lovers' meeting place in the House of Antiquity – are imagined in terms of natural imagery (a 'motley splurge of colours and forms, wild, unorganised, insane . . .'). Unlike Wells, who sees destruction of the repressive city as a possible prelude to a utopian rebuilding, Zamyatin has distinctly primitivist leanings, manifest in his hostility to the finality and order implicit in perfectly planned architectural forms. In consequence, it is only possible to imagine the dislodging of entrenched power if the revolutionaries succeed in razing 'this Wall – all walls – so that green wind may blow over all the earth' (*We*, pp. 41, 154).

Huxley, who was, like Orwell, strongly influenced by Zamyatin, uses both the English landscape and savage society to provide the context for his critique of technocracy, with the interior scenes as well as the panoramas of the 'brave new world' defining the nature of the biological control. Just as Zamyatin's rigid shapes demonstrate man's subordination to the mathematically exact laws of social engineering, Huxley's Central London Hatchery and Conditioning Centre reflects exactly the strict order being genetically engineered within it: enormous rooms, the 'wintriness' of 'glass and nickel and bleakly shining porcelain', white-clad workers, 'frozen, dead' light, test-tubes, conveyors and 'the spidery steelwork of gallery above gallery' (*Brave New World*, pp. 1–9). From a helicopter, there is a hint of the natural world of the forest, but the city's regulation of everything organic is clearly signalled by the 'fierce electric brilliance' of the twenty-storey Internal and External Secretions factory and by the 'majestic buildings of the Slough Crematorium' (p. 64). For those conditioned to enjoy urban consumerism, there is no point in moving beyond such civilised 'landmarks' to explore the unspoiled rural landscape, since it offers no Electro-magnetic golf or Tennis, and the idyllic English countryside is therefore left to provide a fleeting hope of a retreat for the Savage when he makes his attempt to live 'alone and undisturbed' (pp. 223–4). The Savage's own Indian village provides Huxley with another sort of counterpointing, a primitive culture not technologically ordered and sanitised. This primitive world is not, like Zamyatin's, a repository of lush, vibrant energy with 'mute fountains jetting green' (p. 152); it is harsh and dangerous. Huxley himself felt that he had provided the Savage with too limited a range of alternatives. He would, he said, offer another possible way of life if he were to rewrite the book – the implication perhaps being that technological change is not, after all, ungovernable, and that he felt himself, in *Brave New World*, to have been too inclined to technological determinism. His suggested third alternative is the middle ground which is deliberately excluded from the conventional technological dystopia, a decentralised and co-operative body politic in which, as he says in his Forward, 'Science and technology would be used as though, like the Sabbath, they had been made for man, not (as at present and still more so in the Brave New World) as though man were to be adapted and enslaved to them.'

The disjunction between nature and the city is closely related to the opposition between man and the machines that dominate urban life. Pessimism about man's ability to 'use' science and technology, or to resist the application of modern techniques by those in power, can be expressed through the motif of the helplessly dependent individual, surrounded by technology which he is not himself able to manipulate. The isolation and impotence of the human figure in the technological super-city can often be seen, for example, in the image of the protagonist who, in trying to escape entrapment, is confronted by a closed door which offers no visible means of control. Shortly after Wells's Sleeper wakes, he is left in an unfamiliar room, shut in by a 'noiseless door' which is 'securely fastened in some way he never came to understand' (*The Sleeper Awakes*, pp. 57–8). This incomprehension adds to his sense of being very small and ineffectual in the vast mechanical spaces of the city, which are 'complex beyond his understanding' (p. 188). Mechanisms which apparently cannot be affected by human actions also figure prominently in Jack Williamson's *The Humanoids* (1949): the sinister humanoids transport the hero in a 'mirror-bright tear-drop' cruiser in which a flat deck covers all controls, the door has 'no handle a man could work', and the ship itself is powered by a beam from another planet; he is kept in a luxurious bedroom, 'more dreadful to him than any nightmare', sealed in by doors and windows secured with inaccessible relays.[33] In contrast to the old-fashioned disorder of the rooms that so often act as refuges in dystopian tales (in the House of Antiquities in *We*, over Mr Charrington's shop in *Nineteen Eighty-Four*, in the old farmhouse in Vonnegut's *Player Piano*), the technically perfected room is a microcosm of the totally controlled society. It has become an advanced and comfortable 'machine for living', but in return for service, the human occupant must relinquish his wish for mastery.

Equally helpless is the man trapped within a mechanical routine, unable to see how the whole of the machine functions and without any individual influence on what is produced. Winston, in *Nineteen Eighty-Four*, working on the production line of totalitarian truth-subversion, is able to operate the machinery of the Ministry of Truth, but within so limited a sphere of competence that he can have no knowledge of the larger process he serves. Sitting in his Ministry cubicle, surrounded by orifices (pneumatic tubes and a 'memory hole') he has no detailed knowledge of what happens in the unseen labyrinth to which the tubes lead or of the anonymous directing brains who co-ordinate everything (pp. 42–5). What Winston is servicing is in effect a massive device for the destruction of human memory, and hence of human identity, an activity which Orwell takes to be essential to the maintenance of totalitarian power. It is in the threat they pose to individual human identity that totalitarianism and mechanisation are seen to be most closely allied. At the heart of the dystopian nightmare is the image of lifeless mechanism joining hands with totalitarian political control (*Nineteen Eighty-Four*, *We*) or creating its own form of totalitarianism (*Brave New World*, *The Humanoids*). In *Brave New World Revisited*, Huxley comments on the totalitarian implications of a determination to order political life efficiently: 'the theoretical reduction of unmanageable multiplicity to comprehensible unity becomes the practical reduction of human diversity to subhuman uniformity, of freedom to servitude . . . the Will to Order can make tyrants out of those who merely aspire to clear up a mess' (pp. 38–9). The association of this 'subhuman uniformity' with mechanised ways of thinking is so strong that even in a non-technological dystopia like Joseph O'Neill's *Land Under England* (1935) the most recurrent metaphors for total political control are those of automatism: the narrator (another of those who is temporarily trapped in a smooth-walled room with no apparent doors) finds that the inhabitants of the subterranean world he visits behave like automatons, showing no trace of individual identity. He reflects that trying to talk to them was as rewarding 'as trying to get in touch with a gramophone or a motor-car'. They have been taken over by a system created by their own fear, which grew until it began to function for its own sake, becoming a 'monstrous machine'. The narrator is thus the only human being left in that world 'outside the machine', having – as is the way in most science fiction dystopias – to 'make a stand for humanity' and to resist the underworld attempt to deprive him of his own memories and associations.[34] As in much other science fiction, narrative suspense is primarily created by the struggle between human individuality and a highly efficient, systematic effort to eliminate every 'messy' human fact in the interests of a unified political whole.

The application of a machine metaphor to politically or technologically created human cogs involves variations on the idea of the machine as composed of parts that are rigidly organised and work in a regular fashion to produce a standardised product. The themes developed in this way are loss of autonomy (men only functioning as parts of a whole); loss of uniqueness (identical components designed for repetitive tasks); and loss of individual wholeness (men only identified as a cluster of functions).[35] Pessimistic analysts of the technological state have constant recourse to the image of man-as-machine. Gabriel Marcel, for example, writes of 'submen' who are reduced to their own strict function in a mechanised society, without any will of their own (*Man Against Mass Society*, p. 72); Juenger thinks in terms of nightmare images of a vast and powerful mechanism covering the whole earth, with all mankind harnessed mechanically to it – a world of functional thinking 'wherein all things lose face and form' (*The Failure of Technology*, p. 76). The numbering of people within a strictly hierarchical system is perhaps the most common dystopian sign of reduction to strict function and of the concomitant loss of full human identity. As the young couple in Wells's *Story of the Days to Come* suffer descent into the lower orders, their decline is marked not only by their donning of the Labour Company's blue canvas clothing but by their interview with a manageress who assigns them to their new roles in industrial society: '*You* nought nought nought, type seven, sixty-four, b.c.d., *gamma* forty-one, female; you 'ave to go to the Metal-beating Company' (pp. 64–5). A fully categorised population is one that is fully functional, whether they are the elaborately tested and labelled inhabitants of Vonnegut's Ilium, Zamyatin's numbers or Huxley's Bokanovsky Groups.

The creation of these classifications assumes various kinds of selection, whether arbitrary whim (Wells) or rigorous testing (Vonnegut). Zamyatin and Huxley push the selection process a stage further, achieving perfect functional adaptation by means of genetic engineering. What this in essence involves is breaking down the differences between the natural and the artificial, pushing a stage further the coalescence between organic and inorganic forms. Critics of mechanisation have long argued that human techniques are in themselves acting to condition human behaviour. Jacques Ellul, for example, referring back, as Foucault does, to the eighteenth-century work, *L'homme-machine*, maintains that in the coupling of man and machine, the gap will not be bridged mainly by the adaptation of machines to men, but by the emergence of 'the complex "man-machine", the formula of the future', the complete adaptation of men to machines. The next logical step from this objectivisation (thinking of man on the model of a mere physical object) is seen as the attempt to design man as the machine itself is designed, to serve a particular function. What Foucault calls the new regime of 'bio-power', the manipulation of an objectified human body, is at the core of those dystopian fictions in which biological adaptation produces the behaviour required for a smoothly functioning political and economic structure.

Enthusiasm over the prospects opened up by biomedical advances had long given rise to scientific optimism: T.H. Huxley, for example, had in the 1880s predicted a 'molecular mechanism' capable of curing disease; Emil Fischer, accepting the Nobel Prize for Chemistry in 1902, foresaw 'as if half in a dream, the rise of a purely synthetic chemical biology which will manipulate the living world'. Haldane, in his widely debated essay *Daedalus, or Science and the Future* (1924), speculating on the influence of biology on twentieth-century history, imagines a piece of work read by 'a rather stupid undergraduate' to his supervisor in the year 2073. Taking as his starting point the 'conscious attempt at the application of biology to politics in the so-called eugenic movement' in the first decade of the twentieth century, the hypothetical student describes universal ectogenesis as established by the mid twenty-first century, with less than 30 per cent of children 'born of woman'. Haldane speculates on future elections ('if such quaint political methods survive') fought over the issue of which character traits should be developed by selective breeding, and proclaims biologists to be the most romantic of figures: 'They do not see themselves as sinister and revolutionary figures. They have no time to dream. But I suspect that more of them dream than would care to confess it.'[36]

Haldane's prophecies, combined with other biological possibilities discussed in the twenties, prompted many to reflect in the literature of the time on the revolutionary potential and the moral implications of the biologist's dream. C.S. Lewis's 'Space Trilogy', beginning with *Out of the Silent Planet* (1938), was written in part in reaction against Haldane, and also against Olaf Stapledon, who, in *Last and First Men* (1930), projects over a vast time-scale (2,000 million years) the possible development of successive biological variations. Although many of Stapledon's species of men attain higher orders of wisdom, he also uses his speculative framework to survey some of the dangers represented by biological engineering – most notably by the development of a vast super-brain. In a bizarre account of the half-natural, half-artificial system that constitutes 'the first true individual of the fourth human species', Stapledon pictures a giant brain created after centuries of experimentation by inducing embryonic brain cells to spread outwards into an artificial 'cranium' (a 'roomy turret of ferro-concrete'). The great brain serves to illustrate the tyranny inherent in a purely detached and scientific approach to experience.[37] Alternatively, rather than anticipating the creation of an all-powerful super-brain, opponents of genetic engineering feared the biologically programmed uniformity of a large subject population. This had, in the twenties, been briefly sketched in by Zamyatin, who conceived of it as a prelude to the complete depersonalisation necessary to totalitarian control. But the possibility was, of course, most fully imagined by Aldous Huxley. Huxley was rather less unequivocally opposed to a hierarchical system based on genetically engineered differences than *Brave New World* might lead one to suppose, continuing, for example, to advocate compulsory sterilisation of defectives even after many members of the British eugenics movement had moderated their views (distancing themselves from Nazi sterilisation laws). *Brave New World* itself nevertheless supplies some of the best-known satiric images of future-world biological intervention, with its embryos ectogenetically developed on a production line and chemically adapted for life in the appropriate caste. 'Progress', paradoxically, is ensured by arrested development: bokanovskification, 'a series of arrests of development', produces budding – 'making ninety-six human beings grow where only one grew before. Progress' (pp. 3–4). Pharmacology and conditioning continue what Bokanovsky's Process begins, producing the efficient social arrangements needed to sustain the organisation of a technologically advanced society, protecting the great machine of social stability: 'Wheels must turn steadily . . . . There must be men to tend them, men as steady as wheels upon their axles, sane men, obedient men, stable in contentment' (pp. 37–8).

The counterpart of the mechanisation of men is the humanisation of machines. Numerous science fiction robot stories written during the thirties and forties represent robots as friendly, loveable allies, but for writers hostile to technological advance, the robot's mimicry of human qualities creates profound unease. Dystopian plots involving the transference of human traits (will and passion) to robots and androids are closely related to what commentators on technological society call 'the emancipation of techniques' – that is, they are an expression of the fear that technological *means* can come to be valued and cultivated for their own sake and hence acquire determining power in human social and political organisation. The machine that ceases to be strictly derivative in its powers and functions becomes a kind of demonic other, capable of imitating the human and thus not only jeopardising our self-definition but threatening to supplant its inventors.[38] Juenger, for example, shows clearly the tendency of the time towards the demonisation of the automaton in his reference to the old superstitious 'but by no means erroneous' idea 'which held that some man-made apparatus might acquire a demoniacal life, might unfold a will of its own, a rebellious and destructive will' (*The Failure of Technology*, pp. 114–15); in *La Révolte des machines*, there is at the beginning a vision of progress towards a world in which godlike man will control everything from his armchair, but masterful man is ultimately dehumanised and deposed by machines that, in a frenzy, tease, torment and destroy the helpless human onlookers.[39]

The prototypical robot story is Čapek's *R.U.R.*, which introduced the word 'robot' into the English language (from the Czech 'robotit', to drudge). The play shows, in Čapek's own account, the heir to scientific materialism (young Rossum) undertaking to make Rossum's Universal Robots, following the principles of Taylorism, technocratic efficiency and mass-production: 'Immediately we are in the grip of industrialism, this terrible machinery must not stop . . . .'[40] The determining power of inhuman, large-scale technology, mastering those who thought themselves masters of industry, is embodied in the revolt of the machine-men of *R.U.R.*, synthetic androids who exactly resemble human beings. Each robot can replace two and a half workers, thus offering mankind the prospect of a technological utopia in which all work is done by the 'living machines': 'The Robots will clothe and feed us . . . everybody will be free from worry' (p. 25). Manufactured in a way that emphasises the crude materialism of their conception (a kneading-trough for the paste, a spinning-mill for nerves and veins), the robots apparently lack the most important human qualities (will, passion, soul). But one of the scientists gives them 'a twist' (the irritability that is the start of 'soul') and this, combined with the sheer momentum of their rapid production, carries the robots towards a confrontation with their creators (pp. 70–5). Behind Čapek's fantasy, there is a vision of the inevitable violence inherent in capitalist industrial technology – of inhumanity as well as dehumanisation. The direction his fable takes is therefore the total destruction of the human species, which is punished for its offence against nature by being reduced to the same condition as inorganic matter – first sterile, then lifeless. Human beings become, like machines, unable to reproduce themselves, thus erasing one of the most important distinctions between man and machine; then, as the play reaches its climax, the prime goal of the technological utopia (to 'extend human dominion' by eliminating human labour) is defeated when the machines take it upon themselves to eliminate the human element in a more comprehensive fashion: 'Robots throughout the world, we enjoin you to murder mankind . . . . Then return to work. Work must not be stopped' (pp. 66, 59).

By no means all stories of machine–man reversal imagine so sanguinary an end as *R.U.R.* They may seize not on the possibility of mechanical annihilation but instead on the questionable blessing of mechanical beneficence – the insidious ascendancy of the ubiquitous servant. The prospect of machines feeding and clothing everyone is gradually extended, until there is a surrender of all human tasks, judgements and responsibilities to the machines men have invented. Vonnegut's *Player Piano*, for example, which satirises technocratic tyranny of a distinctly American variety, imagines power in the hands of an elite of engineers, managers and scientists, and almost all other work done by machines, including the classification of every citizen's job and the elimination from official files of jobs rendered redundant. The blackly comic fantasy of 'people gettin' buggered by things they made theirselves' ends with a Luddite smashing of the automatic factories in a movement to give America back to the people – though with the wry recognition at the end of people's eagerness to recreate 'the same old nightmare'.[41] A darker, more exaggerated version of the oppressively helpful machine nightmare can be seen in Williamson's *The Humanoids*, in which a thoroughly utopian intention (the promotion of human welfare and the removal of class distinctions, poverty, toil and crime) produces intergalactic mechanical tyranny. It is an ill-conceived transference of responsibility, with men protected from themselves by the 'serene solicitude' of the sleek black android 'mechanicals', leading to a suppression of all the more interesting human desires and qualities. Williamson's oxymoronic phrase 'ruthless benevolence' conveys the same ironic vision we found in Forster's 'The Machine Stops': the most comprehensive guardianship of mankind is the ultimate act of aggression by the Machine, which has 'robbed us of the sense of space . . . blurred every human relation . . . paralysed our bodies and our wills' (pp. 130–1).[42]

INDIVIDUAL/MASS

The humanoid masters of Williamson's dystopia prepare themselves against human dissent with a drug called euphoride, capable of removing all unhappiness. Those to whom it has been given are looked after in an environment that is vacuously soothing – luminous, satin-surfaced walls, colour views of scenic wonders, softly glowing tapestries decorated with childlike pictures, the all-enveloping scent of 'Sweet Delirium' (*The Humanoids*, pp. 68–9). Anyone whose 'unhappiness' threatens to destabilise the technologically guaranteed harmony is provided with an instant escape from reality. Chemically induced euphoria is, of course, even more crucial to the control mechanisms of *Brave New World*. Huxley, who had a strong sense of the human need for both traditional mind-changing drugs and 'the latest products of psycho-pharmacological research' (and who returns, in *The Doors of Perception*, for example, to write far more positively of 'chemical vacations from intolerable selfhood and repulsive surroundings'), gave dystopian fiction its most famous drug: soma.[43] This self-administered defence against all unpalatable facts and uncomfortable emotions separates people from reality as effectively as the barriers of the dystopian civilisation separate it from the natural world: 'that second dose of *soma* had raised a quite impenetrable wall between the actual universe and their minds. Bottled, they crossed the street . . . .' This 'bottling' does not mean a withdrawal into isolated subjectivity but into a self relentlessly formed by the conditioning and propaganda of a highly organised collective ethos. Soma assists in generating the collectively endorsed feelings of solidarity, happiness and benevolence that are celebrated at the communal rituals of self-abnegation – 'I drink to my annihilation' (pp. 70–2).

Pharmacology, of course, is only one of the aids to ensuring conformity in dystopia. Insistence on collective as opposed to individual ways of thinking is a distinguishing feature of the dystopian vision. This can be a development of the banal consensus of a future of consumer capitalism (*Brave New World, Player Piano*), the unplanned result of technological 'progress' (*The Humanoids*), or the consequence of a collectivist political mystique, carefully contrived by those bent on preserving their own power (*Nineteen Eighty-Four, We*). But whatever the ideological foundation and however arrived at, this uniform mind set is a *sina qua non* of the dystopia. Of the texts we have looked at, only *R.U.R.* (which is not generally classed as a dystopia) lacks the theme of enforced harmony, and this is because, in Čapek's fantasy, absence of dissension is achieved with more brutal simplicity, by the complete elimination of humanity itself. Formally, the element of conformity is necessary to the creation of the dystopia, which is only genuinely horrifying as an all–encompassing system – the counter-image of the self-contained utopia, which must, as Wells says in *A Modern Utopia*, 'have a clear common purpose' that overrides 'all these incurably egotistical dissentients' (p. 128). As in fantasies of the megamachine, autonomy and uniqueness disappear, but here, instead of coldly rational, functional thinking and objectivisation, the threat is the irrationalist one of immersion in a collective experience made more durable and uniform by techniques for extension and replication. This is in a sense, then, a technologically generated substitute for charismatic followership, releasing participants from the constraints of the reasoning, discriminating mind. As Juenger argues, it is possible to see a close connection between technical progress 'and the efforts to turn our minds against rationalism itself' (*The Failure of Technology*, pp. 141–2). The key oppositions stressed are between mass and individual; happy and free; popular art and high art; subservience to the dominant ideology and antagonism to it; unconsciousness (lack of awareness) and consciousness (critical awareness) – or, in old-fashioned Marxist terminology, between those who suffer from 'false consciousness' and those without illusions who either break away or who (villainously) manipulate and brainwash the masses. 'The masses', both as a symbol of the society of the future and as a subject of contemporary investigation, was a central term in the language of social and political debate. Accordingly, in the dystopian vision, the 'universal harmony' of the Wellsian utopia is rephrased as 'mass conformity', and the horror evoked is fuelled by a strong distaste for popular culture, as well as by a liberal–humanist sense of individualism, tinged with romantic nostalgia. The dystopian writer generally imagines a world enslaved by a powerful elite, but the real sense of horror is most often evoked not by a representation of those in control but by the thought of a malleable mass of humanity, united in shallow and mind-numbing amusements.[44] The machinery of the plot is routinely set in motion by the deviant individual, or revolutionary group of individuals, for whom mass-produced cultural satisfactions and recreations have become a hollow sham.

The polarisation of happiness and freedom is mainly, of course, a characteristic of those dystopias which see social coherence achieved through the sharing of positive rather than hostile emotions. Orwell deliberately counters what he sees as the overly hedonistic nature of Huxley's dystopia – of his attack on 'the more fat-bellied type of perfectionism'[45] – by creating in *Nineteen Eighty-Four* a future world dominated by fear, loathing, sadistic punishment and masochistic submission, the collective emotion generated being epitomised in the 'Two Minutes Hate'. Even Orwell, however, acknowledges the need for a certain degree of low-level happiness. The machinery of oppressive power is only really brought to bear on the Middle, the intellectuals who mediate between the High and the Low. But *their* function is to ensure the contentment of the proles, to control them, not only by an extension of terror but by the provision of propaganda and entertainment. As critics have often observed, Orwell failed to see the potential of television for the provision of mass amusement, imagining the telescreen as being used mainly for surveillance, with most of the proles, in any case, not possessing one. What he did see, however, was a massive effort to shape popular opinion: 'The possibility of enforcing not only complete obedience to the will of the State, but complete uniformity of opinion on all subjects, now existed for the first time.' The masses, who 'never revolt of their own accord' and never develop articulate discontent without leadership, are kept in submissive ignorance, distracted by the outpourings of cheap fiction mass-produced on novel-writing machines, by songs composed 'without any human intervention', telescreen broadcasts, manufactured rumours and atrocity pamphlets (pp. 214–16, 154–5). In spite of Winston's secretly expressed view that whatever hope there is lies in the proles, he suspects, as Orwell himself does, that the lower orders are capable of remaining all too contented on a diet of Prolefeed.

Whatever the prevailing mood of the dystopian society, and whether the basis of extrapolation is totalitarian or democratic conformity, the distaste for mass culture remains constant. There is some truth in Kingsley Amis's charge that science fiction writers of the time are characterised by 'a certain triumphant lugubriousness, a kind of proleptic *schadenfreude* (world copyright reserved)', a satisfaction taken in issuing Jeremiah-like warnings about the decline of culture.[46] This nightmare vision of popular culture is not, of course, confined to the fictional dystopia. The intellectual and cultural level of the man in the street was despised equally by right- and left-wing intellectuals. On the Right, cultural elitists like Huxley, Yeats and Lawrence pondered the question of how intellectual aristocracy could be protected from the incursions of popular taste and democratic vulgarity. On the Left, we have, for example, the critique of industrial mass society developed by German social thinkers seeking to account for the rise of fascism in Germany and the development of a theory of mass culture by members of the Frankfurt Institute. In this blend of Marxist and Freudian thinking, repressed industrial man, subject to the selfish manipulation of those in control, has his instinctual drives perverted and his judgement led astray. Adorno and Horkheimer, in *Dialectic of Enlightenment* (1944), argue that 'culture now impresses the same stamp on everything'. They see an 'iron system' in which films, radio and magazines impose uniformity, with deliberately produced rubbish swamping the individual consciousness: the radio authoritatively subjects all listeners to programmes which are exactly the same, with no possible rejoinder and no real broadcasting freedom; the lightning-fast spread of popular songs in America (like rapidly-disseminated Nazi propaganda) leads to the reification of the most intimate reactions, so that, for ordinary men, 'the idea of anything specific to themselves now persists only as an utterly abstract notion: personality scarcely signifies anything more than shining white teeth and freedom from body odour and emotions'. Technology has become psycho-technology, a procedure for producing false consciousness, for manipulating and overpowering, for using 'the assembly-line character of the culture industry, the synthetic, planned method of turning out its products' to achieve the same effects as the propaganda slogan – mechanical repetition which numbs the mind and helps to guarantee that power will remain in the same hands. Democratic mass media thus usurp individual consciousness as effectively as the ceaseless propaganda of a totalitarian regime – of Nazi Germany or of the Soviet Union in the Stalinist era. The actual methods of dissemination (radio broadcasts, for example) are seen as an inevitable degradation of thought; all amusements in which the machine plays a part are regarded as empty, dominated by compulsion and repetition. Views such as these combine hostility to technologically-assisted entertainment with contempt for the mass men who have supposedly lost the faculty of amusing themselves, and whose spare time can only be filled by 'automatic regulation'.[47]

The dystopia extrapolates on the basis of just such suspicion of mass culture, projecting a society in which there is near-universal submission to ideas and entertainments centrally produced by a power structure determined to stifle all individual thought, initiative and difference. Although mass man is already seen as almost uniformly mindless, the dystopian emptying of the common mind is yet more thoroughly accomplished by all of the conditioning and educational refinements that future-world technology and 'ideal' social–political structures can provide. Utopia is, of course, often founded on conditioning. Modern utopian thinking has generally emphasised the importance of moulding human character by means of scientific psychology, the most comprehensive and controversial example of 'behavioural engineering' being B.F. Skinner's *Walden Two* (1948), which is the most detailed utopian treatment of the procedures needed to perfect the race and to condition men to be virtuous. Skinner quotes T.H. Huxley's reflections on being turned into a clock to support his argument that virtue should be made as near-habitual as possible, with conditioning enabling men to be good without thinking about it. Wells gives comparatively less attention to the question of how man is to be improved. But *Men Like Gods* (1923), although written too early to use the word 'conditioning', describes in general terms the training of the Utopian child 'by the subtlest educational methods', so that kindness and civility become habitual and 'all its desires are made fine', thus obviating the need for rule and government. Benign though this may sound, Wells imagines the fight to stop the advent of the universal scientific/educational state in utopia as having lasted for nearly five centuries, and, in his own dystopia, even he seems to have created a negative image of the officially conditioned child emerging from state nurseries and mechanical nurses.[48]

The grounds for objecting to the ideal of fully conditioned human behaviour are evident in many dystopias. Antipathy to behaviourism is particularly important to Huxley, who launches, in *Brave New World Revisited* (1974), a strong attack on the 'Behaviourist fervour' of J.B. Watson and B.F. Skinner, which he sees as a development of the trends he fictionalised in *Brave New World*. Huxley contends that, in order to fit into the organisations of a technologically advanced society, individuals already have to 'de-individualise' themselves, deny their native diversity and conform to a standard pattern; to augment this tendency, the rulers of tomorrow will increasingly try to impose uniformity on their populations (*Brave New World Revisited*, pp. 26, 38–9). Like others who are opposed to behaviourist conditioning, Huxley sees it as aiming for perfect adjustment at the cost of free will, self-determination and human dignity, and as entailing a loathsome democratisation of virtue. As Mustapha Mond says in *Brave New World*, 'Anybody can be virtuous now' (pp. 216–17). The point is driven home in *Brave New World* by having the infants conditioned against nature and against high culture. In a world in which science has contrived an almost painless adjustment, the pain has been shifted to an early stage in the dehumanisation process, administered by technicians so effectively as to render needless the adult pain inflicted by thought police: the identical babies released from their shelves, crawling happily towards the books and flowers, are stopped by explosions, sirens, alarm bells and electric shocks, which, after two hundred repetitions, will keep them 'safe from books and botany all their lives' (pp. 17–18). As in prenatal conditioning, the key elements are denaturing and repetition. Huxley's choice of books and flowers is obviously in part an effort to achieve the strongest possible demonstration of the standard anti-utopian case against the remorselessness of scientific conditioning; it also underlines the differences between conditioning and education, viz., conditioning as the creation of behaviour which bears no normal or natural relation to outside conditions and as 'the creation of behaviour where the subject does not understand why the behaviour is created'.[49] Most importantly, of course, flowers and books signify the diverse stimuli of vital nature and high culture from which the uniform dystopia is invariably cut off. The appalling repetition of the conditioning process produces a world in which only repetition is possible. The individual is associated with high culture, the mass with formulaic, sterile repetition. Huxley, who famously described himself as an 'amused, Pyrrhonic aesthete', had arguably become, by the mid thirties, less contemptuous of mass society and more humanitarian, but he nevertheless writes of the 'infinitely precious experience of being in a superior minority' and, as he looks down on mankind, proclaims that 'about 99.5 per cent of the entire population of the planet' are 'stupid and philistine' and that, since nothing can be done about imbecility so appalling, all that is important is to keep the superior 0.5 per cent up to the highest level. Popular culture is for Huxley indistinguishable from the mechanical repetition of the production line, incapable of range, variety or diversity. As he writes in 'Boundaries of Utopia': 'to extend privileges is generally to destroy their value. Experiences which, enjoyed by a few, were precious, cease automatically to be precious when enjoyed by many.'[50]

The juxtaposition of popular and high culture is central to the construction of *Brave New World*. The Savage, a child of nature whose mind is filled entirely with Shakespeare, measures the new world against high art and finds it 'stupid and horrible'. In the climactic confrontation of the novel, he discovers that the Controller, too, has read Shakespeare, but that he cynically suppresses what he knows to be disruptive. They have, Mustapha Mond explains, created a 'non-vicious' circle, that is, a 'blissfully ignorant' population is kept happy by feelies and scent organs, sustaining a socially stable society which would be incapable of producing great tragic literature. As with the antithesis between nature and the city, this is presented as a choice of opposites: 'You've got to choose between happiness and what people used to call high art. We've sacrificed the high art' (pp. 200–1). In his Foreword of 1946, Huxley explicitly recommends the ersatz satisfactions of popular art to any dictator wishing to retain his hold on power, since the freedom to daydream 'under the influence of dope and movies and the radio . . . will help to reconcile his subjects to the servitude which is their fate'. The combination of drugs and popular culture – both here and throughout *Brave New World* – implies that technoculture is addictive and mind–numbing, separating the quiescent 'user' from the real world. Although Huxley's views are those, in Wells's phrase, of 'a brilliant reactionary',[51] he in fact shares considerable common ground with the many critics of the Left who are similarly distressed by evidence of the creation of a mass mind. Wells himself, in a utopia such as *Men Like Gods*, projects a world in which there has been a total elimination of popular entertainment for the 'mere looker-on' – indeed, 'the common life' seems to have been completely swept away; in his dystopias, on the other hand, one important measure of his distress is the prevalence of mass culture (pp. 64, 125). In *The Sleeper Awakes*, the crowds have the kinematograph-phonographs and the 'newfangled Babble Machines' which, having replaced printed books, are 'easy to hear, easy to forget' (pp. 110, 145). These are the same themes elaborated by Herbert Marcuse, for example, in *One-Dimensional Man* (1964), which analyses what he sees as a process of integration, an end to artistic alienation, with the diffusion of culture by technological means turning all artistic productions into 'cogs in a culture-machine' and removing the possibility that high art can act as an 'antagonistic force' (instead, all media being mobilised for the defence of 'the established reality', one sees no possibility of sustaining solitude or of refusing 'to behave').[52] Similarly, in *Brave New World*, the inevitable end is the failure – in the face of something very like what Marcuse calls 'Happy Consciousness' – of the solitary integrity of Huxley's Savage and of the weak resistance of his representative artist, Helmholtz Watson.

Artists can, of course, serve the one state of dystopia not just by churning out mindless amusements but by producing the propaganda which shapes the specific political preferences of the multitude. Poets, as the narrator of Zamyatin's *We* says, have 'come down to earth' and 'are striding side by side with us, keeping in step with the austere, mechanical March, issuing from the Musical Factory' (p. 78). The future art represented in the conventional dystopia is not the antagonistic work of the renegade, but the lies and distortions of the propagandist and the glorifications of the state produced by future-world artists, or by the machines that have replaced them. The image of the artist marching in step with the masses catches both the mechanical nature of the creation and the irresistible momentum of mass activities – a rhythm which, like the timed motions of the assembly line, allows no individual to vary the pace or step out on his own. Some of Zamyatin's most detailed descriptions of the future-world of *We* are given over to capturing the compelling force of mechanical rhythms, their 'diurnalness . . . repetitiveness . . . mirrorousness'. When the 'blue unif-waves' of ten million numbers assemble to praise The One State, they are all permeated by the vivifying currents of the music mathematically composed by turning the handle of the musicometer. The complete harmony of the occasion is only broken by the antique costume of E-330, who stirs quite different rhythms in the narrator's mind – 'wild, spasmodic', Dionysian rhythms that would lead you to 'tear everything off yourself' (p. 49). Huxley, much less of a primitivist, suggests affinities between a tribal dance and the Solidarity Services and Ford's Day celebrations. The sado-masochistic reservation ceremony, however, has some claim to be more closely in touch with natural energies, whereas Orgy-Porgy is no more than a comically diminished expression of the libidinous id, contained within a service designed to maintain a 'balanced life'. The experience is one of being caught up in mass emotion, forced away from individual unity of personality towards absorption in the social body and dissolution of the reasoning self.

Bernard, in *Brave New World*, though he feels nothing himself, finds that the urge to conform has him waving his arms and shouting 'with the best of them' (p. 74). For other would-be resisters of dystopia the sense of self is still less secure in the face of collective irrationalism. One of the things that makes the world of *Nineteen Eighty-Four* a far more disturbing, claustrophobic place than Huxley's brave new world is the fact that Orwell concedes no islands to the self – no remote Falklands to which the isolated individual can retire, and no room within the existing body politic for a mere pretence of conformity. Winston, to his shame, finds it impossible to avoid joining in the Two Minutes Hate and impossible not to experience the 'ecstasy of fear and vindictiveness, a desire to kill . . . seemed to flow through the whole group of people like an electric current' (p. 16). This violation of his own will to resist is a foreshadowing of the end, when, broken into submission, he has his final 'victory over himself' (p. 311). In representing the victory of the collective emotion over self, dystopian writers repeatedly come back to the use of brainwashing and other forms of indoctrination which break down men's connection with the past and erode any sense of independence. Winston's act of self-hypnosis at the beginning of *Nineteen Eighty-Four*, when he deliberately drowns consciousness by means of rhythmic noise, prepares us for an end in which he is asked to accept that reality exists only in the collective mind and is crushed by techniques capable of leaving 'a large patch of emptiness, as though a piece had been taken out of his brain' (p. 269). This emptying or hollowing out of the individual personality, leaving a vacancy into which mass emotions can flow, is a recurrent feature of dystopia, and one of the most frightening, leaving no one to resist. Fear of science is coupled with a deepseated fear of the loss of mind, of the last place where the individual self can retreat to escape the domination of the powerful. As O'Brien tells Winston, control over matter is already absolute, but what the Party has achieved is power over the human being, not just over the body but over the mind.

In mainstream science fiction, more elaborate forms of mind-control, such as telepathy, are used to establish the ultimate in totalitarian mastery. Telepathic powers, when they signify freedom to communicate, have perhaps most commonly been possessed by superior beings, persecuted by normal society – a pattern established, for example, by van Vogt's *Slan* (1940).[53] On the other hand, telepathy can be represented as an all-powerful form of the total mind-control more conventionally accomplished by psychological manipulation. Thus, Joseph O'Neill's *Land Under England*, which is strongly anti-Nazi in its political orientation, uses telepathy to image the obliteration of individual identity by means of powerful psychological control mechanisms. Telepathy is so far developed that the idea of individual will has become incomprehensible, leaving only the distinction between the Submissive Ones and the High Ones, the 'hypnotic dominators' who have completely subjected the underground race of the dystopia – just as, in terrestrial totalitarian regimes, the masses hand themselves over to the hypnotic suggestion of their leaders (pp. 105–7, 130). In Williamson's *The Humanoids*, we see another plot that hinges on the importance of controlling mind as opposed to matter. There are operations to remove conflict and hate from the human mind, together with any part of the memory that is dangerous to the Prime Directive, and the next stage in the projected take-over is complete psychic control, to be achieved by the building of a huge grid that will 'operate men'. The Psychophysical Institute has developed a new kind of psychology, 'an actual science of the mind', which, by repairing 'mental injuries', can convince those who have been treated that 'freedom' is guaranteed by the elimination of man's 'dangerous traits' (pp. 175–8). As is often the case in stories involving strong mind control, the perceptions of the central figure undergo such radical transformation that the narrative tension is dissolved in a final acquiescence. Conventionally, this is so heavily ironised that it is clear to readers that there has been a pessimistic closing off of the possibility that the protagonist might resist: Winston loves Big Brother; the narrator of *We*, always very uneasy in the role of a rebel, is brought back to wholehearted belief in the rectitude of The One State. In Williamson, the ending is more ambiguous, but this is primarily because powers of complete mind-alteration *would* ultimately abolish all antagonistic perspectives. The ending can be read either as an account of the hero, Forester, coming to his senses and accepting the new order or as a darkly ironic image of a completely dehumanised hero, whose smooth, reconditioned face all too quickly erases unwelcome thoughts and 'the fleeting trouble of his frown' (pp. 188–9).[54]

ENERGY/ENTROPY

A reader's uncertainty at the end of Williamson's *The Humanoids* is in part created by a pattern of imagery which runs counter to dystopian expectations. The hero is about to move on with old friends, like him reconditioned, to embark on new colonial projects in far-flung parts of the universe. The 'preposterous notion' seems to haunt Forester that he would once have been reluctant to help with the importation of humanoids to 'virgin planets of another island universe', but his sense of youth and adventure (the grid having made him young again) sweeps him away with 'bright expectation'. Though the parenthetic doubts seem to ironise Forester's final judgements, such an ending cuts against the conventionally closed and static image of dystopian society – if only, perhaps, because the whole of the universe is about to be swallowed by the 'wise benevolence of the Prime Directive' (pp. 188–9).

In many of the best-known examples of the genre, the claustrophobia of a dystopian future-world is established by an ending in which outward movement is severely circumscribed. Even where remote islands remain for malcontents (as in *Brave New World*) or where possible rebellion stirs at the margins, the closing image is likely to be one of near-motionless defeat: the dead Savage rotating 'slowly, very slowly' (*Brave New World*, pp. 236–7); the gin-sodden Winston not stirring from his seat, looking lugubriously at the portrait of Big Brother and dreaming of 'the long-hoped-for bullet . . . entering his brain' (*Nineteen Eight-Four*, pp. 310–11); the narrator of Zamyatin's *We* impassively watching E-330 suffer under the Gas Bell Glass, having had his head emptied by the extraction of 'some sort of sliver' in a fantasiectomy (the surgical removal of fantasy) which has cured him of his 'former malady, the soul sickness' (*We*, pp. 220–1).

In the fully dystopian future-world, although narrative tension is created by the intrusion of more dynamic impulses, there is ordinarily a deathly absence of any real, purposive movement. There is inaction as opposed to action – a shutting out of the world of heroic adventure. This is not (as in the thriller) a nostalgically viewed homeland which must be protected from violence; it is a state of utter paralysis. Zamyatin sees in the dystopia two contrary forces: energy and entropy. The totalitarian imposition of closed, repressive, monolithic ideological forms is represented by Zamyatin as the entropic pull towards ossification, as, finally, a cessation of all that is truly alive. The image is based on the Second Law of thermodynamics, which states that all forms of energy tend to dissipate within a closed system – entropy being the measure of unavailable energy within a system, and so reflecting the tendency of things to 'run themselves down'. In developing the law of entropy metaphorically, Zamyatin omits the implication of increasing disorganisation, since the object of his attack is a system so oppressively ordered that all energising and differentiating signs of the human have disappeared. This non-living system he associates with the cold lifelessness of ageing suns: 'the fiery magma becomes coated with dogma – a rigid, ossified, motionless crust'. Its 'quiescence' also suggests a dull planet rather than a sun, that is, a comfortable and convenient place with smooth highways and 'dispassionate computations in a well-heated room'. In terms of the controlling metaphor, it is a closed system not receiving energy from outside. Against this, he sets the uncomfortable, unsettling explosion of new energy, of revolutionary acts breaking up homogeneity. Zamyatin

269

grafts the language of romanticism on to the physical notion of an energising force. The kind of revolution he has in mind, he stresses, is 'not a social law' but an eruption of individuality – unfamiliar ideas, new tensions, the anti-entropic force of 'harmful' literature, the absurd romanticism of the heretic, by means of which the planet will be 'kindled into youth again'.[55] It is an aggressive energy, acting to destroy equilibrium and ensure 'excruciatingly perpetual motion' . As Zamyatin's heroine in *We*, E-330, develops the argument, humanity will drift downward unless people recognise that, just as there is no ultimate number, there can be no ultimate revolution – no 'full stop' of achieved perfection (pp. 161, 169–70).

Zamyatin's elaboration of this metaphor is distinctly his own, but many others (Spengler, for example) had borrowed the concepts of entropy and energy for the purposes of social prophecy, and the meaning Zamyatin extracts from the image is repeatedly echoed in the dystopian opposition between stasis and change. He locates the true 'utopian' in the absurdly romantic individual gesture – the antithesis, in fact, of the conventional literary utopia, to which he attributes the soul-destroying fixity of perfect form (what he calls 'petrified paradisiac social equilibrium'). The two generic and invariable features of the traditional utopia are, he argues, the content, representing an ideal society (an ordered and 'completed' totality), and the form, which is always static – that is, there is an absence of story-line which reflects the changeless conception of the utopian vision. Dystopian transformations always start from the premise that the gap between real and ideal has been closed, that the utopian vision has been immutably established. The counter-vision aims to expose the contradiction between change and changelessness, the irony of progress towards a dream of perfection which, once realised, becomes a frozen form, denying all possibility of progressive dynamism.[56]

Zamyatin distinguishes Wells from the creators of purely utopian visions, arguing that his stories have sufficient tension and complexity to avoid the stock elements of classic utopia. Wells himself, recognising that the notion of static perfection fatally undermined the appeal of the utopian vision, carefully separates his own 'kinetic' conception of utopia from the more traditional static form: 'Modern Utopia . . . must shape not as a permanent state but as a hopeful stage, leading to a long ascent of stages.'[57] It can be objected that Wells does not really make adequate institutional allowance for the dynamism he values, but what he more successfully does is to accommodate within his fictional utopias points of view that counteract the sense of static perfection. In *Men Like Gods*, for example, he stresses that his utopian order is not 'sclerotic', not so lacking in energy that it declines into motionless homogeneity. The charge that the fixed pattern of a utopian scheme is bound to eliminate the possibility of free individual choice is met by Wells with the picture of an Edenic world in which great beasts roam free and the childlike inhabitants experience a 'wonderland of accomplished human desires' (pp. 186–9). In this Eden, no knowledge is forbidden, and both childhood and Eden carry strong positive connotations: like Zamyatin, who sees children as 'the boldest of philosophers', Wells represents the childlike as the antithesis of the ageing and intellectually unadventurous, not as dependent or immature but filled with 'an insatiable appetite for knowledge and an habitual creative urgency'. This childlike population is, like the artist and scientist, simply doing whatever appeals to the imagination.[58]

Wells supports his belief in the possibility of a kinetic utopia with an argument of images that anticipates some of the main motifs of later dystopian science fiction. At the centre of the plot of *Men Like Gods* are contemporary human interlopers who threaten the ordered calm of a superior civilisation, thus raising within a utopian future questions about the dynamic elements in human society as we know it – about freedom of choice, scientific progress, the spirit of adventure and political activity itself. These are manifestations of individual human will and energy which would arguably have no more function in a perfectly adjusted system and which might therefore threaten to destabilise a peaceful, harmonious state. Wells uses the characteristics of his intruders to define more precisely (by contrast) the kinds of dynamism that *do* have a place in utopia. The visitors' cars are driven by 'internal conflict', which, as the plot makes clear, is a dangerous and undesirable form of forward motion. In contrast, the positive utopian energies are suggested by images of surging motion, both natural and mechanical, enabling intellectual exploration of 'the world without or the world within'. It is a society of constant discovery and 'adventure into the unknown and untried' (pp. 125–6). Though the right way to do things has been found (and hence, politicians and lawyers are unnecessary), utopia is not a place of tranquillity. Life marches, strides and progresses at a great velocity, and the apparent calm the observer sees is only 'the steadiness of a mill-race'. The energies from our own Age of Confusion, however, are recklessly disruptive. A thinly disguised Winston Churchill (Rupert Catskill, Secretary of State for War) presents the standard case against a utopian vision of the future, summing up, in a parodied politician's speech, the 'earthly' view of all that is left out of a society too rigorously planned and ordered. His characteristic gestures are thrusting and clenching; his language –

tides, vitality, thunder, urging, titanic, toughness, 'tormented energy', 'perpetual struggle' – implies that intensity and strife are inseparable. The argument he develops is one implicit in many dystopian future-worlds, that is, that the 'weeding and cleansing' necessary to create a perfectly ordered system would also eliminate the energy and beauty that are 'begotten by struggle' and 'wrought in hardship'. As the plot develops, Catskill and the other earthly visitors (excepting Barnstaple) are shown acting out the role of dynamic men of action – a negative counterpart of the adventure and individual enterprise motif around which the standard dystopian plot is centred. The most romantic of images are undermined by their application to Catskill and the others, who emerge as a band of base conspirators. Barnstaple, whose own political views are anti-nationalistic and anti-imperialistic, sees Catskill as a man who has been 'be-Kiplinged': like pirates with desperate ambitions, these destructive men would drag utopia back to 'terrestrial conditions' (pp. 149–50). Wells distinguishes, then, between destructive and creative energies (opposing scientist and artist to warrior and adventurer). Dystopian fiction, on the other hand, tends to react against totalising patterns by marshalling all unruly human energies against the entropic 'ideal society'. The adventurer, the warrior and the scientist are, from this perspective, allied figures, standing for individual human enterprise and curiosity, for movement as opposed to stasis.

In science fiction as a genre, linked as it is to voyaging out, the act of 'journeying on' often serves not only as the essential connecting thread of the narrative but as an image of man's skill in dynamic expansion. The idea of travel in space or time carries suggestions, as do all tales of adventure, of man's conquest of the material world or his capacity for empire-building. It celebrates the force and growth of Western man. The impossibility of such adventure implies the loss of all capacity for constructive growth. Men might travel, but they cannot actually discover anything that is unknown. The image of the static machine-state which pretends to a progressive form is a characteristically romantic-organicist way of countering the claims of the progressive technomyth. As Mumford argues, resistance to machine civilisation has historically been blunted by a sense that the machine is allied with life and energy and adventure, and that technological advance, having youth on its side, offers 'fresh revelations and new possibilities of action', bringing with it 'revolutionary elan'. Wells, in *A Modern Utopia*, includes free travel as an indicator of openness and dynamism. In dystopia, however, such apparent freedom would always be illusory – as Juenger writes, motion becomes a consumer good, and modern man 'worships uninhibited, dynamic, throbbing life – but worships it as a weakling who cherishes an illusion of strength' (*The Failure of Technology*, p. 160). In *Brave New World*, for example, Huxley repeatedly represents locomotion without progression. Tourists want to fly West as long as their destination promises a sufficient number of Escalator Squash Courts; or they go on the ultimate trip, the 'complete and absolute' soma holiday, an embarkation for 'lunar eternity' which requires no more space than a bed and leaves time behind (p. 127). To the Savage, it is a world devoid of romantic tasks for the questing hero to perform. There are no wolves or lions to kill, no adventures, no opportunities to 'undergo something nobly' (pp. 172–3). The justification for this way of life is lucidly and cynically supplied by Mustapha Mond, as he develops the case for contentment and happiness as opposed to spectacular instability, 'the glamour of a good fight', the picturesque struggle. Undifferentiated human mediocrity (the Bokanovsky Groups) is the stabilising force within a state which ironically lays claim to being an emblem of progress – an onrushing 'irresistible machine', the 'rocket plane of the state on its unswerving course' (p. 202). In the same way, Forster's 'Machine' provides substitutes for purposeful locomotion and itself lays sole claim to all dynamism and modernity. Civilisation exists *within* the Machine and has reversed the old function of the communication system, now bringing things to people rather than people to things. It is still possible to travel, but for a wholly static population there is a terror of direct experience. The hero's mother travels in an airship, but chooses to cover the windows, since the natural scene gives her 'no ideas'; the hero himself, on the other hand, finds his own way out on to the surface of the earth and proceeds on foot – a rare accomplishment in an age which has not only lost the sense of space but has deliberately destroyed the human potential for heroic conquest, killing at birth any infant who shows signs of undue strength and future athleticism ('The Machine Stops', pp. 120–5).

Even for the gentle Forster, it seems natural to connect this tentative questing with the spirit of great warriors: the only remedy to machine-induced paralysis, the hero reflects, is 'to tell men again and again that I have seen the hills of Wessex as Ælfrid saw them when he overthrew the Danes' (p. 131). An inescapable undercurrent in dystopian fiction involves the adventuring hero in acting courageously in human conflict. There is often a nostalgia for violent action. At the beginning of *Player Piano*, for example, the feeling that there might be too much peace is there in the initial description of the site of the Ilium works, once a battleground of tribes and nations, where men 'howled and hacked at one another' (p. 13). Contemplating the insipid 'fruits of peace' in an all too safely removed future world, the dystopian writer often romanticises heroic battles and the 'be-Kiplinged' bellicosity satirised by Wells. The impulse is effectively analysed by George Kateb, who argues that, while it would seem that no one in his right mind would object to peace, there are in fact many who, while not defending the material utility of war, nevertheless find 'something distasteful in the thought of perpetual peace'.[59] Even after the horrors of the First World War, there are often echoes of the sort of sentiments expressed by William James in 1910 – of his worries that, without war, such human qualities as heroism, exertion and manliness would have an inadequate outlet, the possibility of violent death being 'the soul of all romance'. Wells himself, in *The Time Machine*, speculates that, in the absence of conflict, a decadent and enfeebled race of men might evolve.[60] The controlling powers in dystopia can either expunge the martial instinct entirely or find alternative outlets for the 'primitive strengths' expressed in battle: Huxley, who imagines these urges as virtually eliminated, sees only the soma-less maladjusted longing to test their inner resources in 'some great trial' (pp. 92–4); Vonnegut pictures aggression discharged in the absurdly trivial games at the annual Meadows competition, when the White Team threatens to batter with fury the Blue Team. In Orwell's darker vision, the *pretence* of war is necessary because it justifies scarcity, without which the masses would become too comfortable, and because an atmosphere of national conflict generates the moods of 'fear, hatred, adulation and orgiastic triumph' which can be canalised by the state (p. 200). The need for heroes is also recognised – and is met by the wholly fictitious biographies of the Party's shining exemplars, like 'Comrade Ogilvy', who rapidly ascends from infant war games to manly slaughter and death in action (pp. 49–50).

In terms of scientific progress, the Orwellian phoney war functions as the occasion for pseudo-research: technical progress is no longer called for, but it is socially useful to give the appearance of conducting relevant research. Truly scientific modes of thought, however, must, like non-fictional heroism, be excluded from the static dystopia. The assumption is always, as in *Nineteen Eighty-Four*, that technical progress, invention and experiment have ceased – generally speaking, because, as Orwell suggests, empirical habits of thought are a source of energy too disruptive to a regimented society. Wells, in *Men Like Gods*, sees our own time divided into periods of diastole and systole. He acknowledges that human experience so far has led people to think of the development of civilisation in terms of periods of initiative, expansion and great scientific discovery (diastole) followed by the commercialisation and application of science in a world which neglects pure science (systole). It is necessary to the closed horizon of dystopia that the development of science is imagined as having been arrested in a period of systole. Whilst opposing the technologically perfected future world, dystopian fiction often preserves a romanticised attachment to a purer ideal of scientific enquiry.

The figure of the scientist, like that of the martial hero and adventurer, has often been associated with images of heroic endeavour. Spengler, for example, in his sweeping vision of Faustian culture, assesses the role of 'the Vikings of the blood and the Vikings of the mind' – the latter (for example, Copernicus and Galileo) embarking on 'Viking voyages of the intellect', motivated wholly by the 'delight of strong men in *victory*'. It was this intellectual boldness and passion that secured the advance of Western European technics, Spengler argues, and it is this that is betrayed by the conversion of technics into a materialistic religion, under the sway of the 'progress–philistine of the modern age'. Spengler's analysis is, of course, a melodramatic one, but the basic opposition between heroic and tame science is recurrently used to define the intellectual horizons of dystopia. The scientist-adventurer, who is the hero of conventional science fiction, appears in dystopia either as a distant memory or as a present threat to stability, a restless explorer, never content, defending the right to acquire new knowledge, which those in power seek to suppress. The dystopia that persecutes or excludes him is not a genuinely scientific state: as technology has progressed, it has gradually made the scientist its servant; as pure science declines, emphasis is put on application and the disciplines of science 'become auxiliary disciplines of technology'.[61]

Thus the hero of *The Humanoids* is an archetypal questing scientist, making discoveries and looking through his telescope, but one who has been enslaved by the applications of the techniques he has himself developed. Similarly, *Nineteen Eighty-Four* makes a point of the suppression of true science and even *Brave New World*, the most scientific of perfected states, can give no house room to the restless and disruptive energies of scientific enquiry. It is the enemy of stability and must be 'chained and muzzled'; the only science tolerable in dystopia is 'a cookery book' – 'an orthodox theory of cooking that nobody's allowed to question, and a list of recipes that mustn't be added to except by special permission from the head cook'. The scientist has the choice of exile or collaboration – like Mustapha Mond, once an inquisitive young scullion doing a bit of 'illicit cooking', now a cynical head cook, suppressing any scientific writing which seeks to look 'somewhere beyond' instead of concentrating on the maintenance of well-being (pp. 204–5, 160–1). In *We* the image is much more central, since the completion of a great scientific enterprise is being used as a metaphor for the betrayal of science in a monolithic system. The scientist-narrator, D-503, builder of the gigantic rocket ship, the Integral, ironises the imagery of the heroic scientific quest. The Integral itself is to be launched not for scientific but for political purposes, to lift into 'universal space' the message of complete homogeneity, carrying propaganda celebrating the 'integration' of all life in The One State (p. 19). Neutral science empowers and transmits the dominant ideology. It is the bearer of the concept of a 'final change', the contradictory nature of which Zamyatin's imagery repeatedly exposes. Throughout, he opposes images of motion, flight and speed to the immobility of The One State, perfected in its 'sedentariness', the final entropic stage in man's long transition from nomadic to settled life (pp. 27–8). The scientific calculations relating to the trial flight of the Integral are all suggestive of explosive energy and impetuous movement. Metaphorically, the speed of an 'aero' is linked with liberty ('let the speed of an aero = 0, and the aero does not move, let the liberty of man = 0, and man does not commit crimes'); it is associated with the inner vitality that threatens to disturb the perfect harmony of the system, and with the exhilaration of living dangerously (climbing at top speed in an aero, with the window open and wind buffeting your face). The explosive energy of the rocket ship seems the antithesis of its ideological function: it is a 'fiery Tamerlane', bearing the message of perfect repose. In the same way, what the narrator produces is turning out, it seems, to contradict his official purpose: 'I perceive with much regret that instead of a well-constructed and strictly mathematical poem glorifying The One State I am turning out some sort of romance of fantastic adventure' (pp. 47–9, 108–9). The perfection of the state means an end of flight and fear of motion: 'We have finished our flight, we have found what we were after'; and now 'it seems to me that everybody is just as afraid of the least motion as I am' (pp. 96, 146). This fear is set against the excitement and openness of a rocket launch which triggers erratic human emotions, such as the abortive plan of revolutionary forces to use the energies of the flight themselves.

Zamyatin's representative and 'asymmetrical' poet, R-13, relates The One State to the Myth of the Fall – with the closed, entropic totalitarian world as an Eden to which men can return if they leave behind their destructive energies. The 'Fortunate' Fall – *felix culpa* – is fortunate because human life is given its moral stature by man's acquaintance with, and struggle to overcome, evil. The utopian society has chosen, as R-13 bitterly proclaims, happiness without freedom and so has attained 'Paradise once more': 'None of that crazy jumbled stuff about Good, about Evil; everything is . . . childishly, paradisiacally simple. The Benefactor, the Machine, the Cube, the Gas Bell Glass, the Guardians – all this is good, all this is majestic, splendidly beautiful, noble, exalted, crystal-pure. Inasmuch as all this safeguards our unfreedom – our happiness, that is' (p. 72). The mythic pattern most often echoed in the dystopian technocratic state is a reversal of the Fortunate Fall, achieving a denatured and de-moralised Eden. As Orwell says in his review of *We*, 'In the Garden of Eden man was happy, but in his folly he demanded freedom and was driven out into the wilderness. Now the Single State has restored his happiness by removing his freedom.'[62] In *Nineteen Eighty-Four*, Orwell points out quite directly, in Winston's reading of the 'forbidden book', that twentieth-century totalitarianism only pays lip-service to 'the Utopianism of past ages', having in fact completely abandoned the idea of an earthly paradise at the very moment when it became realisable. In the hedonistic dystopia, however, the lip-service paid to the old utopian ideal finds expression in the shape of the society itself, providing its means of social control – in the pretence, that is, of peace, harmony and brotherhood that masks the real inequalities of the power structure. Edenic images are correspondingly more important, for example, in Vonnegut's description of an 'Eden of eternal peace', in which technological perfection replaces flawed humanity (*Player Piano*, pp. 280–2); in Čapek's closing images of the ultimate Edenic renewal of the humanised robots as Adam and Eve, who will presumably fall again, into the richness of human perfection; or in Forster's juxtaposition of the completely self-contained, all-providing paradise of the individual room with the truly paradisal earth above ground – from which perspective the Machine can be seen for the evil it is, not paradise but the serpent, with the long white worm of the Mending Apparatus dragging the hero back down, 'intertwined into hell' ('The Machine Stops', pp. 132–3). This sort of ironic reversal – seeing hell in the Edenic absence of human pain and conflict – is also at heart of O'Neill's *Land under England*, in which the elimination of human strife produces a kind of happiness which is the death of full humanity. Again, we have underground people who have attained peace at the cost of 'all the things that seem to us worth living for' (p. 241); rage and violence are gone, but so are passion and all impulse to act. The narrator, as he journeys through the society, is repeatedly threatened with absorption into its human immobility: 'I was . . . paralysed . . . motionless under that fixed stare'; to submit would be to attain 'the complete peace of complete loss' (pp. 120, 244). It is an artificial paradise which enslaves its automaton workers like 'damned souls working in a state of stupefaction' (p. 170). *Brave New World* similarly depends on our valuing the Fortunate Fall and therefore seeing the irony in the Savage's Edenic images of a new world – the 'Other Place' viewed from the Reservation is 'a heaven, a paradise of goodness and loveliness' (pp. 182–3). He will, of course, come to see the contrast between painless beauty and 'awful' significance in a different light as he broods on the impossibility of tragedy in this completely stable and happy world. 'You can't make tragedies without social instability' – and so tragedy has been, along with science, art and religion, one of the necessary sacrifices. The Savage discovers the latent horror in the elimination of all difficulty and speaks for living dangerously with what is flawed and uncertain, rather than accepting the resolution of the brave new world: 'Neither suffer nor oppose. You just abolish the slings and arrows. It's too easy' (pp. 200–1, 217–19).

In the rejection of the technological Eden, we see very clearly the fundamental contradiction that surfaces in many ways in the literature of the time. On the one hand, a 'humane' prospect of the rational control and technological betterment of human life; on the other, a romantic suspicion that a simpler, more primitive, more robust life allows our humanity fuller expression. These seemingly incompatible dynamics – the belief in 'automatic progress' and the celebration of struggle – were widely evident in the first half of the twentieth century. One of those who best sums up the conflicting pull of atavistic and progressive impulses is Orwell, who writes in *The Road to Wigan Pier*:

> The truth is that many of the qualities we admire in human beings can only function in opposition to some kind of disaster, pain or difficulty; but the tendency of mechanical progress is to eliminate disaster, pain and difficulty . . . . In tying yourself to the ideal of mechanical efficiency, you tie yourself to the ideal of softness. But softness is repulsive; and thus all progress is seen to be a frantic struggle towards an objective which you hope and pray will never be reached.
>
> (pp. 180–2)

In developing his paradoxical image of optimistic progress towards an unappealing goal, Orwell is referring mainly to socialism, which has, he argues, become too closely linked in everyone's minds with a hedonistic vision of progress, with 'a sort of glittering Wellsworld' that is so ordered and efficient that it has 'no loose ends, no wildernesses, no wild animals, no weeds, no disease, no poverty, no pain' (p. 176). Fascism, too, however, could be said to harness together the contradictory elements of the urge towards modernisation and the rebellion against its consequences.[63] As Orwell points out, fascism equally aims for the kind of collectivist (if non-egalitarian) future that favours the advance of machine-technique, and thus both ideologies seem to face an ultimate conflict between admiration for the tougher human virtues and a technically perfected future-world. Chief amongst the values destined to be outmoded in all versions of the technological world state are, as we have seen, those of the heroic adventurer. And here, Orwell himself is ambivalent: he acknowledges his fear that fascism will attract more adherents because of its greater power to give politics a spiritual dimension by appealing to the primitive emotions of patriotism and militarism; he makes it clear that, even if the fascist sees himself as 'Roland in the pass at Roncevaux', his methods are indistinguishable from those of the bully with a rubber truncheon. But however alarming he finds this contemporary candidate for the role of hero to be, Orwell also shares with many others of the time a strong distaste for a future-world which would have no room for such displays of romantic political vigour – that would all too peacefully exclude the dangerous barbarian, 'the champion of anachronisms' (pp. 199, 181).

NOTES

1. Huxley T.H. On Descartes' 'Discourse touching the method of using one's reason rightly and of seeking scientific truth' (address to Cambridge Young Men's Christian Society, 24 March 1870), in *Methods and results: essays by Thomas H. Huxley* Macmillan 1898 pp. 192–3; Zamyatin Y. *We* pp. 28–9.
2. Huxley A. *Proper studies* 1927 pp. ixff.
3. Juenger F.G. *The failure of technology* (1939) 1949 Chapter 7; and Mumford L. *The myth of the machine* 1971 p. 97.
4. Foucault M. *The Foucault reader* 1987 pp. 180–1; Mumford *Myth of the machine* pp. 84–5 and 98–100; Ferkiss V.C. *Technological man* 1969 p. 75; and see Frye N. *Anatomy of criticism* (1957), Princeton University Press, Princeton, New Jersey 1973 pp. 228–31.
5. Anti-socialist dystopias included, for example, Conde B. Palen's *Unborn tomorrow* (1933) and John Kendall's *Anthem* (1938); anti-fascist dystopias, Joseph O'Neill's *Land under England* (1935) and Rex Warner's *Wild goose chase* (1937). See Barron N. (ed) *Anatomy of wonder* 1987 pp. 58–61.
6. Scholtz-Klink G. (*Die Frau im Dritten Reich*) and Goebbels J., quoted by

Koonz C. *Mothers in the Fatherland* 1988 pp. 178–80; Hitler A., Speech to the Reichsstadthalters (6 July 1933) quoted by Fest J. *Hitler* 1974 p. 418; Lindholm C. *Charisma* 1993 pp. 111–12.

7. Ferkiss *Technological man* pp. 67–8; see also Bertrand Russell *The impact of science on society* (1952) 1990 pp. 33–54; Williams R. *Politics and technology* 1971 pp. 34–5; Orwell G. *Road to Wigan Pier* (1937) 1989 pp. 193–4; Raleigh W. *England and the war* (1918), quoted by Pick D. *The war machine* 1993 p. 138; Churchill W., Their finest hour (18 June 1940) in *Churchill speaks* 1981 p. 720.

8. Zamyatin Y., H.G. Wells; Tomorrow in *Yevgeny Zamyatin* 1991 pp. 259 and 51–2.

9. Ferkiss *Technological man* p. 28.

10. Čapek K. *R.U.R.* (1923) 1991 p. 45.

11. Pick *War machine* p. 67; Spengler O. *Man and technics* 1932 p. 90; Mumford L. *Technics and civilization* 1946 p. 322.

12. See, for example, the arguments summarised by Williams *Politics and technology* p. 14.

13. Russell B. *Icarus* 1924 pp. 23–4; and Russell *Impact of science* Chapter 6.

14. Orwell *Road to Wigan Pier* p. 193; Juenger *The failure of technology* p. 70; Ellul J. *The technological society* 1954 pp. 387–391.

15. Hillegas M.R. *The future as nightmare* 1967 p. 66; see also the discussion of dystopias in Nicholls P. (ed) *Encyclopedia of science fiction* 1979 and Aldiss B.W., Wingrove D. *Trillion year spree* 1988 Chapters 5–8.

16. Wells H.G. *A modern utopia* (1905) 1967 p. 102.

17. See, for example, Foucault M., Truth and Power in *The Foucault reader* pp. 51–75; Williams *Politics and technology* pp. 58–61.

18. On the importance of Spengler, see Hughes H.S. *Consciousness and society* 1979 pp. 368–9 and 379.

19. Zamyatin, H.G. Wells, in *Yevgeny Zamyatin* p. 286.

20. Huxley A. *Brave new world revisited* 1974 pp. 11–12.

21. Mumford *Technics and civilization* p. 287; and see Frye *Anatomy of criticism* p. 228.

22. Marcel G. *Man against mass society* (1951) 1985 p. 93; Warner R. *The aerodrome* (1941) 1982 pp. 14–15 and 225.

23. See Nicholls *Encyclopedia of science fiction* and the general surveys provided by Amis K. *New maps of hell* 1961; Parrinder P. (ed) *Science fiction: a critical guide* 1979; Suvin D. *Metamorphoses of science fiction* 1979; Clarke I.F. *The pattern of expectation* 1979; Barron N. (ed) *Anatomy of wonder* 1987.

24. Juenger *The failure of technology* pp. 73 and 77; Adorno, T., Horkheimer M. *Dialectic of enlightenment* (1944) 1979 p. 120; Kateb G. *Utopia and its enemies* 1963 pp. 163–4.

25. Hillegas M.R. *The future as nightmare* 1967 pp. 86–7; Forster E.M., The machine stops (1910) in *Collected short stories* (1947) 1954 pp. 137–8.

26. See Wells *Modern utopia* p. xxi.

27. Pick *War machine* p. 67; and see Jackson R. *Fantasy: the literature of subversion* Methuen 1981 p. 167 on these themes in fantasy literature generally.

28. Rolland R., Masereel F. *La révolte des machines ou la pensée dechainée (1921)*, discussed by Pick *War machine* pp. 208–9; Mumford *Myth of the machine* pp. 80–1.

29. Wells H.G. *The sleeper awakes* (published in 1899 as *When the sleeper wakes*) 1925 pp. 44 and 79.
30. Wells H.G. *Story of the days to come* (1927) 1976 pp. 40, 34 and 49–50.
31. See Mumford *Technics and civilization* pp. 286–7 on indiscriminate nature of the romantic reaction against the city; Orwell G. *Nineteen eighty-four* (1949) 1989 p. 131.
32. Foucault *Foucault reader* pp. 18–19.
33. Williamson J. *The humanoids* (1948) 1977 pp. 65–6 and 92.
34. O'Neill J. *Land under England* (1935) 1978 pp. 104–110, 159 and 239.
35. Ferkiss *Technological man* pp. 74–5.
36. Stansky P. (ed) *On 'Nineteen eighty-four'* 1983 p. 79; Haldane J.B.S. *Daedalus* 1924 pp. 49–80.
37. Stapledon O. *Last and first men* (1930) 1963 pp. 211–15.
38. See, for example, Nicholls *Encyclopedia of science fiction* p. 503; Marcel *Man against mass society* p. 71.
39. Pick *War machine* pp. 208–9.
40. Capek K., The Meaning of *R.U.R.*, *Saturday Review* **86** (21 July 1923), quoted by Hillegas *The future as nightmare* p. 96.
41. Vonnegut K. *Player piano* (1952) 1992 pp. 282, 278 and 317.
42. Forster, The machine stops, pp. 130–1.
43. Huxley *Brave new world revisited* pp. 103–6; Huxley A. *The doors of perception* (1954), Grafton 1977 p. 52.
44. On the centrality of the notion of 'the masses', see Briggs A., The language of 'mass' and 'masses' in nineteenth-century England, in *Ideology and the Labour movement*, ed Martin D.E., Rubinstein D.; Carey J. *The intellectuals and the masses* 1992; and Pick *War machine*.
45. Orwell *Road to Wigan Pier* p. 189.
46. Amis *New maps of hell* p. 109.
47. Adorno and Horkheimer *Dialectic of enlightenment* pp. 120–2 and 162–7; Marcel *Man against mass society* pp. 49ff and 54; and Juenger *The failure of technology* pp. 155–6.
48. See Carey *The intellectuals and the masses* passim; Skinner B.F., Freedom and the control of men, *The American Scholar* **25** (Winter 1955–56) p. 61; Kateb *Utopia and its enemies* pp. 158–60; Wells H.G. *Men like gods* (1923) 1987 pp. 162–4; and see Wells *Story of the days to come* pp. 59–60. Hillegas *The future as nightmare* p. 118 notes Wells's approval of Pavlov's book on conditioned reflexes, which was published in 1928.
49. Kateb *Utopia and its enemies* pp. 142–3.
50. Huxley, Forward to *Brave new world*; Huxley A., Boundaries of Utopia, *Virginia Quarterly Review* **7** (January–October 1931): 54; and see Bradshaw D., Introduction to *The hidden Huxley* 1994 pp. viii and xx.
51. Wells H.G. *The shape of things to come* (1933), quoted by Hillegas *The future as nightmare* p. 121.
52. Marcuse H. *One-dimensional man* (1964) 1991 pp. 57 and 65–71. Although the phenomenon Marcuse comments on in contemporary society is more thoroughgoing than that represented by Wells and Huxley – that is, the incorporation of high art into the established order and its reproduction and display on a massive scale – the essence of the argument is the same.

53. See discussion of the science fiction representation of telepathic powers in Nicholls *Encyclopedia of science fiction* p. 200.

54. See Aldiss and Wingrove *Trillion year spree* pp. 265–6; Nicholls *Encyclopedia of science fiction*, in its entry on Williamson, notes that one explanation of the end simply posits that it was supplied by someone else.

55. Zamyatin Y., On literature, revolution, entropy, and other matters (1923), in *Yevgeny Zamyatin* pp. 108–9.

56. Myers G., Nineteenth-century popularizations of thermodynamics and the rhetoric of social prophecy, *Victorian Studies* **29** (1): 35–66; Zamyatin, On literature, revolution, entropy, p. 109; Zamyatin, H.G. Wells, in *Yevgeny Zamyatin* pp. 288–9; more recent utopian studies (for example, Levitas R. *The concept of utopia* 1990 p. 164) have worked to rescue the concept of utopia from this difficulty of conception.

57. Zamyatin, H.G. Wells, in *Yevgeny Zamyatin* pp. 286–8; Wells *Modern utopia* p. 5. In this respect, Wells has been followed by later defenders of utopian modes of thought: Darko Suvin, for example (*Metamorphoses of science fiction*), insists on a distinction between a true and 'fake' novum, the only consistent novelty being one that constitutes an open-ended system, 'as befits the unfinished state of the world' (Bloch E. *Experimentum mundi*, quoted by Suvin p. 82).

58. Kateb *Utopia and its enemies* p. 79 (see also Alexander P., Gill R., eds, *Utopias* 1984 p 10 on what is required for dynamism); Zamyatin, On literature, revolution, entropy, in *Yevgeny Zamyatin* p. 110. The child here is not to be taken as an emblem of puerile childishness (in contrast, for example, to Huxley's image of life inside 'an invisible bottle of infantile and embryonic fixations' – *Brave new world* pp. 203–4).

59. Forster, Machine stops, p. 131; Vonnegut *Player piano* p 13; Kateb *Utopia and its enemies* p. 113.

60. James W., The moral equivalent of war (1910), quoted by Kateb *Utopia and its enemies* p. 116; and see Kateb pp. 113–17.

61. Spengler *Man and technics* Chapter 11, pp. 81–9; Juenger *The failure of technology* p. 84.

62. Orwell G., Review of *We* (4 January 1946), in *The collected essays* 1968 vol. 4 p. 73.

63. See Skidelsky R. *Oswald Mosley* 1981 pp. 299–300.

Bibliography

Adamson J. *Graham Greene: the dangerous edge: where art and politics meet.* Macmillan 1990

Adorno T., Horkheimer M. *Dialectic of enlightenment* (1944) trans Cumming J. Verso 1979

Aldiss B.W, Wingrove D. *Trillion year spree: the history of science fiction* (1986). Paladin (Grafton Books) 1988

Alexander P., Gill R. (eds) *Utopias.* Duckworth 1984

Ambler E. *Cause for alarm* (1938). Fontana 1988

Ambler E. *Here lies: an autobiography.* Weidenfeld & Nicolson 1985

Ambler E. *Journey into fear* (1940). Fontana 1989

Ambler E. *The dark frontier* (1936). Fontana 1988

Ambler E. *The mask of Dimitrios* (1939). Fontana 1988

Ambler E. *Uncommon danger* (1941). Fontana 1988

Amis K. *New maps of hell: a survey of science fiction.* Victor Gollancz 1961

Apter D.E. *The politics of modernization.* University of Chicago Press, Chicago 1965; 1967

Apter T.E. *Thomas Mann: the devil's advocate.* Macmillan 1978

Arendt H. *Between past and future: six exercises in political thought* (1954). Faber & Faber 1961

Arendt H. *On violence* (1969). Harcourt, Brace and World Inc. 1969

Arendt H. *The human condition.* University of Chicago Press, Chicago 1958

Arendt H. *The origins of totalitarianism* (1951). Allen & Unwin 1967

Armstrong N., Tennenhouse L. *The violence of representation: literature and the history of violence.* Routledge, 1989

Aron R. *Main currents in sociological thought* (2 vols., 1967) trans Howard R., Weaver H. Penguin 1990

Auden W.H. *The dyer's hand and other essays* (1963). Faber & Faber 1987

Ayers D. *Wyndham Lewis and Western man.* Macmillan 1992

Bailes K.E. *Technology and society under Lenin and Stalin: origins of the Soviet technical intelligentsia 1917–1941.* Princeton University Press, New Jersey 1978

Baines J. *Joseph Conrad: a critical biography* (1960). Penguin 1986

Bance A.F. (ed) *Weimar Germany: writers and politics.* Scottish Academic Press 1982

Barker E. *Principles of social and political theory* (1951). Clarendon Press 1967

Barron N. (ed) *Anatomy of wonder: a critical guide to science fiction.* R.R. Bowker Co., New York 1987

Beauvoir S. de *The second sex* (1949) trans Parshley H.M. Pan (Picador) 1988

Belloc H. *The servile state* (1913). Constable 1950

Benson F.R. *Writers in arms: the literary impact of the Spanish Civil War* (1967). University of London Press Ltd 1968

Bentley E. *The cult of the superman* (1944). Robert Hale 1947

Berdyaev N. *The end of our time* trans Attwater D. Sheed and Ward 1933

Berendsohn W.E. *Thomas Mann: artist and partisan in troubled times.* University of Alabama Press, Alabama 1975

Berki R.N. *Security and society: reflections on law, order and politics.* Dent 1986

Berle A.A. *Power.* Harcourt, New York 1967; 1969

Berlin I. *Personal impressions.* Hogarth Press 1980

Bernal J.D. *The world, the flesh and the devil: an enquiry into the future of three enemies of the rational soul.* Kegan Paul 1929

Berthoud J. *Joseph Conrad: the major phase.* Cambridge University Press 1978

Blake N. (Day-Lewis C.) *The smiler with the knife* (1939). Hogarth Press 1985

Bloom C. (ed) *Spy thrillers: from Buchan to le Carré.* Macmillan 1990

Bloom C. (ed) *Twentieth-century suspense: the thriller comes of age.* Macmillan 1990

Bloom C. et al. (eds) *Nineteenth-century suspense: from Poe to Conan Doyle.* Macmillan 1988

Bloom H. (ed) *Graham Greene.* Chelsea House Publishers, New York 1987 (Modern Critical Views)

Bowering P.E. *Aldous Huxley: a study of the major novels.* Athlone Press 1968

Boyd I. *The novels of G K Chesterton: a study in art and propaganda.* Paul Elek 1975

Bracher K.D. *The age of ideologies: a history of political thought in the twentieth century* trans Osers E (1982). Methuen 1985

Brander L. *Aldous Huxley: a critical study.* Rupert Hart-Davis 1969

Bridgewater P. *Nietzsche in Anglosaxony: A Study of Nietzsche's impact on English and American literature.* Leicester University Press 1972

Brittain V., Holtby W. *Testament of a generation: the journalism of Vera Brittain and Winifred Holtby* (ed Berry P., Bishop A.). Virago 1985

Buchan J. *Mr Standfast* (1919). Penguin 1988

Buchan J. *Prester John* (1910). Penguin 1956

Buchan J. *The three hostages* (1924). Penguin 1988

Buitenhuis P. *The great war of words, literature as propaganda 1914–18 and after.* Batsford 1989

Bullock A. *Hitler and Stalin: parallel lives.* Harper-Collins 1991

Burdekin K. *Swastika night* (1937). Lawrence & Wishart 1985

Burnham J. *The managerial revolution: what is happening in the world* (1941). Greenwood Press Publishers, Westport, Connecticut 1972

Calder J. *Heroes.* Hamish Hamilton 1977

Canetti E. *Crowds and power* (1960) trans Stewart C. Penguin 1973

Canovan M. *G.K. Chesterton: radical populist.* Harcourt Brace Jovanovich, New York 1977

Canovan M. *Hannah Arendt: a reinterpretation of her political thought.* Cambridge University Press 1992

Čapek K. *R. U. R. and the insect play* (1923). Oxford University Press 1991

Caplan J. Introduction to female sexuality in Fascist ideology. *Feminist Review 1979* **1**: 59–66

Carey J. D.H. Lawrence's doctrine. In Spender S. (ed) *D.H. Lawrence: novelist, poet, prophet.* Weidenfeld & Nicolson 1973

Carey J. *The intellectuals and the masses: pride and prejudice among the literary intelligentsia 1880–1939.* Faber & Faber 1992

Carlyle T. *On heroes, hero-worship and the heroic in history* (1841). Centenary Edition, London 1897

Caudwell C. *Studies in a dying culture* (1938). John Lane 1948

Cawelti J.G. *Adventure, mystery, and romance: formula studies as art and popular culture.* University of Chicago Press, Chicago 1976

Cawelti J.G., Rosenberg B.A. *The spy story.* University of Chicago Press, Chicago 1987

Charmley J. *Churchill: the end of glory.* Sceptre 1993

Chesterton G.K. *George Bernard Shaw* (1909). John Lane 1935

Chesterton G.K. *Heretics.* John Lane 1919

Chesterton G.K. *The Napoleon of Notting Hill* (1904). Oxford University Press 1994

Churchill W. *Churchill speaks: Winston S. Churchill in peace and war: collected speeches, 1897–1963* ed Rhodes James R. Windward 1981

Churchill W. *Savrola* (1900). Cedric Chivers Ltd 1973

Clarke I.F. *The pattern of expectation, 1644–2001.* Jonathan Cape 1979

Coates J.D. *Chesterton and the Edwardian cultural crisis.* Hull University Press 1984

Cockburn C. *Bestseller: the books that everyone read, 1900–1939.* Sidgwick & Jackson 1972

Colls R., Dodd P. (eds) *Englishness: politics and culture 1880–1920.* Croom Helm 1986

Conquest R. *The great terror: Stalin's purge of the thirties.* Penguin 1971

Conrad J. *Autocracy and war* (1905). In *The works of Joseph Conrad in twenty volumes.* John Grant 1925, vol 19

Conrad J. *Heart of darkness* (1902). Penguin 1973

Conrad J. *Lord Jim* (1900). Penguin 1989

Conrad J. *Nostromo* (1904). Penguin 1990

Conrad J. *The collected letters of Joseph Conrad* ed Karl F.R., Davies L. (2 vols). Cambridge University Press 1986

Conrad J. *The rescue* (1920). Penguin 1950

Couto M. *Graham Greene: on the frontier: politics and religion in the novels* Macmillan 1988

Cranston M. *The mask of politics and other essays.* Allen Lane 1973

Crick B. *In defence of politics* (1962). Penguin 1971

Cunningham V. *British writers of the thirties.* Oxford University Press 1989

Cunningham V. (ed) *Spanish front: writers on the Civil War.* Oxford University Press 1986

Daniell D. *The interpreter's house: a critical assessment of John Buchan.* Thomas Nelson 1975

Darroch R. *D.H. Lawrence in Australia.* Macmillan, Melbourne 1981

Delany P. *D.H Lawrence's nightmare: the writer and his circle in the years of the Great War.* Harvester Press 1979

Denning M. *Cover stories: narrative and ideology in the British spy thriller.* Routledge & Kegan Paul 1987

Dodd W.J. *Kafka and Dostoyevsky: the shaping of influence.* Macmillan 1992

Edelman J.M. *The symbolic uses of politics.* Illinois University Press, Urbana, Illinois 1964

Einstein A., Freud S. *Why war?* International Institute of Intellectual Co-operation, League of Nations 1933

Ellul J. *The technological society* trans Wilkinson J. Jonathan Cape 1954

Ferkiss V.C. *Technological man: the myth and the reality.* Heinemann 1969

Fest J.C. *Hitler* trans Winston R. and C. (1973). Penguin 1974

Fischer K.P. *History and prophecy: Oswald Spengler and the decline of the West.* Peter Lang, New York 1989

Flathman R.E. *The practice of political authority.* University of Chicago Press, Chicago 1980

Fleishman A. *Conrad's politics: community and anarchy in the fiction of Joseph Conrad.* The Johns Hopkins Press, Baltimore, Maryland 1967

Flower J.E. *Writers and politics in modern France (1909–1961).* Hodder & Stoughton 1977

Forster E.M. *A passage to India* (1924). Penguin 1964

Forster E.M. *Abinger harvest* (1936). Edward Arnold 1961

Forster E.M. *Selected letters* ed Lago M., Furbank P.N. Collins 1985, vol. 2

Forster E.M. The machine stops (1910). In *Collected short stories* (1947). Penguin 1954 (pp. 109–46)

Forster E.M. *Two cheers for democracy.* Edward Arnold 1951

Foucault M. *The Foucault reader* ed Rabinow P. (1980). Penguin 1987

Freud S. *Civilization, society and religion* trans Strachey J. Penguin (Penguin Freud Library, vol. 12) 1985; 1991

Freud S. *On metapsychology: the theory of psychoanalysis* trans Strachey J. Penguin (Penguin Freud Library, vol. 11) 1984; 1991

Fromm E. *The anatomy of human destructiveness* (1974). Penguin 1990

Fromm E. *The fear of freedom* (1942). Routledge & Kegan Paul 1966

Fussell P. *The Great War and modern memory.* Oxford University Press 1975; 1977

Fussell P. *Wartime: understanding and behaviour in the Second World War.* Oxford University Press 1989; 1990

Geddes G. *Conrad's later novels.* McGill-Queen's University Press, Montreal 1980

Girouard M. *The return to Camelot: chivalry and the English gentleman.* Yale University Press, New Haven 1981

Glover E.G. *War, sadism and pacifism: three essays.* Allen & Unwin 1935

Gorky M., From Prometheus to the hooligan. In *Collected works in ten volumes.* Progress Publishers, Moscow 1982, vol. 10

Graves R., Hodge A. *The long weekend: a social history of Great Britain 1918–1939* (1940). Cardinal 1988

Green M. *Dreams of adventure, deeds of Empire.* Routledge & Kegan Paul 1980

Green M. *Seven types of adventure tale: an etiology of a major genre.* Pennsylvania State University Press, Pennsylvania 1991

Greene G. *A gun for sale* (1936). Penguin 1979

Greene G. *A sort of life.* Penguin 1972

Greene G. *Brighton rock* (1938). Penguin 1971

Greene G. *England made me* (1935). Penguin 1977

Greene G. *It's a battlefield* (1934). Penguin 1980

Greene G. *Journey without maps* (1936). Penguin 1980

Greene G. *Stamboul train* (1932). Penguin 1977

Greene G. *The confidential agent* (1939). Penguin 1971

Greene G. *The lawless roads* (1939). Penguin 1982

Greene G. *The Ministry of Fear* (1943). Penguin 1979

Greene G. *The power and the glory* (1940). Penguin 1971

Greene G. *Ways of escape.* Penguin 1981

Griffiths J. *Three tomorrows: American, British and Soviet science fiction.* Macmillan 1980

Grossvogel D.I. *Mystery and its fictions.* The Johns Hopkins Press, Baltimore, Maryland 1979

Haggard H.R. *Allan Quatermain* (1887). Penguin 1990

Haggard H.R. *King Solomon's mines* (1885). Oxford University Press (World's Classics) 1992

Haldane J.B.S. *Daedalus, or science and the future.* Kegan Paul, Trench & Trubner 1924

Haldane J.B.S. *Possible worlds and other essays.* Chatto & Windus 1929

Hampshire S. *Innocence and experience* (1989). Penguin 1992

Harden I., Lewis N. *The noble lie: the British constitution and the rule of law.* Hutchinson 1986; 1988

Harper R. *The world of the thriller.* Press of Case Western Reserve University, Cleveland, Ohio 1969

Harrison J.R. *The reactionaries. Yeats, Lewis, Pound, Eliot, Lawrence: a study of the anti-democratic intelligentsia.* Gollancz 1969

Hay E.K. *The political novels of Joseph Conrad: a critical study.* University Press of Chicago, Chicago 1927

Haynes R.D. *H.G. Wells: discoverer of the future.* Macmillan 1980

Held J. *The cult of power: dictators in the twentieth century.* Columbia University Press, New York 1983 (East European Monographs, Boulder)

Heller E. *Kafka.* Collins (Fontana Modern Masters) 1974

Hibbert C. *Benito Mussolini* (1962). Penguin 1975

Hilfer T. *The crime novel: a deviant genre.* University of Texas Press, Austin, Texas 1990

Hillegas M.R. *The future as nightmare: H.G. Wells and the anti-utopians.* Oxford University Press, New York 1967

Hobson J.A. *Imperialism: a study* (1902). Allen & Unwin 1938

Hochman B. *Another ego: the changing view of self and society in the work of D.H. Lawrence.* University of South Carolina Press, Columbia, South Carolina 1970

Hodgkinson C. *The philosophy of leadership.* Basil Blackwell 1983

Hoffer P.T. *Klaus Mann.* Twayne Publishers, Boston 1978

Holroyd M. *Bernard Shaw* (1988–91). Penguin 1991, vols 1–3

Hook S. *The hero in history* (1943). Beacon Press, Boston 1962

Hopkins J. An interview with Eric Ambler. *Journal of Popular Culture 1975* **9** (2): 285–93

Horsley L. *Political fiction and the historical imagination.* Macmillan 1990

Hoskins K.B. *Today the struggle: literature and politics in England during the Spanish Civil War.* University of Texas Press, Austin, Texas 1969

Hough G. *The dark sun: a study of D.H. Lawrence* (1956). Penguin 1961

Houghton W.E. *The Victorian frame of mind* (1957). Yale University Press, New Haven 1985

Household G. *Rogue male* (1939). Penguin 1989

Howe I. *Politics and the novel.* Horizon Press, New York 1957

Howe M.B. *The art of the self in D.H. Lawrence.* University of Ohio Press, Athens, Ohio 1977

Hughes H.S. *Consciousness and society* (1958). Harvester Press 1979

Hull E.M. *The Sheik* (1919). A.L. Burt Company, New York 1921

Hunter A. *Joseph Conrad and the ethics of Darwinism.* Croom Helm 1983

Huxley A. Boundaries of utopia. *Virginia Quarterly Review 1931* **7** (Jan–Oct): 47–54

Huxley A. *Brave new world* (1932). Flamingo (Harper–Collins) 1994

Huxley A. *Brave new world revisited.* Chatto & Windus 1974

Huxley A. *Point counter point* (1928). Flamingo (Harper–Collins) 1994

Huxley A. *Proper studies.* Chatto & Windus 1927

Huxley A. *The hidden Huxley: contempt and compassion for the masses* ed Bradshaw D. Faber & Faber 1994

Huxley A. *The olive tree and other essays.* Chatto & Windus 1947

Hynes S.L. (ed) *Graham Greene: a collection of critical essays.* Prentice-Hall, New Jersey 1973

Jablonsky D. *Churchill, the great game and total war.* Frank Cass 1991

Jackson B.S. *Law, fact and narrative coherence.* Deborah Charles Publications 1988

Jameson F. *Fables of aggression: Wyndham Lewis: the modernist as Fascist.* University of California Press, Berkeley 1979

Jameson F. *The political unconscious: narrative as a socially symbolic act.* Methuen 1981; 1983

Johnstone R. *The will to believe: novelists of the nineteen-thirties.* Oxford University Press 1982; 1984

Juenger F.G. *The failure of technology: perfection without purpose* (1939). Henry Regnery Company, Hinsdale, Illinois 1949

Kafka F. *The trial* (1925) trans Muir W. and E. Minerva 1992

Karl F. *Joseph Conrad: the three lives.* Faber & Faber 1979

Kateb G. *Hannah Arendt: politics, conscience, evil* (1983). Martin Robertson 1984

Kateb G. *Utopia and its enemies.* Free Press of Glencoe 1963

Katz W.R. *Rider Haggard and the fiction of Empire: a critical study of British Imperial fiction.* Cambridge University Press 1987

Kennedy P. *The realities behind diplomacy: background influences on British external policy 1865–1980.* Harper–Collins (Fontana) 1981; 1985

Kermode F. *Lawrence.* Collins (Fontana Modern Masters) 1973

Kershaw I. *The 'Hitler myth': image and reality in the Third Reich* (1987). Oxford University Press 1989

Kipling R. *Selected stories* (ed Rutherford A). Penguin 1987

Kirschner P. *Conrad: the psychologist as artist.* Oliver and Boyd 1968

Koestler A. *Darkness at noon* (1940) trans Hardy D. Penguin 1964

Kollontai A. *A great love* (1923) trans Porter C. Virago 1991

Koonz C. *Mothers in the Fatherland: women, the family and Nazi politics* (1986). Methuen 1988

Lasswell H.D. *The political writings of Harold D Lasswell.* Free Press, Illinois 1951

Lawrence D.H. *Aaron's rod* (1922). Penguin 1950

Lawrence D.H. *Apocalypse* (1931). Penguin 1981

Lawrence D.H. *Fantasia of the unconscious* and *Psychoanalysis and the unconscious* (1921–22). Penguin 1986

Lawrence D.H. *Kangaroo* (1923). Penguin 1981

Lawrence D.H. *Reflections on the death of a porcupine and other essays* ed Herbert M. Cambridge University Press 1988

Lawrence D.H. *Selected essays.* Penguin 1950; 1981

Lawrence D.H. *Selected literary criticism* ed Beal A. Heinemann, Melbourne 1955

Lawrence D.H. *The plumed serpent* (1926). Penguin 1990

Lee S.J. *The European dictatorships 1918–1945*. Methuen 1987

Leites N., Bernaut E. *Ritual of liquidation: the case of the Moscow trials*. The Free Press, Glencoe, Illinois 1954

Lesér E.H. *Thomas Mann's short fiction: an intellectual biography*. Associated University Presses 1989

Levene M. *Arthur Koestler*. Frederick Ungar, New York 1984

Levitas R. *The concept of utopia*. Philip Allan, New York 1990

Lewis W. *An anthology of his prose* ed Tomlin, E.W.F. Methuen 1969

Lewis W. *Paleface: the philosophy of the 'melting-pot'*. Chatto & Windus 1929

Lewis W. *Snooty baronet*. Cassel 1932

Lewis W. *The art of being ruled* (1926) ed Dasenbrock R.W. Black Sparrow Press, Santa Rosa 1989

Lewis W. *The diabolical principle and the dithyrambic spectator*. Chatto & Windus 1931

Lewis W. *The Hitler cult*. Dent 1939

Lewis W. *The revenge for love* (1937). Penguin 1982

Light A. *Forever England: femininity, literature and conservatism between the Wars*. Routledge 1991

Lindholm C. *Charisma*. Basil Blackwell 1990; 1993

Lukes S. *Marxism and morality* (1985). Oxford University Press 1990

Lukes S. (ed) *Power*. New York University Press, New York 1986

Lukes S., Scull A. (eds) *Durkheim and the law*. Martin Robertson 1983

Macciocchi M. Female sexuality in Fascist ideology. *Feminist Review 1979* **1**: 67–82

Mack Smith D. *Mussolini's Roman Empire* (1976). Penguin 1979

Mackenzie W.J.M. *Power, violence, decision*. Penguin 1975

Majumdar R., McLaurin A. (eds) *Virginia Woolf: the critical heritage*. Routledge & Kegan Paul 1975

Mann K. *Mephisto* (1936). Penguin 1983

Mann T. *Mario and the magician and other stories* (1936). Penguin 1975

Mannheim K. *Ideology and utopia: an introduction to the sociology of knowledge* (1936). Routledge & Kegan Paul 1976

Marcel G. *Man against mass society* (1951). University Press of America, Lanham, Maryland 1985

Marcus J. *Virginia Woolf and the languages of patriarchy*. Indiana University Press, Bloomington, Indiana 1987

Marcuse H. *One-dimensional man* (1964). Routledge 1991

Marder H. *Feminism and art: a study of Virginia Woolf.* University of Chicago Press, Chicago 1968

May K.M. *Aldous Huxley.* Paul Elek 1972

Mays W. *Arthur Koestler.* Lutterworth Press 1973

McClure J.A. *Kipling and Conrad: the colonial fiction.* Harvard University Press, Cambridge, Massachusetts 1981

McConnell F. *The science fiction of H.G. Wells.* Oxford University Press, New York 1981

McNeile H.C. *'Sapper': the best short stories* (1920–37). Dent 1986

Melman B. *Women and the popular imagination in the twenties: flappers and nymphs.* St Martin's Press, New York 1988

Merleau-Ponty M. *Humanism and terror: an essay on the Communist problem* (1947) trans O'Neill J. Beacon Press, Boston 1969

Meyers J. *D.H. Lawrence and the experience of Italy.* University of Pennsylvania Press, Philadelphia, Pa. 1982

Meyers J. *The enemy: a biography of Wyndham Lewis.* Routledge & Kegan Paul 1980

Meyers J. (ed) *Graham Greene: a revaluation – new essays.* Macmillan 1990

Meyers J. (ed) *Wyndham Lewis: a revaluation.* The Athlone Press 1980

Miller J. *Women writing about men.* Virago 1986

Millett K. *Sexual politics* (1969). Virago 1985

Milosz C. *The captive mind* (1953) trans Zielonko J. Penguin 1985

Mitzman A. *The iron cage: an historical interpretation of Max Weber* (1969). Transaction Books, New Brunswick, New Jersey 1985

Modleski T. *Loving with a vengeance* (1982). Routledge 1990

Moi T. *Sexual/textual politics: feminist literary theory* (1985). Routledge 1993

Monteith M. (ed) *Women's writing: a challenge to theory.* Harvester 1986

Morris J.A. *Writers and politics in modern Britain (1880–1950).* Hodder & Stoughton 1977

Mumford L. *Technics and civilization.* Routledge 1946

Mumford L. *The myth of the machine: the pentagon of power* (1964). Secker & Warburg 1971

Myers G. Nineteenth-century popularizations of thermodynamics and the rhetoric of social prophecy. *Victorian Studies 1985* **29** (1): 35–66

Nicholls P. (ed) *The encyclopedia of science fiction.* Granada 1979

Nietzsche F. *The philosophy of Nietzsche* ed Clive G. New American Library (Mentor) 1965

O'Neill J. *Land under England* (1935). New English Library 1978

Orwell G. *Collected essays* (1946–53). Secker & Warburg 1961; 1975

Orwell G. *Inside the whale and other essays* (1957). Penguin 1974

Orwell G. *Nineteen eighty-four* (1949). Penguin 1989

Orwell G. *The collected essays, journalism and letters of George Orwell* ed Orwell S, Angus I. Secker & Warburg 1968, vols 1–4

Orwell G. *The road to Wigan Pier* (1937). Penguin 1989

Paglia C. *Sexual personae: art and decadence from Nefertiti to Emily Dickinson* (1990). Penguin 1992

Palmer J. *Thrillers: genesis and structure of a popular genre.* Edward Arnold 1978

Palmer P. *Contemporary women's fiction: narrative practice and feminist theory.* Harvester Wheatsheaf 1989

Panichas G.A. (ed) *The politics of twentieth-century novelists.* Hawthorn Books Inc, New York 1971

Parrinder P. (ed) *Science fiction: a critical guide.* Longman 1979

Patai D. Orwell's despair, Burdekin's hope: gender and power in dystopia. *Women's Studies International Forum, 1979* **7** (2): 85–95

Payne R. *The great man: a portrait of Winston Churchill.* Coward, McCann & Geoghegan, New York 1974

Pick D. *War machine: the rationalisation of slaughter in the modern age.* Yale University Press, New Haven, 1993

Plank R., The Golem and the robot. *Literature and Psychology 1965* **15** (1): 12–28

Pritchard W.H. *Seeing through everything: English writers 1918–1940.* Faber & Faber 1977

Raphael D.D. *Problems of political philosophy.* Macmillan 1970

Reich W. *The mass psychology of Fascism* (1946) trans Carfagno V.R. Souvenir Press 1991

Rieselbach H.F. *Conrad's rebels: the psychology of revolution in the novels from 'Nostromo' to 'Victory'.* UMI Research Press, Ann Arbor, Michigan 1985

Roth J.J. *The cult of violence: Sorel and the Sorelians.* University of California Press, Berkeley 1980

Russell B. *Icarus.* Kegan Paul 1924

Russell B. *Power* (1938). Unwin Paperbacks 1975

Russell B. *Roads to freedom* (1918). Unwin Paperbacks 1989

Russell B. *The impact of science on society* (1952). Unwin Paperbacks 1990

Rutherford A. *The literature of war: five studies in heroic virtue.* Macmillan 1978

Sagar K. *The art of D.H. Lawrence.* Cambridge University Press 1966

Said E.W. *Culture and imperialism.* Chatto & Windus 1993

Sanders S. *D.H. Lawrence: the world of the major novels.* Vision Press 1973

Sandison A. *The wheel of Empire: a study of the Imperial idea in some late nineteenth- and early twentieth-century fiction.* Macmillan 1967

Sauerberg L.O. *Secret agents in fiction: Ian Fleming, John le Carré, and Len Deighton.* Macmillan 1984

Schiffer I. *Charisma: a psychoanalytic look at mass society.* University of Toronto Press, Toronto 1973

Schneider D.J. *D.H. Lawrence: the artist as psychologist.* University of Kansas Press, Lawrence, Kansas 1984

Schwarz D.R. *Conrad: 'Almayer's folly' to 'Under Western eyes'.* Macmillan 1980

Schwarz D.R. *Conrad: the later fiction.* Macmillan 1982

Shaw G.B. *Agitations: letters to the press 1875–1950* ed Laurence D.H., Rambeau J. Frederick Ungar, New York 1985

Shaw G.B. *Back to Methuselah* (1921). Penguin 1990

Shaw G.B. *Everybody's political what's what?* Constable 1944

Shaw G.B. *Man and superman* (1903). Penguin 1946

Shaw G.B. *Plays pleasant* (1898). Penguin 1946

Shaw G.B. *Saint Joan* (1923). Penguin 1946

Shaw G.B. *Selected non-dramatic writings of Bernard Shaw* ed Laurence D. H. Houghton Mifflin, Boston 1965

Shaw G.B. *Shaw offstage: the non-dramatic writings* ed Crawford F.D. Pennsylvania State University Press, University Park, Pennsylvania 1989

Shaw G.B. *The intelligent woman's guide to socialism and capitalism.* Constable 1930

Shaw G.B. *Three plays for Puritans* (1901). Penguin 1946

Sherry N. *Conrad's Western world.* Cambridge University Press 1971

Sherry N. *The life of Graham Greene, volume one: 1904–1939.* Penguin 1990

Shirer W.L. *The nightmare years, 1930–1940.* Bantam Books, Toronto 1985

Siegel P.N. *Revolution and the twentieth-century novel.* Monad Press, New York 1979

Simpson H. *D.H. Lawrence and feminism.* Northern Illinois University Press, Illinois 1982

Skidelsky R. *Oswald Mosley.* Macmillan 1975; 1981

Skinner B.F. *Walden two* (1948). Macmillan, New York 1976

Spender S. *Trial of a judge.* Faber & Faber 1938

Spengler O. *Man and technics: a contribution to a philosophy of life* trans Atkinson F.C. Allen & Unwin 1932

Spengler O. *The decline of the West: perspectives of world history.* Allen & Unwin 1922, 2 vols

Stansky P. (ed) *On 'Nineteen eighty-four'.* W.H. Freeman and Company, New York 1983

Stapledon O. *Last and first men* (1930). Penguin 1963

Steinhoff W. *George Orwell and the origins of '1984'.* University of Michigan Press, Ann Arbor, Michigan 1975

Stern J.P. *A study of Nietzsche.* Cambridge University Press 1979; 1981

Stern J.P. *Hitler: the Führer and the people.* Collins (Fontana) 1975; 1979

Stern J.P. The law of *The trial.* In Kuna F. (ed) *On Kafka: semi-centenary perspectives.* Paul Elek 1976

Strachey J. *The coming struggle for power.* Victor Gollancz 1932; 1934

Suvin D. *Metamorphoses of science fiction: on the poetics and history of a literary genre.* Yale University Press, New Haven 1979

Swinden P. *The English novel of history and society, 1940–80.* Macmillan 1984

Sypnowich C.E. *The concept of socialist law.* Clarendon Press 1990

Talmon J.L. *Political messianism: the romantic phase.* Secker & Warburg 1960

Talmon J.L. *The origins of totalitarian democracy* (1951). Norton Library, New York 1970

Taylor R. *Literature and society in Germany 1918–1945.* Harvester Press 1980

Thatcher D.S. *Nietzsche in England, 1890–1914.* University of Toronto Press, Toronto 1970

Thorburn D. Conrad's romanticism: self-consciousness and community. In Thorburn D, Hartman G (eds) *Romanticism: vistas, instances, continuities.* Cornell University Press, Ithaca 1973

Trilling L. *The opposing self* (1950). Viking Press, New York 1955

Turco A. (ed) *Shaw: the neglected plays.* Pennsylvania State University Press, Pennsylvania 1987

Usborne R. *Clubland heroes. A nostalgic study of some recurrent characters in the romantic fiction of Dornford Yates, John Buchan and Sapper* London (Barrie and Jenkins) 1953; (Constable) 1974

Vonnegut K. *Player piano* (1952). Flamingo (Harper–Collins) 1992

Walsh C. *From utopia to nightmare.* Greenwood Press, Westport, Connecticut 1962

Warner R. *The aerodrome* (1941). Oxford University Press 1982

Warner R. *The cult of power* (1947). Kennikat Press, New York 1969

Watson G. *Politics and literature in modern Britain.* Macmillan 1977

Watts C. *A preface to Conrad.* Longman 1982

Weatherhead A.K. *Stephen Spender and the thirties.* Associated University Presses Inc 1975

Weber M. *Economy and society: an outline of interpretive sociology* (1922) ed Roth G., Wittich, C. Bedminister Press Inc, New York 1968

Wells H.G. *A modern utopia* (1905). University of Nebraska Press, Lincoln, Nebraska 1967

Wells H.G. *A story of the days to come* (1927). Corgi 1976

Wells H.G. *Men like gods* (1923). Penguin 1987

Wells H.G. *The holy terror.* Michael Joseph 1939

Wells H.G. *The new Machiavelli* (1911). Dent 1994

Wells H.G. *The sleeper awakes* (1899, as *When the sleeper wakes*). The Literary Press 1925

Welsh A. *Strong representations: narrative and circumstantial evidence in England.* The Johns Hopkins University Press, Baltimore 1992

West R. *Harriet Hume: a London fantasy* (1928). Virago 1980

West R. *The strange necessity: essays and reviews* (1928). Virago 1987

Whitman R.F. *Shaw and the play of ideas.* Cornell University Press, Ithaca, New York 1977

Wiener N. *Cybernetics: or control and communication in the animal and the machine* (1948). The MIT Press, Cambridge, Massachusetts 1961

Wiener P.P., Fisher J. (eds) *Violence and aggression in the history of ideas.* Rutgers University Press, New Brunswick, New Jersey 1974

Wilding M. *Political fictions.* Routledge & Kegan Paul 1980

Williams R. *Politics and technology.* Macmillan 1971

Williamson J. *The humanoids* (1948). Sphere Books 1977

Willner A.R. *The spellbinders: charismatic political leadership.* Yale University Press, New Haven 1984

Winegarten R. *Writers and revolution: the fatal lure of action.* Franklin Watts (New Viewpoints), New York 1974

Wisenthal J.L. *Shaw's sense of history.* Clarendon Press 1988

Wisenthal J.L. *The marriage of contraries: Bernard Shaw's middle plays.* Harvard University Press, Cambridge, Mass 1974

Woolf L. *Quack, quack!* Hogarth Press 1936

Woolf V. *Three guineas* (1938). Hogarth Press 1986

Zamyatin Y. (trans Guerney B.G.) *We* (1920). Penguin 1983

Zamyatin Y. *Yevgeny Zamyatin: a Soviet heretic* (1970) trans Ginsberg M. Quartet Books 1991

Index